MW00618204

Upstart

"An insightful framework for illuminating China's rise to challenge the U.S."
—**Graham Allison**, Douglas Dillon Professor of Government
at the Harvard Kennedy School and Former US
Assistant Secretary of Defense

"*Upstart* is a must-read. Mastro provides a new way to understand how China has built its national power over the past thirty years. In doing so, she provides a clearer way forward for policymakers hoping to get China right."
—**Stephen Hadley**, former National Security
Advisor of the United States

"*Upstart* applies the logic of business competition to China's drive for great power status, a framework that provides an original and illuminating perspective on Sino–U.S. relations. According to Mastro, although Beijing is modeling itself on America as a "great power," more often than not, it chooses not to emulate American-style power projection in order to avoid provoking a backlash. My take-away from Mastro's analysis is that while China's ambition is inevitable, a smart U.S. strategy can avoid war by channeling it into peaceful competition."
—**Susan Shirk**, U.S. Deputy Assistant Secretary of State in the
Bureau of East Asia and Pacific Affairs, founding chair of the 21st Century
China Center and author of *Overreach: How China Derailed Its Peaceful Rise*

"A fresh and insightful approach to understanding China's rise. Drawing on the business literature on competition, *Upstart* is theoretically stimulating and empirically sound. It is well worth reading by scholars and practitioners alike."
—**David Shambaugh**, George Washington University,
and author of *China Goes Global*

"Oriana Skylar Mastro's book offers an original, provocative, and persuasive thesis of China's rise as a great power. Its meticulous research and lucid analysis illuminate China's grand strategy that has enabled the country to reach near parity with the U.S. Mastro's masterpiece not only helps us gain a better understanding of the past, but also provides valuable insights for policy makers as they wrestle with the China challenge today."
—**Minxin Pei**, Professor of Government, Claremont McKenna
College and author of *The Sentinel State: Surveillance
and the Survival of Dictatorship in China*

"*Upstart* is the rarest of books: serious and scholarly, yet still fun and punchy. By drawing on the business literature on competition, Oriana Skylar Mastro has given us an invaluable new intellectual framework with which to understand the Chinese Communist Party's grand strategy. Students, scholars, and policymakers at all levels should read Upstart to not only understand how China managed to close the gap with America over the past thirty years, but also jumpstart America's efforts to compete more successfully over the next thirty years."

—**Rep. Mike Gallagher**, Chairman of the Select Committee
on the Chinese Communist Party

"*Upstart* provides a sophisticated framework for measuring great power status, and explains how China succeeded in rising to this status using a combination of approaches that capitalized on US weaknesses and Beijing's unique strengths. The book is invaluable for understanding both China and geopolitical competition today."

—**Francis Fukuyama**, Olivier Nomellini Senior Fellow, Freeman Spogli
Institute for International Studies and Director, Ford Dorsey Master's
in International Policy, Stanford University

"Oriana Skylar Mastro's *Upstart* provides a comprehensive explanation of China's dramatic rise to great power status in a competitive international environment. Mastro shows how the Chinese Communist Party leadership employed a strategy based upon a combination of emulation, exploitation, and entrepreneurship to gain influence in foreign policy, increase its military capabilities, and build its economic power. Her book will find an eager audience among scholars and policy makers alike.

—**Thomas G. Mahnken**, Senior Research Professor, Merrill Center
for Strategic Studies, Johns Hopkins SAIS and President
and CEO, Center for Strategic and Budgetary Assessments

Upstart

How China Became a Great Power

ORIANA SKYLAR MASTRO

OXFORD
UNIVERSITY PRESS

OXFORD
UNIVERSITY PRESS

Oxford University Press is a department of the University of Oxford. It furthers the University's objective of excellence in research, scholarship, and education by publishing worldwide. Oxford is a registered trade mark of Oxford University Press in the UK and certain other countries.

Published in the United States of America by Oxford University Press
198 Madison Avenue, New York, NY 10016, United States of America.

Library of Congress Cataloging-in-Publication Data
Names: Mastro, Oriana Skylar, author.
Title: Upstart : how China became a great power / Oriana Skylar Mastro.
Description: New York, NY : Oxford University Press, 2024. |
Includes bibliographical references and index.
Identifiers: LCCN 2023057234 (print) | LCCN 2023057235 (ebook) |
ISBN 9780197695067 (hardback) | ISBN 9780197695074 (epub)
Subjects: LCSH: China—Foreign relations—21st century. | China—Foreign
economic relations. | China—Military policy. | Great
powers—History—21st century. | World politics—1989–
Classification: LCC JZ1734 .M385 2024 (print) | LCC JZ1734 (ebook) |
DDC 327.51—dc23/eng/20240108
LC record available at https://lccn.loc.gov/2023057234
LC ebook record available at https://lccn.loc.gov/2023057235

ISBN 978–0–19–769506–7

DOI: 10.1093/oso/9780197695067.001.0001

Printed by Sheridan Books, Inc., United States of America

To Cyrus and Didi—tutto quello che faccio, lo faccio per voi

Contents

Figures and Tables

Figures

Tables

Acknowledgments

I have been very lucky to receive a great deal of support and motivation throughout the process of writing this book. Dan Kurtz-Phelan was the first to encourage me to write down my argument about China's unique rise, which was published as "The Stealth Superpower" in the January/February 2019 issue of *Foreign Affairs*. I was fortunate to receive support through the Smith Richardson Foundation's Strategy and Policy Fellows Program and the Asia Pacific Foundation of Canada's John H. McArthur Distinguished Fellowship to expand and refine the idea that eventually became this book.

The American Enterprise Institute (AEI) provided me with a policy home for almost seven years, and with it an amazing amount of support. The development team helped with the grants, and the media team with the graphics found throughout this book. It is an understatement to say this book would not have been possible without the hard work of my AEI research assistants, Emily Carr and Thomas Causey. Thomas coordinated all the research assistants effortlessly to ensure I had what I needed, and he did it without ever seeming overwhelmed or stressed (which I greatly appreciate, as an easily stressed and overwhelmed person). AEI also hosted a book workshop for me during the initial stages of the writing process—the comments from external reviewers Thomas Mahnken and Jessica Chen Weiss, along with Bonnie Glaser, Mark Montgomery, Nathan Beauchamp, Michael Beckley, Dan Blumenthal, Zack Cooper, Thomas Ehrhard, Bonny Lin, Frank Miller, and Al Song, helped me refine my thinking at that critical stage.

I started this book during my first year as a center fellow at Stanford University's Freeman Spogli Institute for International Studies (FSI). The Center for International Security and Cooperation at Stanford and the Stanton Foundation provided generous support for researching and writing on the nuclear dimensions of this book. The China Fund and the Shorenstein APARC faculty research award program at FSI provided generous funding for the travel, supplies, and research support necessary to see this book through to fruition. Aspects of these funds also supported a book workshop at Stanford in May 2023. I am in debt to Jenny Lind, Tyler Jost, and Tom Christensen for flying across the country to provide critical feedback, as well as to my Stanford colleagues Scott Sagan, Ken Schultz, Larry Diamond, Mike Brown, Thomas Fingar, Jean Oi, Mike McFaul, and Laura Stone—this book is much, much, much better thanks to you all. Last but not least, this book would not have been possible without my research dream team at Stanford: my lead RAs Janpal LaChapelle, Vivian Zhu, Jerome He, and Chengyang Zhang, but also Linda Liu, Zhenwei Gao, Kasha Tyranski, George San Miguel, Hannah Kohatsu, Joshua Goodwin, Kevia McComb, Jaden Morgan, JB Lim, Shirley Cheng, Jaden Kaplan, Tianyi Chen, Yifan Xu, Isabel Cai, Khushmita Dhabhai, and Nicholas Welch.

I am grateful to my team of editors: David McBride at Oxford, who supported the project from the beginning and helped make this book more readable, and Phoebe Aldridge-Turner, who expertly stewarded it through the production process. My agent, Don Fehr, at Trident Media, helped craft the proposal and took me on, even though I was a somewhat unknown entity. Morgan Kaplan, your insights are always on point. Roger Haydon, who stewarded me through my first book, was kind enough to read through the second (multiple times) to try to make it more readable. Allison Van Deventer provided expert copyediting skills that ensured the book was as concise as possible, and Birgitte Necessary stepped up to put together the index.

I have been lucky to enjoy such institutional support. But the truth is, like the process of writing this book, my acknowledgments must be untraditional as well. When the pandemic hit, I had a newborn and a twenty-month-old. With the latter now at home—and the need to organize his preschool days to make sure he did not fall behind, while trying to survive with the baby who would never take a bottle (so I was on call for feedings)—the idea that I could produce a work like this seemed impossible.

And if it were not for a few people and institutions, it probably would have been. So, for the untraditional thanks. First and foremost, to the government of Australia. When we needed a place to flee to, you welcomed us. After four months in lockdown in DC with two immunocompromised kids, I cannot tell you what a relief it was to be in a place that was safe for my children. This allowed us to get childcare help (thanks, Alba!) and for me to work at a nearby café, so I was out of the house but available for feedings. A big thanks to the Sweet Spot and Clovelly Social House for always welcoming me, bringing me my usual (thanks, V!), and not once giving me a hard time about the hours I sat at your tables. Alex Korolev helped set up an academic home for me at the University of New South Wales. And to Richard MacGregor and family, who let me use their home office once those cafés closed.

They say it takes a village to raise a child, but it probably takes a country to support me and my ambitions. To all the childcare workers at Bing Nursery School and Madera Grove Childcare Center—you hardly ever see me, but that is only a testament to how much my kids are learning and enjoying their time with you. To Rosa Hernandez, Jade Reidy, and Haidee Storms, I literally do not know how I would have managed our household without your help. Your commitment to me and my family, without judgment, helps me be a better mother and wife. To Dr. Laurence Kaplan, for seeing to my mental health through it all. And a special thanks to Aynne Kokas, the original warrior woman. If the pandemic brought anything good, it was the deepening of our friendship. The weekly calls, filled with career advice, confidence boosters, and tips on enjoying the best life has to offer, gave me the strategies and motivation I needed to push through with this book.

Thanks to my parents, James and Claudia, who literally came across the country whenever we needed them, to fill in where I fell short and who instilled in me the grit and drive that saw me through this project. To my in-laws, especially Amy Tarapore, whose help with the kids during our time in Australia gave me some much-needed respite. And to the Muttoni family, who continue to remind me that life is more than just work.

There are really no words to describe my gratitude to the man brave enough to embark on this life adventure with me, Arzan Tarapore. The night wakings, the masterly solo parenting when I'm traveling, the endless months unexpectedly managing the kids at home before kids' vaccinations became available, the nutritious meals—all this was beyond amazing. But it's so much more than the day-to-day support—it's also the intellectual companionship and leaps of faith in every major life decision we make. You create the feeling that whatever happens, we will be okay. And that allows me to take the risks in work and in life that have brought the most rewards. Johnny Cash was right: we are the best partners this world has ever seen.

Lastly, to my sons, to whom this book is dedicated. You fill my days with joy and laughter, but also purpose. I want the world to be a beautiful, open, and safe place for you two to explore. I hope this book contributes to that vision.

Abbreviations

ADIZ	Air Defense Identification Zone
AEW	air early warning
AFB	Air Force Base
AI	artificial intelligence
AIDP	Artificial Intelligence Development Plan
AIIB	Asia Infrastructure Investment Bank
APEC	Asia-Pacific Economic Cooperation
ASBM	anti-ship ballistic missile
ASEAN	Association of Southeast Asian Nations
A2/AD	anti-access and area denial
B3W	Build Back Better World
BDN	Blue Dot Network
BEV	battery-electric vehicle
BRI	Belt and Road Initiative
C3I	command, control, communications, and intelligence
C4ISR	command, control, communications, computers, intelligence, surveillance, and reconnaissance
CASCF	China–Arab States Cooperation Forum
CASS	Chinese Academy of Social Sciences
CBDC	central bank digital currency
CCG	Chinese Coast Guard
CCP	Chinese Communist Party
CCTV	Chinese Central Television
CEE	Central and Eastern European
China-CELAC	Forum of China and Community of Latin American and Caribbean States
CGTN	China Global Television Network
CIPS	Cross-Border Interbank Payment System
CMC	Central Military Commission
CNP	comprehensive national power
COSCO	China Ocean Shipping Company
COVID	coronavirus disease
CPEC	China–Pakistan Economic Corridor
CPPTC	China Peacekeeping Police Training Center
CSTC	Central Science and Technology Commission

CUES	Code for Unplanned Encounters at Sea
DCRI	Digital Currency Research Institute
DRAM	dynamic random access memory
EEZ	exclusive economic zone
EU	European Union
EV	electric vehicle
FAO	Food and Agriculture Organization
FBI	Federal Bureau of Investigation
FDI	foreign direct investment
FOCAC	Forum on China–Africa Cooperation
FTA	free trade agreement
FYP	five-year plan
GATT	General Agreement on Tariffs and Trade
GDI	Global Development Initiative
GDP	gross domestic product
GGE	Group of Governmental Experts
GGF	government guidance funds
GPU	graphical processing unit
HADR	humanitarian and disaster relief operations
HKD	Hong Kong dollar
HKEX	Hong Kong Stock Exchange
IADS	integrated air defense system
IAEA	International Atomic Energy Agency
IC	integrated circuit
ICAO	International Civil Aviation Organization
ICBM	intercontinental ballistic missile
IMF	International Monetary Fund
IPO	initial public offering
IRBM	intermediate-range ballistic missile
ISA	International Seabed Authority
ISR	intelligence, surveillance, and reconnaissance
ITU	International Telecommunication Union
JCET	Jiangsu Changjiang Electronics Tech
JCPOA	Joint Comprehensive Plan of Action
LACM	land attack cruise missile
LDCs	least developed countries
LMIC	low-income and middle-income countries
MLP	Medium and Long-Term Program of Science and Technology
MMCA	Military Maritime Consultative Agreement
MOOTW	military operations other than war
MPS	Ministry of Public Security
MRBM	medium-range ballistic missile
MTCR	Missile Technology Control Regime

NDS	National Defense Strategy
NEO	non-combatant evacuation operation
NGO	non-governmental organization
NPT	Nuclear Non-Proliferation Treaty
NSC-68	National Security Council 68
ODA	official development assistance
OECD	Organization for Economic Co-operation and Development
OOF	other official flows
OSRD	Office of Scientific Research and Development
PAFMM	People's Armed Forces Maritime Militia
PAP	People's Armed Police
PKO	peacekeeping operations
PLA	People's Liberation Army
PLAAF	People's Liberation Army Air Force
PLAN	People's Liberation Army Navy
PLARF	People's Liberation Army Rocket Force
PPWT	Prevention of the Placement of Weapons in Outer Space and of the Threat or Use of Force Against Outer Space Objects
PRC	People's Republic of China
PSC	private security contractors
PSI	Proliferation Security Initiative
RCEP	Regional Comprehensive Economic Partnership
RMB	renminbi
R&D	research and development
SDR	Special Drawing Rights
SEI	Strategic Emerging Industries
SIPRI	Stockholm International Peace Research Institute
SMIC	Semiconductor Manufacturing International Corporation
SOE	state-owned enterprises
SRBM	short-range ballistic missile
STRATCOM	Strategic Command
SWIFT	Society for Worldwide Interbank Financial Telecommunication
S&T	science and technology
THAAD	Terminal High-Altitude Area Defense
TIV	trend-indicator value
TPP	Trans-Pacific Partnership
TSMC	Taiwan Semiconductor Manufacturing Company
UAE	United Arab Emirates
UAV	unmanned aerial vehicle
UK	United Kingdom
UN	United Nations
UNCLOS	United Nations Convention on the Law of the Sea

UNESCO	United Nations Educational, Scientific, and Cultural Organization
UNGA	United Nations General Assembly
UNICEF	United Nations Children's Fund
UNIDO	United Nations Industrial Development Organization
UNMISS	United Nations Mission in Southern Sudan
UNPKO	UN peacekeeping operations
UNSC	United Nations Security Council
US	United States
USAID	United States Agency for International Development
USCGC	United States Coast Guard cutter
USNS	United States naval ship
VPN	virtual private network
WHO	World Health Organization
WMD	weapons of mass destruction
WTO	World Trade Organization
WWI	World War One
WWII	World War Two

Introduction

China's Rise to the Great Power Club

Thirty years ago, the idea that China could challenge the United States economically, globally, and militarily was unfathomable. The United States had won the Cold War and emerged as the most powerful country the world had ever seen. As the world's wealthiest nation, the United States also boasted the world's largest economy, which grew an average of 4 percent per year between 1992 and 1999. It enjoyed a vast military alliance network and a gross domestic product (GDP) over sixteen times that of China. It had created a constitutional order after World War Two (WWII) consisting of dozens of international institutions that, along with its allies, it dominated.

And then there was China. In 2000, China's economy was a mere 3 percent of global GDP, less than that of France. Fewer than 7 percent of Chinese had cellphone subscriptions in 2000, and the number of internet users was below 2 percent of the population. It had a large military, with roughly 4 million people under arms, but that was more a sign of its backwardness than anything else. With obsolete equipment and poor training, China barely had what could be considered an air force and a navy. Its pilots could not fly over water, at night, or in bad weather. In 1999, fewer than 2 percent of its fighters were fourth-generation, fewer than 4 percent of its attack submarines were up to current standards, and none of its surface ships were modern. Indeed, its navy was a glorified coast guard with ships that, lacking air defense systems, had to hug the coastline when on patrol. Its nuclear weapons, solid-fueled and housed mainly in fixed silos, were at risk of being taken out in one fell swoop. And Beijing was still internationally isolated at the end of the Cold War, lacking representation in influential international institutions such as the World Trade Organization (WTO) and without formal diplomatic ties with dozens of countries, including regional powers such as South Korea.

This is where our story begins—with Chinese leaders recognizing a vast disparity in power and hoping to close the gap. The United States enjoyed a unipolar moment that no country was in a position to challenge, a fact highlighted by the US military's spectacular performance in the 1991 Gulf War.[1] Since then, all Chinese leaders from Jiang Zemin to its current leader Xi Jinping have wanted to build China up, to regain the nation's standing in the international system as a great power after decades of humiliation and subjugation at the hands of the powerful.[2] This drive for power and influence is not the only motivation for China's behavior—this book shows that, unsurprisingly, the Chinese Communist Party's (CCP) insistence on strong state control to maintain domestic power also shapes how China competes, often in ways that are problematic both for the US-led world order and for China itself. But at the beginning of the new millennium, the domestic imperatives only underscored the necessity of a careful strategic approach if Beijing was to compete for power and influence in a US-dominated world, one in which the United States could undermine China's rise if Washington felt threatened.[3]

What happened next was nothing short of a transformation. In 2010, China's economy surpassed Japan's to become the second-largest in the world, and it has since become larger than the Japanese, Indian, and German economies combined. Between 1990 and 2010, Beijing doubled its membership in international institutions and became proactive in others, such as the United Nations (UN). China also normalized relations with twenty-eight countries during the 1990s. Over the ensuing thirty years, China went from diplomatic isolation to having as much diplomatic and political power on the world stage as the United States (by some measures, slightly more).[4] By 2021, China had become the number one trading partner to 120 countries, including all the United States' Indo-Pacific allies.

The military modernization of the People's Republic of China (PRC) has been equally awe-inspiring. Thanks to a 790 percent increase in defense spending from 1992 to 2020, most Chinese military equipment in service is now modern, meaning that anything from fighter planes to anti-satellite laser technology is sufficiently advanced to pose a danger to cutting-edge technology. In other words, China can credibly threaten the world's most advanced militaries and can be confident that it will not lose engagements solely because of inferior technology and equipment. China's nuclear force is now survivable, meaning that enough Chinese nuclear warheads and delivery systems would survive a preemptive attack that Beijing could threaten a retaliatory nuclear strike. In October 2021, China tested hypersonic nuclear missiles, the first country ever to do so, prompting former Chairman of the Joint Chiefs of Staff General Mark Milley to say, "They have gone from a peasant army that was very, very large in 1979 to a very capable military that covers all domains."[5] Indeed, with 20,000 more scientists than the United States and a 15 percent per year average growth in research and development (R&D) spending over the past twenty-five years (compared to 3 percent for the United States), it is no surprise that China is now considered more advanced than the United States in many emerging technologies relevant to warfare, such as artificial intelligence (AI), hypersonics, and quantum computing.

Conventional military metrics also show how far the People's Liberation Army (PLA) has come. While earlier its pilots could not navigate the roughly forty miles off the coast to the centerline between China and Taiwan, now they do so almost daily. Between September 2020 and September 2021, PRC aircraft flew into Taiwan's Air Defense Identification Zone (ADIZ) 250 days of the year, with the number of incursions and aircraft involved trending higher over time.[6] While earlier its ships had rarely seen the waters beyond its coasts, they now roam the South China Sea, the East China Sea, and the Indian Ocean. China does not yet possess a blue-water navy—meaning a naval force capable of operating globally, far from home shores—but it has some global presence thanks to a military base in Djibouti and routine port calls. The People's Liberation Army Navy (PLAN) is now the world's largest navy, with 355 platforms (though it does not yet equal the US Navy in tonnage). China also boasts the largest, most advanced ballistic and cruise missile programs in the world, including an anti-ship ballistic missile (ASBM) that can hit moving ships at sea—a weapon that the United States currently does not have in its inventory.

To close the gap in relative diplomatic, economic, and military power, China's strategy had to be not only effective but also efficient. If it were not, China would never catch up, and it might risk internal collapse. Beijing also had to avoid a strong backlash from the United States, which could spoil its efforts, make them prohibitively expensive, or even cause an internal collapse or preventive war that would end its rise definitively. China needed to navigate these trade-offs between power maximization, great power reaction, domestic stability, and prosperity, and it had to do so while adapting flexibly to changing circumstances. The answer was the upstart strategy.

The Upstart Strategy

In March 2021, President Biden's newly minted team made their way to Alaska to meet with their Chinese counterparts for the first time. Despite initial heightened expectations, the meeting was far from friendly. The Chinese were in no mood to listen to the US list of complaints regarding China's violations of human rights in Tibet, Hong Kong, and the Xinjiang region and regarding China's assertive foreign policy, despite the legitimacy of these concerns. China's top diplomat, Yang Jiechi, actively pushed back against the accusations and made China's views clear: "The United States does not have the qualification to say that it wants to speak to China from a position of strength."

While there were some theatrics to China's behavior at the summit, Yang's statement was not untrue. The relative power between China and the United States had narrowed significantly, with China pulling ahead in some cases. As Xi stated in his report to the 20th Party Congress in October 2022, "China now has more solid material foundations and stronger institutional underpinnings for pursuing development. The rejuvenation of the Chinese nation is now on an irreversible historical course."[7]

How has China tried to build power and influence over the past thirty years? What factors have determined the strategies Beijing has pursued? In these pages I present my answer: the "upstart" strategy. An upstart is an entity that has risen suddenly from a low position to achieve power, wealth, or rank.[8] It is often used pejoratively to describe a person thought to be cocky, arrogant, or aggressive—one who has recently begun an activity and become successful without showing proper respect for older and more experienced people.[9] But the term does not necessarily have a derogatory meaning; it is used in a neutral fashion to describe start-up enterprises. The inspiration for the upstart strategy comes from the business literature on competition. While rising powers and major conflicts are rare in international relations, disruptions to industries and firm bankruptcies are common, leading to a mature research tradition in the business literature, tested and refined across a greater number of cases, about how established firms may be pushed out by upstarts.

My upstart strategy has three components, defined by the areas of competition and the rising power's approach: emulation, exploitation, and entrepreneurship (the three E's). Emulation is when a country competes in the same way as the established hegemon in existing areas of competition. Most of the existing literature focuses on this form of competition; it argues that to become a great power, an ambitious state will build and exercise power in a proven way. The second component, exploitation, refers to situations in which a rising power adopts approaches like those of the great power, but in new areas of competition. For example, China exploits opportunities where competitive forces are the weakest—where the United States is not active or suffers vulnerabilities, where there are cracks in the international order, or where the normative environment is weak. The last component, entrepreneurship, involves taking new approaches in domains of competition both new and old. The Venn diagram in Figure I.1 demonstrates this.

The business literature on competition provides some insights into the pros and cons of each approach. For example, in certain domains, emulation may be the quickest and most efficient way to rise. It can be seen as "playing by the rules," which helps an upstart build power while avoiding backlash or counterbalancing. But emulation can be costly and slow or, at worst, risky and wasteful if it increases the great power's competitive reaction and the rising power lacks the competitive advantages to respond.

In the second component of the upstart strategy, exploitation, countries follow the example of enterprising competitors with low market share who become market leaders by exploiting incumbent firms' blind spots and becoming better at executing their existing strategies within those areas.[10] This strategy is only an option if (1) there are blind spots to exploit—areas in which the established power is not actively competing because of oversight or inability, or because it sees little room left for growth in that area—and (2) the rising power has some strengths to leverage in these areas.[11] The

Figure I.1 The Definition of the Three E's
Source: Author's creation.

rising power then can employ a proven approach, but without having to compete directly with the established great power. This is a relatively efficient way to build power if the rising power also possesses competitive advantages in the right areas.

The last component, entrepreneurship, also has its perks. A novel approach may not be seen as a direct challenge to the hegemon's position, and thus may not attract immediate balancing. And although innovation may be riskier than emulation (which is a tried-and-true approach), success can lead to a quicker and more efficient rise than emulation can.[12] More innovative approaches may also allow an upstart to gain a first-mover advantage in new strategic areas or leverage its unique competitive advantages. Challengers who successfully dethrone a leader have often "creatively destroy[ed] entrenched beliefs" about how to best build and exercise power.[13] But there is no clear road map, and a different approach can also lead to the rising power's demise.[14]

From this discussion, we can derive five main factors that shape which of the upstart strategy's three E's is pursued: the effectiveness of the established hegemon's strategy, the hegemon's most likely interpretation of the behavior, efficiency of a particular approach (shaped largely by competitive advantages), liabilities of an approach, and existence of gaps and blind spots. In the case of China's rise, this has meant China tends to emulate the United States when it assesses the US approach to be effective, when emulative behavior would reassure Western powers, and when it enjoys competitive advantages in that domain to ensure strategic efficacy. China's attempts at diplomatic outreach, mediation, and new participation in international institutions fall into this category. When the first condition holds but China is unable to compete directly because of its own limitations, China identifies gaps to exploit and applies the same strategy there.

The last component of the upstart strategy has been the most critical to China's rise. China pursues entrepreneurial pathways to power when the US approach is believed to be ineffective or a liability for the CCP, or when pursuing US approaches is likely to spark strong negative threat perceptions. China then devises a new way to build a particular type of power that uniquely leverages its competitive advantages (and mitigates its weaknesses). For example, China builds commercial port facilities (instead of overseas military bases) to protect its overseas interests, or it trains local law enforcement (instead of foreign militaries) to build goodwill.

Investigating How China Competes for Power

Our narrative begins in the mid-1990s, which is generally considered the beginning of China's broader geopolitical rise.[15] It was around this time that Chinese leaders made the strategic decision to move beyond domestic economic growth to build political, military, and economic power on the international stage. This book tries to understand these efforts by looking deeply into twenty-two cases in which Chinese leaders had to decide how to achieve certain strategic objectives.

These thirty years, roughly from 1993 to 2023, also correspond with China's understanding of its own trajectory. Deng Xiaoping referred to the thirty years after the Cold War as a period of "catching up" and remarked on the importance of "seizing opportunities."[16] The prominent Chinese intellectual Zheng Bijian began speaking of China's "peaceful rise" in the early 2000s, and official Party texts and speeches began to openly discuss China's rise after prime minister Wen Jiabao's 2003 speech at Harvard University on the topic.[17] Moreover, official and scholarly assessments began right before the COVID-19 outbreak to accept China as a country that had sufficiently closed the power gap with the United States to be considered a great power.

This book aims to describe what China has done, why it did things a certain way, what the approach has done for China, and how these strategies have contributed to the idea that China is a great and influential power. Using granular data and authoritative Chinese sources, I contextualize China's choices and describe its path up the global power hierarchy through twenty-two cases of Chinese economic, diplomatic, and military strategy. In each case, I present objective measurements and Chinese assessments of the five factors that shape which component of the upstart strategy China chooses—strategic effectiveness, strategic efficacy, domestic political factors, potential US response, and existence of gaps. The upstart framework reveals which of the three strategies is most likely to be pursued given the values of those variables. Because "competitiveness" is a relational term, each section evaluates China's strategic approach compared to the main tenets of US strategy. I draw inferences about whether Beijing emulated, exploited, or pursued entrepreneurship based on how the Chinese allocated their limited resources. I then evaluate whether the impact on China's power position was as predicted.

The results are detailed explanations for why China chose a particular pillar of the strategy—emulation, exploitation, or entrepreneurship—based on the real and perceived pros and cons of emulation, exploitation, and entrepreneurship. We should expect several data points to emerge if the upstart framework captures China's approach to power accumulation. First, US strategy should be the primary reference for Chinese decision-makers as they determine whether to imitate, exploit, or innovate. We should expect Chinese writings, official and authoritative, to evaluate China's competitive advantages and weaknesses against US strategy, and we expect that this evaluation will shape how China competes. Second, I evaluate in the case studies whether the Chinese logic behind a particular approach is consistent with upstart thinking. The data should show that China's choice of strategy results from a cost-benefit calculus that considers strategic effectiveness, strategic efficacy, US perceptions, China's competitive advantages and vulnerabilities, and the existence of gaps. Chinese leaders might not always make the best decisions, as they do not have complete information, but I do assume they are rational insofar as they monitor China's performance and its environment and then respond to underperformance and changes in the strategic environment.[18]

The first key feature of my approach is that it is data-driven. The analysis in this book is based on six original datasets and dozens of existing datasets on Chinese activities, which can all be found in an online appendix.[19] The second key feature of this approach is that it relies on Chinese perceptions and assessments. The Chinese-language research for the book has encompassed hundreds of primary sources, from government publications and leadership speeches to media commentary and academic papers. Of the 856 sources I have examined, 128 are books published by military-affiliated presses; 37 are books published by Party-affiliated presses; 69 are academic volumes (biographies of leaders, studies of events such as the Gulf War, and other publications from Social Science Academic Press and World Affairs Press); 150 are government white papers and other government publications such as speeches, news releases, reports, official websites, and datasets; and 472 are media reports and academic articles, most from state media outlets and publishing houses.[20]

My goal is to explain how China has built power over the past three decades—to explain the conditions under which China emulates, exploits, or is entrepreneurial in its approach. One extension of the upstart thesis is that how a rising power builds power is context dependent; if the conditions had been different, China would have chosen a different combination of emulation, exploitation, and entrepreneurship in its strategy. The case studies, which show that during the same period (and thus under similar domestic and international conditions) China chose different components of the upstart strategy based on variation in the five main variables I laid out earlier, put the upstart theory on sound footing. I do not claim that China has never erred; I include several cases in which other motivations caused China to deviate from the upstart strategy, leading to policies that were costly, suffered setbacks in execution, or provoked significant pushback consistent with the logic of the upstart strategy.

There is a second possible extension of the upstart thesis: if China had chosen to emulate the United States, it might not have succeeded in becoming a great power (or, to put it another way, the upstart strategy is the reason for China's success). The information found in this book does not prove this hypothesis beyond a doubt. It is theoretically possible that China could have become a great power by pursuing a different strategy. (A quick thought experiment, however, calls this possibility into question: What if an overly ambitious leader had built bases around the world, sought alliances in Latin America and with rogue states, or even attacked its weaker neighbors in the 1990s or 2000s, as John Mearsheimer and other strategists predicted? The United States would have responded in ways that constrained China. China would not be a great power today and might not even exist in its current form.)

Complicating matters, the methodological challenge of assessing "success" is a perennial issue in international politics. I try to address this issue through two strategies. First, I present both objective and relevant metrics of success for each case study in addition to providing Chinese assessments of success and evaluations from other observers, for perceptions of power can be as important as power itself. Second, while the case studies will show that China pursued the upstart strategy, the next section demonstrates that China has been successful at least in building power in the aggregate.

Metrics for Success: China as a Great Power

The necessity of understanding China's strategy and its drivers is based on the premise that Beijing has been largely successful at closing the relative power gap with the United States to the point of achieving great power status. Here I follow conventional practice in using "power" and "influence" interchangeably to refer to the ability to convince actors to do things they would not otherwise do.[21] (Interestingly, Chinese writings mainly use "power" to describe US approaches, while "influence" is reserved for China.)[22] Both power and influence can be repressive and facilitative, deliberately wielded, or latently impactful; both can be dispositional factors, a resource, or measured by outcome.

Although "great power" is a term in common usage, there is no one accepted definition or set of metrics for measuring power.[23] Some scholars define the term by latent characteristics—population, land, natural resources—that tie the potential for great power status to big countries.[24] Smaller countries may achieve significant economic growth and wield great geopolitical weight but lack the ability to protect themselves against external pressures or to convince countries to accommodate their preferences.[25] With respect to these indicators, China is undoubtedly a great power. It hosts the world's second-largest population (India took over first place in 2023), and its territory is comparable in size to that of the United States, replete with significant stocks of traditional minerals as well as those used in modern manufacturing like rare earth elements.

But these are at best necessary conditions, not sufficient ones. Russia is the largest country in terms of land mass, and no one would say Moscow is outcompeting the United States or China (or that Canada can give the United States a run for its money, even though it is bigger). Additionally, according to this metric, the PRC has been a great power since its founding in 1949, which is obviously false. Lastly, many countries such as Portugal, England, and Japan did not have the population or territory initially, but through their historical rises to great power status accumulated it through territorial expansion and colonization.

Military power is considered the critical necessary condition for great power status, especially among realist scholars. Over the past two decades, "the PRC marshalled the resources, technology, and political will . . . to strengthen and modernize the PLA in nearly every respect."[26] The result is a military commensurate with great power status: one that meets Paul Kennedy's threshold of "holding its own against any other nation," Jack Levy's "high level of military capabilities relative to other states" with "relative self-sufficiency with respect to security," and John Mearsheimer's "sufficient military assets to put up a serious fight in an all-out conventional war against the most powerful state in the world."[27] Indeed, in several areas (shipbuilding, land-based conventional ballistic and cruise missiles, and integrated air defense systems [IADS]), Chinese military capabilities now surpass those of the United States.[28] Some argue that nuclear weapons are a necessary condition for great power status.[29] China possesses the third-largest nuclear arsenal in the world, one that is currently undergoing a major modernization.[30]

Other scholars have been critical of this narrow focus on military power, calling for greater consideration of economic might. Metrics for economic power vary widely, from GDP (with various refinements) to more abstract indicators like managerial organization, industrial innovativeness, and techno-industrial superiority.[31] Still, with each of these measurement methods, China's economic power is undeniable. China possesses the second-largest economy in the world and has been the world's largest exporter since 2010. General education levels and technological innovation are also strong (if regionally unequal); China enjoys around 97 percent literacy rate, and its national intellectual property office processes about 46 percent of the globe's patent applications.[32]

But one must be cautious about overreliance on economic variables. Post-reunification Germany and postwar Japan became the economic and political leaders of their regions without achieving great power status (arguably by choice).[33] India has been a rising power for decades and undoubtedly has the resources to be a great power, but it is "widely seen as a nearly-power that cannot quite get its act together."[34] During the period of China's rise, Brazil has also periodically been viewed as a rising power, yet "the conversion of a giant economy and political activism into actual, tangible regional and global power status seems to have eluded Brazil so far."[35] States also need the ability to consistently leverage economic resources for broader political gains and the ambition to be a great power.

Perceptions play a big role as well: power and influence are not only earned but conferred by other nations. According to Manjari Miller, global acceptance of great power status is predicated on external perceptions (derived from relationships with the international community and material capabilities) as well as internal perceptions (domestic support for a shifting international position).[36] In terms of external perceptions, the 2017 US national security strategy described the defining feature of contemporary international politics as great power competition with Beijing, a formulation that basically continues to this day.

Chinese internal perceptions also suggest that China has successfully risen to great power status. In the 2000s, most Chinese scholars were interested in measuring China's comprehensive national power (CNP), the overall ability to pursue its strategic goals.[37] About ten years ago, the consensus was that China had yet to reach great power status.[38] But by 2020, it was more common domestically to consider China a great power, either second to the United States in a multipolar system or an equal in a bipolar system.[39] At a meeting with his US counterparts in 2021, top diplomat Yang Jiechi emphasized that "both China and the US are global great powers."[40]

What This Book Is Not About

My aim is to determine how China has built power and influence, not to determine the exact balance of power between the United States and China at various intervals. My argument rests on two conclusions about relative power: (1) China has reduced the power gap with the United States since 1993, and (2) the current gap is now small enough that US strategists and thinkers consider China a great power competitor. These are relatively conservative conclusions.

Even though this book focuses on the *how*, it provides some insight into *what* China currently wants. The debate about whether China wants to be a "global" or "regional" power falls into the trap of assuming that China will pursue its ambitions like the United States has, and thus that having global ambitions means challenging the US global equities by employing similar strategies. The upstart approach assumes that China wants the ability to influence or dictate outcomes, especially in issues or in regions of importance to its interests.

But China does not have to compete everywhere and in the same manner to achieve this outcome. The case studies in this book show that China wants to have a global reach, but primarily for the purpose of consolidating its position at home and in its region. In other words, China does not have to be a global peer competitor to be a superpower—indeed, an attempt to compete in every domain globally would place China's power position in jeopardy. Moreover, perceptions of revisionism, defined as a desire to change or modify the status quo in some way, usually through use of force, are somewhat subjective.[41] The upstart strategy takes this fact into account. One of the factors that determine whether China chooses emulation, exploitation, or entrepreneurship is whether the United States will perceive emulation as status quo or revisionist behavior.

Although I do not empirically test my approach across other histories of successful rising powers, I do provide anecdotes that suggest that China's strategy is not unique. Though I suspect that countries that have followed the upstart strategy have been the most successful at building power and influence (the United States often chose entrepreneurship during its rise, opting for global military presence, international institutions, soft power, and a free trade system over the British ways of colonies, protectionism, and occupation), I do not attempt to prove this hypothesis. But showing that China's meteoric rise is not the result of emulation alone makes a powerful case that *how* countries build power is just as critical to their success as the material inputs they enjoy. Other great power histories might warrant reconsideration, a topic I discuss in the conclusion.

Lastly, this book is not meant to be a condemnation of China, nor is it meant to praise the country. When I say that a strategy is effective or successful, I do not condone that approach. I am making a statement about China's ability to build power and influence efficiently and effectively, not presenting a normative conclusion about Beijing's methods. Ingenuity has historically been applied both for good and for evil, and this continues to be true in the present day.

A Sketch of What Comes Next

This book lays out how China managed to reach great power status in a competitive international environment. In Chapter 1, I lay out my main argument regarding the upstart strategy. I discuss the basic propositions of competition theory, showing why actors are sometimes driven toward tactics, activities, and strategies that differ from those of their primary competitors. I lay out the three components of the upstart strategy—emulation, exploitation, and entrepreneurship—and discuss the pros and cons of each, which set the conditions under which each component is likely to be the preferred pathway to power.

Chapters 2 and 3 assess the degree to which China has adopted the upstart approach to its attempts to build political and diplomatic power. Chapter 2 focuses on the conditions that motivated the cases of emulation, some (mediation diplomacy, for example) more successful than others (soft power). I also present the conditions that led to exploitation and discuss the details of those behaviors, including how China has competed with similar strategies where competitive forces are weakest. Some examples include China's approach to arms sales, diplomatic outreach, and manipulation of international institutions.

Chapter 3 demonstrates how consideration of the five main factors led to the entrepreneurial approach and how that approach manifests itself in the diplomatic realm. For example, the United States strives to be the external security partner of choice to many countries. In contrast, China strives to be the internal security partner of choice, helping to train law enforcement personnel and supply internal surveillance equipment. China also eschews alliances in favor of strategic partnerships. The result is that China can be flexible in putting together issue-oriented coalitions while avoiding alienating any state or group of states—Beijing seeks to be a friend to all, an enemy to none.

Building military power without sparking a strong response from the established great power is the hardest and most pivotal task for any aspiring great power. Chapters 4 and 5 show how China managed to build a military befitting a great power without provoking the United States to strangle its modernization efforts for most of its rise. Given that global military power is the foundation of US power and influence in the world, Chapter 4 focuses on how China's views of possible US responses and strategic effectiveness led to emulation in pursuing the ability to fight wars in the information age, carrying out "legitimate" military activities like humanitarian and peacekeeping missions, and participating in arms control regimes. It also covers one case in which different motivations caused China to diverge from the upstart strategy—China's aircraft carrier program. Lastly, it discusses an example in which China exploits US gaps and vulnerabilities, a strategy that lies at the heart of China's military challenge: its ability to keep most US forces out of Asia and disrupt those operating there (known as its anti-access/area denial capability [A2/AD]).

Chapter 5 begins by laying out how the United States has leveraged its military in foreign military intervention and global power projection to promote its interests. I show that, contrary to what the concerned voices within the US defense establishment say, China has yet to pursue similar strategies largely because it sees those strategies as ineffective and overly threatening to the United States. China also largely avoided a strong US military response to its rise by initially delaying military modernization. It then focused on innovative ways to build and exercise military power: gray zone activities, a distinct nuclear strategy, and unique ways of protecting overseas interests that do not rely on overseas bases or military intervention. By avoiding emulation, China has been able to navigate through the period when it was most vulnerable to US military coercion and build a military capable of taking on the United States in many regional contingencies.

Although China's approach to building military power has been impressive, it is nothing compared to the economic clout China has managed to muster over the past three decades. Chapter 6 provides examples of emulation and exploitation in China's pursuit of free trade, its use of economic coercion, and its somewhat failed internationalization of its currency, the renminbi (RMB). Chapter 7 also discusses examples of China's entrepreneurship in gaining economic power through industrial policy, foreign economic assistance, and its Belt and Road Initiative (BRI). The chapter shows how China uses these tools to dominate the activity of standard setting and gain access to natural resources. In all economic cases, China weighed what would be the most strategically effective and efficient against potential domestic and international costs given US strategy, US perceptions, and Chinese competitive advantages.

What can we expect from China moving forward, and what is the best US policy response? Understanding the upstart approach can help policymakers around the world predict Chinese activities, assess their potential benefits, and increase the costs to China of engaging in particularly problematic competitive approaches. To this end, the conclusion of *Upstart* points out areas where China is likely to focus its competitive efforts and the approach Beijing may adopt in the future. The conclusion weighs in on the major theoretical and policy debates, such as whether China's power has peaked and whether it will eventually overtake the United States (and whether such an outcome even matters). I argue that part of the answer depends on whether China continues with the mix of emulation and entrepreneurship that has led to its current success or shifts to more direct competition through more emulation. Lastly, I provide recommendations for how the United States could adopt aspects of the upstart approach to maintain and increase its competitive edge.

1

The Upstart Strategy

Competition for power in its various forms is a defining feature of the international system. Striving to gain or win by establishing superiority over others is not necessarily conflictual or destabilizing; two countries could theoretically compete for influence by seeking to be the more generous provider of foreign aid, the greener nation, or the country with more open-door immigration policies. But the competitive dynamics inherent in the relationship between rising powers and established hegemons tend to be zero-sum in nature; twelve out of the sixteen such contests in modern history culminated in major war.[1]

While these power-transition wars are rare in international politics, so too are countries that build enough power and influence to enter the league of great powers. Cultivating the domestic resource base to become a great power is difficult; translating those resources into power on the international stage is arguably even harder. And a rising power must do all this under the watchful eye of the incumbent hegemon, which is inclined to undermine efforts it deems threatening.

This chapter lays out the strategy that has allowed China, as a rising power, to enter the great power club and the factors that have determined the contours of its strategic approach. Innumerable books have examined historical cases of rising powers and then applied those findings to China assuming China will behave like other aspirants before it. Some believe China will follow in the footsteps of other rising powers, falling victim to the structural constraints of "Thucydides's Trap."[2] Others argue that China—like other rising powers in history—will become more aggressive to achieve its ambitions before its power fades.[3] Indeed, why should we expect China to behave any differently than its historical predecessors?

This chapter provides an explanation for why a rising power might do things differently from an established great power, and what those strategies might entail. In doing so, I provide a clearer conceptualization of emulation and its role in international politics.

Emulation in International Politics

The conventional wisdom is that states emulate in the hope of becoming powerful themselves. One of the first versions of this argument was Kenneth Waltz's "sameness effect," which famously predicts that states will imitate the successful practices of others.[4] The idea is not new. Machiavelli, writing in the early sixteenth century, counseled leaders to emulate, stating, "Above all he must do what some great men have done in the past: take as model a leader who's been much praised and admired and keep his example and achievements in mind at all times."[5] Arguments about imitation are widespread in political science. In the military realm, states often copy innovations in tactics and weaponry; for example, many states respond to opponents' development of nuclear capability with nuclear weapons of their own.[6] Similarly, in technology and medicine, global leaders often try to "emulate proven models of success."[7]

The emulation argument is popular beyond realists as well. Prestige, status, and legitimacy are concepts that rely on emulation, because an action is imbued with a recognition of importance only when a state of a certain type has taken that action beforehand. Emulation stems from comparing the "feats and qualities" of different states.[8] States may be driven to develop certain military capabilities such as nuclear weapons or aircraft carriers; contribute peacekeeping forces or foreign aid; or dive into competitions in which they repeatedly copy each other, such as arms races, naval buildups, or even colonial expansion in Africa—all in a competition for prestige.[9] A small state may emulate acknowledged middle power practices to be recognized as a "good" state so as to "climb the global pecking order."[10] To gain status benefits, countries outside an alliance grouping may mimic the alliance's central strategy to show they "pursue foreign policy goals validated by the hegemon."[11] Indeed, mimicking, including copying the behavioral norms of a group, can be a rational decision-making heuristic that is especially valuable under uncertainty. It reduces the time and effort an actor must expend to gather and evaluate information before reaching a decision.[12]

Other schools of thought in social science highlight that differences between countries are eliminated as countries develop—a phenomenon known as convergence. Countries that modernize trend toward homogeneity or "a restricted set of alternatives" that force them to become similar.[13] Whether it is because of competition, coercion, emulation, mimicry, or normative pressures, a common view is that "the forces making for uniformity among different societies become stronger than those perpetuating diversity" as countries industrialize.[14]

Sociologists have identified a similar emulative phenomenon called diffusion, which they use to explain how practices (behaviors, beliefs, technology, or structures) from one culture or group spread to another. These studies focus on why and how the diffusion occurs. For example, it can occur when two groups are in close, frequent contact with each other, though adoption is more likely to occur when the actors are culturally similar.[15] The homogeneity in organizational fields, in contrast, can be explained by coercion (pressures from culture or others the organization is dependent on), mimetic behavior (when organizations model themselves after other successful organizations in response to uncertainty in organizational technologies, goals, or the environment), or normative behavior (applying common filters to help define work conditions, methods, and legitimization).[16]

Though powerful and pervasive, the emulation argument is surprisingly underdeveloped. First and foremost, there is lack of clarity about what is considered emulation. Emulation can describe a country's strategy or the area in which it competes. For example, China's participation in international institutions can be a form of emulation (since the United States also participates), but so too can its building of separate institutions (since the United States built power by founding institutions). Indeed, some scholars consider it emulation if the rising power merely engages in "the conscious and careful search for exemplars and success stories [and] a dissection of the reasons for their success."[17]

Second, what is the target of this careful assessment? Realist arguments clearly point to great powers, but this could mean the approaches of past great powers or contemporary ones. There might even be a distinction between the strategies the established great power pursued to achieve its status and the policies it implements to then maintain it. For those that focus on how countries are socialized into adopting certain practices, the great power could be the target of emulation, but whether certain norms and practices are adopted might also depend on how many and what types of countries engage in that practice. Diffusion points to the similarity of societies as a key predictor of the source of adoption practices, and a country might reasonably have learned lessons from its own history.

Third, how comprehensive must the adoption be for it to be considered emulation? Does the rising power need to adopt values or domestic political processes like those of the established power for its power accumulation strategy to be considered emulation? This seems unlikely, as multiple studies point to the adopter's need to reconstruct the practice or norm to a degree to better fit with local conditions.[18] But then it is still unclear at what point adaptation leads to practices so different that the strategy can no longer be considered emulation.

Fourth, the emulation approach to competition is incomplete. It fails to capture critical and novel ways countries attain and maintain their great power status. Some very powerful countries have built and exercised power differently from the prevailing norms and practices of their times. The builders of the Roman Empire were the first to connect their conquered lands with roads and provide them with basic social services like aqueducts and sewage systems.[19] The Persians built an empire by allowing their conquered peoples to maintain their cultures, traditions, languages, and religions, while still standardizing the currency and providing regional governance.[20] Early Chinese dynasties defeated enemies with new chariot technology and bronze weapons and were the first to build a tributary system.[21] Great Britain pioneered naval dominance as a winning strategy and redefined the word "empire," co-opting locals to run their bureaucracies.[22] The Soviet Union was the first Marxist-communist state in the world and proactively sought to disseminate its ideology, which allowed it to establish a bloc of allies.[23] The United States chose to build international institutions and protect its interests not through permanent occupation but through global power projection and democratization.[24]

Lastly, the emulation approach fails to acknowledge the potential downsides of taking the well-trodden path. Indeed, although many scholars recognize that imitation of the dominant state's strategy sometimes does not occur, they incorrectly assume this is a suboptimal outcome in need of explanation.[25] But there are rational reasons not to emulate. First-mover advantages may mean that the progress gained by emulating is too slow or costly. If achieving great power status does not require the riser to gain strength in a particular area, then emulating in that area can be a waste of resources. Also, when the rising power emulates the incumbent, there is less plausible deniability about what it is trying to achieve (great power status), especially in strategic domains. For example, Germany's efforts before World War One (WWI) to build battleships and gain colonies—key components of Great Britain's great power status—generated grave concern in London. Britain responded by increasing naval spending and constructing a new class of battleship: the dreadnought, which impeded Germany's attempt to compete with Britain.[26] In the case of China, Beijing initially tried to compete directly with the United States for preeminence after the end of the Cold War, but Chinese elites realized that this strategy "fed into the 'China threat' theory, increasing the risk that a coalition of states would try to contain China's rise."[27] As a result, Chinese leaders shifted to a strategy of "social creativity" that involved "identifying areas outside the geopolitical paradigm, where they could assume prominent roles."[28]

The upstart approach contributes to our understanding of how states build power by providing a clear conception of what behavior constitutes emulation. I provide justification for my measurement strategy and address competing conceptions in the alternative explanations section. I also build a more complete theory by adding exploitation and entrepreneurship to fully capture the range of a rising power's international activities. After clearly describing the components of the upstart strategy, I turn to its determinants and specify the conditions under which emulation benefits the rising power and when different pathways to power in the form of exploitation or entrepreneurship make more sense.

The Components of the Upstart Strategy

Leaders using the upstart strategy continuously choose a mix of imitation and innovation to facilitate power accumulation while balancing the need to reduce the costs and risks associated with their nation's rise. The upstart strategy has two elements: a defined area of competition and a method of competing. Emulation involves taking established approaches to old areas of competition, exploitation involves taking established approaches to new areas of competition, and entrepreneurship involves new approaches regardless of the area of competition. These different approaches are captured in Table 1.1.

In the case of China's rise, emulation involves taking established approaches to old areas of competition. Simply put, China's behavior and activities are largely the same as those of the United States and are carried in the same areas of competition: China and the United States are both seeking leadership roles in international institutions, attempting to mediate the same international conflicts, and striving for a large navy with aircraft carriers and a financial system dominated by their currency. Within emulation, there can be minor adjustments to adapt to different cultural, political, and normative

Table 1.1 Theory Table with Approach Type and Area of Emulation

		Approach Type	
		Imitative	Innovative
Area of Competition	Old	Component 1: Emulation	Component 3: Entrepreneurial
	New	Component 2: Exploitation	Component 3: Entrepreneurial

Source: Author's creation.

domestic circumstances, but the strategy is largely the same. Thus, China's involvement in international institutions and its creation of new institutions are emulative, as the US approach includes both activities. There is overlap between cooperation and emulation when the great power's strategy is cooperative, but there are many instances in which China could emulate a US practice that is more unilateral or conflictual in orientation.

With the second component, exploitation, China employs similar strategies to new areas of competition, thus exploiting US blind spots or gaps in the international order. The structure of the international system, together with a state's position in that system, determines the profitability of different approaches to building international power.[29] China has been trying for thirty years to shape the strategic environment to assist its rise while simultaneously searching for a better strategic position. One way it does so is to engage in niches within functional areas (norms, arms sales, military power projection, development assistance, etc.) and geographic areas (Asia, the Global South, developing rather than developed countries) where the United States is not active.[30] The blind spots of the established great power and whether China has advantages in those precise areas greatly influence whether exploitation is a viable strategy.

A blind spot is something that is not on the radar of the great power; it is an "untapped" segment of the market for international power and influence in which the great power is not actively participating. These blind spots exist for numerous reasons. The United States may discount certain areas, such as poor or developing countries, as being of low strategic importance. Washington may also believe it has already met the global demand for a certain public good—for instance, by backing the World Bank and International Monetary Fund (IMF) to provide international financial assistance. Blind spots can exist due to a lack of focus or suboptimal policies on the part of the great power.

Great power neglect can also be rational. Rising powers and great powers may have different "cost structures" of strategies: an area of engagement that is profitable for one may not be profitable for the other. China can gain power in Central Asia at a lower cost than the United States can since it enjoys less pushback from Russia and, as a bordering country, can provide benefits such as greater physical connectivity. In such matters, China is not outcompeting the United States; rather, the United States is not competing at all. States also have differing levels of satisfaction with the incumbent great power and the nature of its order, and China will find it easier to make inroads with the less-satisfied players. The established great power has vulnerabilities to exploit— inherent weaknesses that it has overlooked. A rising power may also free ride, benefiting from the system that the great power has established and pays to maintain without contributing its fair share.

There are also gaps in the international order that can be exploited—areas where ties are "thin," informal, and irregular, and where norms and rules are disputed (i.e., actors attach different meanings to symbols and events). Contradictions create structural holes in the system that allow for competition within these relatively unestablished areas.[31] Not all countries are involved in all institutions, of course, and there is great asymmetry between those that benefit from aspects of the order and those that are not intimately involved. Contested orders and fragile networks create openings for a rising power like China. The rising power can then play the role of agenda-setter and rule-maker, establishing its own institutions or guiding a consensus among like-minded states, without clearly attacking the main pillars of the hegemon's world order and thus delaying recognition of threat. Finally, a rising power can add to the international order by addressing new issues or engaging with countries that are somewhat isolated from aspects of the current order.

Component three captures a common feature of countries that successfully rose to great power status: entrepreneurial actions.[32] A rising power is entrepreneurial if it looks for new sources of power and accumulates and exercises influence in a way that sets it apart from its main competitor.[33] The specifics of entrepreneurial action change throughout history as the nature of power and the international order evolve. What makes an action entrepreneurial is not only what is done but how it is done; it is the seeking of opportunities and then the actualization of innovation.[34] Entrepreneurial actions allow a state to produce significant structural change, tearing down outmoded organizations while simultaneously laying the groundwork for their replacements.[35]

Many types of actions can be considered entrepreneurial. A country can engage in value creation by introducing new types of international organizations, providing new services or benefits to other countries, or using tools like foreign aid in a different way. Like corporations, countries can identify supply shortages and respond by providing new knowledge, products, or services that the incumbent power cannot or will not supply. China's provision of financing for infrastructure construction, as opposed to the US practice of providing aid mainly for medical and governance improvements, is one example.

The rise of the United States is a good illustration. Scholars suggest that the United States' approach of creating political orders that limit its ability to exercise its power is uniquely American—a leadership approach that did not mirror that of the British Empire, which led through threats and inducements instead of requiring willful deference.[36] The United States proved exceedingly successful at accumulating power while delaying an unfavorable reaction from the United Kingdom. By the early twentieth century, the United Kingdom had already determined that it could not challenge US ascendency. In the words of Lord Salisbury, "It is very sad, but I am afraid America is bound to forge ahead and nothing can restore the equality between us. If we had interfered in the Confederate Wars, it was then possible for us to reduce the power of the United States to manageable proportions."[37]

In the upstart strategy, the three E's are defined in reference to the established great power's current approaches. This claim will be further justified when I explore the cost-benefit analysis behind each strategy later in this chapter. But intuitively, this idea makes sense: during China's rise, the United States was the most powerful country in the international system, and thus the greatest role model for any rising powers seeking to emulate great powers. China also needed to close the power gap with the United States to become a great power, and US responses have a disproportionate impact on the success of China's strategy.

Additionally, the reference point for the rising power is the strategies of the contemporary established hegemon, not the strategies it employed during its own rise. This is because the world in which one country rises is often fundamentally different from the strategic environment that existed for the previous great power, changing the relative costs and benefits of different strategies. This is not to say that China does not value lessons from its own past or from other countries, but the potential costs and benefits of each component of the upstart strategy are determined by their relationship to US strategy.[38] Great power competition is a main driver here; as one prominent Chinese scholar posits, "The nature of a nation's rise is to surpass the strongest nation in the world, and the strongest nation in the world can only be its barrier and not supporter."[39] The United States is also the main reference point because what the United States is doing and how it responds to China largely determine how effective and efficient China's approaches will be.

The case studies provide empirical support for this measurement decision, as Chinese strategists tend to consider US approaches and practices far more than those of any other country. I also explore the alternative hypothesis that Chinese behavior is emulative of countries other than the United States throughout this book. I give special attention to whether China looks to other sources of inspiration in two situations: (1) when Chinese thinkers believe a US strategy is ineffective and (2) when the Chinese system does not allow for adoption. These are the most likely scenarios in which China might turn to other countries—those deemed more successful in that area or that have attributes like China's—as the source of emulative inspiration.

Determinants of the Upstart Strategy

Rising powers implement strategies to increase their aggregate power, but ideally not at the expense of the other (arguably more important) goals of maintaining domestic stability and avoiding a major confrontation with the established power. These goals require effectiveness and efficiency in power accumulation, which relates to the strengths and vulnerabilities of the regime in power as well as the nature of the international system. Rising powers manage these trade-offs by choosing different components of the upstart strategy. In this section, I discuss the five main variables that shape the decision to emulate, exploit, or embrace entrepreneurship: established power/hegemon perceptions, strategic efficiency, strategic effectiveness, domestic political considerations, and the nature of the international system.

Factor One: Perceptions of the Established Great Power

Theories of emulation might correctly explain how some countries improve their power position, but they ignore some unique factors that a rising power must consider if it hopes to become a great power. A rising power like China must avoid (or at the very least delay) pushing the incumbent great power into intense forms of competition such as containment or preventive war. Imitating the great power can signal that the intent to challenge the existing great powers, and so the optimal strategy is to choose ways to build power and influence that are unlikely to spark a negative great power response. The rising power needs to balance expanding global influence against dampening the security pressure imposed by the dominant power.[40]

This balance is not easy. As a prominent professor at Tsinghua, Sun Xuefeng, notes, the great power is extremely sensitive about whoever is challenging its dominant position, a sensitivity that poses a significant security threat to the rising power.[41] Direct challenges, like Wilhelmine Germany's challenge to British sea supremacy in the eastern Atlantic, are likely to backfire.[42] It doesn't help that a rising power inherently challenges the current power structure of the international order and will therefore likely make "the order's current beneficiaries wary."[43] It is a common Chinese refrain that China "must not only confront the Cold War mentality of Western capitalist great powers to hinder China's integration into the international community and its fair participation in building a more just international order, but also the strategic intentions of hostile forces to westernize and divide [the country]."[44] As former deputy foreign minister Fu Ying warned in 2020, the closing of the power gap between China and the United States, will "inevitably bring about tension."[45]

Ideally, the rising power will delay recognition of the threat it poses until the great power has few attractive options to deal with it. If the rising power provokes a strong competitive reaction too soon, it may be drawn into costly conflicts that extinguish its capacity to rise.[46] Indeed, Chinese leaders and thinkers have generally believed that the greatest threat to China's ambitions of becoming a great power would be the hostility of other states, especially the United States.[47] This was the ultimate logic behind Deng Xiaoping's strategy of "biding your time and hiding your strengths" (*taoguang yanghui*): to "avoid making enemies everywhere" and create an international environment conducive to China's rise.[48] Former Chinese leader Hu Jintao declared in 2009 that China "tries its best to avoid becoming the focus of major international conflicts and falling into the vortex of conflict and confrontation" to "minimize external pressure and resistance to China's development."[49] Chinese leaders and strategists agreed; the first two decades of the twenty-first century were the critical time for China to focus on catching up, and as the United States reacted to maintain its position in world affairs, it would become more difficult to do so.[50] Beijing's strategic approach "needed to negate other nations' abilities to constrain its foreign policy pursuits and related economic objectives" while simultaneously "avoid[ing] generating the very antagonism that could most directly derail its objectives."[51]

These considerations highlight the first factor that influences a rising power's choice of upstart pathway: an assessment of how the established great power will perceive a particular strategy. In some cases, emulation can be reassuring. Here China's emulative policies "succeeded" partly because countries were reassured by them and wanted them to succeed; the United States and its Organization for Economic Co-operation and Development (OECD) allies wanted to enmesh China in the international economic order partly because it viewed a developed China as preferable to a poor and unstable one. The incumbent may understand emulation as cooperation or a form of appeasement ("playing by their rules"), which in turn can help distract from, shield, or obfuscate the rising power's more problematic behavior in other areas. In others, these behaviors overlap with what would be considered "cooperation" and thus not engaging in such activities could spark concern. Relatedly, incumbents will have a difficult time labeling the riser's emulation as "illegitimate" behavior (a common tactic used to shore up allies and global public opinion) if they themselves engage in similar behaviors.

In other cases, a rising power's attempts to accumulate power in the same fashion as the incumbent power might be seen as a direct challenge to the established powers' equities and thus a threat. Doing things differently creates uncertainty about the nature of the action itself—the established great power may not recognize the rising power's achievements because its strategy is at odds with the great power's understanding of how to compete. Such a strategy "lie outside of the routine tasks which everybody understands."[52]

On the individual level, confirmation bias plays a role. Leaders tend to fit incoming information into their existing theories and images. Consequently, they resist information that suggests their country's power is waning, especially if such information is ambiguous.[53] This situation prevents a convergence in views about the rising power's intentions, and its actions are therefore discounted, mischaracterized, or absent from the great power's radar. Established great powers might "misjudge a challenging rival's actions . . . [by] apply[ing] traditional critical success criteria" without updating their understanding of how those criteria have changed.[54]

The greater the uncertainty about the implications of the rising power's actions, the greater the likely delay in the great power's response.[55] A rising power's preferences have to be revisionist for leaders to update their position and devise strategies to counter threats.[56] On the domestic political level, a lack of elite consensus or cohesion in the hegemon can hurt a state's willingness to balance.[57] Chinese strategists explicitly recognized the need to avoid appearing "as if [China] actively seeks to undermine US power and influence" since "such steps could precipitate outright rivalry with the United States and some of its allies," which would ultimately defeat the purpose of their power accumulation efforts.[58]

Factor Two: Strategic Efficiency

Another unique characteristic of a rising power is that it must build power on the international stage efficiently.[59] Expending more resources to achieve the same marginal gain in power is a losing proposition, especially since the rising power has by definition fewer resources than the great power.[60] Efficiencies can stem from internal or external factors. The anti-statist political tendencies of the United States, for example, inspired certain decisions—like adopting an all-volunteer military force instead of using conscription—that were more efficient than the Soviet approaches.[61] Michael Beckley builds on this logic to come up with a new metric of net power that deducts from aggregate power the domestic liabilities associated with building wealth and military capabilities.[62] On external factors, "the relative costs of the United States' 'empire by invitation' were not nearly as large as the imperial costs faced by the Soviets, who arguably confronted modern history's worst case of imperial overstretch."[63]

The need for efficiency might push a country toward more emulative policies. A competitor might be able to adapt successful practices later, when the approach becomes viable, and so reap all the benefits without the start-up costs.[64] Aggressive free riding can allow a country to avoid the costs of trial and error and leapfrog directly to successful strategies, bypassing the intermediate stages of development.[65] A rising power may also be particularly well suited to compete in a certain area due to its historical, cultural, political, or economic characteristics. In other words, it enjoys competitive advantages in that area or mode of competition. When these characteristics align with those of an established power, the emulator can optimize their second-mover advantage, which is the benefit derived from observing the successes and failures of the first mover, allowing the emulator to avoid costly mistakes and improve upon existing strategies. Also, doing something new might be risky; without a tried-and-true method, a new strategy could turn out to be ineffi-cient or ineffective, leading to a slower rise, if not the end of the rise.

Conversely, acute competition could incentivize rising powers to do things differently.[66] There may be few marginal gains in areas where the United States has perfected an approach. Indeed, rising powers are at a "dis-tinct competitive disadvantage in relation to well-endowed rivals that are probably capable of matching almost any move."[67] New approaches through exploitation or entrepreneurship can also lead to a quicker rise than copying one's competitor, which allows the rising power to catch up. They might also allow the rising power to gain a first-mover advantage in new strategic areas in which the incumbent may one day need to be competitive.

Additionally, the fact that the United States did something in the past does not mean that China can do something analogous today at an affordable price. The international system is constantly in flux; the costs of a strategy now may be higher than when the incumbent embarked on it. The norms of appropriate international behavior can evolve as some past practices and approaches become progressively unacceptable to the point that it is no longer beneficial to engage in them. Similarly, technological innovation can increase or reduce the costs of certain approaches. Long-term occupation of foreign territory, for example, became a less efficient option as the costs of repression increased and the benefits of holding land decreased.[68] It also becomes more expensive over time to make technological progress—ships can sail only so fast. Furthermore, gains may diminish as other countries de-velop counterstrategies or different approaches.

Factor Three: Strategic Effectiveness

Theories of emulation implicitly assume that the notion of success is what draws an actor to emulation. While great powers are successful on aggregate at building power, that determination does not necessarily apply to all their policies, practices, and approaches. If strategies are seen as effective, they are more likely to be emulated, or at least exploited in new areas of competition. However, an established great power may pursue strategies that the rising power sees as ineffective even for the great power. Chinese leaders, for example, think that certain US strategies have never been particularly effective or that they once were effective but no longer are. The US military, for example, has identified the need to adapt to the changing geopolitical and technological environment but has found it difficult to do so. Although many top US Navy leaders constantly emphasize the need for innovation to counter this threat and numerous Department of Defense war games demonstrate that the navy's ships are increasingly susceptible to attacks, the navy finds itself shackled to political and economic forces that prioritize job creation over adaptability in ship procurement. They are reluctant to break from the tradition, and they "have an arrogance" in their tried-and-true methods of the traditional fleet that has hindered the navy's progress.[69]

The reasons the United States continues to engage in ineffective strategies lie outside the scope of this book, but research suggests that Washington might have difficulty changing tack because of complacency, the stickiness of institutions, and general resistance to change from the known to the unknown. Part of the reason for the cyclical rise and fall of great powers is the possibility that what made a country great will eventually cause its decline.[70] China points to the United States' willingness to use force, its involvement in international conflicts, and its consequent need for a global military presence as factors that are depleting US power and hastening its decline.[71] To exercise its global leadership, moreover, the United States relies heavily on military power, which has arguably been ineffective, even in conflicts with weak states such as Afghanistan and Iraq.[72] From China's perspective, aspects of the United States' global economic strategy are also ineffective. Washington requires states to adhere to its preferred economic and political development models.[73] China, in contrast, is not constrained by such requirements and is therefore able to do business in high-risk, politically unsavory areas where Western companies are largely absent.

Factor Four: Domestic Political Considerations

Strategists often see competition between the United States and its challengers as "a test of systems—an audit of whose political-economic model is best placed to generate resources, craft sound policies and act effectively on the global stage."[74] Relatedly, a large number of political science theories hold that a domestic political system's strengths and vulnerabilities affect outcomes. The concept of liberal internationalism—with its emphasis on the pacifying role of global trade, the need for interstate arrangements to prevent physical conflict, and strategic restraint—largely assumes that democracies are best "suited to lead and operate within" the system.[75] Democracies tend to win more of the wars they fight than authoritarian regimes do, perhaps because they are more cautious about the wars they fight, or because the flexibility in their military systems and high morale lead to greater military effectiveness.[76] Authoritarian regimes are less stable than democracies, for internal threats can more readily be exploited to undermine the regime.[77]

By the same token, the centralized, non-transparent nature of authoritarianism allows for greater speed and secrecy in a state's foreign policy, while the ability to mobilize resources and infrequent changes in leadership make autocracies relatively predictable and potentially reliable allies.[78] In the area of technological competition, some argue that the United States is better positioned than China because its domestic political system encourages innovation; others say that a whole-of-government commitment and deep pockets are more important, and thus autocratic China has the advantage.[79]

I will address the validity of these arguments in the case studies, but for now the important takeaway is that different systems generate different competitive advantages, and this difference can create incentives for emulation, exploitation, and entrepreneurship.[80] Different power accumulation strategies will suit different countries, varying with their ideologies and domestic political structures. It is not surprising, then, that many of the rising power/great power competitions have involved states that were fundamentally different. Athens and Sparta, the Protestant Dutch Republic and Catholic Spain, and the United States and the Soviet Union during the Cold War—the countries in each pair had different competitive advantages and thus pursued different approaches to building and exercising power.

In the case of China, domestic political considerations can impact this calculus in two main ways: through competitive advantage and through domestic liabilities. Competitive advantage is the unique set of attributes and strengths that enables a country to outperform its competitors in the international system. It is a measure of how well a firm can differentiate itself from its competitors—for example, through its ability to provide a good or service at a better value (either at a lower price or with higher quality).[81] Competitive advantage thus also shapes the relative efficiency and effectiveness of a rising power's strategies.

While a state's political system, bureaucracy, and military organization may limit the ability to adopt innovations, the upstart strategy recognizes that these different internal conditions also create different competitive advantages.[82] One of the main reasons emulation may not be an attractive strategy is that what works well for one country may not work well for another, due to geography, history, and culture. One of the primary determinants of a country's competitive advantage—and of how a state can best translate national resources into international power—is its domestic political system. Indeed, the diffusion literature predicts that emulation is most likely when the source and adopter have similar attributes; close social or cultural ties can also lead actors to conform.[83]

Another type of domestic political consideration that impacts strategic choices is the motivation of the governing regime to maintain control. In the case of China, this imperative might make emulation of US practices, particularly those that could undermine the Communist Party's position, unattractive and untenable. As Xi has stressed repeatedly, "The party, government, military, people, and academia; east, south, west, north, and center—the Party leads all."[84] The CCP has made numerous decisions it deemed necessary to maintain Party control, even if the decisions led to suboptimal results for power or prosperity (the COVID-zero policy being a recent example). In other words, while China hopes to rise and enhance its position in the world, its leaders also must consider whether a given approach might diminish the Party-state's control. (For a democracy, the need to get reelected could shape the relative attractiveness of certain strategies.)

The need to maintain regime legitimacy could also encourage exploitation or entrepreneurship when it is important for China to see itself as different from the United States inside and out. Xi Jinping criticizes those who equate reform with moving toward Western values and political systems; for him, the best path is toward socialism with Chinese characteristics.[85] As Xi said when speaking at a 2015 high-level meeting addressing the education provided by Party schools:

> If [China] molds its practices according to Western capitalist value systems, and measures our development against the West's capitalist standards . . . and we judge everything that does not fit that standard as backwards and outdated, as needing to be criticized and attacked, the consequences would

be disastrous! If we do this, we would either be dancing to their tune or forever be scolded by them for not being "good enough."[86]

Factor Five: Exploitable Gaps, Blind Spots, or Vulnerabilities

The last factor that can influence whether a rising power chooses emulation, exploitation, or entrepreneurship depends on the nature of the area of competition, and specifically on whether there are gaps in the international order or blind spots and vulnerabilities of the established great power that can be exploited. Such exploitation can be beneficial because states consider another state's political intentions "revisionist" only if they seem to undermine, weaken, supplement, or change the "explicit principles, rules and institutions that define the core relationships between the states that are party to the order."[87]

But in some aspects of political behavior, the international order is nonexistent, weak, unstable, ambiguous, or incomplete. If the rising power builds influence in these areas first, while simultaneously enmeshing itself in and interacting comprehensively with well-established aspects of the order, it can strengthen its relative position without triggering alarm.[88] US strategists are looking for "clear violations of rules and norms."[89] In blind spots, "a competitor will either not see the significance of events at all, will perceive them incorrectly, or will perceive them very slowly."[90] There is also an efficiency aspect of this competitive strategy; pursuing tried-and-true strategies in areas where competition is weak can lead to significant gains at the cost of fewer resources than direct competition would require.

The Upstart and the Three E's

In this section, I lay out how these five factors interact to create incentives for emulation, exploitation, and entrepreneurship. China may assess the US strategic approach to be effective or ineffective at building power and certain approaches China may take as reassuring or threatening to the United States. The main domestic factor in the case of the CCP is whether a particular strategy might undermine Party control (or ideally could even serve to strengthen it). Chinese leaders will also consider whether there are competitive gaps and how efficient it would be to build power in that way—that is, whether China enjoys competitive advantages with respect to that strategy. Figure 1.1 depicts this decision tree. While it is a useful simplification, ultimately the decision depends on the weighing of the costs and benefits of all these factors simultaneously. Below I provide some examples of the combination of factors that lead China to emulate, exploit, or take entrepreneurial actions.

When China Emulates

The conventional wisdom holds that emulation is the key to power and influence. Indeed, sometimes China competes in the same area in the same way. Beijing has embassies, participates in most international institutions, and has built ground, naval, and air forces. But emulation does not make sense in all cases. The upstart framework lays out the conditions under which emulation allows a rising power to build power while managing the risks of external and internal pressures. In the case of China, Beijing considers emulation only when it judges the US approach in question to be effective. If it also concludes that emulation will be reassuring to the United States because the behavior is considered a legitimate course of action for a responsible country, China has an incentive to model US behavior. In other words, China is most likely to choose emulation in activities that are considered "legitimate" and "appropriate" within the contemporary international order—things all states do, and thus are expected to do. Engaging in such activities can give China prestige and status, especially if it is emulating something that only great powers can do. (This is assuming such an approach is not prohibitively costly to China due to competitive disadvantages.)

Strategic efficacy can also encourage emulation in certain cases. For example, a rising power may be able to build power efficiently where high fixed costs of an approach are borne by the great power, as in the case of US-led international institutions.[91] It is thus unsurprising that China wanted to participate in certain aspects of the world order such as the UN and WTO. The United States paid the fixed costs of setting up these institutions (and continues to take on a larger burden than China in maintaining them), and China was able to build power without provoking the United States. If the rising power builds influence in these areas first, interacting with established aspects of the established order, it can strengthen its position without triggering the alarm. China has even managed to reassure countries of its

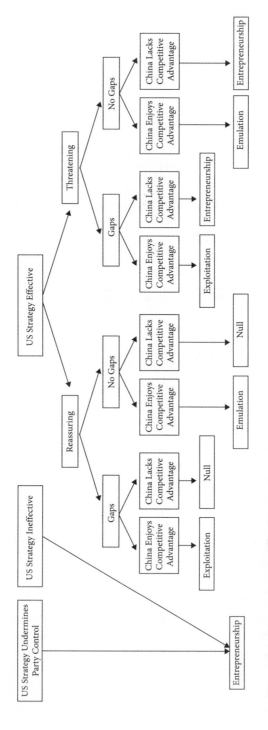

Figure 1.1 Determinants of the Upstart Strategy
Source: Author's creation.

peaceful intentions by emulating cooperative behavior.[92] China might also have unique attributes or strengths that allow it to compete efficiently in that competitive approach or area of competition. It is possible China emulates in this case, even if it sparks threat perceptions, because the relative power gains are so significant.

When China Exploits

If a US approach is considered effective, China may consider exploitation the best option under certain conditions. First, if Beijing cannot compete efficiently in direct competition, it will seek areas where competitive forces are relatively weak due to gaps in the international order or the blind spots and vulnerabilities of the United States. If any of these weaknesses exist, China can employ a tried-and-true approach in these new areas of competition to make gains efficiently and at a lower relative risk of provocation.

Areas of competitive uncertainty are ripe with prospects for marginal gains. Order involves "well-defined boundaries, common rules and practices, shared causal and normative understandings, and resources adequate for collective action."[93] But in some domains and issue areas, things are unsettled, boundaries are not well defined, principles are contested, and understandings diverge, resulting in ambiguity about "appropriate actions." Competing in areas dominated by the United States might be seen as a challenge, whereas activity elsewhere perceived as compliance. Thus focusing efforts on building power within competitive gaps may be an effective way of building power without provoking the hegemon.[94]

While exploiting competitive uncertainty and blind spots does not provoke sudden and extreme reactions, the approach is not wholly unproblematic. Sometimes competing on the margins, in niches and gaps, is not efficient, or it can upset the established great power. In such cases, the rising power can pursue power differently, through entrepreneurial actions that cater to its competitive advantages.

When China Is Entrepreneurial

Competition can incentivize a rising power to differentiate itself, instead of converging with the behavior of others, to exploit its competitive advantages and minimize the attention it attracts.[95] There are three pathways to entre-preneurial actions. First, if the United States' approach to a similar goal is viewed as ineffective, then China will choose an alternative entrepreneurial approach. Second, if the approach is seen to undermine Party control, China will eschew emulation in favor of entrepreneurial actions regardless of how effective and efficient the US strategy is thought to be. Third, when US strategy is considered effective, but emulation is likely to be perceived as threatening, there are no significant gaps to exploit, and China does not enjoy competitive advantages that makes the risk of emulation worthwhile, it will embrace an entrepreneurial approach to build that type of power. Ideally (from China's perspective), its entrepreneurial approach would simulta-neously strengthen Party control, leverage its competitive advantages, and undermine US policies in that area, all at an acceptable cost in terms of US threat perceptions and thus response.

Observable Implications of the Upstart Strategy

What would we expect to see in the case studies if the upstart approach has significant explanatory power? First and foremost, there should be a core re-lationship between US strategy and Chinese strategy. Externally, the United States is the driving factor. In all the cases, we should see indications that China is assessing the relevant US strategy—its costs, its benefits, whether China can compete, and how the United States might respond. Whether there is strategic uncertainty to exploit, an opportunity for innovation, or incentives for emulation depends largely on the United States. But what China does in these various categories—choosing BRI, for example—will be largely determined by its own competitive advantages and impact on Party control.

There should also be a strong correlation between the key determinants of the upstart strategy and the component Beijing chooses, as described in the preceding section. When China chooses imitative approaches even though the cost-benefit calculus per the upstart strategy suggests an alternative path would be better, we should expect a suboptimal result—greater concern about China's rise with little to show for it in terms of power and influence.

While the components of the upstart strategy should capture Chinese behavior, its explanatory power increases when Chinese thinking reflects the pros and cons of imitation versus innovation. For this reason, a section of each of the case studies evaluates Chinese perspectives on the competitive strategy. Though the internal deliberations of the CCP are notoriously opaque, there are indications that Chinese leaders are thinking along the lines of the upstart approach. Chinese leaders recognized that China was starting to compete in the 1990s from a relatively weak political, economic, and military position. According to a popular internal metric called Comprehensive National Power (CNP), China's self-assessed scores were poor in the 1990s; China had a little more than a third of the United States' power and still lagged countries such as Canada and France.[96] Even so, China's ambition of achieving great power status was clear.[97] And building power was not enough. Chinese leaders understood they needed to ensure that it could protect its interests "with[in] the stark constraints of a unipolar world in which a potentially hostile US would long remain the dominant power."[98] As one high-level military officer explained, China needed to avoid a major war at all costs while "the foundation of our country's economic construction is still weak."[99]

Alternative Arguments

My argument that China built enough power to reach great power status through the upstart strategy challenges the conventional wisdom.[100] Throughout these pages, I evaluate the main alternative explanation: China became a great power by emulating the United States. A corollary to this explanation is that the main source of emulation is not the United States but other states. My framework allows for China to seek inspiration from other countries (and even its own history), and I note in the case studies where this occurs, but I contend that the United States is the main reference point because of its relative success.[101] Additionally, great power competition with the United States shapes many of the factors that determine the relative attractiveness of emulation, exploitation, and entrepreneurship.

The second alternative hypothesis is that China's strategic choices are based on factors other than those presented in the upstart strategy. Perhaps capabilities alone drive competitive decisions: China will mimic the US strategy when it has the capabilities to do so, and when it lacks those capabilities, it will pursue a different strategy until those capabilities are developed. But the upstart strategy is based on the premise that, for rising powers, there are additional reasons not to imitate great power efforts, such as concern about how the great power will perceive and respond to the challenge. To be sure, capabilities shape the contours of the upstart strategy. US failings define weak competitive spaces; Chinese competitive advantages determine the new pathways to power upon which they embark. But I argue that it is not right to say China does not emulate the United States because it cannot.

Perhaps unique ideational factors such as strategic culture or different preferences (a desire for prosperity over power, for example) explain China's strategic decisions. I do present some case studies in which, from the perspective of the upstart strategy, China did not make the correct strategic choice about how to build power. In these cases, factors other than the five I list are likely the culprit. But I show in the case studies that for the most part, the five factors I highlight have the greatest impact on China's strategic decisions about how to build power and influence.

Lastly, one could argue that there is already a sufficient explanation for China's approach—it is pursuing an asymmetric strategy, meaning that China uses its strengths against its adversary's weaknesses instead of "attempt[ing] to match the adversary in all of his capabilities."[102] Like Gaddis's concept of asymmetric strategies, the upstart strategy is resource-conscious and involves trying to "shift the nature and location of competition" to press asymmetric advantages. But it is more complex in that it helps the rising power determine which capabilities to develop in the first place. China often pursues parallel strategies, such as striving to be the internal security partner when the United States is the external security partner. It also pursues strategies like those of the United States but in areas where competitive forces are weaker. It courts African countries through high-level visits, for instances, whereas the United States largely focuses its diplomatic efforts on the developed world. Even when China wants to achieve a common goal—security for its overseas interests—it may do so through exploitation of commercial access and reliance on host nation security forces rather than overseas bases.

None of these examples of China's upstart approach can be considered asymmetric. This is not to say that China does not also embrace asymmetric approaches, but only that this characterization is insufficient to explain China's strategic choices. Additionally, a country can imitate another broadly and yet pursue asymmetric strategies to counter influence in particular areas. For example, during the Cold War, George Kennan believed the United States should seek to compete with the Soviet Union militarily by "reinforcing its own strengths and those of its allies, but with no effort to duplicate Soviet force configurations."[103] But the characteristics of the United States' asymmetric strategy—development of nuclear weapons, pursuing alliances, covert activities, and psychological warfare—were not unique to the United States; the Soviet Union employed the same tactics.[104]

This chapter provides a way to understand how China competes and what factors shape its approach. I argue that the upstart strategy—which entails emulation, exploitation, and entrepreneurship—is what best characterizes how China competes for power. It also explains how China has built power over the past thirty years while balancing the competing demands of maintaining internal stability and avoiding a hegemonic war (or at least ensuring that it reaches power parity before war occurs).[105] In other words, the United States did not simply fail to respond to China's rise. Rather, China has designed strategies to encourage delayed responses to its relatively effective and efficient accumulation of power.[106]

In the following chapters, I explore how the upstart strategy manifested itself in the geopolitical, military, and economic realms. I demonstrate that differentiation, not emulation, is often China's main driver. While this book focuses on demonstrating how the upstart strategy has captured past Chinese behaviors, it presents some significant implications for the future of Chinese power and competition. As China's power grows, its competitive advantages, as well as the costs of provoking the United States, will change. This means that the mix of exploitation, entrepreneurship, and emulation could change over time as well. The rationale for each decision over time, which is captured in the case studies, will provide insight into how we can expect its competitive approach to evolve.

2

Emulation and Exploitation in Chinese Foreign Policy

The 1990s were a time of seismic shifts in Chinese foreign policy. China emerged from its post-Tiananmen isolation determined to build its power on the international stage by expanding bilateral relationships and playing a greater role in international institutions. China normalized relations with twenty-eight countries during the 1990s, including major players like South Korea. From 1989 to 2022, China's participation in intergovernmental organizations increased by a factor of twenty and its participation in non-governmental organizations rose by a factor of seven.[1] Jiang Zemin, the leader of China from 1989 to 2002, created guidelines for managing US–China relations in this initial period of its rise, including growing confidence, reducing complications, increasing collaboration, and avoiding opposition.

Chinese thinkers had recognized that China was weaker than the United States but nonetheless had to figure out in the post–Cold War period how to escape international isolation while simultaneously carving out space to maneuver within this bilateral relationship.[2] China managed to transform from a diplomatically isolated country to a country that possessed as much diplomatic and political power on the world stage as the United States (or by some measures slightly more).[3] Even though the United States dedicates far more resources to foreign policy—it has twice as many diplomats stationed abroad and twenty times as many contributions to international organizations—in 2022 many perceived Beijing to be "winning the race for global influence."[4]

China has achieved this feat by embracing the upstart strategy. China tends to emulate the United States where the US approach is thought to be effective and where such behavior is seen as legitimate and reassuring, and thus useful for improving China's image at minimum cost. This chapter examines two cases that meet these criteria: mediation diplomacy and participation in international institutions. I also examine a case of emulation—soft power—in which Chinese leaders chose emulation even though the ideal conditions for emulation were not present. I include this deviant case to show that China does not always follow the logic of the upstart strategy (possibly because motivations beyond power drive that particular decision), but when it does not, it pays a cost. Such cases enhance our confidence about the centrality of the upstart strategy to China's successful rise.

Where US strategy is effective but not all-encompassing, China pursues exploitation, embracing the same strategy but implementing it in areas where competitive forces are weak in ways that cater to its competitive advantages. Through this approach, China has expanded its base of influence among countries largely ignored by the United States. I look at two cases in which China has exploited US blind spots and gaps in the international order: arms sales and diplomatic outreach. In these cases, China is not so much outcompeting the United States as being active where the United States is absent.

Playing the Mediator

Conflict mediation has been a key tool of US foreign policy since the end of WWII and has been fairly successful at ending violent behavior and creating stability.[5] The United States has mediated fifty-six civil conflicts from 1945 to 1999.[6] Some of the highest-profile success stories include the Good Friday Agreement, which brought an end to Irish Republican Army violence in Northern Ireland, and the 1978 Camp David Accords, which resolved territorial and political disputes between Egypt and Israel.[7] The focus has primarily been on preventing conflicts from spiraling out of control, which would damage the interests of the United States and its allies. In addition to recognizing the effectiveness of mediation diplomacy, Chinese officials and strategists realize that mediation diplomacy is largely perceived as a legitimate way to promote or secure one's economic interests and political influence.[8] Embracing this strategy would thus enhance China's image as a responsible great power while also dampening threat perceptions.[9]

China enjoys some competitive advantages in this area. Unlike the United States, China often has good relations with all parties in the dispute, including some problematic states, and thus has the potential to influence the participants and position itself as an unbiased mediator. In some prominent situations, the United States does not even formally recognize the parties in question (e.g., Iran, North Korea, the Taliban in Afghanistan), which makes it even harder to engage. China may be able to host political elites from such countries without suffering the reputational consequences that the United States would incur. American officials seemed to recognize these competitive advantages when they reportedly asked their Chinese counterparts to intervene to help avert a Russian invasion of Ukraine.[10]

Given mediation's effectiveness and legitimacy, as well as China's competitive advantages, the upstart strategy encourages emulation. Indeed, China has positioned itself as a peacemaker in several high-profile crises. China championed the UN Security Council (UNSC) resolution urging India and Pakistan to sign the Nuclear Non-Proliferation Treaty (NPT) in 1998 after nuclear tests had created tensions. Beijing again conducted shuttle diplomacy between Pakistan and India after the 2008 Mumbai attacks, and between Afghanistan and Pakistan in 2017, when Afghanistan charged Pakistan with harboring Taliban militants. China has been intermittently involved as a mediator in Myanmar's internal security and peace process since 2010, hosting various talks with Burmese officials and the eight ethnic armed organizations.

China was critical in bringing North Korea and other participating countries to the negotiating table in the six-party talks, a multinational effort from 2003 to 2009 to achieve North Korean denuclearization through a diplomatic agreement. (China has since continued to call for the resumption of negotiations.)[11] Beijing also intervened more than once in Sudan, helping warring parties conform to the 2005 Comprehensive Peace Agreement and the 2015 South Sudan Peace Agreement. After the US withdrawal from Afghanistan in 2021, China met with the Taliban to demonstrate China's pivotal role in any peace process there. In 2023, China mediated a Saudi-Iran agreement to restore diplomatic ties and put forward its own proposal for a Russo-Ukrainian peace. While arguably of little substance, Party outlets have touted these efforts as a sign of China's benevolence in world affairs and the advantages its approach to diplomacy confers compared to that of Western counterparts.[12]

China's approach to mediation diplomacy is deliberate and strategic. Since 2016, China has nominated special envoys for the Korean nuclear issue, African affairs, Middle Eastern affairs, the Afghan issue, and the Syrian conflict. In November 2022, China's Ministry of Foreign Affairs announced it would establish a new international organization for conflict resolution.[13] Unsurprisingly, Chinese mediation efforts are more likely in areas where the country has a strategic stake (like in countries participating in the BRI).[14] China's mediation efforts in Sudan, where its state-owned enterprises (SOEs) hold a 40 percent share in one of Sudan's oil field projects, are a compelling example.[15] Mediation is also an effective way to control events in bordering countries like Afghanistan, India, Myanmar, Nepal, North Korea, and Pakistan, where strife threatens to spill over into China.[16] Figure 2.1 is a map of the locations of China's most significant mediation activities, 2006–2023.

Whether mediation leads to conflict resolution is, for our purposes, a secondary consideration. China's willingness to engage seems to be enough to win favor, legitimacy, and recognition. Former President Trump famously argued that Beijing had "been a big help, bigger than most people know," with North Korea.[17] China received kudos for pressuring the Sudanese government to accept UN-African mission forces in the 2005 Darfur crisis and for facilitating follow-up peace agreements. In 2017, when China attempted to restore talks between the UN and the Houthi movement in Yemen, the leaders of the latter "thanked China for taking an objective and impartial stance on the Yemen issue and said they would be willing to maintain close communication with Beijing."[18] China's involvement in negotiations with Iran was seen as pivotal to the signing of the Joint Comprehensive Plan of Action (JCPOA). Myanmar's Aung Sang Suu Kyi publicly thanked China for its role in Myanmar's national reconciliation process.

Mediation, furthermore, helps China minimize the political costs associated with its trade relations with rogue states. China was heavily criticized for buying oil from the Sudanese government while Sudan engaged in genocide, for sourcing gas from the Iranians as they moved toward nuclear weapons, and for trading with the North Koreans. To counteract this criticism, China worked hard in all three cases to bring countries to the negotiating table. In 2023 Beijing also brokered an agreement between Riyadh and Tehran, two large suppliers of energy to Beijing.

Another reason emulation is attractive is that China does not need to dedicate significant resources to these efforts before reaping its benefits, making it highly efficient. As one Chinese diplomat joked in reference to China's role in the six-party talks, for the sake of stability on the Korean peninsula China was willing to provide the coffee, which cost a few dollars.[19] Much of it is public theater; China favors high-profile methods—host diplomacy, special envoy diplomacy, top-level visits—over tools such as multilateral contact groups, document diplomacy, leveraged aid, and shuttle diplomacy. The influence China gains in return is often welcome, thus reassuring countries of China's intentions and boosting its international image.[20] China also uses these opportunities to criticize US policy and distinguish itself from

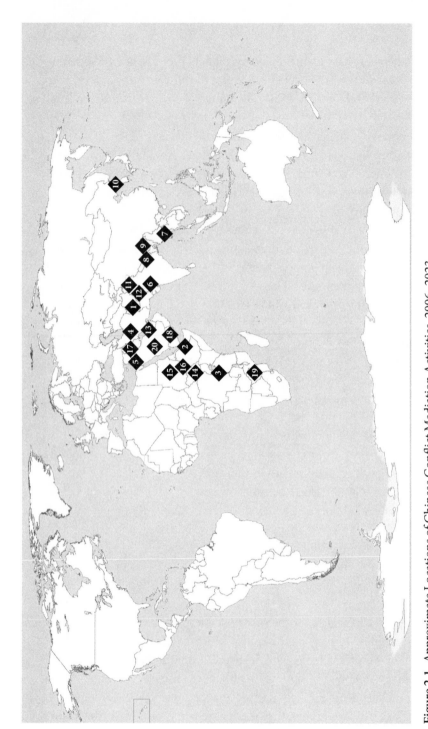

Figure 2.1 Approximate Locations of Chinese Conflict Mediation Activities, 2006–2023

Source: Data from Helena Legarda, "China as a Conflict Mediator: Maintaining Stability Along the Belt and Road," MERICS, August 22, 2018, https://merics.org/en/short-analysis/china-conflict-mediator; supplemented by author's own research.

the United States. In May 2021, when offering to host talks between Israelis and Palestinians, Chinese foreign minister Wang Yi noted that the proposal was part of China's desire to be a "constructive" player in the region, unlike the United States, which was "standing on the opposite side of international justice."[21]

In its approach, China has attempted to minimize any risks associated with embracing mediation diplomacy. To protect the Communist Party's position on human rights issues and areas like Tibet, Hong Kong, Xinjiang, and Taiwan, China tries to mediate in ways that support its non-interference principle, such as by making sure countries officially request China's involvement before taking action.[22] The plethora of articles on how China's mediation style differs from that of the United States—impartial, not forceful, welcomed, without ulterior motives—indicates China's desire to make sure its efforts do not unintentionally enhance threat perceptions.[23] And to ensure that its strategy is effective and efficient, China avoids overinvolvement. As the prominent scholar Wang Jisi noted, China must "strike a balance between 'intervening creatively' and being tied down into national crises in the region, as did the West."[24]

Manipulating International Institutions

After the devastation of WWII, the United States created a series of international institutions to encourage cooperation and shape the nature of international politics. Diplomacy would be conducted through the UN, which was also tasked with codifying major principles of international law, maintaining international peace and security, and suppressing acts of aggression. The General Agreement on Tariffs and Trade (GATT), which would become the WTO in 1995, was set up to facilitate free trade among nations. The World Bank, which was founded as the International Bank for Reconstruction and Development in 1944, focused initially on postwar reconstruction and eventually on international cooperation for development. The International Monetary Fund (IMF) has overseen exchange rates and other arenas of monetary policy, such as capital flows, since 1944. The World Health Organization (WHO), established in 1948, manages international public health. A wide range of international institutions with more limited charters have also been established, including UN subsidiaries such as the United Nations Children's

Fund (UNICEF) and the United Nations Educational, Scientific, and Cultural Organization (UNESCO).

International institutions were part of the American means of building and exercising power in an entrepreneurial fashion. They have allowed the United States to set the agenda, rules, norms, principles, and procedures for other states to follow, facilitating information sharing and reducing the transaction costs of cooperation among states.[25] As John Ikenberry argues, institutions provide a democratic hegemon like the United States with a mechanism to preserve its dominant position in a favorable order, partly by making its power more palatable to weaker states.[26]

The United States was so confident in the ability of international institutions to constrain state power in accordance with US preferences that thirty years ago many thought China's inclusion in the world order would compel Beijing to liberalize and establish a domestic political and economic system more in line with that of the United States. Even in the wake of the 1989 Tiananmen massacre, President George H. W. Bush's 1990 National Security Strategy insisted that China's ties to the outside world were "crucial to China's prospects for regaining the path of economic reform and political liberalization."[27] The logic that institutional enmeshment would lead to reform encouraged the United States to grant China most-favored-nation status in the 1990s and support its accession to the WTO.

In other words, participation in international institutions is an effective way of building and exercising power. Moreover, China could use its participation to expand its power while simultaneously reassuring other countries about its rise.[28] According to China's top diplomat during the Hu era, Dai Bingguo, China's top priority in the mid-2000s was to reassure Washington by being a willing participant and "constructive builder" in the international system.[29] This tactic promised efficiency as well: the United States would continue to pay to uphold the international order (the United States continues to contribute about 5.5 times more to the UN than China does as of 2021).[30]

By the beginning of the twenty-first century, China had joined fifty international governmental organizations and 1,275 international nongovernmental organizations.[31] Emulation was clearly a better pathway to power than trying to work outside these institutions in a more entrepreneurial fashion. In the words of Wang Yizhou, an international relations theorist and vice dean of the School of International Studies at Peking University:

The existing international rules under Western leadership are problematic, including many places of unfairness and injustice, but the options for a disadvantaged developing country are few; they must first be a part of it and then work toward long-term reforms when strengthening themselves. The idea of "setting up a separate kitchen" is unrealistic and may bring more harm to oneself.[32]

Chinese strategists called for emulating the United States when it came to leveraging international institutions, and specifically for "combin[ing] forces" with other rising and developing states "to usher in a more reasonable and just international system."[33]

Within these institutions, China subsequently sought a greater leadership role akin to that of the United States and its allies with the aim of controlling the agenda and outcomes and inspiring reform.[34] The proportion of elected Chinese management and executives in international organizations indicates that China wields relative power within those institutions through two mechanisms: first, the influence over international organizations required to place Chinese citizens in those positions in the first place, and second, the Chinese bureaucratic power necessary to determine organization agendas and outcomes once in control.

According to my dataset on thirty major international and regional organizations (2000–2021), China has greatly expanded its share of top-level executive roles and senior management roles held by its citizens in international institutions over the last two decades, especially in standard-setting organizations.[35] In 2000, none of the twenty-seven organizations surveyed were led by a Chinese official, and only eight out of 232 senior managers were Chinese. By 2015, China had increased its top-level leadership representation to six out of twenty-nine (the two new organizations being UN Women and the Asian Infrastructure Investment Bank [AIIB], both of which were created after 2000), or 21 percent.

By 2021, Chinese representation had begun to level out: four out of the twenty-nine organizations surveyed were led by a Chinese citizen—one more leadership position than the United States held in the same year—and Chinese citizens occupied 19 out of 301 senior management positions. This change represents an increase of 13.8 percent in top-level executive representation and 2.8 percent in senior management positions over the entire twenty-one years surveyed. In 2021, four of the fifteen UN specialized agencies were headed by Chinese nationals, including the Food and

Agriculture Organization (FAO), the International Telecommunication Union (ITU), the United Nations Industrial Development Organization (UNIDO), and the International Civil Aviation Organization (ICAO), while the United States headed only one.[36]

US reduction in its participation in such institutions facilitated China's increased influence, which hints a bit at exploitation as well. In 2000, the United States accounted for 15 percent of executive positions and 13 percent of senior management positions, peaking in 2010 with 17 percent of senior managers. By 2021, the United States' representation had fallen to 12 percent of senior management positions, a decline of approximately 5 percentage points in eleven years. By 2021, China was regularly holding as many top-level executive slots as the United States, or even more, although US citizens held nearly twice as many senior management positions at this time. However, Europe, a longtime ally of the United States and party to its current international order, continues to fill a large proportion of the remaining leadership positions.

Another example comes in the International Seabed Authority (ISA). The ISA, part of the United Nations, regulates the mining of seabeds for important minerals. For years, China has taken an active role in this body, while the United States is only an observer, not a full member. And while the rules governing seabed activities may not have interested Washington policymakers earlier, that is no longer the case. Access to the massive deposits of critical minerals on the ocean floor, such as the nickel-rich Clarion-Clipperton Zone in the Pacific Ocean, will be critical for any nation interested in making the green transition (nickel and other materials are crucial for making electric batteries). The ISA is currently deliberating over rules for seabed mining, but if they do not come up with a regime, companies will be free to start mining in 2025. The short time window to finalize regulations, China's sway over the organization, and the United States' contrasting lack of power means that Beijing will likely be able to bend this new legal regime to its interests. This is an example of how China competes in the gaps, exploiting areas where the United States has failed to pay enough attention.[37]

China has some unique attributes that facilitate its approach. For example, China does not shy away from problematic approaches like bribery and coercion. In 2019, as elections approached for the top position in the FAO, allegations arose that China was playing dirty. China, in fact, was using both carrots and sticks to build its coalition. The carrots included forgiving $78 million of Cameroon's debt and purportedly providing voting officials with first-class plane tickets and other luxuries. The sticks included threatening to bar certain South American exports should the countries fail to support Beijing's candidate and purportedly demanding that voters send screenshots of their China votes, circumventing the secret ballot process. China's efforts paid off, and today it wields substantial control over agricultural institutions by directing priorities, international standards, and international responses to global hunger.[38]

Emulation in international institutions has increased China's influence and power in the international system. First, China uses its position in international organizations to its benefit (as do most countries), often with a focus on gaining power to support the CCP's control and legitimacy at home. For example, China lobbied successfully for the Interpol presidency, which former vice minister for public security Meng Hongwei assumed in 2016.[39] During his tenure, the agency spent more manpower on arresting Chinese dissidents and corrupt officials, who were sent back to China for trial thanks to extradition treaties with countries like Italy, Bulgaria, Greece, Spain, Hungary, and France.[40]

China had a seat on the UN Human Rights Commission for ten of the fifteen years between 2006 and 2020, largely to mitigate domestic liabilities.[41] One diplomat recounts that, thanks to the advice of other developing countries, China realized that the best way to win support for its position on human rights was to change the question from a substantive one to a procedural one—bringing up resolutions that other nations under US pressure found it in their interests to support.[42] For example, China submitted proposals to redefine human rights as economic and social rather than political and civil. According to a National Bureau of Asian Research report:

> Through the use of economic leverage, threats, intimidation, inducements, the mobilization of networks, and skillful manipulation of procedures, China . . . now has the votes and support to implement . . . its vision for the HRC . . . with China's norms, values, and discourse at the center . . . where "win-win cooperation" means that governments can avoid scrutiny and escape accountability for human rights abuses and victims are unable to find redress for their grievances.[43]

In 2019, when twenty-two nations—including the United States, Australia, Germany, and the United Kingdom—issued a joint letter to the UN Human Rights Council condemning China's mass detention of Uyghur Muslims and other minorities in the Xinjiang region, China was able to respond with a letter of its own, signed by twenty-three Islamic-majority nations (including three that host US military bases), calling the accusations "groundless" and criticizing the pressure attempt. This shows China's ability to exercise influence in international institutions to achieve its national objectives, including the protection of the regime. In October 2022, China was able to defeat a UN Human Rights Council vote, brought by the United States and seven other Western countries, to hold a "debate on the situation of human rights in the Xinjiang Uyghur Autonomous Region, China."[44] Analysts saw this defeat as a result of China's campaign to undermine the Western, universal conception of human rights.[45] A 2018 report lists twelve instances between 1990 and 2005 in which China was able to defeat a vote on its own human rights record.[46]

A Heavy-Handed Push for Soft Power

At first glance, building soft power, or the ability to get what you want through persuasion or attraction rather than coercion or payments, seems like a good candidate for emulation, given the strategy's effectiveness for the United States. The United States has been the primary beneficiary of soft power, with its globally recognized brands, pop culture, fast-food chains, world-renowned universities, liberal political values, and moral authority dominating the international stage.[47] Soft power is one of the great innovations of US foreign policy and is often credited with helping the United States win the Cold War.[48]

In China's case, however, soft power is an area where emulation makes little strategic sense. Soft power lies at the heart of US power, and thus China's attempts to build soft power would likely be seen as a direct challenge. China also does not enjoy competitive advantages in this area given its domestic political system, because soft power is created organically, mainly through civil society. It is no wonder that most competition for soft power comes from other open societies (Great Britain's Premier League, Bollywood, K-pop, and Japanese tech brands are only a few examples). Exploitation of gaps—trying to build soft power where the United States is not as dominant—would have been the better choice here. Indeed, China has invested billions in securing a media stronghold in Africa, and its tech brands have made headway there as well.[49] Similarly, poorer and less politically free countries are the primary beneficiaries of Beijing's scholarships.[50]

But China has not tried to build soft power only in the gaps and blind spots. Despite the disincentives for emulation, the CCP announced in 2007 its intention to pursue soft power as "an important component of comprehensive national power and international competitiveness."[51] Possibly because their authors recognized the limitations of China's appeal as an autocratic country, official documents focused heavily on Chinese culture as the most promising source of soft power, although its socialist value system and "unity of Chinese ethnicity" were also highlighted.[52] Top leaders echoed the call. A then-powerful and influential Bo Xilai (years before he would be charged with corruption and ousted from the Party) argued that "among nations, ideas and culture are advantages of competition that are more internal, long-lasting and irreplaceable."[53] The top military news outlet warned that "solely relying on hard power such as military and economics not only bears huge costs of resources, but also faces accusations from the global society."[54] Chinese strategists and scholars took the hint and began to focus their efforts on how to measure and build soft power.[55]

In the end, the Party tried to increase its attractiveness through heavy-handed top-down approaches and clumsy propaganda.[56] In 2004, the government established Confucius Institutes, which promote a particular version of Chinese language and culture abroad. At their height in 2017, there were over 500 institutes and 1,000 Confucius Classrooms (a primary and secondary school version of the program) operating in over 130 countries.[57] Chinese media started going global; the Xinhua News Agency added almost forty new foreign bureaus between 2009 and 2011 alone, and as of 2023 it was operating more than 180 overseas bureaus, about five times more than CNN.[58] In 2016, the Chinese state broadcaster China Central Television (CCTV) launched its international news arm, China Global Television Network (CGTN).[59] Xi Jinping urged officials to "raise [China's] soft power, tell China's story well, and do a good job of external propaganda."[60] Since then, Xi has doubled down on rhetoric along these lines, urging officials to build up soft power to allow China to take charge of its narrative and portray itself "truthfully, three-dimensionally, and comprehensively."[61]

But, predictably, China's emulative attempts have fallen short. After a decade and a half of sustained efforts to build soft power, China still ranks tenth in the world; the United States has generally ranked first.[62] As Beijing ramped up its soft power efforts, negative views of China in Australia, the United Kingdom, Germany, the Netherlands, Sweden, the United States, South Korea, Spain, and Canada increased from 2002 to 2020. A median of

78 percent of individuals surveyed in fourteen countries in 2020 said they had no confidence in Xi to "do the right thing regarding world affairs.[63] As of 2023, a record low of Americans—15 percent—viewed China favorably.[64] A 2022 poll of respondents in forty-three countries showed that opinions of China had become dramatically less favorable worldwide, with the notable exception of some developing nations in Africa and the Pacific, which remained relatively positive compared to more highly developed nations.[65] In another 2021 poll of Association of Southeast Asian Nations (ASEAN) countries, China performed abysmally in terms of preferred location for tertiary education or a holiday destination, with only 3.3 and 2.9 percent of respondents, respectively, choosing China.[66]

China's censored and propaganda-infused pop culture predictably has low appeal.[67] *The Battle of Lake Changjin*, a 2021 film about China's involvement in the Korean War commissioned by the Central Propaganda Department with a budget of over $200 million, currently holds the domestic Chinese record for box office sales. But the film fell flat abroad; sales were too low in Singapore to even be recorded.[68] China's second-highest-grossing film, *Wolf Warrior II*, has been criticized for its racist portrayal of Africans, which is not surprising coming from a country that once broadcast a skit in which a Chinese actress portrayed an African woman through blackface, adding on a large posterior and a pet monkey in tow.[69]

China has experienced similar struggles with its global brands. Chinese companies are spending huge sums of money on advertising around the world. Half the 2018 World Cup sponsors, for instance, were Chinese. But these efforts are not increasing the attractiveness of Chinese brands. Of the top ten highest-valued global brands, all but two are American (Samsung and Louis Vuitton). Chinese brands do not even break the top fifty—and these are rankings from 2020, when the US economy took a much bigger hit than China's due to the pandemic.[70] Chinese brands receive low recognition outside the Chinese market; a 2019 poll shows that almost 80 percent of Americans cannot name one Chinese brand.[71] Additionally, the United States retains a soft power edge in Asia, with one 2023 poll showing that 75 percent of respondents retain positive views of US soft power, while only 33 percent have a positive view of China.[72]

China's emulative efforts have even been seen as a direct threat. China's attempts to take advantage of historical, economic, and cultural ties to build soft power in Southeast Asia, for example, worried some analysts, who called China's project a "Monroe Doctrine for Southeast Asia" that would reduce

US alliances in the region.[73] Rather than facilitate more positive perceptions of China and its government, Confucius Institutes, cultural exhibitions, a globalized media, and scholarships for higher education in China have attracted international suspicion.[74] Over 90 percent of Confucius Institutes in the United States have shut down, and Chinese media companies have received pushback for manipulating content to favor the CCP.[75] In the United Kingdom, a similar pattern emerged; a 2019 inquiry held by the Conservative Party Human Rights Commission found that Confucius Institutes "threaten academic freedom and freedom of expression in universities around the world and represent an endeavor by the [CCP] to spread its propaganda and suppress its critics."[76] Confucius Institutes have also been closed in countries such as Denmark, Finland, Sweden, and Japan.[77]

Chinese scholars have recognized China's weaknesses in soft power. Some believe the cause is the limitations of China's domestic institutions, while others blame "anti-China political forces" in the world.[78] A former Chinese ambassador, Fu Ying, conceded in 2020 that the United States still held "greater sway in the international court of public opinion," partly because China remains "isolated from the Western information ecosystem."[79] In other words, the Communist Party and its propaganda machine have difficulty capturing the hearts and minds of people across the world. Perhaps this is why there has been less strategic focus on this pathway to power in recent years; The People's Daily published about 435 articles on soft power in 2012, but fewer than 150 in 2022.[80]

This case provides several insights into the upstart strategy. First, it provides evidentiary support for the argument that emulation helps countries build power only under the right conditions: those laid out by the upstart strategy. When a rising power deviates, emulation can prove threatening, as well as an ineffective and inefficient way of competing with the great power. The elaborate and highly orchestrated 2008 Beijing Olympics is one such instance; it enhanced China's great power image, but with a $2 billion price tag in direct costs and an estimated $40 billion in non-sport infrastructure investments, it was a stark contrast to Greece's $16 billion spending on the 2004 Olympic Summer Games.[81]

This case also shows us how the need to bolster the CCP at home can dominate other strategic considerations and consequently get in the way of China's ability to compete with the United States. The CCP seems to be selling the Chinese culture and system to explain to its own public that its regime is legitimate even though it is undemocratic. Xi has argued that cultural soft power is central to realizing the China dream.[82] Judged by this metric, perhaps China's soft power approach should be considered a success. While China's aggressive media strategy has not led to positive views of China, it has pushed media coverage in East Asian, Southeast Asian, and Pacific Island nations from negative to neutral.[83] China's enormous movie market has even helped it influence Hollywood portrayals of the country.[84] According to one Chinese author, China's overall Party diplomacy—which "aim[s] at branding the CCP as a capable and responsible ruling party"—has been well received by some foreign counterparts.[85]

Exploiting Niche Markets in Arms Sales

Countries, especially great powers, use arms arrangements to cement positive relations with foreign governments or to achieve political gains such as basing agreements and alliance commitments.[86] Arms sales, according to the US State Department, are "tangible implements of US foreign policy with potential long-term implications for regional security."[87] The past two decades have seen considerable growth in arms transfers, with the United States accounting for just over 30 percent of global arms transfers between 2015 and 2020. Nearly half of those sales were to countries in the Middle East.[88] In 2020 authorized US arms exports rose to approximately $175 billion, with major equipment going to Japan, Morocco, Israel, Singapore, Egypt, France, and Indonesia.[89] The amount fell in 2021, but it remained massive at $138 billion.[90] The United States is also currently using arms sales to balance against China; US sales to countries in East Asia and the Pacific increased by two and a half times from 2018 to 2019, and by another 41 percent between 2019 and 2020.[91] Arms sales are also the defining feature of US Taiwan policy: from 1979 to 2020, the United States has supplied Taiwan with more than 75 percent of its arms imports.[92] In short, the United States has used arms sales as "foreign policy writ large" to build long-term relationships and gain leverage in the foreign policy arena.[93]

Chinese analysts recognize that arms sales have been an effective tool of power acquisition for the United States, especially during the Cold War.[94] Even after purchase, militaries need technical support, spare parts, and additional ammunition, all of which ensure long-term dependency. Chinese experts also recognize that the United States accrues financial benefits through its arms sales, which support domestic industry and job creation.[95]

Many write about how the United States achieves a level of control over its partners, and possibly military access, through partner reliance on US supply.[96] Chinese writings are uncharacteristically generous in their assessments; many note that US arms transfers aim to sustain regional stability and that the United States is largely successful in this endeavor.[97]

Even as Chinese thinkers recognize the contributions of arms sales to diplomatic power, emulation is not considered the smart approach because China would have a hard time competing directly with the United States. For one thing, arms sales involve first-mover advantages. Because of the fierce competition for influence between the Soviet Union and the United States during the Cold War, most countries in the world get their supplies from either Russia or the United States. Changing suppliers is costly and comes at an operational cost, as systems purchased from a new supplier may not integrate well with those from another country. And countries prefer to get their equipment, weapons, and platforms from a single source so that they integrate.

Second, given the choice, most states would prefer to buy from the United States. Chinese platforms are cheaper, but they suffer from reliability, serviceability, and quality issues. From faulty submarines sold to Bangladesh and Myanmar to malfunctioning frigates sold to Kenya and Pakistan, Chinese military equipment has repeatedly disappointed buyers.[98] For those that need cheaper alternatives to US technology, Russian equipment is still the better option in most cases. The United States also subsidizes some purchases for countries that cannot afford to buy US equipment at market rates. Additionally, most US arms sales involve military aircraft and engines, where China struggles to perform.[99]

The last reason Chinese emulation makes little sense is obvious: the United States often sells to entities competing with China militarily, such as Japan, the Philippines, India, and Taiwan. Unsurprisingly, Chinese sources express concern about how the United States is using arms sales to strengthen its Asian alliances and to pursue new partnerships with India, Indonesia, and Vietnam.[100] China could sell to countries that balance against US partners and allies, as it does to Pakistan, but for the most part building up its own military is its best means of counterbalancing in Asia.

Indeed, China's arms sales record demonstrates that it is not emulating the United States. In quantity, China's sales are almost negligible compared to those of the United States. During this period the United States sold about nine times as many arms, about 30 percent of the share of total global arms transfers (China made up less than 4 percent). This is not a case of China's early figures dragging down the average; in 2022, the United States still transferred over seven times as many arms as China did.[101]

Moreover, China is not seeking out the same client base. Out of the 195 countries in the world, the United States has sold weapons to 169 since 2001, and China to 82.[102] Even with respect to developing countries, which is an area where China often seeks to outcompete the United States, the United States still dominates; from 1995 to 2015 the Chinese transferred around $40 billion worth of conventional arms to developing countries, compared to the United States' $285 billion.[103] The United States still enjoys about twice as many arms export relationships worldwide.[104] The top five arms companies in the world are American. Even as four Chinese companies have entered the top twenty-five, they do not present any real challenge to the US position in the market.[105] The graph in Figure 2.2 shows the huge disparity in Chinese and US arms transfers.

Given the view that arms sales are an effective tool of US foreign policy, and given China's ability to produce arms but not to directly compete with the United States, the upstart approach suggests that exploitation is the best option if there are gaps in US arms sales activity. In this respect, China is in luck: there are areas where competitive forces are weaker, making Chinese systems more appealing. First, some countries cannot afford US weapons and are unlikely to receive subsidies, loans, grants, or gifts if they are not of crucial strategic importance to the United States. Second, gaps exist because US domestic law prevents sales to countries with a history of human

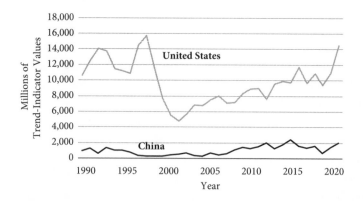

Figure 2.2 US and Chinese Arms Transfers, 1990–2022

Source: Data from "SIPRI Arms Transfers Database," Stockholm International Peace Research Institute, https://www.sipri.org/databases/armstransfers.

rights abuses. Third, US domestic law prohibits the export of certain types of technologies.

Chinese arms sales fit this pattern of congregating where competitive forces are weaker. Bangladesh is one of the poorest countries in the world and happens to get 80 percent of its arms imports from China.[106] Other customers, like Pakistan, Myanmar, and Sudan, are even poorer.[107] China has sought to use its resulting leverage, for example, to dissuade Bangladesh from cooperating with members of the Quadrilateral Security Dialogue (a bloc composed of India, Japan, the United States, and Australia and aimed at managing China's Indo-Pacific aggression) and to limit India's influence.[108]

Three of China's top four customers from 1990 to 2022—Pakistan, Myanmar, and Iran—are hardly beacons of freedom. The United States has arms embargoes of some form on two of the four (Iran and Myanmar).[109] The case of Myanmar demonstrates how China moves in to fill the void when an opportunity arises. The United States and the European Union stopped all defense cooperation with Myanmar after the military refused to accept the results of the 1990 democratic elections and placed the leader of the victorious party, Aung San Suu Kyi, under house arrest. The first major shipment of Chinese arms and ammunition arrived in Rangoon on August 10 of that year. Since then, China has moved to capture a large share of the country's arms imports. From 2014 to 2019, China supplied half of Myanmar's major arms purchases.[110] About 86 percent of Chinese arms sales in Latin America go to one country, Venezuela, which China relies on for oil and which is under a US arms embargo.[111]

China also exploits US restrictions on exports of certain types of technology. US obligations under the Missile Technology Control Regime (MTCR), to which China is not a signatory, restricted the export of cruise missiles because long-range unmanned aerial systems were initially characterized by US law as cruise missiles.[112] Even after the law was amended in 2002, a host of US regulations, international agreements, and precedents made it difficult for the United States to export its drone technology beyond a fairly narrow group of countries such as France, Japan, Australia, and the United Kingdom.[113] These factors have created a ripe market opportunity for China, which has made its unmanned aerial vehicles (UAVs) available to countries such as the United Arab Emirates (UAE), Saudi Arabia, Egypt, and Serbia.[114] Between 2003 and 2018, China delivered 181 drones to thirteen countries.[115] The Chinese company DJI is a world leader in the export of consumer drones, holding 74 percent of the global market share in 2017.[116]

Russian and Ukrainian soldiers use small consumer drones for surveillance and scouting purposes, as well as to drop grenades on unsuspecting enemies below.

Through this niche approach, China has been able to gain some ground. China's arms sales grew by 120 percent from 1990 to 2022.[117] The country has strengthened its relationship with states like Pakistan, Saudi Arabia, Venezuela, and the UAE, pivotal players in their regions and major oil suppliers to China.[118] The United States has not imposed major costs on China because of its approach, though it has in some cases tried to minimize China's effectiveness; both the Obama and Trump administrations loosened export controls to facilitate the sale of drones, for example. China's approach has not sparked enough concern to encourage seriously costly US responses, perhaps because China has been careful to minimize the potential for such responses. For example, China does not sell much to Latin American countries (accounting for about 2 percent of the region's purchases), where the United States is particularly sensitive to outside involvement.[119] (Interestingly, as competition between China and the United States has heated up in the past few years, China has sold even less to Latin America.) Chinese scholars are cautious about spelling out the benefits of China's growing impact in the global arms market even though they believe the strategy augments China's geopolitical influence.[120]

Chinese elites also try to minimize any domestic costs of its arms sales policies. First, the strategy is not loudly broadcasted in China, partly because many view US arms sales as a tool to control allies, suppress opponents, and interfere in regional affairs—and it is important for the CCP to project a different image at home and abroad.[121] In fact, Chinese official media often openly criticize the United States for being the world's largest "warmonger," claiming that the United States has a strong incentive to keep the world in turmoil to serve the interests of its domestic military-industrial complex.[122]

Domestic political reasons prevent China from emulating a related aspect of US strategy—using arms embargos to signal its distaste for certain regimes and their policies, especially those that violate human rights norms. In 2022, the United States had in place eight arms embargos (on Belarus, China, Cuba, Iran, Myanmar, North Korea, Syria, and Venezuela) and three military end-use/end-user licensing requirements (on China, Russia, and Venezuela).[123] In contrast, China has never initiated a unilateral arms embargo against any nation and has voted only in favor of select UN arms embargos.[124] In general, China avoids policies that make interference in internal affairs for human rights reasons a legitimate international action, since such interference would threaten Party control.[125]

In sum, China is not emulating this US pathway to power, nor has Beijing come up with an innovative alternative. Instead, China has pursued exploitation, in which it sells to certain countries and certain technologies where US competition is minimal.[126] This practice has allowed China to become a significant, though still minor, player and gain influence with countries that have become dependent on Chinese arms.

Exploiting US Absence with Diplomatic Outreach

It is hard to argue with the idea that diplomacy is an effective way of building power and influence in international politics. Expanding diplomatic engagement with the world, especially bilaterally, supports all aspects of power; it is an important tool for accomplishing foreign policy goals and a peaceful way of mediating "the clash of hostile interests."[127] Moreover, compared to coercive foreign policy tools, diplomacy is less threatening. For China, it offers progress toward the strategic goal of minimizing US responses to Chinese activities.

Unsurprisingly, building up its diplomatic portfolio was one of China's first tasks during its rise. In 1996, CCP general secretary Jiang Zemin proclaimed that China needed to "go out" and engage beyond its borders to facilitate its growth and development.[128] China had its work cut out for it. Between 1990 and 2011, China established official ties with thirty-four additional countries, including major players like South Korea.[129] China has invested heavily in its diplomatic network during its rise, especially in Asia, where its network is now slightly larger than that of the United States.[130]

But the story does not stop there. An additional factor beyond effectiveness, reassurance, and efficiency pushes China beyond emulation to exploitation: the presence of gaps in US diplomatic outreach. Specifically, China has been focusing its efforts on the developing world, and compared to the United States, it makes more extensive use of approaches like host diplomacy and subnational engagement.

First and foremost, China visits countries along its periphery and in the developing world that the United States often ignores.[131] US leaders have visited only sixteen of the fifty-four nations in Africa (President Bush visited the most, at eleven).[132] In contrast, China's senior leaders made seventy-nine visits to forty-three countries in Africa in just the decade from 2007 to 2017. These visits include twenty-six of the thirty-three least-developed countries in Africa.[133] Since 2013, US presidents have made four visits to South Asian countries (two to India and two to Afghanistan).[134] In the same period, Xi visited Pakistan, Bangladesh, and Nepal, in addition to three trips to India.[135] No US president has ever visited Central Asia, whereas Xi has visited Kazakhstan, Kyrgyzstan, Tajikistan, and Uzbekistan multiple times.[136] Between 2013 and 2020 Xi was particularly active, visiting sixty-nine countries across six continents, more than any of his predecessors.[137] Forty percent of Xi's overseas trips have been to Asian countries, and 33 percent were to countries with which China shares a maritime or land border. In contrast, 43.7 percent of President Obama's and President Trump's trips were to Europe, mainly to Germany and the United Kingdom.[138] This difference is especially notable because diplomacy consists largely of just showing up.[139]

China has also focused more on host diplomacy. Leaders from Asia, Africa, Oceania, North and South America, and Europe visited China more than they did the United States between 2010 and 2019. In particular, Asian leaders visited China 287 times, more than triple the 90 times Asian leaders visited the United States. African leaders visited China 172 times, whereas they visited the United States just 83 times. This was a new instrument of power accumulation taken on by a rising China; in the early 2000s, visits to the United States were more common.[140]

China has also built regional fora to increase coordination among states largely ignored by US multilateral diplomacy, such as the Shanghai Cooperation Organization with Russia and Central Asian states in 2001, the Forum on China-Africa Cooperation (FOCAC, 2000), the China–Arab States Cooperation Forum (CASCF, 2004), the Forum of China and Community of Latin American and Caribbean States (China-CELAC, 2014), and the 17 + 1, which is a multilateral cooperation forum established in 2012 with Central and Eastern European (CEE) countries.

These trends are not a coincidence. Instead, they are the result of a deliberate strategy to build power effectively while minimizing negative backlash. Since 2002, both the Hu and Xi administrations have embraced "multifaceted diplomacy" (quan fangwei waijiao), characterized by the slogan "Great powers are key, the periphery is first, developing countries are the foundation, and multilateralism is an important platform."[141] Xi Jinping Diplomatic Thought has also explicitly called for a shift to focus on cooperation with developing nations.[142] According to one prominent Chinese international relations scholar, China's focus on areas like Central Asia is effective because it avoids direct competition with the United States in traditional regions of contention and instead focuses on places in which "rules for competition" do not yet exist.[143] Chinese strategists believe that focusing on peripheral countries will reduce the United States' ability to obstruct China's rise.[144] Writing in 2014, former Chinese foreign minister Li Zhaoxing highlighted the "tremendous long-term political support" Africa has offered to China.[145]

Lastly, Xi Jinping reinvigorated China's efforts in another gap: subnational diplomacy, or diplomacy that takes place below the national level. From the China-US Governors Forum (founded in 2011, ended by the United States in 2020 due to concerns about influence), the China-US Sub-National Legislatures Cooperation Forum, and the China and Central and Eastern European Countries Mayors Forum to various direct meetings with mayors and governors from provinces and cities involved in BRI projects, Chinese officials have pursued subnational ties.[146] US and Chinese commentators alike point to subnational diplomacy's ability to circumvent ideological differences with democracies at the national level by appealing to local economic interests.[147] Subnational entities frequently have more leeway and less federal oversight, making them a preferred counterpart. For example, China used subnational exchanges with US governors to make deals with major US solar companies and eventually captured the solar market, which the United States once led.[148]

Subnational exchanges are a means of pushing Beijing's political agenda. Agreements are often implicitly accompanied by expectations of political solidarity. For example, all sister-city agreements with cities in the United States include a provision that activities be carried out "in accordance with the principles on the establishment of diplomatic relations between the United States of America and the People's Republic of China"—principles that might be invoked to preclude exchanges with Taiwan. Some, like the agreement to join the BRI signed by the premier of the Australian state of Victoria, lack any contractual obligations, creating concerns that the Victoria government agreed to endorse the CCP's foreign policy doctrine in exchange for "shadowy political favors."[149]

China's exploitation of gaps in regulation at the subnational level was initially successful, but countries have caught on and have tried to limit Beijing's subnational diplomacy. In 2020, secretary of state Mike Pompeo ended the US partnership with the China-US Governors Forum, accusing his Chinese counterparts of "directly and malignly influenc[ing]" state and local leaders.[150] Victoria's BRI agreement was invalidated by Australia's federal government in April 2021, after internal reviews warned that the agreement would bolster Chinese influence and weaken Australia's regional position. And in July 2022, a US intelligence report warned that Beijing was using subnational forums as outlets to pressure state and local actors and exert its influence within the United States.[151]

Given the United States' absence in some parts of the world and lack of attention at the subnational level, China has had an "unrivaled playing field over several years for its public diplomacy efforts to consolidate influence."[152] Weak competition in these areas is important because China is no better at diplomatic engagement than the United States. In high-level meetings, most Chinese officials still follow strict talking points, which inhibits candid discussion and can hamstring efforts to establish effective diplomatic networks.[153] And while many countries would prefer not to choose between Beijing and Washington, China's increasingly large presence abroad has been met with pushback in some countries. In Africa, for example, one RAND report found that "labor unions, civil society groups, and other segments of African societies criticize Chinese enterprises for poor labor conditions, unsustainable environmental practices, and job displacement."[154] Countries tend to welcome, if not favor, US engagement. In other words, if the United States were more diplomatically active across the board, China would find it more difficult to compete.

But this isn't the end of the story of China's rise in diplomatic power. Emulation and exploitation alone would not have allowed China to become a global power. But China could not be exactly like the United States, and in any case, Beijing didn't want to be. In 2016, former state councilor Dai Bingguo stated, "No matter how well it develops, China will not replace the US . . . no [one] can replace the US as the No. 1 in the world, and no one can stop China's peaceful rise or renewal."[155] Displacing, not replacing, the United States was the goal. And doing things differently—competing in new areas and new ways—was critical to achieving this goal.

3

Entrepreneurship in Chinese Foreign Policy

In April 1974, Deng Xiaoping, then vice premier, delivered a speech to the UN that contained a surprising statement. "China," said Deng, "will never become a superpower." But Deng wasn't saying that China would not become *powerful*. Rather, Deng continued with a question: "What is a superpower? A superpower is an imperialist country that invades, interferes, controls, subverts, and plunders other countries everywhere." If the Chinese government were to engage in such activities, he argued, then other countries would be welcome to join the Chinese people in opposing the Chinese government.[1] With his signature rhetorical flair, Deng made it clear that China intended to do things differently than both the United States and the Soviet Union.

Deng's pronouncement shows that doing things its own way has long been a component of China's approach, and successive generations of leaders have followed suit. Jiang Zemin's innovation came in the form of building strategic partnerships, and Hu Jintao's in the concepts of the "harmonious world" and China's "peaceful development."[2] Today, Xi asserts that China must "make clear that its diplomatic outlook and patterns of action are different from those of traditional Western powers."[3] Additionally, according to Party sources, China's "unique style" of diplomacy "promotes innovation through practice, constantly doing new things on the international stage by opening new platforms, unlocking new paradigms, and actively championing new international agendas and advocating for the establishment of new international rules."[4]

These are more than grand statements designed to build up the Party's image at home. Practical reasons have pushed China to experiment with alternative ways of building diplomatic power. This chapter explores these entrepreneurial activities. Specifically, China has avoided the US strategies of forming alliances, acting as the external security partner of choice, and pushing others to adopt its governance model. China has judged that following in the United States' footsteps in these cases is not worth it, because doing so would heighten US threat perceptions and fail to cater to China's competitive advantages. Some gaps exist in the US approach, but not in areas that promise real returns. Beijing has therefore embraced new pathways to power by building strategic partnerships, becoming the internal security partner of choice, and observing regime neutrality.

These entrepreneurial approaches are part of the reason China has managed to catch up to the United States in diplomatic power. Admittedly, China was more successful at avoiding sharp reactions during the first two decades of its rise, while its more aggressive diplomacy under Xi Jinping, often referred to as "Wolf Warrior diplomacy," has led to greater concern. But these changing perceptions have yet to translate into concrete obstacles. States are still not interested in taking sides against China, even after years of increased Chinese assertiveness. The United States is far from implementing any sort of containment policy; on the contrary, American outbound investment and securities holdings in the PRC more than doubled between 2011 and 2020.[5] And even as many states criticize aspects of China's domestic politics, Beijing's influence still manages to minimize real action. For example, only four countries (the United States, the United Kingdom, Australia, and Canada) participated in a diplomatic boycott of the 2022 Winter Olympics in Beijing over genocide in Xinjiang, and even those states still chose to send athletes.

Strategic Partnerships: China's Answer to US Alliances

It is rare that American strategists, scholars, and government officials all agree, but they concur on the centrality of alliances to US power. The US alliance network is considered by most to be "one of the most enduring and successful elements of US foreign policy since World War II."[6] The benefits of alliances are not limited to military affairs; allies vote with the United States in international institutions, coordinate development assistance, and help each other become more prosperous through trade and investment.[7] US allies also pay for the privilege of hosting US military forces abroad. This system has allowed the US military to maintain a global presence at a far cheaper cost than the British colonial empire or the Soviet Union's repeatedly contested occupation of neighboring countries.[8]

Given that alliances have been such a major source of US power, they seem to provide an attractive target for emulation. But the situation is more complicated, and as a result, Chinese thinkers have concluded that seeking alliances would put Beijing at a competitive disadvantage vis-à-vis the United States. First, many question the effectiveness for China of setting up an alliance network. The current strategic environment is fundamentally different from the one faced by the United States in the post-WWII period. Alliance diplomacy helped the United States rise to great power status and outcompete the Soviet Union, but Chinese thinkers see less utility for them in the post–Cold War period.[9] As one Chinese scholar pithily asserts: "Alliance diplomacy no longer accords with the times."[10] China expert Adam Liff agrees, writing that the "US alliance system traces its roots back to historically unique geopolitical conditions that are unlikely to recur."[11]

Second, there are few gaps worth exploiting. Given China's limited expeditionary capabilities and historically tense relationships with many US allies in Asia, poaching US partners is not a feasible option. This leaves few attractive alliance candidates to pursue.[12] Russia and India are less than ideal partners given the reluctance of the former to concede to China's leadership and the distrust and hostility from the latter.[13] Russia's invasion of Ukraine served as a stark reminder of the liabilities of having close relationships with unpredictable actors.[14] China could attempt to form a coalition of many smaller countries by offering them security guarantees, but most Chinese analysts believe that such a strategy would not significantly improve Chinese security.[15] In other words, adding allies from countries that the United States has not pursued would not increase Chinese power enough to counter the increased liabilities.

One of the most powerful arguments against alliances is that they would alienate the United States and its allies, especially if China reached agreements with countries hostile to the United States.[16] To rise over the past few decades, China needed to strengthen ties precisely with the countries most deeply integrated into the US alliance system, because they are some of the richest and most powerful in the world.[17] In short, China's rise depended on these trade and investment relationships.[18] Setting up its own alliance network would have impeded productive relationships with countries outside the alliance and made it difficult to oppose the countries within the alliance that acted counter to Chinese interests.[19]

Thus, China has not emulated the US approach. Instead, China's leaders have proudly and purposely eschewed military alliances.[20] The United States has more than fifty defense pacts; China has only one defense-oriented agreement that qualifies as a traditional alliance (the 1961 Sino–North Korean

Mutual Aid and Cooperation Friendship Treaty), and this agreement hails from a time before China's rise began. Even though China is close to Russia, Beijing has no desire to be dragged into its overseas adventures. To be clear on this point, the Chinese foreign minister downgraded slightly the relationship in January 2023 from one of "no limit, no forbidden area, and no upper boundary" to "no alliance, no enmity, and no targeting third parties."[21]

Given the lack of exploitable gaps and the downsides of building its own alliance system, the upstart strategy predicts an entrepreneurial approach, one that leveraged its competitive advantages, did not alienate countries, and did not spark perceptions of threat while at the same time ensuring that Beijing built the leverage it needed in bilateral relationships to protect its domestic interests.[22] Beijing's answer was strategic partnerships (*zhanlüe huoban guanxi*), an alternative path into the great power hierarchy.[23]

Strategic partnerships are "organized around a general (security) purpose known as a system principle (such as championship of a multipolar world), rather than a specific task, such as deterring or fighting a hostile state . . . tend to be informal in nature and entail low commitment costs, rather than being explicitly formalized in a specific alliance treaty that binds the participants to rigid courses of action."[24] Beijing has leveraged them to institutionalize, regulate, and assuage relations with important global players as well as to coordinate foreign policies to promote China's preferred norms, like non-interference in internal affairs.[25] In the words of former premier Wen Jiabao, such partnerships "transcend the differences in ideology and social system and [are] not subjected to the impacts of individual events that occur from time to time."[26] From Beijing's perspective, the establishment of a strategic partnership indicates a "partner's political willingness to recognize China's legitimate rise, to manage areas of disagreement in order to steadily improve the overall bilateral relationship, and to enhance coordination in promoting their common preferences in the international arena."[27]

Since the first of these agreements in 1993, partnership diplomacy has become one of the most notable dimensions of Chinese diplomacy. Jiang Zemin first established partnerships with most major powers in the late 1990s. Hu Jintao then prioritized other countries that had a disproportionate impact on China's rise, such as those in the Middle East. More recently, Xi has focused on countries around China's periphery, such as BRI participants.[28]

China is not the first country to employ strategic partnerships—the EU has ten such relationships. China's innovation has been to use strategic partnerships as the organizing principle of its foreign policy, "a dominant tool

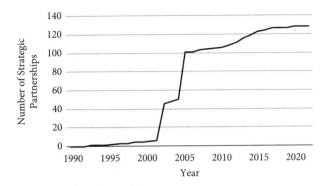

Figure 3.1 Chinese Strategic Partnerships, 1990–2022
Source: Full dataset can be found at www.orianaskylarmastro.com/upstart.

for managing relations and as a replacement for more competitive alliance thinking," according to a review of Chinese writings on the topic.[29] Strategic partnerships are not just quasi-military alliances under a different name; 75 percent of Chinese partnership agreements do not contain any provisions for security cooperation.[30] China has also embraced this strategy on an unprecedented scale: by 2022, 128 countries' economic and political goals were linked to those of China through partnership agreements. Figures 3.1 and 3.2 show China's increased reliance on this unique organizing principle over the past three decades of its rise.[31]

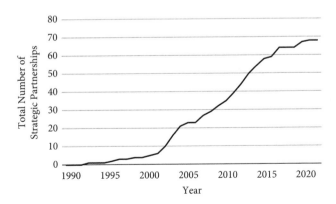

Figure 3.2 Chinese Strategic Partnerships (Bilateral and Multilateral), 1990–2022
Source: Full dataset can be found at www.orianaskylarmastro.com/upstart.

This entrepreneurial approach has several advantages. First, it allows China to leverage its competitive advantage as an economic power to minimize criticism of the Communist Party. Strategic partnerships establish a clear linkage: if countries choose to pressure Beijing on sensitive matters like human rights or Taiwan, they jeopardize trade and investment opportunities. Indeed, all the strategic partnership agreements mention trade, investment, and economic cooperation, as well as working together in the UN, and all but three include a provision in support of Beijing's position on Taiwan.[32] As one Chinese scholar explains, this foreign policy approach makes it possible for China to gain the support of those who want to benefit from China's rise and weakens US resistance.[33]

Strategic partnerships also allow China to compete in the developing world, which Chinese leaders have long identified as an untapped source of political strength and economic opportunity.[34] Chinese thinkers assess Beijing's principles of "non-alignment, non-confrontation, and non-targeting the third country" as more attractive to developing countries than the "interventionist" style of the United States.[35] Making common cause with developing countries by condemning alliances, which facilitate the allegedly American approaches of hegemonism, expansionism, and power politics, contributes to Beijing's global power and influence.[36] Chinese partnership diplomacy with Algeria, Egypt, Saudi Arabia, Iran, the UAE, Israel, and Turkey, for example, has "objectively 'diluted' the influence of other great powers" in the Middle East, according to one Chinese academic's analysis.[37] Non-OECD countries in strategic partnerships with China exhibit greater trade flows and greater alignment in voting in the UN after the conclusion of a partnership than they did before.[38]

Perhaps most importantly, strategic partnerships allow China to establish strong relationships with many more countries than alliances would have permitted.[39] They do not restrict partners to those with ideological affinities or the same political system, relationship with the United States, or level of economic development.[40] Indeed, shared domestic political traits, shared threat perceptions, and even shared ideology are not good predictors of China's partnerships—about 38.50 percent of the partnerships are with countries rated as "free" by Freedom House, 22.66 percent with countries that are "partly free," and 39.84 percent with those that are rated "not free."[41] China has managed to convince about half of US allies to sign on. China also saw an opportunity to strengthen ties with middle powers like New Zealand, Australia, and Finland, because they were more flexible in the security domain and open to closer cultural and economic ties.[42] With this approach, China can even maintain positive relations with both sides of a rivalry: Iran and Saudi Arabia, North Korea and South Korea, Pakistan and India, and Israel and Palestine.[43]

This is not to say that China's partnership diplomacy has been without complications. The Sino-Russian "comprehensive strategic partnership of coordination for a new era," arguably China's deepest strategic partnership, created problems for Chinese foreign policy after Russia's invasion of Ukraine. But with the entrepreneurial approach, China can manage these trade-offs more dexterously than it could with a traditional alliance. In the case of Russia, while the United States has been unhappy with China's weak stance on the war, China's friendship with Russia has yet to alienate its European partners. In April 2023, French president Emmanuel Macron visited Beijing, where he sought to strengthen France–China business, and in late 2022, the German government stated that Germany had no intention of "decoupling" from China, its largest trading partner. In contrast, if China formed a military alliance with Russia, European countries' security considerations might trump the economic imperative for friendly relations with China.

There is one glaring failure in China's strategy: the inability to convince the United States to sign on to a comprehensive strategic partnership. In the late 1990s, President Bill Clinton and Jiang Zemin discussed the possibility, and although President George W. Bush defined China as a "strategic competitor" during his 2000 campaign, he and Jiang Zemin agreed to build a "constructive relationship of cooperation" in 2001.[44] But in the twelve years that followed, the relationship was never elevated.

Xi tried to reinvigorate the idea in 2013 with a "new type of great power relationship." In the relaxed, informal setting of Sunnylands, Xi attempted to sell the idea to President Obama.[45] While multiple Obama administration officials used the phrase "new model of great power relations" to describe Sino-American relations, Japan complained to Washington that China's goal was to use the framework to credibly promote its status as equal to the United States, thereby influencing the ways other countries interacted with China and likely helping Xi foster nationalistic pride and political capital at home. The concern was this would contribute to China's goal of gradually pushing the United States out of Asia militarily to facilitate its takeover as the regional hegemon.[46] It was also apparent that China was trying to constrain the United States in the same way it was constraining the choice set of other countries—by linking strong political and economic relations to acceptance of China's "core interests."[47]

Some might argue for an alternative explanation, that China's approach was driven by purely ideational factors: "Ideological and historical opposition to alliances appears firmly ingrained in the CCP and PLA, manifests powerfully in interpretations of contemporary real-world developments, and will not be easily overcome."[48] China's failed alliance experiment with the Soviet Union (which stemmed in large part from the ideological row between Khrushchev and Mao) discouraged many Chinese leaders, most notably Deng Xiaoping, from using alliances as a path to global influence.[49] But the debate within China does not lend support to the argument that this is the only, or even the dominant, factor influencing its leaders' thinking. Moreover, Chinese leaders have jettisoned long-standing traditional approaches when doing so enhances their power at home and abroad (building an overseas military base in Djibouti and joining international institutions are two examples). And ideational explanations alone provide little insight into what China might do instead. The upstart strategy reveals that China is likely to pursue a pathway that caters to its competitive advantage, minimizes a threatening image, and creates a stark contrast to the US approach. Within these parameters, an appealing option is to create a framework that focuses on ties based on the economy rather than security.

Internal Security Partner of Choice: China's Answer to US Foreign Military Training

A related but independent pillar of US foreign policy on the international stage is the commitment to being countries' external security partner of choice.[50] The United States' training of foreign militaries, through means that include joint exercises, "is the foundation for US supremacy in security cooperation."[51] The Military Assistance Program started in 1949 as a way for the United States to counter Soviet influence in Europe, but the program's focus shifted to Latin America, the Pacific, the Middle East, and Africa as Europe recovered.[52]

Nowadays, the United States leverages this competitive advantage in its regional competition with China by increasing its security cooperation not only with allies like South Korea, Japan, the Philippines, and Australia but also with other regional players like India and partners in Southeast Asia, including Vietnam, Indonesia, and Malaysia. The US Departments of Defense and State together earmark about $19 billion a year to train foreign militaries.[53] By building up countries' military competency and capacity, the United States can reduce its defense burdens and build goodwill that helps protect its overseas interests at lower costs.[54] Research suggests that US assistance programs also successfully helped socialize former Warsaw Pact countries into the US-led community by instilling US values, thereby stabilizing Europe and improving partner states' internal stabilities.[55]

Even given this approach's centrality and effectiveness in US foreign policy strategy, several factors discourage Chinese emulation. First, China would have difficulty usurping the United States' role. The PLA has not fought a war since 1979; this lack of operational experience makes it a less attractive partner than the battle-tested United States for training and advising on traditional military operations. And courting countries that rely on the United States for their defense would be an ineffective approach because defense pacts and extended deterrence are not on offer. Trying to directly outcompete the United States could backfire if the United States thought China was trying to displace its pivotal position or if China enhanced the capabilities of the "wrong" countries—those that threaten US interests.

As a result, Washington's drive to be the external security partner of choice does not face serious competition from China. While China's 2019 national white paper boasts about conducting twenty joint exercises from 2012 to 2019, NATO conducted 103 such exercises in 2018 alone.[56] In 2018, China participated in sixty military exercises and thirty-one port calls. Meanwhile, the US Seventh Fleet, the part of the Navy assigned to the Indo-Pacific, typically participates in 100 bilateral and multilateral exercises and roughly 200 port visits each year.[57] Even across Africa, "the United States has far more training engagements and partnerships" than China does.[58]

It is not only the scale that gives the impression that China is not emulating the US path; it is also the nature of the exercises themselves. China is using the tool more to reassure than to create demand for its military expertise or to enhance the combat capabilities of the participating countries. Most of the 310 military exercises with sixty-three countries that China conducted between 2003 and 2018 were non-combat multilateral exercises, and the United States was among its top five partners.[59] Most of the PLA's joint exercises in 2010–2019 were with the five US Asian allies.[60] China does not provide combat advisory support, direct action, or defense institution building in these engagements. Instead, Beijing offers financing and infrastructure, professional military education, and intelligence and surveillance, especially to countries that do not receive much support from the United States.[61]

The conditions thus invite an entrepreneurial approach. In fact, a look at Chinese competitive advantages and the imperative of Party control reveals a new area where China does have a leg up over the United States—internal security. Unsurprisingly, China, an autocratic country that suppresses internal dissent, has dedicated vast resources to perfecting its internal security system. China spends around one-fifth more on internal security than on its military.[62] The Party has created the "Great Firewall," which restricts the flow of information within China through the internet, including blocking foreign technology platforms like Facebook and Twitter that threaten control. China has also built a surveillance state that "utilizes artificial intelligence, facial recognition technologies, biometrics, surveillance cameras, and big data analytics to profile and categorize individuals quickly, track movements, predict activities, and preemptively take action against those considered a threat in both the real world and online."[63] The degree of control borders on the ridiculous. In January 2020, Suzhou city officials used street cameras and facial recognition technology to publish photos and identifying personal details of residents wearing pajamas in public as part of a public shaming campaign.[64]

China's entrepreneurial approach to becoming the internal security partner of choice is extensive. From goose-stepping Qataris to the Presidential Guards of the Central African Republic, China has trained many other countries' internal security forces.[65] I have compiled an original dataset to capture this training, which includes police, forensics, cybersecurity, military, and coast guard training. The most common categories are military and police training. China has trained police officers, immigration officers, presidential bodyguards, and other personnel from 110 countries. Nearly three-quarters of African countries, just over two-thirds of the countries in the Americas, and over half of Asian countries have received police training from China. Additionally, about a quarter of European Union member states received some form of Chinese law enforcement training (Bulgaria, Croatia, France, Italy, Latvia, and Spain).[66]

China institutionalized some of its efforts in 2002 when it built Asia's largest police training center, the Academy of the Chinese People's Armed Police Force in Beijing, which trains forces for UN missions.[67] By October 2020, the China Peacekeeping Police Training Center (CPPTC) within the academy had held a total of eighty-eight foreign police training courses and sent faculty to conduct training programs in various other countries.[68]

The University of Public Security (*zhongguo renmin gongan daxue*), a government institution, also operates a foreign training program that in 2019 held thirty-one training sessions with 677 students.[69] Even smaller police academies, like those in Henan and Zhenjiang provinces, and vocational schools like the Railway Police College started hosting their own training programs for foreign counterparts in 2017 and 2018.[70]

The Chinese Coast Guard (CCG), the largest in the world, is expanding its partnerships with Russia, France, Indonesia, Malaysia, and Pakistan to build both a regional and a global law enforcement network at sea.[71] China has pursued coast guard cooperation with twenty-six countries in Africa, the Caribbean, and Southeast Asia. For example, in 2017, the coast guards of the Philippines and China organized reciprocal visits and joint maritime training exercises (though the ties have deteriorated in recent years). This cooperation continued into 2020, when the CCG held a "joint maritime exercise on search and rescue and combating fire at sea in waters off Manila in the South China Sea" to strengthen the participating countries' interoperability at sea.[72] The CCG also participates in the ASEAN Regional Forum Disaster Relief Exercises, aimed at promoting exchange of expertise among participants, and co-hosted the 2015 iteration with Malaysia.[73] Beyond Southeast Asia, the CCG has conducted educational exchanges and joint exercises with the South Korean coast guard.[74]

Part of grand strategy involves finding effective and efficient ways to protect one's interests. The United States trains foreign militaries partly to reduce its defense burden. Similarly, China trains foreign internal security forces to protect its interests at minimal cost. For example, in December 2011, in reaction to drug violence, China set up a Mekong River Joint Patrol Command Center in Yunnan and has been conducting joint coastal patrols with Laos, Myanmar, and Thailand ever since.[75] December 2020 saw the 100th time the four countries collaborated along the Mekong River.[76] These anti-drug patrols are largely self-serving, as they prevent drugs and criminals from entering southwest China. In addition, governments are less likely to be critical of China's internal security measures if they are adopting similar ones.

China also runs training sessions on how to control information on "new media" (internet censorship), which have attracted government officials from at least thirty-six countries.[77] Rather than relying on internet shutdowns, the CCP favors an approach that makes accessing information inconvenient. These covert censorship techniques are in many ways more effective than cutting off information completely, since users are less aware of them.[78] China's International Liaison Department has sent representatives from state-run media conglomerates such as Xinhua to train other countries' state-run media outlets.[79] China also advises countries on how to craft cybersecurity legislation to open the door to their approach.[80] In 2014, China founded the World Internet Conference, an annual forum for countries to discuss internet practices and policy. In 2022, China built upon these efforts by founding the World Internet Forum Conference in Beijing, which could, according to Freedom House, allow the Chinese government to promote its vision for a state-centric, authoritarian internet.[81]

States have clamored for Chinese expertise, technical guidance, and material support at this new frontier in internal security.[82] Chinese companies (and longtime targets of American sanctions) such as Huawei and ZTE are at the forefront of internal surveillance technology.[83] In 2012, only twenty countries had adopted Chinese surveillance tech. By 2018, that number had quadrupled. At least seventy-five countries have adopted it since 2008 for three main purposes: smart city/safe city platforms, facial recognition systems, and smart policing.[84] Hikvision, a Chinese state-owned civilian and military technology company, and Huawei are two of the world's leading vendors of 5G technology.[85]

These Chinese wares are attractive not only to autocratic regimes; over 50 percent of advanced democracies deploy some type of AI surveillance system, in contrast to 37 percent of closed autocracies and 50 percent of electoral/competitive autocracies.[86] While the United States and allies such as Canada, South Korea, Australia, and Japan have not adopted Chinese internal security technologies, it is noteworthy that US allies like the Philippines, Great Britain, France, Germany, Spain, and Italy have done so.[87]

China has a competitive advantage in this surveillance technology, partly because of its own immense internal market (of the 770 million surveillance cameras worldwide in 2019, over half were in China).[88] But evidence suggests these decisions are not motivated by commercial calculations alone. The Chinese government provides support to companies providing internal security support: for example, it pays directly for training programs through the Ministry of Commerce and sometimes chooses to subsidize Chinese companies, which increases their willingness to enter smaller, underserved markets. Chinese companies then offer their equipment at steep discounts to developing countries, often requesting access to data in exchange for favorable loan terms.[89] Additionally, national champions—that is, particularly successful firms that the government sees as advancing some larger national interest—have easy access to financing and government subsidies (Huawei received $222 million in government grants in 2018).[90]

In sum, China has built power and influence with other countries by becoming the internal security partner of choice. China's training programs have also improved the ability of foreign law enforcement to protect the Communist Party's interests abroad and, on a grander scale, to garner international support for Chinese positions on national security and law enforcement.[91] Not only does China use this position to enhance its political, military, and economic relationships with democracies and autocracies alike, but its dominance in AI surveillance creates influence that overshadows that of the United States and other democracies in shaping norms in these critical areas. This entrepreneurial strategy also allows Beijing to guide the industry in ways that give its companies economic advantages.[92]

Regime Neutrality: China's Answer to US Democracy Promotion

Democracy promotion, or "foreign policy activities intended to encourage the transition to or improvement of democracy in other countries," has been a central feature of US foreign policy since the end of WWII.[93] Since the end of the Cold War, the idea that "representative governments responsive to their people are least likely to turn to aggression against their neighbors" and "democracies [are] better equipped to support economic freedom, and promote stability" have become American mantras.[94] George H. W. Bush, Bill Clinton, and George W. Bush all listed democracy promotion as a key pillar of their foreign policy. President Obama named democracy promotion as a crucial value in his first National Security Strategy, and President Biden chose to emphasize "strengthening democracy," helping already democratic states build up their institutions rather than encouraging democratic revolutions.

In practice, US attempts to promote democracy post–Cold War have largely taken the form of US foreign aid. An average of $2 billion is allocated annually through the State Department, the United States Agency for International Development (USAID), the National Endowment for Democracy, and other entities. Some programs within the US Department of Defense may also be counted as democracy promotion; over $7.5 billion was allocated for FY2021.[95] Covert action, military intervention, and electoral interference are other tools of US democracy promotion. From 1946 to 2000, the United States intervened in eighty-one foreign elections.[96] Between 1948 and 2017, the United States conducted 234 military interventions, some in the name of democracy.[97]

Democracy promotion has a mixed record. A 2006 study commissioned by USAID to measure the effects of its democracy promotion activities found a significant positive impact on democracy.[98] By 2000 more than half the world's population lived under a democratic government, more than at any time in recorded history, and many saw the United States as the reason.[99] But since 2005, democracy has been on the retreat, with the countries experiencing declines in political rights and civil liberties outnumbering those experiencing gains.[100] "There has been no net expansion in the number of electoral democracies" since 2006, "which has oscillated between 114 and 119 (about 60 percent of the world's states)."[101] Part of the problem is that after the invasions of Afghanistan and Iraq, democracy promotion became associated with disastrous military interventions.

It goes without saying that emulation of democratization is out of the question for China, as it would present a direct threat to CCP control. But China has its own model to promote. The concept of the "China model" has evolved over the past decade to describe authoritarian capitalism, the "interrelationship of a strong government and a market economy."[102] Key components include the rejection of multiple political parties, the separation of powers among government branches, and adaptation to fit other ideologies when politically convenient.[103] On the economic front, a country following the China model might selectively integrate itself into the global economy and pursue infrastructure-led development.[104]

Even with respect to the promotion of its own system, China faces disincentives to emulation. Chinese strategists believe that imposing its model on other countries and attempting to topple democracies would be a costly and counterproductive way of competing. Democracies are generally more stable and prosperous than authoritarian states.[105] A policy of autocracy promotion would also immediately alienate rich, powerful democratic countries. Of China's top ten trading partners, eight are democracies; 60 percent of China's strategic partnerships are with democracies.[106] As Andrew Nathan succinctly puts it, "Attempting to undermine a foreign democratic regime would, in business terms, cost more than it would be worth."[107] Complicating matters, the US strategy is based on the premise that a world full of democracies is safer, and consequently a deliberate Chinese attempt to promote autocracy would be immediately perceived as a threat.

Moreover, Chinese writings present the general view that the US approach has been an ineffective way of building and maintaining power. Imposing one's economic and political system on others is a difficult, expensive, and complicated way to win other countries' support for one's objectives.[108] Chinese scholars comment that neither the US path nor their own is universally applicable.[109] As one scholar puts it, the unitary party leadership system was necessary for China's high efficiency and consistency in policy implementation.[110] But the broader consensus is that China's system of authoritarian capitalism cannot be easily imported by states with weaker government control, fewer resources, and no Communist Party.[111]

Due to the threatening and ineffective nature of emulation in this case, the upstart strategy predicts an entrepreneurial pathway to power. Indeed, China is not trying to remake the world in its image. Political scientist Seva Gunitsky wrote in 2018 that "so far, China has been the first non-proselytizing great power since the Dutch Golden Age."[112] Chinese leaders themselves have long proclaimed they have no intention of exporting the China model.[113] Deng argued that "countries can only develop their own development strategies and methods and approaches to adapt to the actual situation on their own . . . having only a single model cannot work."[114] Although Hu Jintao proposed to promote the Chinese model to the outside world, he also expressed the acceptance of different models. Painting a clear contrast with the United States, Xi articulated in 2017 that China "does not 'export' its own model and does not require other countries to 'replicate' its own way of development."[115] Chinese writers often argue that China has never advocated for its model to be widely adopted, nor has it asked other countries to copy Chinese practice.[116]

Instead of attempting to spread authoritarian capitalism, China is innovating by promoting a regime-neutral foreign policy. China's message is that every country has the right to choose how it operates according to its own situation, and any imposition is a failure to treat the country in question "with respect as an equal member of the international community."[117] For Chinese leaders and scholars, China's "unique style" of diplomacy is characterized by opposition to the rigid application of a particular philosophy and to the imposition of any preferred path and political system on others.[118] Beijing promotes the idea that each country's development path will be different, requiring experimentation—"groping for stones to cross the river"—and, perhaps most importantly, freedom from the interference of larger countries.[119]

It might be easy to dismiss this idea as propaganda, but there is substantial evidence to support the argument that China does not give preferential treatment to autocracies. First, it must be acknowledged that in the post-Mao era, China has stopped attempting to export proletarian revolution or topple democracies.[120] Chinese official development assistance (ODA) does not target specific governments according to their level of autocracy or corruption; democracies such as South Africa, Kenya, Tanzania, Indonesia, and Brazil are major borrowers.[121] China has not used multilateral economic sanctions or arms embargos to encourage adoption of its political or economic system. Xi Jinping publicly congratulated the winners of almost all forty democratic elections of an executive that took place in 2020.[122] In its congratulations to President Biden, the Chinese Foreign Ministry stated that the PRC "respects the choice of the American people."[123]

China's regime agnosticism resonates with many countries, especially in the developing world. While people around the world generally consider democracy to be desirable, international surveys show that nearly half of those polled view governance by non-elected experts as "very or somewhat good."[124] China's rejection of the principle of conditionality in granting foreign aid is popular with states that have grown tired of attempts by the World Bank and Western governments to leverage inducements to compel improvements in human rights and democratic practices. They are drawn to illiberal leaders who can help them build stable, prosperous societies without having to cater to demands for democratic progress.

While China has not imposed authoritarian capitalism on others, its approach has a darker side: China is trying to make the world safe for autocracies (and thus for its own Communist Party). Chinese strategists take a cynical view of US democracy promotion, believing that these are "efforts by Western powers to weaken rivals and expand their own influence."[125] Especially since the Tiananmen Square protests, CCP leaders believe that the United States is pursuing a policy of "peaceful evolution," or attempting to bring about a democratic China via peaceful means.[126] To rise to great power status, China has focused on blunting these efforts to protect CCP rule. China has become increasingly aggressive on this front, with efforts ranging from verbal criticism and the reshaping of international norms to more nefarious campaigns of political interference.

First, China has worked to delegitimize democratization on the international stage, advocating instead for the principles of sovereignty, non-interference, cultural pluralism, and mutual respect.[127] China has also tried to reshape conceptions of human rights and the ways they are applied within international institutions. For example, China is actively seeking to alter procedures at the UN to minimize the organization's oversight of its own and other governments' approaches to human rights.[128] As deputy assistant secretary of defense for South and Southeast Asia Lindsey Ford argues, "Beijing doesn't need to build carbon copies of its system to exert influence. It simply needs to encourage greater adoption of the institutions and tools that enhance its power."[129]

Second, Chinese leaders are becoming more publicly critical of US-style democracy. In the first high-level meeting between China and the Biden administration in Anchorage in February 2021, Chinese foreign minister Yang Jiechi explicitly cited racism, the January 6 storming of the Capitol, and the United States' disastrous handling of the COVID-19 pandemic as evidence of the inferiority of its system.[130] "We believe," he stated, "that it is important for the United States to change its own image and to stop advancing its own democracy in the rest of the world."[131] A Chinese State Council report underscores this point: "The US government, instead of introspecting on its own terrible human rights record, keeps making irresponsible remarks on the human rights situation in other countries, exposing its double standards and hypocrisy on human rights."[132] Such vocal critiques are designed to encourage the United States "to lower the tone on democracy and human rights" to protect the CCP's legitimacy.[133]

Third, China has been entrepreneurial in ensuring that other countries' preferences align with its own. Instead of trying to shape other countries in its own image, it engages in a multifaceted campaign to influence how governments, companies, and individuals address what it considers internal affairs. Its methods vary in their degree of legality, coercion, and harm. On one end of the spectrum are largely legal activities, such as lobbying, cultural exchanges, and paid media inserts. China tries to influence academic institutions, especially in Western democracies, through tuition dollars, cash donations, and lucrative prestige partnerships. Notably, Chinese students and scholars at US academic institutions who openly criticize China can face swift reprisals from Chinese authorities. China has targeted overseas Chinese scientists and engineers through its Thousand Talents Plan, a CCP program designed to encourage both legal research collaborations and illegal theft of intellectual property.

Controlling the image of China in overseas media is the fulcrum of this strategy. The state-sponsored *China Daily*, for example, has paid millions to place its propaganda insert "China Watch" in mainstream US newspapers, including the *Washington Post, Time*, the *Los Angeles Times*, and the *Wall Street Journal*.[134] Chinese state media have formed over 200 content-sharing agreements with Chinese-language media inside and outside the main-land.[135] Chinese state media inserts content into foreign news outlets in over thirty countries, and fifty-eight stations in thirty-five countries were carrying China Radio programming by 2018. In Africa in particular, the Chinese TV service StarTimes has helped over thirty countries and over 10 million subscribers transition from analog to digital, and through this process has shaped what information viewers can access.[136] More recently, China's propa-ganda efforts have gone "social," and many state-sponsored news outlets now have over 100 million followers across Twitter, Facebook, and Instagram.[137] According to Freedom House, China has negatively affected freedom of ex-pression between 2019 and 2021 and has sought to influence media coverage in thirty countries outside China.[138]

At the other end of the spectrum are covert, coercive, and corrupt activi-ties designed to reduce criticism of the CCP. China has tried to co-opt elites and opinion makers, sometimes through generous economic assistance and trade deals, other times through payoffs and bribes.[139] In one instance, a former Chinese military officer donated 220 motorcycles to Cambodian prime minister Hun Sen's personal force and subsequently received approval for a $5 billion resort.[140] China's United Front, which is in charge of "coopting influential figures and groups that the CCP finds useful but does not trust," has funneled money toward pro-CCP, or even CCP-affiliated, politicians in New Zealand and Australia.[141] One Australian Labor Party official, later re-vealed to be a recipient of Chinese funds, resigned after opposing freedom of navigation operations and influencing immigration decisions in ways favor-able to CCP associates.[142]

China has a competitive advantage in these types of state-directed activi-ties. No parallels exist in the US system for the main Chinese agencies re-sponsible for foreign influence—the Party's United Front Work Department, the Central Propaganda Department, the International Liaison Department, the State Council Information Office, the All-China Federation of Overseas Chinese, and the Chinese People's Association for Friendship with Foreign

Countries.[143] Unlike Chinese media, most influential US media outlets are neither state-owned nor state-controlled. US journalists at US government agencies such as Voice of America also adhere to journalistic codes of ethics that enshrine accuracy and transparency and "recognize a special obligation to serve as watchdogs over public affairs and government."[144] By contrast, the professional code of ethics for Chinese journalists highlights the importance of safeguarding social stability.[145] The CCP's efforts to influence overseas Chinese populations to expand its global influence also lack a parallel in the US system.

China's upstart approach has undoubtedly been more effective than imposing its system on other countries would have been, and it requires fewer resources. As Kurt Campbell and Jake Sullivan argued in 2019, China "ultimately present[s] a stronger ideological challenge than the Soviet Union did, even if it does not explicitly seek to export its system."[146] Nearly half of survey respondents in Mexico said they would prefer a China-led world order, although this view is somewhat unusual in the developing world: respondents in Brazil, Nigeria, and India hold positive views of the United States.[147] In countries that prioritize stability and economic growth, the China model appears to be an efficient "post democratic" fix.[148]

Countries throughout the world are becoming less democratic (though China's regime-neutral non-interference strategy is only one of the reasons), and China has an easier time working with these countries than the United States does. The United States often has few ways to impose costs on problematic states because of its limited bilateral relations. Strong ideological and political differences often result in severed relations, like those between the United States and Cuba. The United States often limits its diplomatic and economic ties to protest states' poor human rights records, sponsorship of terrorism, and pursuit of weapons of mass destruction (WMD). This tactic is exemplified by the United States' lack of diplomatic relations with Syria, North Korea, and Iran and its sanctioning of those states plus Cuba, Sudan, and Venezuela. Ironically, US support for human rights and democracy has made the United States reliant on China's support in efforts to coerce these regimes to be more responsible actors at home and abroad.

Additionally, China has succeeded in undermining anything that might encourage liberalization of its domestic political system. If anything, Party control has increased over the past ten years under Xi Jinping.[149] The Party has reversed the march toward free market principles, creating a system of "state control on steroids."[150] State surveillance has become sophisticated and uses a wide range of tools, including mobile apps, biometric data collection, AI, and big data.[151] China has used the COVID-19 pandemic to accelerate the implementation of tracking programs and to continue cracking down on virtual private network (VPN) usage.[152] Given these trends, China's Freedom House–assigned score has consistently declined within the "not free" category over the past five years.

Not all aspects of China's strategy have been successful. Beijing made a serious misstep in underestimating the extent to which political interference—the use of nefarious or underhanded tactics to influence another country's elections, political discourse, or civil society—would affect democracies' views of China. Many democracies have taken significant steps to interdict China's influence operations. In 2022, the Federal Bureau of Investigation (FBI) charged thirteen individuals for "alleged efforts to unlawfully exert influence in the United States for the benefit of the government of the PRC."[153] In 2018, Australia's parliament passed laws aimed at limiting foreign political influence in the country. Taiwan passed similar measures that enabled the government to prosecute nefarious Chinese lobbying. The European Parliament has since 2021 refused to implement an investment agreement with China unless Beijing drops its sanctions against members of the European Parliament that had put sanctions in place against Chinese officials complicit in human rights abuses in Xinjiang.[154]

Xi Jinping's regime neutrality approach is also evolving from demanding that the world respect China's system of political governance to presenting its model as an inspiration. Chinese strategists and leaders, including Xi himself, have become bolder in declaring that other countries can learn from China's approach even if China does not insist on it.[155] Xi has stated brazenly that his country is "offering a China solution to humanity's search for better social systems" and is "blazing a new trail for other developing countries to achieve modernization."[156] China seems to be cashing in on domestic economic success, as "regimes become morally appealing simply by virtue of their triumph.'"[157]

Since the mid-1990s, China has pursued a foreign policy strategy designed to propel it into the great power club. Like all great powers, China wants influence and international support for the issues it deems important. But China would have been hard-pressed to build power and influence on the international stage by building an alliance network, molding itself into the external security partner of choice, and imposing its model on other countries. In some cases, China simply could not compete; where the United States is dominant and experienced, emulation would have been high-risk and low-reward. In others, emulation would have placed Beijing in direct conflict with the most prosperous and powerful countries in the international system. The risk of provoking a countervailing coalition made those approaches unadvisable. China has thus eschewed some core US tactics, choosing approaches that maximize its power while decreasing the risks to its rise and to CCP control at home.

Almost twenty years ago, China scholars Evan Medeiros and M. Taylor Fravel warned that as China expanded its influence and refined its diplomacy, it would get better at protecting its own interests—even when they conflict with those of the United States.[158] This prediction seems especially accurate in light of China's emerging Wolf Warrior diplomacy, in which Chinese officials have gone on the offensive to defend China and its interests.[159] Indeed, China has apparently transitioned from "conservative, passive, and low-key" diplomacy to "assertive, proactive, and high-profile" engagement with other countries.[160] Former foreign minister Tang Jiaxuan describes China's foreign policy as having evolved from finding a place on the international stage to improving the international environment and then to becoming unprecedentedly active in diplomatic efforts.[161] Xi Jinping has called for foreign affairs to be managed in a way that helps China regain its standing as a great power, safeguard its expanding global interests, and acquire the strategic confidence to tackle such efforts as reforming the global governance system and deepening its partnership relationships.[162]

But even as China has become more assertive on the international stage over the past few years, these three cases show that it has maintained its entrepreneurial approach. China's partnership diplomacy, its self-positioning as the internal security partner of choice, and its regime agnosticism are just a few examples of how China, in the words of Xi, is "putting forward new ideas and new initiatives" to develop "its own characteristics of major power diplomacy."[163]

4

Emulation and Exploitation in Chinese Military Strategy

In 2018, after another series of wargames analyzing conflict between China and the United States in the Taiwan Strait, US military officers were frustrated. Conducting more wargames, one participant argued to the Secretary of the Air Force, would be a waste of time. It was clear how the games would end—with a US loss.[1] The once peerless US military had to wrap its head around this new situation: China had modernized its military in the precise ways that created the greatest challenges for US forces. Indeed, in March 2021, Admiral Philip Davidson, then commander of US forces in the Indo-Pacific, warned that within six years, China's military would "overmatch" that of the United States and could "forcibly change the status quo" in East Asia.[2]

Fifteen years previously, the United States would have dominated the Chinese military in any scenario. The Chinese knew it—and they didn't like it. Indeed, as China began its rise to great power status in the mid-1990s, events in the Taiwan Strait were front and center in the minds of Chinese leaders. China had started a series of missile tests to signal its displeasure with Taiwan's president Lee Teng-hui and had continued them into 1996 in the hope of influencing the Taiwan electorate in the presidential election. The United States had sent one aircraft carrier battle group to the vicinity of the strait, and later another, to warn China to back off.

The US show of force worked. China stepped down its provocative military coercion against Taiwan, ceasing the missile tests. Diplomatically, China spent its time trying to convince the United States to steer Taiwan away from any moves toward independence. But internally, Chinese strategists and elites stewed. China vowed not to find itself in such a disadvantageous position again.[3]

Chinese strategists conducted a detailed analysis of US strengths and weaknesses to decide where China should emulate and where it could exploit gaps in US military capabilities. This chapter explains how considerations of strategic effectiveness, efficacy, US perceptions, the existence of gaps, and domestic political factors at times encouraged emulation in military strategy. For example, China became proactive in multilateral military operations and in arms control regimes. In these cases, Chinese strategists believed that emulating US practice would reassure other countries and confer the added benefit of closing the relative power gap by constraining US military power or enhancing that of China. Indeed, the strategy convinced many observers at the time that China's military could be a force for good.

Not all Chinese emulation of US military practice followed this logic. Developing the capability to fight wars under informatized conditions—defined by Chinese military thinkers as "the war pattern of seeking all-area superiority through the 'trinity warfare' formed by the information, electromagnetic, and missile weapon systems"[4]—was seen as so strategically effective, so necessary to China's ability to leap from major to great power status, that it would be worth the trade-off in terms of heightened US threat perceptions.[5] Modernizing China's military also supported Party control; in the words of Hu Jintao, "Defense and military building are directly related to the success or failure of socialism with Chinese characteristics."[6] Beijing tried to minimize backlash through entrepreneurial approaches (discussed in Chapter 5), but there is no doubt that China's spate of building conventional systems sparked consternation and led to negative reactions from the United States.

For the most part, the costs were worth the trade-off in greater capability and thus military power. But in this chapter, I argue that this was not so for one case of emulation: China's aircraft carrier program. China has spent huge sums on the program, which has raised threat perceptions around the region, but it is unable to produce systems comparable to those of the United States in either quality or quantity. This case shows what happens when factors outside the upstart logic drive choices—in this case the desire for prestige and the desire to intimidate regional players.

This chapter also traces how the five factors—strategic effectiveness, strategic efficacy, domestic political factors, potential US response, and existence of gaps—encouraged China to adopt exploitation approaches in its military strategy. I show how the United States' need to project power over vast distances to contend with China creates unique vulnerabilities that China deliberately exploits with an anti-access/area denial (A2/AD) capability strategy. This A2/AD strategy focuses on the ability to impact US operations: to blunt the United States' power projection capabilities, deny the United States entry into an area, and restrict freedom of access once US forces are in the area.

Emulating to Reassure: Pursuing "Legitimate" Military Roles

In 2005, deputy secretary of state Robert Zoellick publicly urged China to become a "responsible stakeholder," a country that would not only benefit from being a member of the open, rules-based international system but also contribute to this system. In part, his address was a response to Zheng Bijian, chair of the China Reform Forum and a counselor to China's leaders, who had posited the "peaceful rise" doctrine, in which China would not seek hegemony but would prioritize economic growth for all.[7] In his address, Zoellick referred to Zheng's position but was clear that words were not enough: "The world," said Zoellick, "will look to the evidence of actions."[8]

Zoellick's speech was symptomatic of a belief among the US strategic community in the 2000s that China's greater participation in international and multilateral military efforts would be a credible signal of its peaceful intentions. As China security expert David Shambaugh noted, if China was more active militarily around the world "under the sponsorship of the UN or other recognized regional organizations, Western publics and governments [would] be accepting—even encouraging—of China's activism."[9]

The call to become a responsible stakeholder was not initially welcomed in China. Hu Jintao, for example, thought it was a ploy to limit China's rise.[10] In his words:

> They don't really want our country to play a greater role in the international community, but place us on a pedestal, pressure us to undertake obligations beyond our capabilities, require us to deal with major international and regional issues according to their logic, and even attempt to influence our country's major domestic policies in this way. Their real intention is to transfer conflicts to our country and hinder our country's development.[11]

From the Chinese perspective, "Western countries only want China to help share the costs of their hegemony, but are not willing to share their global leadership."[12] In the language of the upstart framework, the United States was encouraging China to sacrifice effectiveness and efficacy for a greater ability to reassure.

While contributing to the global public good to the degree Zoellick envisioned did not make sense for the upstart, the fact that the United States was publicly calling for a more active Chinese role created an opportunity for the military. Chinese military leaders were cognizant of the high sensitivity of other countries to anything military-related; a more active, visible PLA could invite scrutiny from the international community.[13] But emulating certain aspects of the US military's role in the world could reassure others China was building "an army of peace" even as it improved critical military capabilities.[14] The United States has long conducted extensive military operations other than war (MOOTW): one RAND analysis identified 846 MOOTW conducted by the US Air Force (or its predecessor) between 1916 and 1996.[15] MOOTW cover a broad range of actions, from arms control to peacekeeping operations (PKOs), combating terrorism to humanitarian assistance.

While the formal distinction between MOOTW and wartime operations was abandoned in 2006 in favor of "a conflict continuum that spans from peace to war," contemporary US doctrine continues to see non-traditional military operations as a means to transform the military into "a political instrument used to shape an international environment favorable to the United States."[16] To China, the United States' MOOTW offered a feasible target for emulation; it could present a peaceful image to the world and "give China more capital when it runs for leadership positions in international organizations."[17] It helped as well that PLA participation in multilateral peacekeeping and humanitarian aid and disaster relief operations abroad was popular with the Chinese people and thus contributed to solidifying the CCP's rule.[18]

Domestic political considerations also encouraged China to consider emulating aspects of the US military's global role. For the first time in its history, China had millions of citizens abroad in any given period and thousands of companies setting up shop in countries around the world. The Chinese government was facing increasing domestic pressure to protect these interests and Chinese nationals abroad.[19] The 2000s and early 2010s saw a steady increase in threats to China's investment footprint around the globe.[20] Following the deaths of fourteen Chinese nationals in Afghanistan and Pakistan in 2004, pressure mounted on the Department of Consular Affairs to establish an office to protect overseas Chinese nationals.[21] These rising threats pushed the Chinese government to include, for the first time, a section on protecting Chinese interests overseas in the 2013 Defense White Paper.[22]

Sensing that expanding China's global military role in "acceptable areas" would strengthen its position at home and abroad, the Party ordered the Chinese military to participate in MOOTW. Its first major contribution was to the Gulf of Aden anti-piracy task force, an international effort established by the UNSC in 2008 that called on member states to combat piracy off the coast of Somalia.[23] The timing was no coincidence; Somali pirates had tried to hijack a Chinese merchant vessel in 2008, which created a strong domestic imperative to participate. Since 2009, PLAN vessels dedicated to these counterpiracy operations have conducted over forty anti-piracy and escort missions in the Gulf, escorting over 6,000 merchant ships.[24]

China also became proactive in UN peacekeeping operations (UNPKOs). At the start of the century, China had a mere fifty-two people participating in UNPKOs; fifteen years later, that number was over 3,000 (twenty-three times more than the Americans had deployed). The Chinese military has participated in twenty-five UNPKOs and has dispatched nearly 50,000 peacekeepers over the past thirty years, about 36,500 of whom were sent out between 2000 and 2020.[25] China is currently the eighth-largest troop contributor to UNPKOs and since 2009 has provided more personnel than any of the permanent members of the UNSC.[26] The nature of China's contribution changed significantly in 2012 when it deployed combat troops for the first time (previous deployments had consisted mainly of engineering, transport, and medical detachments).[27] Figure 4.1 shows the total number of troops the UNSC's permanent five members have provided to PKO missions from 1990 to 2020.

Lastly, China began to conduct its own humanitarian and disaster relief operations (HADRs), with the vast majority occurring after 2010.[28] China has conducted approximately forty HADR missions, and its hospital ship made thirty-eight stops between 2002 and 2022. In 2011, the Chinese military was called upon to assist for the first time in a non-combatant evacuation operation (NEO) of 36,000 Chinese citizens from Libya over the course of ten days (the longest known deployment in People's Liberation Army Air Force [PLAAF] history). Four years later, the Chinese navy was deployed to evacuate more than 600 Chinese citizens and another 279 people from the Republic of Yemen.[29] In April 2023 as unrest grew in Sudan, China evacuated approximately 1,000 of its citizens from the country.[30] Figure 4.2 shows the approximate locations of China's HADR activities.[31] The numbers on the

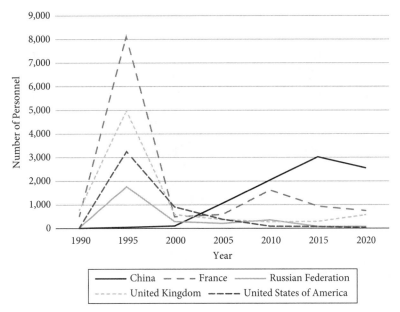

Figure 4.1 UN Security Council Permanent Five Members' Total Personnel Contributions to UNPKOs, 1990–2020

Source: Data from "Troop and Police Contributors," United Nations Peacekeeping, https://peacekeep ing.un.org/en/troop-and-police-contributors.

diamonds correspond to individual activities, and more information on these activities is provided in the corresponding appendix. The dots correspond to stops made by China's *Peace Ark*, a hospital ship under the PLAN.

China's focus on emulating the US approach to MOOTW has helped it build power at minimal cost through several mechanisms. First, its participation has led to improvements in military capacity. According to one congressional report, "During HADR-related exercises with the US military, Beijing has routinely sought—and on a number of occasions successfully gained—access to training that would directly or indirectly improve the PLA's ability to carry out combat operations, such as force projection or a blockade of Taiwan."[32]

Chinese analysts recognized that by "selectively yet actively" participating in PKO, China could improve its image and the PLA's ability to operate globally to include "developing new military practices and innovative military theories."[33] China has indeed learned from other troop-contributing countries, developing foreign language and cultural skills, exposing junior

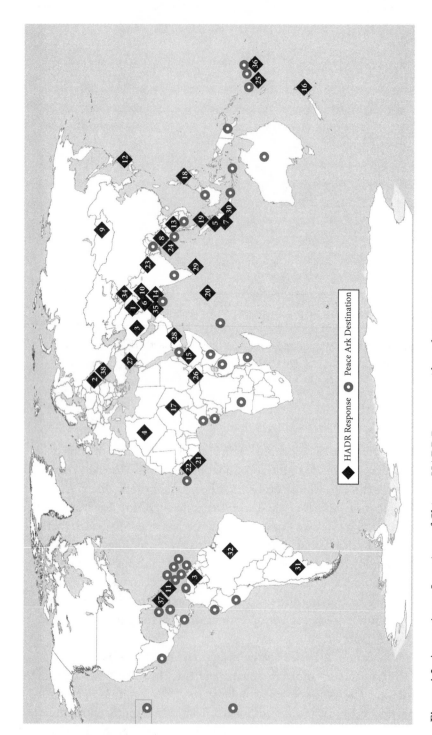

Figure 4.2 Approximate Locations of Chinese HADR Responses Abroad, 2002–2022

Source: Author's creation.

and midranking officers to high-risk environments, improving planning skills relevant to expeditionary operations, and testing its unit readiness.[34] Through PKO, China has also improved its ability to rapidly coordinate, transport (via airlift), and deploy mobile forces over a long range in complex environments.[35] Moreover, such operations buy China influence that helps it promote its other security goals. Indeed, some have criticized China for letting political considerations get in the way of effective participation.[36]

In addition to improvements in capabilities and training, China's participation in the Gulf of Aden anti-piracy mission helped justify China's first overseas base in Djibouti. In 2015, when news of the facility broke, China was careful to label it a "logistical support facility" (*houqin baozhang sheshi*) rather than a "base" (*jidi*). Beijing maintains officially that the base exists to aid in Chinese naval escort missions and humanitarian relief activities.[37] While many analysts worried about the international response to China's first overseas base, China's humanitarian rationale meant that it faced far less international blowback than it would have otherwise. Indeed, China had increased its participation in peacekeeping, anti-piracy, counterterrorism, and humanitarian relief missions with the explicit purpose of "normalizing Chinese military presence overseas, secur[ing] important sea-lanes, and protect[ing] the country's overseas interests."[38]

State media's coverage of these activities shows that Beijing believes they will enhance Party legitimacy. State media praised China's NEO in Yemen as a reflection of the Party's choice to "put the people first and diplomacy for the people," demonstrating the government's strong determination to protect its citizens abroad and its decisive and efficient administration.[39] After another NEO in Sudan, the Chinese government described the operation as a manifestation of Xi Jinping's New Era socialism with Chinese characteristics, arguing that it demonstrated China's strength and commitment, as well as the majestic image of the Chinese military.[40] This majestic image of China-as-protector finds its way to the silver screen, and it is not just popular but a bonafide blockbuster with the Chinese public—the movies *Operation Red Sea* and *Wolf Warrior 2* earned $575 million and $854 million in China, respectively.[41]

To ensure that the benefits outweigh the costs of emulation in this case, China has been careful not to contribute resources to these efforts at US levels. Despite joining the UN mission to escort ships through the Gulf of Aden, the Chinese acted largely unilaterally—for instance, refusing to take orders from other countries or organizations.[42] For decades, the United

States' financial contribution to UN peacekeeping has dwarfed China's; in 2012, China contributed only 6.6 percent of the budget for UNPKOs, in contrast to the United States' 28 percent. China's share has risen to 15 percent since then, but it is still 12.6 percentage points less than that of the United States.[43] Despite bold promises of more troops and funding, Chinese troop contributions have fallen by a quarter since 2015, and China contributes only $20 million a year to Xi's China-UN Peace and Development Fund despite a previous pledge of $1 billion.[44] China contributes to fewer HADRs and much less in each one compared to the United States.[45] Part of this discrepancy is due to limitations in China's expeditionary capabilities, but the fact that it contributes significantly less financially suggests intent to minimize costs overall. For example, in the case of Ebola, China's relief efforts, totaling over $120 million, were dwarfed by the United States' contribution of $2.4 billion to West Africa since the outbreak began.[46] Figure 4.3 shows China's relative contribution to the UN's PKO budget in 2020–2021.

All of this is to say that China has carefully calibrated its participation in MOOTW to capture the benefits in terms of reassurance, Party control at home, and building military capacity, but without spending the resources that might undermine the efficacy of the approach.

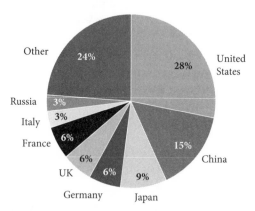

Figure 4.3 Major Contributors to the UNPKO Budget, 2020–2021

Source: Data from "How We Are Funded," UN Peacekeeping, https://peacekeeping.un.org/en/how-we-are-funded, accessed June 26, 2023; "UN Document A/67/224/Add. 1: Scale of Assessments for the Apportionment of the Expenses of the United Nations Peacekeeping Operations," United Nations General Assembly, December 27, 2015, https://documents-dds-ny.un.org/doc/UNDOC/GEN/N12/665/78/PDF/N1266578.pdf?OpenElement.

Emulating to Constrain: Participation in Multilateral Arms Control Regimes

China's participation in arms regimes is widely touted as a success story.[47] In 1980, the country was essentially uninvolved in arms control agreements. But by the late 1990s, its participation rate was on par with that of other major powers.[48] This is a story of emulation, though the upstart framework presents a less positive picture than conventional socialization theory. I argue that China emulated to both disproportionately constrain the United States and enhance reassurance about its own efforts. When China joined the Nuclear Suppliers Group in 2004, for example, it did so with the public support of the Bush administration and others in the US arms control community.[49] China also sacrificed little in terms of potential gains. Arms sales are not a key component of its power accumulation strategy, and Chinese strategists do not see warfighting utility in WMD. It makes sense, therefore, for China to work to constrain US ability in these areas.

Indeed, China has been supportive of international regimes that do just that—constrain the United States in areas of potential strength for Washington. Of the seventeen multilateral arms control regimes, thirteen are primarily about nuclear weapons, two concern biological and chemical weapons, and two regulate sales of conventional weapons.[50] Unsurprisingly, China is particularly supportive of the Arms Trade Treaty, which regulates international trade in conventional weapons (as I discuss in Chapter 2, this is a key source of US power but less so for China) and which it ratified and signed in 2020. Conversely, the United States pulled out in 2019.[51] China has also been more forward-leaning on creating restrictions for the military uses of space, a domain the United States relies on much more heavily compared to China for the projection of military power.[52] Chinese experts like Tang Yongsheng, professor at the PLA National Defence University, have been direct about the strategy, arguing that China should "use the UN arms control and disarmament institutions to restrain US arms development and deescalate the US-China arms race."[53] China has gone further than the current regimes, advocating for a complete ban on and destruction of nuclear weapons.[54]

China experts Alastair Iain Johnston and Evan Medeiros posit an alternative explanation for China's participation in separate studies of China's involvement in such institutions. Medeiros attributes the evolution of China's position to its serial exposure to international arms control during the 1980s and 1990s, particularly through US policy actions and exchanges between American and Chinese non-governmental experts.[55] Johnston argues that the change in the discursive practices of China's arms control community in the 1980s was due to Chinese participation in some of the first major arms control institutions, such as the UN Conference on Disarmament, in which Chinese delegates "mimicked" and adopted some of the habits, language, and organizational models of arms controllers.[56] In this sense, China's participation in arms control agreements was a reaction to its socialization in the international diplomatic community.

The upstart approach also posits that China's accession to these arms control regimes is a story of socialization, in that interactions convinced China of the potential benefits of acceding to them. However, the benefits within the upstart framework are somewhat different: acceding to these treaties would reassure the United States, improve China's international image, and reduce the likelihood of a negative response to its rise while also increasing its relative power. This was especially the case after the end of the Cold War when, according to a Chinese strategist, "the US adjusted the priorities of its arms control policy from focusing on limiting and reducing strategic weapons during the cold war period to focusing on the proliferation of weapons of mass destruction (WMD) and their technology," which required China's cooperation.[57]

Research by Chinese scholars on this history argues that Beijing's participation in arms control negotiations with the United States did reflect a profound change in its attitude toward the Western-dominated international order and international regime.[58] But one of China's key objectives was to build mutual trust with the United States through negotiations and to forge a reciprocal bilateral relationship.[59] In China's view, the United States was undoubtedly the dominant player in the international system, and joining the system could demonstrate that China had no incentive to challenge it.[60] In other words, if Chinese thinkers had decided that a different approach to arms sales or nuclear doctrine would have given it the upper hand in competition with the United States, China would not have signed on to these agreements.

While it is difficult to prove the counterfactual, the upstart approach can explain the variation in China's acceptance of arms control regimes better than the socialization argument can. For example, a more competitive logic explains why China has a spotty record on export controls. China participates in only three of the eight regimes: export control (Nuclear Suppliers Group), non-proliferation (Zangger Committee), and safeguard (International Atomic Energy Agency [IAEA] Safeguards). A quick review of the five China does not participate in—the Australia Group, the MTCR, Wassenaar, the Proliferation Security Initiative (PSI), and the Hague Code of Conduct—hints at why. China enjoys an advantage over the United States in conventional missile technology and relies more heavily on land-based systems for its nuclear deterrent—capabilities that the MTCR and the Hague Code of Conduct would have limited. Signatories to the Hague Code of Conduct, for instance, must provide annual information on their ballistic missile programs, including the number and class of those missiles and information on test launches conducted.[61]

According to Johnston, China supports arms control institutions like the Antiballistic Missile Treaty and the Intermediate-Range Nuclear Forces Treaty but will not join them for "obvious self-interested free-riding reasons."[62] To gain strategic advantage and deter US influence, China has supported the development of arms programs in Saudi Arabia, Pakistan, Iran, and North Korea through state enterprises, even as it committed to follow the rules of the MTCR.[63] Signing these agreements could take away key tools China uses to shape its relationships with Pakistan, North Korea, and Iran.

While China has been supportive of many nuclear arms agreements that constrain the United States more due to its larger arsenal and more aggressive nuclear posture, China has been unwilling to get on board with any agreement designed to limit its nuclear arsenal as a way for the United States to maintain its dominance.[64] Fu Cong, the head of the Chinese Foreign Ministry's arms control department, explicitly stated that "China has no interest in joining the so-called trilateral negotiations, given the huge gap between the nuclear arsenal of China and those of the US and the Russian Federation."[65] This inherent suspicion is illustrated in *Science of Military Strategy*, a core textbook for senior PLA officers, in which arms control is described as a "struggle" between self-interested great powers.[66] Chinese leaders are particularly suspicious of US-led arms control regimes, which Chinese strategists see as a "trap" designed to solidify American nuclear dominance and undermine China's nuclear deterrent.[67] Indeed, China uses arms control mostly to protest against other countries' arms deployment and development.

Emulating to Contend: "Local Wars Under Informatized Conditions"

In the summer of 1990, Iraqi president Saddam Hussein invaded his neighbor Kuwait, triggering a UN condemnation and a mandated deadline for withdrawal. Over the next five months, the United States organized a UN-authorized coalition of NATO and Middle Eastern allies, including Saudi Arabia, Egypt, and Syria, to liberate Kuwait.[68] After an extensive bombing campaign and only 100 hours of ground combat, the 1991 Gulf War left Saddam Hussein's military in ruins.

The conflict also sent a message to Beijing: America excelled in an entirely new way of war, one that China was not ready for. A shocked Chinese leadership, headed at this time by President Jiang Zemin, held three seminars with senior officials to discuss the inspiration and impact of the war on the Chinese military. Jiang, according to state-published sources, believed that the Gulf War should alert China to the possibility of conflict and to the reality that China's technological capabilities trailed well behind those of the United States.[69]

The Chinese military immediately set about reassessing its strategy in a changing security environment.[70] Although decision-makers never mentioned the United States by name, they repeatedly referred to the Gulf War's demonstration of the importance of "coping with local wars and armed conflicts fought under high-technology conditions," a clear indication that China's priority was strategizing against technologically superior foes.[71] These "superiorly equipped enemies" were able to fight "modern wars" that involved multiple battlefields from outer space to the depths of the ocean, an air force capable of "large-scale, uninterrupted, and prolonged air strikes," and an "advanced and mature C3 [command, control, and communications] network that acts as the core of the entire war machine."[72] After witnessing the US war machine and its devastating impact on Iraq in 2003, Chinese leaders concluded that "one of the most important reasons for the strong combat capability of the US military is its leading position in information technology."[73]

The US approach to warfare was seen as so effective that China had to be able to compete in a similar vein.[74] Future wars, military specialists concluded, would showcase weapons with a higher level of informatization, intelligence, and integration, and thus the PLA needed to achieve "the dual historical tasks of mechanization and informatization."[75] In 1993, China formulated a new strategic guideline: "winning local wars under modern especially high-tech conditions" (*daying xiandai jishu tebie shi gaojishu tiaojian xia jubu zhanzheng*).[76] In 2004, the Central Military Commission (CMC) adjusted the guidelines to stress winning local wars under conditions of informatization (applying information technology to all aspects of military operations) to better prepare for the growing unconventional threats to China's national security.[77] In 2015, the guidelines were again adapted to emphasize winning local wars of informatization (not simply wars with informatized conditions), preparing for military struggles on the sea, and effectively controlling major crises.[78]

From that point on, China was determined to "make great efforts to develop the information capability" of its own military.[79] Since 2000, informatization (*xinxihua*) has been a theme in every Chinese national defense white paper, with the 2004 version mentioning it more than forty times.[80] According to top PLA generals, the military needed to improve command and control capabilities to build a unified information system and focus training on the use and implementation of networks.[81] In 2017, Xi articulated that by 2020, the PLA should have roughly realized mechanization, involving the upgrade of the PLA's equipment with modern machinery, and made significant progress toward informatization, which entails the full integration of information technology into the PLA.[82] By 2035, it should roughly achieve modernization in the military's theory, organizational structure, personnel, weapons, and equipment.[83]

To achieve informatization, China required a space command, control, communications, computers, intelligence, surveillance, and reconnaissance (C4ISR) infrastructure to support its informatized needs, from navigation and communication to precision guidance and real-time command and control.[84] At the turn of the century, Chinese military analysts were publishing extensively on how space was the ultimate high ground.[85] Similarly, Chinese scholars believe that space has become the "high frontier," of crucial importance to national security and great power "competition for survival and development."[86] Chinese military thinkers argued that a strong space power is indispensable for "space control" and "information control" on the battlefield.[87] Because the United States' space supremacy would severely worsen China's peripheral security environment and seriously hinder its pursuit of national reunification, China had to adopt suitable countermeasures.[88]

In 2010, China accelerated the development of its space-based military infrastructure. Between 1970 and 2009, China had launched about 130 rockets to deliver 142 payloads into orbit. In 2010, China's annual launches increased significantly, and between 2010 and 2019, it launched 370 payloads on 207 rockets.[89] China now fires more rockets into space than any other country (with a success rate of about 95 percent, comparable to that of the United States and Russia).[90] In June 2020, China put the final touch on its BeiDou Navigation Satellite System, a third-generation network designed to compete with GPS. In addition to commercial uses, this system of thirty-five satellites and over fifty ground stations all over the world aims to enhance the PLA's ability to strike ground targets.[91] By building this system, China hoped to eliminate its dependence on GPS. This was important because the Chinese believed the United States had shut down China's access at least twice previously, including during the 1996 Taiwan Strait Crisis.[92]

Admittedly, China is not poised to catch up with the United States, nor is it particularly efficient in building its space infrastructure. The United States still manages to launch significantly more payloads with each missile—in 2019 the United States put over 200 payloads into orbit on 21 launches, compared to China's much less efficient 79 payloads on 32 launches. As of January 2023, China had about 590 active satellites in orbit, of which approximately three-fifths were for government or military use, compared to the United States' approximately 4,529 active satellites, of which 6 percent are for government or military use.[93] The US approach, largely thanks to cooperation with the commercial sector, is also more cost-effective. SpaceX's Falcon Heavy and Falcon 9 rockets cost about $1,400 and $2,700 per metric ton, respectively, whereas China's Long March 3A and 2D cost upward of $8,000 per metric ton each.[94]

To fight local wars under informatized conditions, China also needed modern conventional platforms with which to conduct network-centric warfare, which refers to "an information superiority-enabled operational doctrine that connects sensors, decision-makers, and weapons platforms into a whole through networks . . . to generate a greater combat capability."[95] Thus, parallel to its A2/AD arms buildup (discussed in the next section), China embarked on a massive modernization plan to create a large force of advanced equipment. In 1999, less than 2 percent of its fighters were fourth-generation, characterized by limited stealth capabilities, older engine technology, and reduced maneuverability, and 4 percent of its attack submarines and none of its surface ships were modern. Today most of its military has modern equipment.[96] China had some advantages to leverage—for example, at the turn of the century, China had an impressive shipbuilding industry at its disposal, third only to Japan's and South Korea's and producing 5 percent of the world's gross tonnage.[97] The culmination of this shipbuilding program came from 2015 to 2020, when the Chinese navy's total number of battleships exceeded that of the US Navy for the first time.[98]

Beijing attempted to minimize the costs in terms of threat perceptions and consequent responses by pursuing other exploitative and entrepreneurial strategies (discussed later in this book)—for example, by delaying key aspects of modernization. In terms of naval power, rather than attempt to match US numbers in the early stages of its rise, the Chinese built their fleet strategically, experimenting with a smaller class of ships before the larger force structure developments.[99] China also benefited from luck: the United States was distracted by the war on terror and therefore may have been slow to respond. Indeed, Jiang Zemin popularized the concept of a "window of strategic opportunity" for China's rise at the 16th National Congress, in which the years 2000–2020 were seen as the critical time partly because of US distraction.[100] The strategy included exercising patience in building up capabilities in ways that avoided large-scale confrontation with potential opponents.[101]

The bottom line is that Chinese thinkers believed that the ability to fight informatized wars was essential to China's ability to build a military capable of achieving its objectives.[102] Chinese leaders needed a larger, more sophisticated military to achieve some of their core objectives, even though a buildup was bound to spark a strong response. As Xi Jinping argued in the 5th Plenary Session of the 19th Central Committee, "In the past we were less developed, which meant we satisfied the needs of others; now that we are more developed, we are competing with them more."[103]

Inadvisable Emulation: China's Aircraft Carrier Program

Perhaps nothing is more emblematic of US military power than the aircraft carrier. In combat, the carrier's main role is to establish local air supremacy, whether that means securing sea lines of communication and protecting convoys from submarine and air attacks or projecting power onshore, such as during the United States' island-hopping campaigns against Japan in the Pacific War. In the 1980s, the Reagan administration's 600-ship navy plan called for a total of 15 carrier battle groups that would serve as the Allied forces' primary instruments of power projection and sea control against

Warsaw Pact forces.[104] The United States has consistently deployed them in conflicts, like the 1991 Gulf War, and for diplomatic purposes, such as conducting freedom of navigation operations in the South China Sea.[105]

In other words, carriers have been an effective way for the United States to project power abroad, respond to crises, reassure allies, and deter potential adversaries. Aside from their operational value, carriers convey a sense of national prestige and pride given their awesome ability to project power.[106] But despite the strategic effectiveness of aircraft carriers, a variety of factors discourage emulation. First, given the aircraft carrier's centrality to US military power, nothing screams "challenger" like building one. Second, while it has been critical to US military power in the past, the carrier is no longer the fortress it once was; the advent of sophisticated intelligence, surveillance, and reconnaissance (ISR) networks and precision-guided munitions seriously undermines the aircraft carrier's utility for power projection.[107] It is also a very expensive pathway to power. The United States' latest carrier, the USS *Gerald R. Ford*, cost $13.3 billion to construct, and the next three ships in the *Ford* class will together cost nearly $40 billion.[108]

Accordingly, for the first fifteen years of China's great power rise, its leaders decided not to pursue this ultimate great power symbol. It is not that a carrier would not have been useful. PLAN commander Liu Huaqing recalled that during a November 1986 meeting on naval strategy, many suggested its utility for pursuing unification with Taiwan and protecting China's territorial interests in the South China Sea.[109] Moreover, Liu commented, at that time Chinese surface ships could not operate outside the range of shore-based aircraft due to limitations in ship-based air defense. An aircraft carrier would have allowed them to extend their range without large expenditures on more aircraft.[110]

Although the Chinese open-source record is vague on the decision, it seems that Chinese leaders initially avoided emulation because the potential costs far outweighed these marginal benefits. Ye Zicheng, a professor at Peking University, argued that given that Chinese spending on the military was limited, the better route was to expend resources on developing the next generation of aircraft and improving the performance of China's missiles.[111] Two experts, Cheng Gang and Zhang Mian, argued in 2003 that China must avoid building aircraft carriers because doing so would feed into the "China threat theory" and because the economic costs and technical difficulties associated with the endeavor made it inadvisable.[112] Indeed, in 1995 Liu Huaqing submitted a report to the Politburo advocating for aircraft carriers, but allegedly the suggestion was turned down because it did not cohere with China's grand strategy at the time, which focused on reassuring countries of its peaceful intentions, especially after Beijing's brutal crushing of the Tiananmen protests.[113] As a result, China went in a more entrepreneurial direction (discussed in Chapter 5), using gray zone tactics in the South China Sea, combining carrots (enhanced economic and cultural ties) and sticks (A2/AD capabilities) to prevent Taiwan from gaining independence, and finally developing adequate ship-based long- and medium-range air defense missile systems like the HHQ-9 and HHQ-16.

In 2012, China shifted strategies, entering the carrier club in a particularly opaque fashion. In 1998, a Macau businessman purchased a former Soviet hull, the *Varyag*, that was lying in disrepair. The ship was towed to a Dalian shipyard in northern China in 2002. Ten years later, in 2012, the PLAN finally announced that the *Varyag*, rechristened the *Liaoning*, had entered the service as China's first aircraft carrier.[114]

Since then, China has built two indigenous carriers, the *Shandong* (commissioned in December 2019) and the *Fujian* (launched in June 2022). Compared with the *Liaoning*, the *Shandong* has an improved radar system and more deck space for berthing aircraft.[115] The *Fujian* is more advanced in that it features electromagnetically powered catapults capable of launching larger and more heavily armed combat aircraft. China plans to have ten aircraft carriers (six conventional and four nuclear) by 2049.[116] Nuclear aircraft carriers will allow Chinese aircraft carriers essentially unlimited range, increased speed, and sufficiently improved power generation to operate a steam-catapult system.

China's decision to emulate despite reduced effectiveness, low efficacy, and sparking threat perceptions came at a predictable price. Since aircraft carriers have long been characterized as the "most tangible symbol of US military dominance," China's strategic shift toward building carriers was likely to set off alarms.[117] Indeed, China's carrier program is mentioned twenty-eight times in the Pentagon's 2021 annual report to Congress, with far fewer references to more "legitimate" Chinese military activities like HADRs.[118] President Biden's China expert on the National Security Council, Rush Doshi, associated China's acquisition of carriers with Beijing's ambitions for regional domination.[119] The launch in June 2022 of the *Fujian* solidified the view that China is vying for Pacific supremacy and will become more confrontational in its attempts to project power, achieve sea control, and conduct amphibious assaults.[120]

In addition to spiking threat perceptions, China has difficulty competing efficiently with the United States in this area. China's carriers are nowhere near the US gold standard. US carriers are bigger and can support more aircraft, and they are nuclear-powered (meaning US carriers do not need to be refueled until after twenty years of service, in stark contrast to the *Liaoning* and *Shandong*, both of which need to be refueled every six days).[121] On the nuclear power front, China is more than sixty years behind the United States, which launched its first nuclear-powered carrier in 1961.[122] This is not for lack of trying—China's present pursuit of a nuclear-powered carrier has been called "relentless" by commentators.[123] But China has had difficulties given shortcomings in the core technology of nuclear reactors.[124]

The PLAN is likely to be at a competitive disadvantage if it tries to form an American-style aircraft carrier strike group that includes forces for aviation combat, surface combat, underwater combat, and support elements.[125] The United States has vast experience with carrier operations—it "can launch and recover waves of [ten to twelve] aircraft more than a dozen times a day."[126] Although similar statistics are not available for the Chinese platforms, the fact that CCTV reported with pride that the *Liaoning* had carried out 200 launches over ten days may reveal something about the Chinese carrier's maximum launch-and-recover capacity.[127] And while the PLAN is improving its ability to conduct under-way replenishment, this remains a weak spot for the service and would present significant logistical challenges.[128]

Given the downsides in terms of strategic effectiveness, efficacy, and US perceptions, why did China deviate from the upstart logic and emulate in this case? The first possibility is that Chinese leaders miscalculated. Perhaps they thought the program would be less expensive, more successful, or less threatening than it proved to be. China did acquire the *Liaoning* at a strategically advantageous time for minimizing backlash—the United States needed China's support for its global anti-terrorism initiative and thus might not have objected much.[129] Chinese leaders also might have thought they could mitigate threat perceptions by repackaging their carrier program. For example, the Ministry of Defense claimed that *Varyag* was being refitted for "scientific research, experiment and training"; it was not officially redesignated as a combat ship until 2019.[130] Chinese propaganda also tried selling the aircraft carrier as an indicator of China's desire to shoulder the great power responsibility to contribute to peace and stability.[131] Numerous official statements and state-sponsored media rhetoric emphasized that China would use aircraft carriers for defensive purposes only, such as to conduct rescue missions, and that its possession of this potentially offensive system would not motivate a more aggressive national defense or naval strategy.[132]

The more likely explanation is that China's aircraft carrier program resulted from other preferences that proved stronger than the five great power competition factors. The first culprit is prestige, which scholars have noted can push countries to emulate despite the downsides. In the eyes of Chinese leaders, the aircraft carrier had always represented the sine qua non for a true great power. In 1973, an ailing Zhou Enlai lamented to foreign visitors that "[he] has been dealing in military and political affairs all [his] life, but has not yet set his eyes on a Chinese aircraft carrier—this is a fact [he] cannot be resigned to."[133] A Chinese military official, speaking in 2011, observed that "all the great powers in the world, including [other] permanent members of the UNSC, have aircraft carriers; it seems that aircraft carriers are a marker of a great power. So I say the Chinese people, as they make their way out into the world, also must pass through this stage."[134] General Liu Huaqing acknowledged that "in the eyes of the world, it is seen as a symbol of comprehensive national power."[135] Liu Zhe, the first captain of the *Liaoning* carrier, recounts a perceived slight by an American, who commented over drinks that Liu's destroyer was "small but beautiful." He was bitter and vowed to become captain of an aircraft carrier one day.[136]

Communist Party leaders might have thought that the carrier program would buy them popularity at home. Indeed, Admiral Liu Huaqing had felt years earlier that the aircraft carrier would be a symbol of comprehensive national power in the eyes of the Chinese people and would thus enhance national prestige.[137] In Xi Jinping's China, the aircraft carrier is the embodiment of the Chinese Dream, a reflection of its economic success, and a source of pride for the Chinese people.[138]

Besides international and domestic prestige, there is one more consideration that seems to have tipped the balance in favor of the program: regional competition.[139] The *Shandong* is assigned to the South Sea Fleet and is tasked with "fill[ing] the last remaining loopholes of the island defense system in the South China Sea."[140] Although China has built military outposts on artificial islands in disputed waters, these stationary facilities are likely vulnerable to enemy bombardment. A carrier strike group, being more mobile and therefore less vulnerable to airborne attacks, would help China protect its sea lines of communication against smaller countries like Vietnam or the Philippines.[141]

The Ultimate Exploitation Strategy: China's A2/AD approach

During the first fifteen years of China's rise, the country was extremely vulnerable to the whims of the United States. At the end of the Cold War, the United States had the largest, most experienced, and best-equipped military the world had ever seen.[142] At the beginning of the twenty-first century, the United States spent more than any other nation on defense, at $320 billion (Russia spent $64 billion, China $46 billion). In 2022, the United States was still dedicating almost three times more than China was to its defense budget.[143]

Chinese leaders had learned from the Soviet Union that competing dollar for dollar with the United States in military spending could lead to its demise.[144] To compete with the United States, Moscow wasted excessive resources on military buildup, hindering economic growth and making it more difficult for the Soviet Union to break away from the rigid Stalinist system.[145] The Soviet economic system did not allow for an efficient civil-military fusion and was therefore not suited for an arms race with the United States.[146]

China's ambitions also made the wholesale emulation of US military power unnecessary; China's goals are largely regional. The Communist Party's legitimacy is wrapped up in its ability to promote its territorial claims in the South China Sea, in the East China Sea, and most importantly over Taiwan. Resolving these disputes in China's favor means (from China's perspective) regaining China's dominant military position in Asia after the hundred years of humiliation in which Western powers and Japan leveraged superior military might to take China's territory and subjugate its people.[147]

Concern for strategic effectiveness, efficacy, and Party control encouraged China to think differently about military competition. China clearly had to "do some things but not other things, catch up in some places but not other places," in the words of Jiang Zemin.[148] Chinese military thinkers settled on developing capabilities to exploit US vulnerabilities in ways that would have a disproportionate impact—or in Chinese military parlance, to "develop what the enemy is afraid of" or "assassin's mace" capabilities.[149] In the words of Zhang Wannian, a PLA general and former vice chairman of the CMC, China needs to "track high and new technologies and select important advanced weapons and equipment to develop" so that the Chinese army owns the most effective means to hurt its adversaries.[150]

Luckily for China, the United States has significant vulnerabilities to exploit. The result was an approach the United States terms an A2/AD strategy. Anti-access refers to the ability to *prevent* an opposing force from entering an area of operations. China has developed capabilities that can slow down the deployment of opposing forces, prevent US forces from operating in certain areas (like the first island chain that extends from the southern tip of Japan to northern Indonesia, to include Taiwan and the Philippines), or compel US forces to operate farther from the conflict than is operationally ideal.

The objective of area denial, in contrast, is not prevention but disruption—to compel a desired behavior by imposing severe costs on the enemy's freedom of action once it has gained access. Chinese integrated air defenses, anti-ship cruise and ballistic missiles, maritime bombers, missile- and torpedo-carrying submarines, and fast patrol boats are all designed to inflict prohibitively high costs on any country that operates near the China mainland. China's increasingly capable layered air defenses, as well as its fighter, ship, and missile assets, could target US bases and assets in the region, hampering operations.

Many US vulnerabilities result from the fact that the United States is not a resident power in Asia and thus, unlike China, is attempting to project power across vast distances. For example, the United States relies on other countries for base access, whereas China can use home bases. This is problematic for several reasons. The number of US bases has diminished since the end of the Cold War, whereas China has many basing options on its massive territory (the United States now has one air base, Kadena, within combat range of Taiwan, while China has thirty-nine).[151]

But the biggest issue is that US aircraft might not be able to get into the sky. A 2015 Rand report estimated that air force bases in Japan and South Korea, including Kadena Air Force Base (AFB), could see thousands of Chinese missiles launched at them, and even Andersen AFB on Guam is within striking range of hundreds of Chinese missiles launched from bombers and fighters. Specifically, the J-20 fighter aircraft, deployed in 2017, greatly increased China's ability to strike regional air bases, logistical facilities, and other ground-based infrastructure.[152] Similarly, Chinese H-6 bombers have undergone several refits enabling them to strike targets as far away as Guam.[153] While the degree of damage would depend on China's strategy, the United States' ability to operate in the region after an attack would be severely limited. US bases could be closed for more than six weeks with almost all aircraft damaged or destroyed.[154]

Chinese military thinkers are well aware of these vulnerabilities, and the resulting development of such a missile arsenal is no accident; Chinese military writings explicitly discuss gaps in US capabilities and how China needs "to deny denial" or neutralize US power projection capabilities.[155] Exploitation is particularly attractive given that China's cruise and ballistic missile programs, the heart of its long-range precision strike capability, are the most advanced in the world. And the size of its arsenal has grown, from about 750 short-range ballistic missiles (SRBMs) and medium-range ballistic missiles (MRBMs) in 2005 to over 1,100 in 2022.[156] In the same time frame, China's intercontinental ballistic missile (ICBM) count grew from 45 to 300 missiles, and intermediate-range ballistic missile (IRBMs) from 20 to 250. China's land attack cruise missiles (LACMs) and SRBMs decreased during this period, perhaps because China is replacing aging systems with more sophisticated variants.[157] China's missiles have improved dramatically in terms of quality as well as quantity. For instance, the DF-16, which only entered service in 2015, is nearly seven times more accurate than the DF-15 and its variant.[158]

China has another competitive advantage when it comes to targeting US aircraft carriers. Five US carriers are assigned to the Indo-Pacific region, with two homeported in San Diego, two in Washington State, and only one in the region, in Yokosuka, Japan. The 2022 movie *Top Gun: Maverick* suggests how critical the carrier has been for deep strike operations: in the film the pilots take off and return to a carrier off the coast of an unnamed hostile country without any concern for the safety of the carrier itself. Indeed, most countries cannot target from their shores a moving ship at sea, especially one as heavily defended as a carrier.

But China is an exception. The PLA's terminally guided ASBM is designed to neutralize "slow-moving targets at sea," which are almost certainly US carriers.[159] Given the DF-21D's estimated range, China may be able to keep the US carriers and their aircraft well outside their most effective operating range in a regional contingency.[160] Even if US aircraft manage to get in the air, they will still be at risk from a robust Chinese air defense system.[161] Chinese radar systems have even been located on the artificial islands China has built in the South China Sea, extending the early warning range farther into the Pacific.[162]

Such capabilities will make it difficult for the United States to surmount Chinese air defenses with its usual tools (e.g., jamming, standoff, and stealth weapons). China's IADS is sophisticated enough to prevent US fourth-generation, non-stealth aircraft from operating over and near the Chinese mainland. As former senior intelligence officer Lonnie Henley told Congress, by denying the US the ability to conduct air operations over the Taiwan Strait, China could blockade the island and continue launching strikes on Taiwan and US Navy ships indefinitely.[163] Although the United States would do better in conflicts in more remote areas such as the Spratly Islands, Chinese capabilities could still stave off rapid defeat. The United States would have to rely on fifth-generation stealth technology, known for its compact, modular, longer-range, and high-speed characteristics, and standoff weapons to strike Chinese targets on the mainland, but China is making progress here too with the HQ-9b medium-range air defense system and the HQ-19 anti-ballistic missile system.[164] Although it is unclear whether Chinese air defense could maintain a constant track on advanced US stealth aircraft, it is certain that the United States would be forced to operate at higher altitudes and disable or destroy anti-aircraft capabilities with long-range missiles before it could establish regional air superiority.[165]

Because the United States would largely be projecting power from Guam, Hawaii, or even the continental United States, its military would have to rely on many "enablers," or assets that main platforms or units need to engage in operations. Enablers also create vulnerabilities that China can exploit. For example, bombers and fighters need aerial refueling on long-range operations, and to provide the fuel they need tankers, which cannot defend themselves. As a Chinese military researcher argues, those US "airborne early warning aircraft, tankers, reconnaissance aircraft, and other large, high-value aerial targets are unable to approach the theater of operations, and their role as enablers in the combat system will decline."[166] China would thus compel the United States to refuel farther away from the conflict zone, which would reduce the amount of combat time for fighters and bombers.[167]

Chinese analysts know how dependent the United States is on space products and services for commanding troops, passing ISR data, and enabling precision targeting.[168] Chinese strategists recognize that anti-satellite operations on communication satellites or cyberattacks on the opponent's command and control system would disrupt how the United States deploys and operates its forces.[169] Indeed, deterrence in outer space is considered "the priority for future deterrence," as space force capabilities are not limited by political or geographical boundaries and have the potential to "project the power of deterrence to every corner on the surface of the earth."[170]

Chinese strategists also are aware that the United States has grown increasingly reliant on cyber capabilities. Between the Gulf War in 1991 and the Iraq War in 2003, US commanders gained access to forty-two times more bandwidth and information flow, a number that continues to increase as more processes become automated and operational units become more accustomed to an informational surplus.[171] To paraphrase an authoritative Chinese military source, cyber operations can be used to disseminate false information, simulate various combat operations to mislead the enemy, disrupt the enemy's information flow, paralyze the enemy's command and control systems, and access the enemy's internet system and destroy information.[172]

Given these realities, Chinese experts have advised that the PLA should emphasize military-civil fusion and develop both offensive and defensive cyber capabilities.[173] As a source published by the CMC's publishing house clearly lays out:

> By focusing on attacking the enemy's electronic countermeasures system, C3I [command, control, communications, and intelligence] system, and other important nodes of the campaign systems, it could destroy the overall function of the enemy's combat forces and achieve the effect of "a huge return for a very small investment [*siliang bo qianjin*]," thus accomplishing the goal of winning with inferior resources.[174]

As a result of this focus, China evolved from "a position of relative backwardness in electronics in the 1990s" to "conduct[ing] large-scale cyber operations abroad, aiming to acquire intellectual property, achieve political influence, carry out state-on-state espionage and position capabilities for disruptive effect in case of future conflict."[175] China is now among the top five source countries for denial-of-service and web-application-based global cyberattacks.[176]

China has also exploited the absence of established norms in areas like cyber and space, putting forth its own norms to cater to its strengths and constrain the United States. For example, China's proposed Prevention of the Placement of Weapons in Outer Space and of the Threat or Use of Force Against Outer Space Objects Treaty (PPWT) would limit offensive weapons in space but do little to restrain anti-satellite weaponry.[177] The United States, which sees little to gain in an agreement that would limit its offensive capabilities while leaving China and Russia's anti-satellite missiles untouched, continues to oppose the PPWT.[178] China has also pushed for the incorporation of concepts such as "cyber sovereignty" through the UN and the Digital Silk Road initiative. The term means that states are free to regulate their information technology industries as they see fit, justifying China's stringent censorship of its internet.[179]

In sum, Chinese strategists identified gaps in US military capabilities and believed that exploitation would be strategically effective and would capitalize on Chinese competitive advantages. In terms of efficiency, it would take only a single $18 million Chinese DF-21D carrier-killer missile to cripple a $13 billion American *Ford*-class aircraft carrier, or a $2 million HQ-9 to shoot down a $26 million F-16.[180] And in terms of effectiveness, as this discussion has highlighted, China can now contend with US military power to a significant degree regionally. After a decade of targeted military modernization, Chinese A2/AD capabilities were such that top brass in the US military believed that the United States was no longer the uncontested global power.[181] Indeed, repeated wargames reveal that the United States could lose if forced to project power into Chinese A2/AD zones, as in war over Taiwan.[182]

After the end of the Cold War, with China entering what we now know to be the initial stage of its rise, Chinese leaders not only embarked upon a series of new foreign policy strategies but also began to rethink Chinese military strategy. China needed to build up its military power and ability to resist the United States, all while avoiding confrontation. Moreover, when its economic foundation was still weak, Beijing needed to avoid costly military competition with the United States and especially a major war.[183]

To balance these demands, China researched foreign militaries, especially that of the United States.[184] Chinese strategists determined that the PLA needed to modernize to be able to fight local wars under informatized conditions. As a result, China embraced legitimate roles for its military, such as HADRs and PKOs, to develop its operational capabilities while minimizing backlash. It joined arms control agreements to further constrain US power projection capabilities while reassuring the world of its peaceful intentions. At the same time, it ruthlessly and deliberately exploited gaps in US capabilities with its A2/AD strategy, significantly narrowing the military power gap despite its limited resources. Not all Chinese military approaches maximized the power gap at minimal cost: notably, the lure of prestige and desire to intimidate weaker regional players pushed China to abandon its initial decision not to pursue aircraft carriers, which was in line with the up-start strategy. This slight deviation came at the costs predicted, but on aggre-gate China's military decisions have followed the upstart logic. As a result, China now has enough military power to impose caution on the United States in the Indo-Pacific region.

5

Entrepreneurship in Chinese Military Strategy

Building military strength without sparking a strong response from the established hegemon is the hardest and most pivotal task for an aspiring great power. The task has perhaps never been as daunting as it was for China, given the sheer power of the US military, a force able to project power farther, faster, and with greater precision and lethality than any other in the history of the world. And yet, since 1995, China has made progress on many of its security objectives, including consolidation of its territorial claims, all while avoiding war with the United States. This is an impressive feat, not only because the United States has significant security interests that are threatened by China's promotion of its territorial claims but also because states tend to be particularly belligerent when it comes to territory and protection of economic interests (such as control over natural resources). Indeed, most wars over the past four hundred years have been fought for these reasons, especially wars between rising powers and established great powers.[1]

In this chapter, I describe several instances in which the need to avoid US backlash, views on effectiveness and efficacy, and Communist Party vulnerabilities have pushed China to pursue entrepreneurial pathways to power in the security realm. Specifically, China deliberately delayed its military modernization, choosing to prioritize economic development. China has also relied heavily on gray zone activities to expand territorial control, especially in the South China Sea. Lastly, China has pursued a unique approach to nuclear weapons and the protection of overseas interests—one that did not rely on a heavy overseas military presence.

A Different Approach: Delaying Military Modernization

Military power makes great powers. Great powers at a minimum need the ability to defend themselves without relying on outside help, and in many historical cases, they need a level of relative power that allows them to impose their will on others.

The United States is therefore not unique in its focus on the necessity of military power to its position in the world. The most important document of the Cold War, National Security Council 68 (NSC-68), concluded that preserving the security of the free world and the United States' leadership required "the military power to deter, if possible, Soviet expansion, and to defeat, if necessary, aggressive Soviet or Soviet-directed actions of a limited or total character."[2] Nearly a decade after the fall of the Soviet Union, President Clinton's 1999 National Security Strategy still declared that a strong military was central to maintaining American security.[3] During the period of China's rise, every national defense strategy (NDS) or equivalent since the Bush administration has argued that America must remain the world's preeminent military power.[4] Most recently, the Biden administration's National Security Strategy points to the immense military power of the United States as a key to its overall influence by "backstopping diplomacy, confronting aggression, deterring conflict, projecting strength, and protecting the American people and their economic interests."[5]

While pursuing military dominance might have been effective for the United States, emulating this approach would have been inadvisable for China. First, it is difficult to emulate military power without heightening threat perceptions. Military competition creates a clear "catching up" dynamic in that military power is based on the number of forces as well as on the technology a country has leveraged for military purposes. While China could (and did) deviate from the US model in many ways, it would be hard for Beijing to improve the quantity and quality of its military forces without the United States noticing and worrying. Indeed, as states rely disproportionately on assessments of an adversary's military power to determine the adversary's intentions, a rising power must be particularly careful to not raise the alarm. The oft-quoted Deng maxim "Hide your capabilities and bide your time" alludes to this dynamic.

Emulation would have also been inefficient, potentially to the point of putting China's rise in jeopardy. As previously discussed, Chinese leaders starting with Deng understood that heavy investment in military power would not allow China to efficiently close the power gap between it and the United States. The Soviets had tried long-term military competition with the United States, and it bankrupted them.[6] Even in the early 2000s, Chinese scholars and analysts were cautioning against "going the way of the former

Soviet Union" by sinking too many resources into the military at the risk of crippling other aspects of national development.[7]

Finally, emulative approaches would never be enough to allow China to catch up with the United States, nor would other countries' methods necessarily be effective in China. Jiang Zemin's commentary on the topic is worth quoting at length:

> Innovation is also the spirit of military progress; an army that has no innovative capabilities can hardly be invincible. The military realm is a realm where opposition and competition are the most fierce, where there exists more innovation than emulation, and innovation is the most rapid. . . . There are no two identical wars in the world, and blind imitation can only cause failure. . . . Our army is a people's army under the Party's absolute leadership, so we must maintain our political character and political advantage and cannot copy the military operation principles of foreign troops. Every country's situation is different, so we also cannot copy foreign armies' mode of modernization construction. Regarding the many good experiences and practices of the foreign armies, we cannot simply take them but must combine them with our army's practical reality to digest, absorb, and innovate, persisting in walking the path of military modernization construction with Chinese characteristics.[8]

Given the threatening nature of military build-ups and considerations of efficiency and effectiveness, military modernization was a ripe area for entrepreneurship. One example of an entrepreneurial approach was China's decision to delay military modernization until it had established sufficient economic and political power to insulate it from a negative US response by creating an international climate favorable to its military development.[9] For instance, in Deng Xiaoping's "four modernizations" framework, national defense came third among the four modernization priorities.[10]

As a result, many of the observable signs of buildup arrived late, with many of the first modern systems coming online in the 2010s and the acceleration of production coming even later. A snapshot in 2010 shows a navy with no aircraft carriers, no *Jingdao*-class corvettes, limited *Luyang*-class guided missile destroyers, and perhaps one advanced submarine.[11] By 2022, China had three aircraft carriers, over seventy *Jingdao*-class corvettes, over thirty *Luyang*-class guided missile destroyers, and fifty submarines.[12] Likewise, it was only in the past decade that China's PLAAF began fielding the J-20, their answer to the F-22, a US stealth fighter aircraft (which originated in the 1980s but achieved initial operating capability in 2005).[13]

China's choice to delay military modernization during its rise was unusual. Historically, rising powers tend to compete primarily in military power. On the brink of World War One (WWI), Germany and the United Kingdom were spending about the same amount on their militaries (Germany was spending about 6 percent more).[14] The Versailles Treaty limited Germany's expenditure following WWI, but Berlin clearly tried to catch up, spending twice as much as the United Kingdom between 1933 and 1939. During the Cold War, US and Soviet defense spending revealed their direct competition. The United States spent on average 32 percent more than the Soviet Union until 1970, when the Soviet Union took the lead by an average of 26 percent until 1988.[15] In contrast, China's spending gradually increased, from only 5 percent of total US defense expenditure in 1995 to 8.6 percent of the US budget in 2000, 10.5 percent in 2005, and 14.97 percent in 2010, jumping to 32 percent in 2017 (where it has remained stable since).[16] Figure 5.1 demonstrates that China has not sought to copy US military force posture wholesale.

To be clear, China's limited defense spending does not translate into limited ambition. Instead, it indicates a more innovative approach that focuses on doing more for less in ways that cater to Chinese competitive advantages and minimized the likelihood of military confrontation while the country was still weak. As the China military specialist M. Taylor Fravel explains,

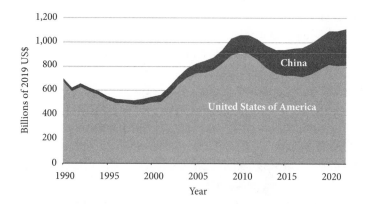

Figure 5.1   Amount of Defense Spending

Source: Data from "SIPRI Military Expenditure Database—2022," Stockholm International Peace Research Institute, https://www.sipri.org/databases/milex, accessed August 25, 2023.

"China had only limited funds with which to modernize its force, which meant that the study of operations should emphasize how to wage high-technology warfare from an inferior position."[17] Even after it embarked on significant military modernization, China continued to rely on entrepreneurial approaches to balance the trade-offs between power maximization and the risks of counterproductively sparking US attempts to undermine its rise or failing on its own due to overspending and overreach. The rest of this chapter covers three cases of China's entrepreneurial approach: expansion through gray zone activities, and its unique approach to nuclear strategy and protection of overseas interests.

Chinese Gray Zone Activities

Control of vast amounts of territory is a defining feature of a great power, and territorial expansion tends to be a central goal of rising powers. Rising powers' attempts to expand their territory often lead to war with the established hegemon. Indeed, territorial disputes are the primary cause of interstate conflict; approximately 80 percent of wars from 1648 to 1990 were over territory.[18]

China has several ongoing territorial disputes. Some of these are in the South China Sea, where Vietnam, Taiwan, and China claim the Paracel Islands (which China occupies) and these parties plus Malaysia and the Philippines claim the Spratlys. China's extensive sovereignty and exclusive economic zone (EEZ) claims conflict with those of Brunei, Indonesia, Malaysia, the Philippines, Taiwan, and Vietnam. In 2013, the Philippines initiated a case against China over disputed features in the South China Sea, including Scarborough Shoal, the Paracel Islands, and other features. In 2016, the Permanent Court of Arbitration ruled against China—a ruling Beijing rejects to this day.[19]

Chinese strategists regard control over the South China Sea as critical to China's great power position. About 50,000 merchant ships, 50 percent of oil tankers, and 64 percent of China's foreign trade pass through the South China Sea each year.[20] Islands across the South China Sea provide natural barriers to China's mainland and, when occupied, support effective power projection to the area between the Malacca Strait and Japan.[21] But as the previous section explained, building up traditional military power for the purpose of territorial control would be a threatening and costly endeavor. Such a buildup might even spark a war China could not win, putting an end to its rise. China needed to find another way to expand its territory, ideally one that drew on China's competitive advantages.

On March 8, 2009, the crew of the USNS *Impeccable*, a US ship that had been conducting routine surveillance in the South China Sea and Western Pacific, faced a unique challenge. Five Chinese vessels shadowed the ship and aggressively maneuvered near it in contravention of accepted naval practice. One of the men on a Chinese-flagged fishing trawler stripped down to his underwear and started messing with the *Impeccable*'s equipment. The crew had the standard means of defending the ship—water cannons—but it was unclear what was happening and whether this strange approach merited a forceful response.

The decision was made to deescalate, and the *Impeccable* radioed its intention to leave the area, asking for safe passage. To further complicate any potential US response, the Chinese government vehemently denied any role in organizing the actions of the Chinese vessels, even though the Chinese ships involved included a navy intelligence collection ship, a Bureau of Maritime Fisheries patrol vessel, and a State Oceanographic Administration patrol vessel. The Chinese "fishermen" knew what the *Impeccable*'s towed array sonar looked like as well as its purpose (to gather acoustic data for submarine tracking), which suggested instruction.

This incident was one of the first instances of what we now refer to as Chinese gray zone activities. Gray zone activities are cohesive, integrated campaigns that make incremental gains with mostly non-military or non-kinetic tools that cloud attribution and thus avoid outright conventional conflict.[22] The gray zone is distinct from traditional warfare, in which military forces apply violence in defined engagements to win a discrete victory. In the South China Sea, for example, Chinese vessels harass targeted vessels by sailing close, firing water cannons, live firing or firing warning shots, sending threatening messages, or threatening to ram targets. They also board target ships, sometimes involve themselves in physical altercations, and arrest sailors.[23] Over the past decade, China has used nearly eighty different gray zone tactics against Taiwan, Japan, Vietnam, India, and the Philippines.[24]

Chinese sources do not explicitly talk about the gray zone activities, largely because the purpose of such activities is to cloud attribution and intent.[25] But China is clearly leveraging its competitive advantages to gain military dominance in Asia. China has many advantages in pursuing gray zone operations given the size of its non-traditional military forces. The Party has access to the People's Armed Forces Maritime Militia (PAFMM), a reserve force of fishermen armed by the state and organized at the grassroots level. This force was created with the advent of the PRC, but its role in the South China Sea began expanding in 2012 and accelerated after 2016.[26] While exact figures are difficult to calculate, it is estimated that nearly 300 militia vessels operate near the Spratly Islands every day—and that is just one of the many areas where the militia operates.[27] The PAFMM is often used for swarming, ramming, and harassing the ships of all claimants and those of the United States, thus making it difficult for these countries to operate safely within their EEZs and in international waters more broadly. China's maritime militia is unique: the only other country in the world with a maritime militia used for resolving sovereignty disputes is Vietnam (whose militia was created in response to China's). Since then, the PAFMM has acted in support of the Chinese Coast Guard (CCG) and navy in establishing control over the South China Sea, including the seizures of Mischief Reef and Scarborough Shoal from the Philippines in 1995 and 2012, respectively.[28]

Additionally, while the United States deploys extremely limited law enforcement capabilities in the region, China has the largest coast guard in the world. This coast guard was formed in 2013 from the maritime branch of the People's Armed Police Border Security Force and other maritime law enforcement agencies in China. At least one Chinese maritime law enforcement vessel has been involved in 73 percent of the major incidents in the South China Sea.[29] In July 2018, the CCG was transferred to the People's Armed Police (PAP), placing it under the command of the CMC and granting it the maritime rights and law enforcement capabilities of civilian law enforcement agencies.

China's one-party Leninist tradition also gives it advantages in shaping the narrative about its territorial claims. The Party maintains absolute power over all media outlets in the country, and the United Front Work Department is well practiced at influencing public opinion abroad.[30] China's political system thus facilitates another aspect of its gray zone approach, the "three warfares": public opinion warfare, psychological warfare, and legal warfare. The three warfares approach has since become a more comprehensive strategy that extends to military training and preparation.[31] China sees this gray zone tactic as a way to alter the status quo in its favor without the costs associated with traditional warfare.[32] If war cannot be prevented, the three warfares approach will ensure that the Chinese military can win an armed conflict at minimum cost.[33]

Public opinion warfare involves shaping views of China domestically and internationally. As Mao Zedong once said, the Communist Party "can only win when it holds pamphlets in the left hand and guns and bullets in the right hand."[34] Domestically, the Party sees the public's willingness to absorb costs as the key variable that determines the victor in a protracted war and is thus actively enhancing resolve through propaganda and national defense education.[35] Internationally, China tries to mobilize overseas Chinese, including Chinese students on college campuses, to support political elites friendly to China and to propagate official narratives. The expansion of overseas Chinese-language media, along with state sponsorship of research and foreign academic institutions, also facilitates information campaigns.[36]

Psychological warfare is about shaping the views and thus the decisions of policymakers. Zhang Yuliang, former director of the Department of Campaign Studies at the PLA National Defense University, defines psychological warfare as "special integrated combat operations" that involve the weaponization of information and communication tools to "secure the greatest possible victory at the smallest possible cost." The purpose is to "improve one's resilience and morale while undermining that of the enemy." Individuals, organizations, companies, and countries can all be the target of psychological warfare.[37] Democracies, like the United States, are ill-equipped to counter information warfare.[38]

Lastly, legal warfare, or lawfare, seeks to create a favorable legal context for Chinese actions. The goal is to employ domestic law, international law, and especially the laws of war to undermine the legitimacy of opponents' activities and establish China's legal advantage.[39] For the South China Sea, China has tried to build legal justification for its actions by misapplying international law and using domestic laws to shape international law.[40] To undermine US attempts at exposing its expansion, China points out that the United States still has not ratified the main international legal framework regarding maritime rights—the UN Convention on the Law of the Sea (UNCLOS). When the Philippines brought a case against China to the Permanent Court of Arbitration, which ruled in its favor in July 2016, Chinese state media argued that China would not follow the ruling of a court given the United States itself is not party to UNCLOS.[41]

The United States, for its part, is not well positioned for gray zone competition. According to political scientist Michael J. Mazarr, the US military typically views prewar and postwar activities as "someone else's responsibility. Pre-war actions are generally limited to 'preparing the battlefield,' actions designed strictly to improve U.S. performance in the main fight."[42] Organizationally, the separation of the political and the military between the State Department and the Pentagon creates an artificial dichotomy. Beijing's incremental approach also makes it hard for other countries to identify threats, and thus to get allies and partners to recognize a threat. This creates fissures in alliances and partnerships that minimize the likelihood of a coordinated response.[43]

China's gray zone approach has allowed it to consolidate control over more territory at a far lower political, economic, and military cost than a traditional military approach would have entailed. Over the past fifteen years, the United States has not managed to stop China from making gains, and it still lacks effective counters to China's gray zone activities.[44] To deal with dangerous behavior, the United States first tried to engage through bilateral dialogues on military professionalism like the Military Maritime Consultative Agreement (MMCA) talks and later the Code for Unplanned Encounters at Sea (CUES). These are fora where the two sides could discuss incidents and agree to rules of the road. But China would not commit its coast guard, law enforcement, and paramilitary forces to these agreements, and it continued to deny that the central government was directing these activities. The United States tried to counter by sending its own coast guard to patrol in 2021. As of 2023, one Coast Guard ship, the USCGC *Munro*, is deployed with the US Seventh Fleet and works with the Japanese Coast Guard and the Philippine Coast Guard.

The United States was slow to respond directly to China's lawfare as well. Washington did not begin routine freedom of navigation operations until 2017 and did not declare China's South China Sea claims illegal until 2020. The United States also has difficulty countering Chinese lawfare because it has not ratified UNCLOS. Moreover, past dismissals of Hague rulings— not only by China but also by the United States and its allies (most recently Taiwan)—undermine the authority of the court. Complicating matters further, the norm of freedom of navigation is still disputed, with some key states arguing that military activities within EEZs require state permission. The United States also was unable to stop China from building and militarizing 3,200 acres of artificial islands in the South China Sea.

While I believe that China's choice of gray zone actions to expand its territorial control was driven primarily by the desire to manage competition with a militarily stronger United States, a few alternative viewpoints merit consideration. First, some might argue that China's selection of gray zone tactics is the result of its strategic culture. Sun Tzu famously said that "to subdue the enemy without fighting is the acme of skill." But the majority of Sun Tzu's text deals with the violent use of military force, and he likely saw "not fighting" as referring to the myriad of preparations taken before fighting begins.[45] Thus, Johnston suggests that "not fighting and subduing the enemy" could be better understood as "first set up maximally advantageous conditions for the defeat of the enemy before fighting, and only then fight and defeat the enemy."[46] Additionally, before China's rise, when the upstart strategy was not yet in place, the country did use traditional military force to make territorial advances against India in 1962, in a border skirmish with the Soviet Union in 1969, a border war with Vietnam in 1979, and its taking of Vietnamese-held islands in the Paracels in 1974 and Johnson South Reef in the Spratly Islands in 1988. This suggests different considerations took hold after the Cold War.

Another critique suggests that gray zone action should not be considered entrepreneurial because other countries also engage in this approach—particularly weak countries. But China is unique in that it does not face capability constraints. It could use its navy, the largest in the world, to press its territorial claims, but it chooses instead to engage in gray zone activities. The upstart strategy is the best explanation for this decision. Furthermore, China has excelled at making simultaneous use of multiple avenues of gray zone activity. One RAND report identifies eighty distinct gray zone actions, from engaging in live fire near the target to purchasing media outlets in the target country.[47] Lastly, an entrepreneurial approach does not need to be completely new. It only needs to be different from the approach of the established hegemon, in this case the United States, which prefers traditional military action and is ill-suited to counter gray zone tactics.

The last common critique is that China's approach has not been effective and should be considered a strategically injudicious way to build power. China's maritime ambitions and aggressive gray zone posturing have led to a regional response. Other countries have bolstered their maritime capabilities and started to coordinate responses, including closer relationships with the United States.[48] China's military buildup in the South China Sea arguably convinced the Obama administration to take more aggressive measures against China.[49] But the question is one of relative costs—whether more traditional military expansion would have sparked a stronger, more decisive US response. The answer is clearly yes.

China's Nuclear Strategy

In 1950, it looked as if the US-led UN coalition might lose the Korean War. On October 19, Chinese forces crossed the Yalu River, and on October 25 they launched their first offensive, which pushed UN forces south out of North Korea. To prevent South Korea from being overrun by communist troops, President Truman said publicly during a press conference that the use of nuclear weapons was under active consideration.[50]

This announcement was the first time, but not the last, that the United States threatened the newly formed PRC with nuclear weapons. Three years later, President Eisenhower threatened to deploy their destructive power to bring an end to the Korean War if the Chinese refused to negotiate its termination.[51] As hostilities continued between China and the United States after the Korean War in the First Taiwan Strait Crisis—when China was bombarding the Nationalist-held islands of Quemoy and Matsu—the Eisenhower administration again issued threats to wage a "limited atomic war" over the islands.[52]

Unsurprisingly, Chinese leaders determined that China needed to develop nuclear weapons, if only to deter nuclear blackmail. In September 1954, Soviet leader Nikita Khrushchev agreed to provide China with technological support for peaceful uses of nuclear energy, a decision that Zhou Enlai celebrated at the State Council Plenary Meeting in January 1955.[53] In his speech, Zhou explicitly associated China's need for nuclear power with American threats, stating that "the Americans want to terrorize us, but they will not be successful."[54] In 1956, Mao himself emphasized the importance of acquiring nuclear weapons to "prevent China from being bullied."[55]

While the dynamics of nuclear deterrence required China to emulate in developing its own nuclear weapons program, the similarities with the United States largely end there. Over the next six decades, China's approach to nuclear weapons, from doctrine and planning to force posture and modernization priorities, was significantly different from that of the United States—differences China embraced during its rise to great power status.

Nuclear policy is an area where factors encouraged China to embrace an entrepreneurial approach, largely because Chinese leaders thought the US approach had been both ineffective (nuclear weapons are not as useful as the United States thinks they are) and inefficient (the United States has wasted a great deal of resources on building and maintaining them). Given

US dominance, there were few gaps to exploit, and a massive buildup of capability was likely to be more threatening than reassuring to Washington.

China's top leaders since Mao have consistently questioned the effectiveness of nuclear weapons in warfighting, claiming that "it is not possible to use nuclear weapons freely" and that "soldiers are more useful than atomic bombs."[56] In 1978, Deng stated that "future wars will mainly be wars with conventional weapons and not atomic wars. The reason is that the destructive power of nuclear weapons is too great and the enemy will not easily use them"—hence China would "mainly develop conventional weapons."[57] Chinese leaders have believed that nuclear weapons are basically unusable on the battlefield and that once mutual deterrence is achieved, "a larger arsenal or arms racing would be costly, counterproductive, and ultimately self-defeating."[58] Because of this thinking, China has refrained to date from building tactical nuclear weapons (small nukes intended for use on the battlefield or for a limited strike), whereas such weapons have been a part of the US and Russian nuclear arsenals since 1950 and the 1960s, respectively.[59] Given their assessment that nuclear war was growing increasingly unlikely, the Chinese decided to largely prioritize the modernization of conventional over nuclear capabilities.[60]

Considerations of efficacy also encouraged entrepreneurship as Chinese leaders assessed that they could achieve deterrence at a lower cost than the approaches pursued by the United States. While the United States and the Soviet Union were building enough warheads to destroy the world many times over, China saw that approach as unnecessary and costly.[61] In Deng's words, "We have a few nuclear weapons. . . . If they want to destroy us, they themselves will also suffer some retaliation. . . . To have even only a few weapons after all is a kind of restraining force."[62] The military doctrine of the PLA's Second Artillery requires that China's nuclear forces must be "small and precise" and tailored to the reality that China is still a developing country. China, according to the doctrine, does not need to match the size of the superpowers if its arsenal meets the need for effective deterrence.[63]

Indeed, in 1998, the United States spent $35.1 billion on its nuclear weapons, more than China's whole defense budget.[64] A conservative projection for the cost of the US nuclear weapons program for the period 2021–2030 is $456 billion.[65] A huge portion of this budget (36 percent) pays for tactical nuclear weapons, on which China has spent almost nothing.[66] The triad, which encompasses the ability to deliver nuclear warheads by aircraft, submarine, and missile, and which resulted more from budgetary struggles between the services than from any strategic rationale, came with a cost: 86 percent of Cold War spending on nuclear weapons went to building this extensive variety of launch systems.[67]

These considerations encouraged China to build far fewer nuclear weapons than the United States possessed. As of 2023, the People's Liberation Army Rocket Force (PLARF) possesses approximately 382 land-based missile launchers, of which about 140 missiles (carrying 240 warheads) can hit the continental United States.[68] China now possesses 410 nuclear warheads capable of delivery by missile, bomber, and submarine. Of these, 72 warheads can be launched by submarine and 20 by aircraft, all of which could have the potential to target the continental United States. The remaining 318 warheads are all missile-launched. For comparison, the United States is estimated to have 400 ICBMs, 280 SLBMs, and nearly 800 warheads capable of being delivered via its bombers. And those are just the launch platforms— the United States maintains over 5,000 warheads in total.[69]

China also developed a distinct nuclear strategy to complement the limited size of its arsenal, choosing to focus on minimal deterrence with assured retaliation, or "deterring an adversary with the threat of unacceptable damage through a retaliatory nuclear strike."[70] The first official articulation of Chinese nuclear strategy in 2006 referred to its "self-defensive nuclear strategy," the need for a "lean and effective nuclear force" as a "credible nuclear deterrent force."[71] Part of this strategy is a no-first-use pledge—the pledge to use nuclear weapons solely in retaliation for a nuclear attack and thus against nuclear states only.[72] With this pledge, China is the only country that makes both negative and positive security guarantees to nuclear-free countries.[73] The pledge also means that China does not provide a nuclear umbrella to any other country (whereas the United States has extended its nuclear deterrent to cover nearly thirty countries).[74] Because of minimal deterrence and this no-first-use pledge, the only campaign the newly named Strategic Rocket Force prepares for is a nuclear counterstrike campaign (*hefang zhanyi*).[75]

The United States, in contrast, has neither committed to no-first-use nor asserted that the sole purpose of nuclear weapons is to deter nuclear use. Indeed, statements of US doctrine often include clauses that allow the United States to use nuclear weapons against non-nuclear states. These threats have ranged in aggressiveness from the George W. Bush–era statement that favored unilateral preventive action to Obama's conciliatory position that nuclear weapons would not be used against non-nuclear states as long as they were members of and acting in accordance with the NPT.[76] Trump's policy of reserving the right to use nuclear weapons in response to "significant non-nuclear strategic attacks," including "attacks on US, allied, or partner civilian population or infrastructure," lowered the threshold for US use.[77] Even President Biden has refused to commit to the idea that the sole purpose of nuclear weapons is to deter nuclear use.

The differences between the Chinese and US approaches to nuclear weapons do not stop with numbers and policy. Because of its different approach, China keeps its readiness and alert levels lower than those of the United States. The PLARF, previously called the Second Artillery, has trained to launch on attack, not warning, whereas the United States has maintained a launch-on-warning policy since the 1970s.[78] China keeps the majority of its nuclear weapons off alert in peacetime, with separate launchers, missiles, and warheads; the United States keeps 45 percent of its nuclear weapons on "hair-trigger alert," meaning that they can be airborne in minutes.[79] Indeed, most of China's warheads are stored separately from delivery vehicles in fixed locations until they are paired in preparation for a strike, which raises further doubts about China's second-strike capability.[80] While shortly after detonating its first nuclear weapons the United States deployed a space-based infrared detection system to establish early warning, China started to create the space-based ability to detect ICBM launches only recently, having only three early-warning satellites in orbit as of 2022.[81] The US Department of Defense, for comparison, asked Congress in 2023 to pay for over fifty satellites as part of its space-based missile warning systems.[82]

China's nuclear deterrent is primarily land-based, whereas the United States (and Russia) has pursued the triad. Indeed, 76 percent of China's force is land-based, whereas 22 percent of the United States' nuclear force is land-based, 54 percent is sea-based, and 24 percent is air-based.[83] China did not even have a sea leg of the triad until 2015, when its *Jin*-class ballistic missile submarine armed with the JL-2 SLBM went on its first patrol. Analysts suggest that a new strategic stealth bomber that could be both conventional and nuclear-capable, the H-20, may enter service by 2025, but China's development of an air leg is still uncertain.[84]

Given the differences in doctrine and force posture, it is unsurprising that the organizational structures in the United States and China are also different. China has always had a separate force in control of its missiles—both conventional and nuclear.[85] The Second Artillery was an independent branch under the direct control of the CMC and was upgraded to a separate service and renamed the PLARF in 2015. From 2017 to 2020, the number of PLARF brigades increased from twenty-nine to forty, half of them operating nuclear-capable ballistic missile launchers.[86] The United States created a single command responsible for all strategic nuclear forces, Strategic Command (STRATCOM), in 1992, while control of conventional land-based missiles still lies primarily with the Army.[87]

While China pursued an entrepreneurial approach to nuclear weapons for most of its rise, the current debate revolves around whether China is abandoning this long-standing approach in favor of emulation. In 2021, anxiety amassed over China's nuclear modernization: satellite imagery showed that China had built about 300 new missile silos at its nuclear facilities in Inner Mongolia, Gansu, and Xinjiang, causing many to worry about a planned buildup. Now, with an arsenal of at least sixty DF-5s, ninety DF-31s, and eighty-four DF-41s coming online, China can deliver ninety missiles with 130 warheads to the continental United States.[88] The number of warheads on China's land-based ICBMs capable of threatening the United States is expected to grow to roughly 200 by 2025.[89] China's recent investment in early warning systems and hypersonic weapons, which pose particular challenges to missile defense because of their long range, low altitude, high maneuverability, and adjustability, create anxiety that China will adopt a more aggressive strategy.[90]

It is too early to tell in which direction China is going, but the upstart strategy provides some guidance. First, incentives are still in place for an entrepreneurial approach. This means that if China does try to emulate the United States by seeking parity in numbers, types of delivery systems, and nuclear doctrine, the effort will come at the expense of its competitiveness. This would impact both what Beijing can achieve despite significant investment of its resources and the reactions from major powers. Second, one of the benefits of the upstart strategy is it allows for changes in approach to adjust to the changing nature of competition. The recent changes in Chinese nuclear modernization appear to be consistent with the previous entrepreneurial approach, even as its contours evolve.

One element of this consistency is the fact that China is still not striving for parity with the United States. In the worst-case scenario, in which each of the approximately 360 silos is meant to house DF-41s carrying three warheads, China plans to have about 875 warheads.[91] Admittedly, China's avoidance of direct competition in nuclear power was starker in the early 1990s, when the United States had forty-seven times more weapons than China.[92] But even the worst-case projection of 1,000 weapons puts the Chinese arsenal at a quarter of the current US level of 5,244 nuclear weapons.[93]

Some might argue that total numbers are not the most relevant metric; instead, strategists need to consider deployed nuclear weapons versus stockpiled weapons. The United States has 1,770 nuclear weapons deployed in accordance with the New START treaty (technically 1,550 are allowed, but bombers count as "one" even though they can carry multiple nuclear weapons). In other words, when comparing arsenals, some might use the number of deployed weapons (1,770) instead of the total number of weapons (5,244).[94] But even here, the evidence that China is striving for parity is weak. Until 2015, China did not have any nuclear weapons that fall under the new START conception of "deployable"—ICBMs on alert, submarines or bombers out on patrols.[95] By 2023, the vast majority of China's arsenal still did not meet that standard, though the PLAN likely now conducts continuous at-sea deterrence patrols using its six Jin-class submarines, which are equipped with twelve nuclear-capable missile tubes.[96]

The expansion and improvements in China's nuclear arsenal by 2050 are also consistent with China's traditional nuclear policy of a minimal retaliation capability with a no-first-use pledge. China has been developing a ground-based midcourse missile defense system capable of intercepting short- and medium-range ICBMs, primarily to protect select fixed command and control sites.[97] This could be a shift to a launch-on-attack posture, but it is also consistent with the need to take measures to maintain a second strike. Advancements in China's early warning radar and satellite capabilities can be used to enhance detection and tracking of incoming threats, not necessarily to launch first.[98]

China's strategy requires that Beijing develop enough weapons to absorb a strike and still impose unacceptable damage from the adversary's perspective. In the strategic doctrine of its missile forces, China's strategic nuclear forces focus on "effective and limited nuclear counterattack" as the core of nuclear deterrence. The focus is on the preservation of nuclear forces as a prerequisite to carry out "focused strikes," as well as "scientific use of nuclear firepower, and carefully crafted strike plans," to "achieve the greatest political and military benefits at a relatively small cost."[99] This posture leaves some flexibility in the numbers. Arguably, the strategic environment has changed in ways that might call for a larger, more survivable arsenal even under China's current nuclear policy. Among the most significant are improvements in US missile defense, which Chinese thinkers see as a serious threat to the relia-bility and effectiveness of China's nuclear counterattack capability.[100]

Protection of Overseas Interests

As China rose economically, its overseas interests proliferated. In 2000, the year before China joined the WTO, its volume of trade with the rest of the world was around $475 billion (less than that of Canada); that same year the United States led the world at just under $2 trillion.[101] Only eight years later, China gained the title of number one exporter in the world and is now the number one trader as well. In 2021, China's two-way global trade surpassed $6 trillion, compared to the United States' $4.7 trillion.[102] During this period, China also became heavily reliant on the import of critical resources like oil and food. Between 1975 and 2018, China's grain consumption alone tripled to 420 million tons, and China imports almost $50 billion more in food than it exports.[103] China is similarly reliant on oil imports—approximately 72 per-cent of oil used domestically in 2021 was imported.[104] China is also tremen-dously dependent on critical technologies like semiconductors, of which it imported over $400 billion in 2021, and certain minerals necessary to be-come a leader in new energy products.[105]

Chinese companies started investing in far-flung places in the 1990s and 2000s, often bringing Chinese labor along. Chinese citizens started going abroad in droves in the mid-2000s, not only as workers but also as tourists. In 1990, some 60,000 PRC citizens worked abroad, but that number has steadily grown to almost 1 million in 2018. There are over 30,000 Chinese businesses operating abroad. Tourism, too, has taken off: in 2019, China boasted 155 million tourists traveling abroad, up from only 10 million at the turn of the century.[106]

The sudden growth in China's overseas interests was driven by the launch of Xi Jinping's major economic initiative, the BRI. By 2020, over 100,000 Chinese had relocated to Africa in search of opportunities along the BRI—bringing the total number of Chinese immigrants on the continent to over one million. Ten thousand Chinese companies were operating in Africa alone.[107] The Chinese Academy of Social Sciences (CASS), which operates under the auspices of the PRC State Council, notes in its 2020 Country-Risk Rating of Overseas Investment from China that 84 percent of China's BRI investments are in medium- to high-risk countries.[108] These reports also consistently characterize countries involved in BRI as "developing, generally with weak, undiversified, and unstable economies," as well as "politically risky due to complex geopolitics and frequent regime changes."[109] According to the Ministry of Commerce, between 2010 and 2015 there were at least 345 security incidents involving Chinese citizens worldwide.[110]

As more Chinese citizens go abroad, the Chinese government felt increasing pressure to protect its citizens against "risk incidents" caused by political instability, unsafe working conditions, and natural disasters.[111] As Zhai Leming, the deputy director-general of the Department of Consular Affairs of the Ministry of Foreign Affairs, lamented in 2015, "No nation has ever dealt with such a huge task where each [overseas embassy] employee has to protect 200,000 citizens."[112] Later that year, when Premier Li Keqiang toured Africa, he promised that protecting Chinese citizens abroad was a "top priority" for the country and that "security should follow in the footsteps of our compatriots."[113] The importance of "taking effective actions to fully protect the security and rights of Chinese citizens" was again emphasized by foreign minister Wang Yi when he visited Africa in 2021.[114] Domestic surveys have revealed that Chinese citizens strongly support NEOs and view protecting Chinese citizens abroad as one of the core functions of government. The second-biggest box office hit in Chinese history was *Wolf Warrior 2*, a movie about a special forces operative who travels to an unnamed African country to save Chinese hostages.

China was far from the first country to face the strategic and domestic imperative to protect its interests overseas. The United States had faced a similar dilemma as it became the world's leading power in the wake of World War II. In that case, the United States chose an entrepreneurial strategy, deviating from the European empires and imperial Japan, which "subjugated other countries and established colonies in part to ensure access to vital resources and markets."[115] Washington decided instead to rely largely on projecting power sporadically from bases located in allied countries.[116]

Since then, global projection of military power has been arguably the central mission of the US armed forces (after homeland defense). The NDS and its precursor, the Quadrennial Defense Review, have addressed global power projection and protection in every published volume since the first in 1997.[117] Operationally, this global focus is integrated into the distinctive missions of the different service branches.[118] For example, of the five core missions of the US Air Force—air superiority; global strike; rapid global mobility; intelligence, surveillance, and reconnaissance (ISR); and command

and control—two are explicitly global, while the remaining three are global in practice.[119]

Overseas territories, bases, and non-contiguous possessions have played an integral role in building US military power.[120] In September 2022, about 13 percent of the United States' active-duty military personnel were stationed abroad (down from 2008, when 26 percent were abroad).[121] In 2012, the United States had approximately 120 bases and major installations in forty-five countries.[122] The number of personnel and the locations of bases and installations abroad have stayed relatively constant since the 1950s, with some adjustments in response to changes in strategic priorities.[123] From 2019 to 2021, the annual cost of maintaining this overseas presence averaged $23.37 billion, not including the costs of overseas contingency operations, which averaged about $62.43 billion per year in the same period.[124]

Since the end of WWII, the United States has used this global force for foreign military interventions. Between 1946 and 2016, the United States undertook 105 distinct military interventions, reaching every continent but Australasia and Antarctica; 75 percent of them involved a ground component.[125] The recent war on terror cost the United States an estimated $6.4 trillion, and an extra $1 trillion to meet veterans' and disability requirements.[126] This amount is over double China's cumulative defense spending from 1995 to 2020, which totaled around $2.9 trillion.[127]

After assessing the US strategy for protecting overseas interests, China had many reasons to eschew emulation. First, a global military presence would not cater to China's competitive advantages. The United States and its allies have overwhelming power projection capability in terms of equipment and access. US basing was gained through wars, initially through conquest (from Spain), then as the result of WWII and the Korean War, and thereafter as part of alliance commitments connected to competition in the Cold War. This type of global military structure rarely happens through negotiations or agreements in peacetime alone.

Second, a global presence has not historically been a strategic necessity for China. Most threats to the United States have occurred far from its shores—military competition with the Soviet Union in Europe throughout the Cold War, and more recently non-traditional threats such as civil wars, piracy, and terrorism primarily from southwest Asia. Chinese leaders perceive the country's greatest security threats to be closer to home in East Asia.[128] Writing in 2015, former Chinese diplomat Zhen Bingxi pointed out that the United States' neighbors, Canada and Mexico, are much weaker in terms of comprehensive national strength, affording Washington a "more simple and controllable geopolitical environment" compared to that of Beijing.[129] According to one high-level Chinese official, these security priorities have been threatened by a meddling Washington with its "rebalance towards the Asia-Pacific."[130] Thus, China has the incentive to minimize military forces committed abroad and, in general, to minimize the expense of overseas commitments.[131]

Third, Chinese strategists see US attempts to protect its interests through fighting foreign wars as costly and ineffective. This belief lies at the heart of Deng Xiaoping's strategy of "hiding and biding," which entailed an avoidance of conflict because "China is not strong enough and cannot afford it" and "no good will come of it."[132] Chinese leaders and analysts, reflecting upon everything from the costly quagmire of the Vietnam War to the British, Soviet, and American experiences in Afghanistan, note the risks of power projection.[133] Wang Jisi, an advisor to Hu Jintao, warned that China should "avoid military adventures on the way to the rise of a great power."[134]

Fourth, in addition to inefficiencies and relative ineffectiveness, emulation would likely spark strong threat perceptions. The CCP has been cautious about its global image and has been trying to convince others that China, no matter how strong and prosperous it becomes, will respect other countries' sovereignty.[135] No one buys the peaceful image wholesale, but China rejects the "Cold War mentality" explicitly to differentiate itself from the United States. Chinese writers are particularly harsh on the negative effects of US military interventions on the developing world, where most of them take place.[136]

Lastly, it is central for the Party's image at home to differentiate itself from the United States. As Isaac Kardon explains:

> If operational requirements were the only consideration, the PLA would have long ago established a substantial overseas logistics network, including dedicated military bases . . . [but] PLA desires are subordinate to the central party-state's broader geopolitical aims, which have dictated a low-key and incremental approach to the projection of military power abroad . . . [T]he whole edifice of China's anticolonial, antihegemonic credentials in the developing world stands primarily on the largely accurate perception that the PRC has not undertaken military adventures abroad.[137]

Indeed, when China established its first and only overseas base in Djibouti, Beijing clarified that it would "never seek for hegemony and will never pursue military expansion and arms race. These commitments will not be changed by the construction of overseas support bases."[138]

This combination of limited strategic effectiveness, a desire to minimize threat perceptions, and an assessment of Chinese competitive advantages led China to embrace an entrepreneurial approach to overseas interests. China has clearly not followed in the footsteps of its great power predecessor. In the late 1990s, China had zero military personnel overseas, and little has changed over the past thirty years. Today the United States still has thirty-nine times more military personnel overseas than China (and that disparity is largely the result of US drawdowns rather than a Chinese buildup). In total, China maintains an average of around 4,000 overseas military personnel each year: out of the 1,600 Navy personnel, 800 operate in Gulf of Aden mission, 70 PLAN special forces are deployed as part of anti-piracy missions and others are in transit or exercises, and about 2,500 Army personnel operate as part of UNPKO missions.[139] In addition, some twenty PLA Air Force personnel are deployed to conduct HADR operations and operate two transport aircraft on an as-needed basis.[140] China has only one overseas base, set up in Djibouti in 2017, which supports a small task force of two guided-missile frigates and one supply ship.

China's expeditionary capabilities have also remained relatively limited. China's first large military transport aircraft, the Xian Y-20, did not come online until June 2016, and China has about 30 to the United States' 223 C-17 Globemaster IIIs.[141] China did not commission its first aerial refueling tanker, the H-6U, until 2015.[142] If China wanted to project traditional power globally, it would also need a blue-water navy, a naval force capable of exerting power on the open oceans at long range. Such a navy would include the ability to engage in under-way replenishment, which involves pumping fuel into the ship and sending over pallets of food, parts, ammunition, people, and so on while the ship is under way. China's first replenishment ships were commissioned into the PLAN in 2015, and a more advanced *Fuyu*-class (Type 901) ship is currently undergoing sea trials. Indeed, when evacuating 35,000 citizens from Libya in 2011, China had to rely on leased ships and aircraft. In other words, China's interests have become decidedly global over the past twenty-five years, but its military power has not. Aside from space, cyber, and ICBMs, China cannot project offensive power beyond its region.

Instead, China has pursued a decidedly hybrid strategy to protect its overseas interests since the strategic imperative arose in the 2010s. It relies heavily on host nation security forces, overseas police presence, private security contractors (PSCs), and UNPKOs to supplement the limited contributions from its own military.[143] This approach accounts for Beijing's limitations (no allies, limited expeditionary capabilities) and bolsters its advantages in political flexibility and abstemious defense spending.

China prefers to rely on local security and law enforcement and its police force to protect its interests in any given country. Through deepened security exchanges, defense diplomacy, economic incentives, and regional and multilateral security cooperation, China wins over partners in its neighborhood to protect Chinese interests and manage transnational issues like terrorism and trafficking. China often funds host nation forces directly, or at the very least provides economic incentives, arms, or training to enable a host nation to improve security in areas featuring Chinese assets and personnel. This strategy is complemented by Chinese training for such forces, as discussed in Chapter 3.

China also leverages its economic clout to bake into agreements host nation responsibility for protection. For example, in 2016 Pakistan announced plans for a 10,000-person special security force to protect Chinese workers in the country, where China is investing in the China-Pakistan Economic Corridor (CPEC) and its commercial port in Gwadar. The agreement came after Beijing pledged billions of dollars of infrastructure investments as part of the economic corridor. Pakistan also protects China's interests and workers at Gwadar Port with "Task Force 88" for the seaward security of the port and sea-lanes, a Coastal Security and Harbor Defense Force, and a Force Protection Battalion (consisting of Pakistani Marines).[144] This effort, coupled with 15,000 Pakistani ground troops known as special security divisions, is financed with CPEC funding.[145]

Pakistan is not the only country that uses its security forces to help China. Burmese police have repeatedly stepped in to suppress unrest by villagers who have lost land and livelihoods to China's Wanbao Mining Company at the Letpadaung Copper Mine.[146] Ethiopia, where Chinese construction and manufacturing projects alone are valued at over $4 billion, is another well-documented case of cooperation between China and local security forces. In 2021, China and Ethiopia signed a memorandum of understanding that established "security safeguarding mechanisms for major [BRI] projects."[147] Just months earlier, hundreds of Chinese nationals caught in violence had been escorted to safety by Ethiopian police, and the Chinese embassy donated security equipment and weaponry to the Ethiopian Police

Commission.[148] Similarly, in its fight against Boko Haram, the Nigerian government secured light arms and UAVs from China, which will likely be used in defense of Chinese firms and nationals working locally.[149] China also committed $60 million to support the African Union's standby military force, specifically to protect the region's economy and by extension Chinese economic interests.[150]

Internal security training is discussed in greater detail in Chapter 3, but a few statistics show that it is an important component of overseas protection. Of the 196 countries in my sample, over half received some form of internal (police, forensics, cybersecurity, military, paramilitary, anti-protest, etc.) training from Chinese agencies. Of the 110 countries that received Chinese training, about one-third received training classified as police-related. As an indicator of economic interests, nearly 90 percent of countries that have received Chinese training also had a BRI memorandum of understanding with China. Moreover, two-thirds of countries with BRI memoranda received some form of Chinese training; only about a fifth of countries without BRI memoranda received Chinese training.

In February 2017, the Ministry of Public Security (MPS) launched new efforts to coordinate the international activities of Chinese law-enforcement agencies through a high-level work conference.[151] At that point, the MPS already had established cooperative relationships with 113 countries and regions, built 129 bilateral and multilateral cooperation mechanisms and 96 communication hotlines, and signed more than 400 cooperation documents with the police departments of 70 states.[152] Later that year, the MPS signed an agreement with Interpol, an intergovernmental organization that connects the criminal police forces of 195 member countries, promising "cooperation on matters of trade security; combating illicit markets, financial crime, and cybercrime; and securing critical infrastructure along the Belt and Road."[153] Since then, MPS representatives have continued dialogue with foreign partners, including international conferences like the 2019 International Police Summit, where 103 police leaders discussed subjects like "investigation cooperation, police training and capacity building."[154]

China's policing activities have extended beyond its borders as well. China has reached agreements with Italy, Serbia, and Croatia to allow its police to patrol alongside host nation police in popular tourist areas to better protect Chinese tourists, primarily from robbery.[155] In other cases, China has extended its policing for more nefarious purposes, and without host country approval. In September 2022, a human rights non-governmental organization

(NGO) released a report investigating "police service stations" that China has set up in embassies across the world, reporting at least fifty-four; in April 2023 the FBI arrested two individuals who had run such a center in New York City.[156] China claims that these facilities are primarily for administrative services like renewing driver's licenses for its citizens overseas, but in practice they allow China to prosecute its "persuade to return" campaign, in which Chinese authorities harass dissidents abroad using social media to encourage them to return to China. This campaign has been successful—China "persuaded" 210,000 people to return home in 2021 alone, according to the MPS.[157]

China has also pursued a more direct role in security provision through deployment of its own forces, mostly the PAP or PSCs rather than traditional military. The PAP is a paramilitary organization, tasked by Beijing with maintaining domestic stability and, when required, providing rear-area support for the PLA. This is the organization responsible for guarding Chinese embassies and consulates, and a 2015 anti-terrorism law provided the legal basis for it to take part in overseas operations.[158] The PAP's overseas operations largely focus on border regions to prevent instability there and facilitate its control of minority populations.

Along those lines, China set up a PAP outpost in Tajikistan and runs counterterrorism patrols in the China-Tajikistan-Afghanistan border area with local police, attempting to interdict terrorists flowing into Xinjiang while denying official "military" intervention.[159] In 2016, China, Afghanistan, Pakistan, and Tajikistan formed the Quadrilateral Cooperation and Coordination Mechanism, which facilitated the deployment of the PAP to Afghanistan for UN missions and joint patrols with Afghan and Tajik forces.[160] Other cooperative frameworks include trilateral forums with Afghanistan and Pakistan, the Conference on Interaction and Confidence-Building Measures in Asia, the Istanbul Process, and the Quadrilateral Coordination Group (with the United States, Afghanistan, and Pakistan). In addition, the PAP conducts exercises with other members of the Shanghai Cooperation Organization at least once every three to four years, including with Kazakhstan, Tajikistan, and Uzbekistan—although these exercises involve basic training, such as hand-to-hand combat, as opposed to advanced tactics.[161]

Beijing also uses PSCs for their ability to project power while maintaining deniability of involvement, especially along the BRI, in the maritime domain, and in training developing nations' police and security forces.[162] In 2009,

China legalized the private security industry, which is under the tight legal, administrative, and political control of the CCP through the MPS.[163] In 2013, thousands of contracting firms licensed in China employed some 4 million security personnel, and by 2016 approximately 3,200 security professionals were deployed overseas.[164] China has deployed PSCs to thirty countries, mostly in Africa and Asia but as far afield as Argentina and Turkey.[165] One major player is DeWe Security Service Group, which handles security for numerous major Chinese SOEs. Since June 2018, this company has carried out over 3,000 in-country trainings for local partners, trained over 70,000 Chinese contractors, and worked with local security forces to successfully handle more than 1,000 incidents involving overseas Chinese targets, according to its website. In 2016, DeWe was tasked with evacuating Chinese workers trapped by warring factions in South Sudan.[166]

There is also some evidence that China is using UNPKOs to ensure the security of its investments in unstable countries. About 70 percent of the countries hosting missions to which China contributed between 2012 and 2018 had seen significant Chinese investments either in the year Chinese peacekeepers arrived or in the three years prior.[167] Beijing is well positioned to lobby for approval of peacekeeping operations in areas where China's economic interests are concentrated.[168] In South Sudan, where China has agreed to acquire one-sixth of the country's oil output in return for infrastructure loans, China lobbied successfully for oil facilities to be included in the United Nations Mission in Southern Sudan (UNMISS) mandate (over the objections of local opposition forces).[169] In the Democratic Republic of the Congo, China has an 80 percent stake in one of the world's largest copper and cobalt mines. China is Lebanon's largest trading partner, with Chinese companies interested in large-scale projects in Lebanon's power, telecommunications, transportation, water conservancy, and other infrastructure projects. Notably, in September 2019, China threatened to veto a UN renewal of the peacekeeping mandate in Afghanistan if the mandate did not include specific reference to the BRI (though it eventually dropped the demand).

While China is clearly not emulating the US approach to overseas presence to protect its global interests, there is one aspect that has been generating anxiety among Western security analysts over the past five years: China's basing ambitions. In 2019, China signed a secret agreement with Cambodia allowing the PLA to use a sixty-two-acre section of a Cambodian navy base at Ream for thirty years. In 2021, rumors of a future Chinese basing facility in the UAE and in Equatorial Guinea shook the US security establishment.

The most alarming development came in 2022, when China signed a deal with the Solomon Islands that would guarantee PLAN access to the country's ports and, ominously, allow China to send troops to the country to protect its citizens and interests, though the details are still unclear. In 2023, news reports revealed (and the US government later confirmed) that China and Cuba had agreed to establish an intelligence base in Cuba that would allow China to eavesdrop on electronic communications emanating from US military bases. According to documents obtained by the *Washington Post*, US intelligence assesses that China wants to have five overseas bases and ten logistics facilities by 2030 scattered throughout Southeast Asia, the Middle East, and Africa.[170]

The US anxiety about Chinese basing is predictable, as emulation in this case would threaten US vested interests. While I speculate more about the future of basing in the conclusion of this book, it is important to note that despite all the concern, nearly twenty years after the first alarms rang about China's desire for a "string of pearls," or a network of bases throughout the Indian Ocean, there is still only one permanent overseas presence for the PLA, in Djibouti. The Solomon Islands deal involves not a specific facility but China's legal rights in the country, specifically the right to make port visits and to send troops, without clarity on the infrastructure to be built. It is hard to determine where the UAE facility and the Cambodia and Equatorial Guinea agreements would lie on this spectrum of control, as the UAE facility was canceled, the Cambodia agreement is not public, and the status of the Equatorial Guinea agreement is unknown.

But change does seem to be under way. In Chinese discourse there is a recognition that the Chinese military needs some expeditionary capability, at the very least to support HADR missions and NEOs as well as to deter the United States from cutting off China's access to the world, closing off choke points with an "offshore control strategy."[171] In 2015, the Chinese navy transitioned its strategy from "near seas defense" (*jinhai fangyu*) to "near seas defense, far seas protection" (*jinhai fangyu yu yuanhai huwei jiehe*) due to a growing need to protect overseas economic activities as well as the original mission of maintaining command of the seas within the first island chain.[172] China has articulated a desire "to address the deficiencies in overseas operations and support" by "build[ing] far seas forces, develop[ing] overseas logistics facilities, and enhanc[ing] capabilities in accomplishing diversified military tasks."[173]

The Chinese do seem to be building some sort of supporting system, though its contours are quite different from those of the US system. An entrepreneurial approach to basing is taking root, one that relies heavily on commercial strategic strongpoints to facilitate its far seas operations, especially non-traditional military operations and intelligence collection. Indeed, Chinese firms own or operate terminals in ninety-six ports in fifty-three countries around the world. Over half of these ports are near major strategic choke points.[174] These activities came to public attention when China Merchants Port took over the Sri Lankan port of Hambantota after the Sri Lankan government defaulted on debt.[175] China Ocean Shipping Company (COSCO) shipping ports garnered international attention for attempting to "buy up Europe" when it secured a concession from the Greek government to operate piers in the port of Piraeus. Gwadar Port, a flagship BRI project in Pakistan, is also a possible location since it has the capability to host large ships and is near a strategic choke point, the Strait of Hormuz.[176]

The upstart factors of efficiency, effectiveness, and need to minimize threat perceptions are encouraging this approach. It is clear from Chinese discourse and behavior as well that the country has deliberately avoided mimicking US strategy over the past thirty years.[177] In most internal discussions, the overseas bases of other countries are considered strategic problems for China rather than a model from which to learn.[178] In contrast, Chinese strategists see commercial logistics hubs as efficient: they come with a reduced cost and an increased availability of necessary basic supplies, ease of access from a diplomatic and administrative standpoint, and the growing availability of facilities that meet certain military standards.[179] Focusing on building dual-use bases not only avoids the trap of exhausting China's resources in pursuing bases but also generates revenue.[180]

Chinese military commentators who advocate for the PLAN to adopt more aggressive strategies along the Maritime Silk Road advocate for an entrepreneurial approach, especially to basing, to minimize backlash. Indeed, by "carefully choosing points, laying out in a low-key manner, prioritizing cooperation, and slowly infiltrating"[181] through civilian facilities, these commentators argue, China will be able to avoid accusations of expansionism and mitigate Washington's perception that the PLAN is becoming a global threat.[182] Many have also recognized the potential utility of these bases for collecting intelligence, as China's network of ports provides a platform for extensive collection of data that is extremely valuable for military intelligence purposes (especially naval intelligence).[183]

While the record is clear that China has not pursued global power projection à la the United States during its rise, the main alternative argument to the upstart approach is that China has wanted to emulate—to build expeditionary capabilities and overseas bases from which it can project offensive military power—but has not managed to do so. In 2010, John Mearsheimer argued that as regional hegemons gain power, they will "invariably be tempted to emulate the United States" simply because the benefits of being a global military hegemon are so "enormous."[184] Similarly, Rush Doshi predicts in his 2021 book that China will pursue greater power projection, though he recognizes in principle that China is unlikely to copy the United States' "complex and costly" global basing system. He still thinks it will rely on traditional military power to protect its overseas interests as soon as it can.[185]

This resource-driven argument—that China will emulate the US strategy once it can—is hard to square with China's resources. The Chinese economy is about six times the size of the French economy and over five times that of India. And yet France had aircraft carriers (the ultimate power projection platform) seventy-one years and India fifty-one years before China; France has twelve overseas bases and India has ten. Russia has military bases in five countries (including some in disputed territory such as Ukraine, Georgia, and Moldova), along with smaller installations and deployments in another three countries.[186] Even Thailand commissioned its first and only aircraft carrier fifteen years before China's *Liaoning* entered service. Both the United States and Russia have more transport aircraft than China, and India has almost as many.[187] In other words, China has had as much ability as other major powers to recreate, even if on a smaller scale, the US model for power projection to protect overseas interests. The evidence supports my contention that China's lack of emulation is due to strategic choice rather than necessity.

Another alternative explanation for the absence of China's capability to project global power is that it free rides on security provided by the United States. The main evidence is that China relies on oil flows from the Middle East but still does not provide sea-lane protection. Moreover, before cooperating with the Taliban, China looked to the United States to protect its Afghan and other Middle Eastern interests.[188] But the US security presence, while vast, does not coincide neatly with Chinese strategic interests, especially in the developing world. China has massive economic investment across Africa, especially East Africa, as part of both the maritime and land routes of the BRI, whereas the United States and other global alliances maintain little security infrastructure in these regions. Furthermore, the United States has been absent from Central Asia, the poster child for the BRI, since 2014, and before that had very little presence. There was speculation that

China might free ride on Russia here, but China's larger security presence in the form of the PAP and coordination with Central Asia countries on counterterrorism patrols shows that Beijing does not feel comfortable leaving its security to other countries.

China, despite possessing fewer resources and limited capabilities, has over the past thirty years made significant advances in its ability to achieve great power objectives in the security and military realm. Although military might has been a key part of China's rise to great power status, Chinese leaders have been keen to avoid the excessive pursuit of military power.[189] China has consolidated control over disputed territory and managed to protect its expanding overseas interests effectively and efficiently, all without provoking major war or destabilizing the Party system. It has accomplished all this by doing things differently—whether regional or globally, in the conventional or the nuclear realm—in ways that cater to its competitive advantages.

6

Emulation and Exploitation in Chinese Economic Policy

In many ways, the story of China's rise to great power status is an economic one. In 1978, 71 percent of Chinese people worked in farming, and the country had a GDP per capita of just US $156 (compared to $10,500 in the United States).[1] But then China adopted a policy of marketization and liberalization of the economy, known as *gaige kaifang*, or "reform and opening up." Deng Xiaoping began to de-collectivize agriculture and open China up to foreign investment. He also created several special economic zones, like Shenzhen, Zhuhai, and Xiamen, cities free of bureaucratic regulations that would become engines for Chinese national economic growth. Later reforms in the 1980s and 1990s would see the state-owned sector reformed and government control of business relaxed.

Over the past thirty years, China's economic power on the international stage has surged. By 2001, China was a member of the WTO following extensive negotiations. By 2005, China's GDP per capita had increased by about 1,000 percent, and nearly 50 percent of its people lived in cities (compared to 20 percent in 1978). Five years later, China surpassed Japan as the second-largest economy in the world. It became the world's largest exporter; today China exports approximately $3.4 trillion of goods to other countries compared to a mere $150 billion in 1995.[2] China's exports also moved up the value chain, from cheap plastic toys to advanced electronics. China now plays a key role in the supply chains for everything from pharmaceuticals to new energy methods.

The world finds itself in a unique position with respect to its economic relationship with China. While this is not the first story of economic competition leading to broader strategic competition, China's international economic trajectory has some unique elements compared to past rising powers. First, China's global position is extensive; China and the United States now trade places year to year as the largest destination for foreign investment. China claims to be the top trading partner for 120 countries (representing about three-fifths of the total number of countries in the world), including key US Indo-Pacific allies like Japan and South Korea.[3] Indeed, the fact that many US allies rely more heavily on China than on the United States for their economic prosperity complicates Washington's ability to compete with Beijing.

The second unique circumstance is that never before have a rising power and the established hegemon been so economically intertwined. China holds at least $860 billion of US public debt, representing 12 percent of the total foreign-owned public debt.[4] Trade volume between the United States and China measured just about $690 billion in 2022 (equal to the entire GDP of Poland).[5] To put this in historical context, the United States and China trade as much in ten days as Germany and Great Britain did in today's US dollars in the full year before WWI broke out (and Germany and Great Britain were considered economically interdependent).[6] The United States also remains the largest destination for outbound Chinese investment in 2022 despite the pervasive call for less dependency on China.[7]

This economic interdependence between China and the United States has generated new interest groups in partner countries that complicate competition. As countries become increasingly reliant on the Chinese market for trade, investment, or aid, a coalition of influential economic players has emerged, advocating for stable and cooperative relations with China to safeguard their own interests, even at the expense of their countries' broader strategic goals.[8] For instance, in 2021, billionaire Ray Dalio, who founded the hedge fund Bridgewater Associates, publicly equated China's human rights abuses with racism in the United States. Elon Musk, whose Tesla has a gigafactory in Shanghai, likewise found himself in hot water after saying that Taiwan would almost certainly be "integrated" into the PRC, comments that drew praise from China and scorn from Taiwan.

Third, the United States has never faced a competitor with such vast economic resources. In the early 1980s, Soviet GDP equaled less than 50 percent of US GDP; in 2021, Chinese GDP was equivalent to around 76 percent of US GDP.[9] China's economic might is palpable: a summer 2020 Gallup poll in fourteen major countries found that the majority in all but three (the United States, South Korea, and Japan) said that China was the world's leading economic power.[10] Objectively speaking, the United States is the world's economic superpower and is likely to remain so, as China's economy has begun to show signs of strain, especially after COVID.[11] But China continues to wield massive economic power, in ways that are felt by other countries.

How did China use economic tools to build power, influence, and leverage in the international system? When the conditions were right, China emulated US approaches and exploited gaps. Free trade, for example, was ripe for emulation because it was perceived to be not only an effective strategy for building power but also one that would reassure the United States and underwrite CCP control at home. China also exploited gaps in its search for preferential trade arrangements, gaining power positions in international economic institutions and expanding its market share in the developing world.

China has also taken the US approach of using economic sanctions to shape the policies of other countries, but it does so via distinctive methods that exploit the vulnerabilities and gaps in the system. Chinese leaders believe this approach to be more effective and less threatening than the use of military force to achieve its objectives. In this case, the Party's need to protect its legitimacy at home does not reduce the effectiveness of the strategy, but it does limit its scope: China for the most part uses unilateral economic sanctions to push trading partners to accept its domestic policies. Specifically, China relies on its massive market to deter countries from engaging in activities it sees as harmful to Party rule.

China pursues both emulation and exploitation in its attempts to buck the US dominance of the global financial system and support economic growth at home. At first Beijing tried to compete directly with the United States by emulating some of its existing practices. China fought for the addition of the RMB to the Special Drawing Rights (SDR) and encouraged international entities to trade in its currency. But this approach had limitations because of the need to maintain Party control over financial tools, which has limited the success of its emulative approach to internationalizing the RMB. Given this situation, the Party has shifted its strategy slightly to try to exploit gaps in accordance with its competitive advantages—encouraging BRI countries to settle accounts in RMB and competing in emerging areas like digital currency to promote the use of its currency.

China's Pursuit of "Free Trade"

The United States' role at the head of the international order has its foundations in the country's massive economy. The durability of the US-led liberal international order is due in part to the free trade principles that have facilitated global prosperity.[12] Chinese thinkers have recognized the value of the US approach. The Chinese Ministry of Commerce regards the WTO and free trade agreements (FTAs) as the two "wheels" that propel economic globalization.[13] Chinese economists also believe that free trade promotes foreign investment; according to the estimates of the ASEAN Secretariat, the establishment of the China-ASEAN free trade area will increase ASEAN's investment in China by 48 percent.[14] In addition, China's leaders believe that free trade with other countries would help to avoid any isolation and containment led by the United States as well as expand China's influence in the global economic order.[15] More trade would cause countries to prioritize economic ties with China over strategic considerations that might drive US policy. For example, as the Chinese economy grew, its participation became necessary for multilateral economic institutions to function. Consequently, countries grew closer to China and became less willing to criticize it for political issues.[16] China also invests strategically in companies, signing lucrative commercial deals, to alleviate other countries' apprehensions about its economic power and incentivize a more favorable policy stance toward China.[17]

Chinese leaders also felt that integration into the global market would be a reassuring move. Beijing had successfully used the prospect of economic cooperation as bait to improve relations after the Tiananmen incident, first with Japan, then with European countries and Canada, and finally with the United States.[18] In 1998, a Chinese official involved in China's WTO accession negotiations feared that the delay or failure of China's accession to the WTO would encourage the spread of the "China threat theory."[19] Long Yongtu, China's chief representative in the WTO negotiations, argued that China's accession had reduced frictions between the United States and China.[20] In other words, China's logic for embracing free trade was about more than just free trade's effectiveness at building power. As Chinese premier Zhu Rongji articulated, China could have had economic growth without the WTO, but accession was "a great concession to preserve the friendly cooperation between China and the US and establish a constructive strategic partnership."[21] This strategy was largely successful, as the notion that China's participation in free trade ensured its peaceful rise persisted for almost three decades.[22]

Free trade was a promising domestic strategy for economic growth and Party control. China deliberately pursued trade to propel its own economic development at home, which was critical for CCP legitimacy.[23] Chinese leaders like Zhu Rongji who wanted to reform the state sector but faced entrenched bureaucratic interests and resistance from conservatives within the regime found success by tying SOE reform to WTO admission.[24] China could take advantage of its large market size, its ability to export low-cost manufactured products, and its near-monopoly control over several critical raw materials to affect supply and demand in international markets.[25] FTAs also facilitated Chinese investment in foreign firms, which is crucial to continued economic growth and the ability to transition to a high-income economy and helps Beijing obtain foreign technology and expertise.[26] All of this allowed the CCP to maintain a growth rate above 6 percent throughout the post–Cold War period until 2019.[27]

Free trade was ripe for emulation given the Chinese perception of its strategic effectiveness, its reassuring nature, and domestic considerations such as China's competitive advantages and need to maintain Party control. Accordingly, China joined the relevant financial institutions as it embarked on its rise. It joined Asia-Pacific Economic Cooperation (APEC) in 1991, the Asian Development Bank in 1986, and the WTO in 2001, and it became a donor to the World Bank by 2007.[28] China then started to pursue bilateral FTAs to compete with the United States' economic power in the 2000s, first with small countries such as Pakistan (which signed in 2006) and New Zealand and Singapore (both in 2008).[29] In 2002, China signed a FTA with ASEAN, four years before the United States signed a similar agreement, creating the most-populated and third-largest (after the North American free trade zone) market in the world.

To further facilitate free trade, China replaced some of its bilateral FTAs with the Regional Comprehensive Economic Partnership (RCEP), first proposed in 2011 by Indonesia and signed in November 2020. The RCEP sought to harmonize the several bilateral agreements between ASEAN and other countries: China, Japan, South Korea, Australia, New Zealand, and India (the last of which would later pull out of the agreements). The RCEP signatories agreed to reduce tariffs by 92 percent over twenty years and eliminate tariffs and quotas for 65 percent of goods traded. RCEP's coverage is impressive: its fifteen members constitute about 30 percent of the global population and the world's GDP. The agreement also marks the first trade agreement between China, Japan, and South Korea.[30] As a leading Chinese scholar who participated in RCEP negotiations argued, RCEP will function to reconstruct the East Asian production network, accelerating regional economic integration and countering US "unilateralism."[31]

China has also exploited gaps in its pursuit of deeper trade relationships. Chinese analysts had always thought the "existing international rules under Western leadership [were] problematic," but they believed it would be unrealistic for China to set up its own system.[32] As discussed in Chapter 2, China began to pursue leadership positions in these institutions, often holding more positions than the United States, with the aim of steering international economic affairs.[33] China has consistently sought to use its participation to accomplish four key aims: to further its multipolar vision and cement its regional leadership, exploit developing countries' resentment of American hegemony to push for its own values, exploit the weakness of the US-led international system after the Asian financial crisis to take leadership in the region, and strengthen its perceived sovereignty.[34] To do all this, China became more assertive in the agenda setting and rule building of the global economic system.[35] After the 2008 global financial crisis, Beijing also saw an opening to support smaller economies in their recovery with the intention of extending its economic influence and creating a better environment for its economic growth.[36]

The American retreat from global leadership under Trump left a power vacuum that China hoped to exploit as well.[37] President Trump pulled out of the Trans-Pacific Partnership (TPP), a regional FTA meant to knit together the United States and major economies around the Pacific Rim, with the notable exception of China. The idea was to encourage China to adopt the practices and policies required for admission to TPP, ensuring a more level playing field for the world's fastest-growing economic regions.[38] Then, in 2018, when the Trump administration imposed significant tariffs on Chinese goods, Xi Jinping availed himself of the opportunity to give a pro-trade and pro-engagement speech at the 2017 World Economic Forum in Davos, where he urged all to "firmly develop global free trade and investment, promote trade and investment liberalization and facilitation through openness, and take a clear-cut stand against protectionism."[39]

Chinese pundits followed in full force, arguing that America had caused the deterioration in the global economy by waging trade wars and adopting protectionism.[40] Exactly what role this rhetoric played in promoting China's image abroad is hard to say, but it may have helped boost its image among developing nations, where Beijing is more popular than ever: in 2022, about 63 percent of respondents in developing nations had a positive view of China.[41]

Today, China has eighteen bilateral FTAs, including the one with ASEAN (which includes ten states), covering 9 percent of global GDP, whereas the United States has twenty bilateral FTAs that together cover 15 percent of global GDP.[42] In other words, the FTAs in which China participates include more states, but US FTAs make up a greater portion of the world's GDP. China is also party to the RCEP, which includes Japan (China had no FTA with Japan prior to RCEP's signing in 2020). The RCEP covers 30 percent of world GDP, but most of that figure comes from China and Japan, which make up 18 and 6 percent of world GDP, respectively.[43] Through free trade, China has expanded its global economic reach, and grown economically to legitimize the Party's domestic rule and have more resources available to pursue its international interests.

Exploiting Countries' Dependencies Through Unilateral Sanctions

Since the end of the Cold War, the United States has increasingly relied on economic sanctions as a tool to punish its adversaries or otherwise shape their behavior. Sanctions can come in several forms, including freezing the assets of an adversary's elites, forbidding US companies or individuals to do business with certain companies, or banning US companies from investing in certain industries overseas.[44]

The United States employs a dizzying array of sanctions against an increasing number of countries and entities. According to the Center for a New American Security's Sanctions by the Numbers dataset, in 2009 the United States implemented 444 individual sanctions actions. By 2021, that number had skyrocketed to 1,552 actions. In the wake of Russia's invasion of Ukraine, the Biden administration has imposed 1,500 such actions in retaliation.[45] The targets of these sanctions can include both foreign firms and individuals. The United States implements sanctions to punish countries (possibly offering a deterrent to would-be imitators) and/or to erode an adversary's ability to pursue its objectives. For example, a Treasury Department official described the goal of current sanctions against Russia: to "constrain Russia's military capabilities, its access to battlefield supplies, and its economic bottom line."[46]

China has learned from the US experience but has adapted its own coercive economic statecraft to cater to its competitive advantages and exploit the vulnerabilities of other countries. Before 2010, China had rarely used unilateral economic sanctions due to concerns about its international reputation and its limited economic power, but from 2011 onward, it has used sanctions to achieve diplomatic goals with rapidly increasing frequency.[47]

Economic sanctions offer China an effective alternative to the use of force in solving problems. In the face of security pressures such as US arms sales to Taiwan and South Korea's deployment of the Terminal High-Altitude Area Defense (THAAD) system, as well as political pressures from other countries that support protection of rights in Xinjiang, Tibet, and Taiwan's democracy, Beijing is unable to resort to direct military means, but it can signal its resolve and force targets to change their behavior through economic sanctions.

China's approach is best considered exploitation in this case because Beijing has pursued economic sanctions like the United States but in new areas to achieve different political objectives. Domestic considerations create incentives to use economic sanctions via a different process and for a different purpose. As James Reilly, a researcher who focuses on China's economic statecraft, explains:

> Unlike US sanctions, which are formalized through domestic law and/or presidential decisions, China rarely openly declares its economic sanctions. Instead, Beijing prefers to use vague threats, variation in leadership visits, selective purchases (or nonpurchases), and other informal measures. Such informal measures enhance the leadership's flexibility, since they can be removed without an embarrassing policy reversal. They also provide Chinese leaders with credible deniability, thus minimizing diplomatic fallout.[48]

The impetus for economic sanctions is different as well. The United States tends to sanction countries for poor behavior—human rights abuses at home, aggression abroad. China opposes this type of sanctions, like those placed on Myanmar, Zimbabwe, Syria, and more recently Russia, often doing so by using its permanent seat on the UNSC. Table 6.1 provides data on China's major economic sanctions activity from 1992 to 2023.

Unlike the United States, China uses sanctions against countries with which it has robust trade relations, in many cases in response to what China considers interference in its domestic affairs and damage to its "core interests." For example, China bought less from France, Japan, and the United States after their leaders met with the Dalai Lama. In September 2010, after Japan detained the captain of a Chinese fishing boat, China enacted a de facto ban on the export of rare earth elements to Japan. As the Chinese Ministry of Foreign Affairs stated, "Given the size of the Chinese market, we don't need to coerce anyone. But one thing is for sure: the Chinese people wouldn't allow foreigners to reap benefits in China on the one hand and smear China on the other."[49]

Table 6.1 China's Sanctions Activities

Years	Target Country	Rationale
1992–94	France	French arms sales to Taiwan
2002	Mongolia	Dalai Lama visits Mongolia
2009	France	Dalai Lama visits France and meets President Sarkozy
2010	USA	US arms sales to Taiwan
2010–2016	Norway	Nobel Peace Prize awarded to Chinese dissident Liu Xiaobo, China sanctioned in response
2010	Japan, USA	Diaoyu Island collision incident
2012–2016	The Philippines	Huangyan Island incident and South China Sea arbitration case
2015	USA	US arms sales to Taiwan
2016–2017	South Korea	South Korea's decision to deploy THAAD anti-missile system
2016	Mongolia	Dalai Lama visit to Mongolia
2016	Taiwan	Election of Democratic Progressive Party presidential candidate Tsai Ing-wen
2006–2016	Iran	Iran nuclear weapons program (Iran was also sanctioned by UN)
2017	Australia	Australian leaders criticized China's relations with South Pacific island countries
2006–present	North Korea	North Korean nuclear weapons program (North Korea also sanctioned by UN)
2019–present	Canada	Canada's detention of Huawei executive Meng Wanzhou
2019–present	USA	July 2019 US arms sales to Taiwan
2019–present	USA	August 2019 US arms sales to Taiwan
2019–present	USA	December 2019 US passage of Hong Kong Human Rights and Democracy Bill
2020	Australia	Australian government's push for international investigation into origins of COVID-19
2021	Taiwan	China's attempt to undermine President Tsai Ing-wen's political campaign
2021	Lithuania	Lithuania opened a new Taiwan Representative Office in Vilnius
2023–present	USA, EU, Japan	Retaliation for US and allies' limits on China's access to semiconductors and related materials

Source: Data from Fang Jiongsheng [方炯升], "Limited Counterattack: China's Economic Sanctions Since 2010 [有限的回击：2010年以来中国的经济制裁行为]," Foreign Affairs Review [外交评论], no. 1 (2020): 65–87; Peter Harrell, Elizabeth Rosenberg, and Edoardo Saravalle, "China's Use of Coercive Economic Measures," Center for New American Security, June 11, 2018, https://www.cnas.org/publications/reports/chinas-use-of-coercive-economic-measures.

China has also weaponized this interdependence to a far greater extent than the United States.[50] Broadly, Beijing deploys two sorts of economic coercion against companies: administrative discrimination and popular boycotts. Administrative discrimination involves the use of regulations to impede a company's ability to conduct business in China.[51] For example, in the aftermath of South Korea's decision to deploy the THAAD anti-missile system, 75 of Lotte's 99 stores were closed in China due to alleged fire code and other infractions, almost certainly because the business had agreed to transfer land to Seoul for THAAD deployment.[52] When Tsai Ing-wen, who was not China's preferred candidate, was elected president in Taiwan, Beijing put restrictions on tourism. By 2019, the number of Chinese visitors to Taiwan had dropped over 50 percent from 2015 levels.[53] Beijing has also gone after foreign organizations, whose popularity in China makes them particularly vulnerable to Chinese influence. For instance, in 2019 when the general manager of the NBA team Houston Rockets tweeted "Fight for freedom, stand with Hong Kong," China was quick to retaliate. CCTV 5, the sports arm of the state broadcasting corporation, stopped airing NBA games altogether for eighteen months, costing the NBA hundreds of millions of dollars in lost revenue.[54]

Most popular boycotts are organized through state media when foreign companies make comments or criticisms regarding Chinese territorial interests (Taiwan and Hong Kong) or human rights.[55] In August 2019, for example, Coach and Givenchy faced a Chinese social media boycott campaign for carrying shirts that implied that Hong Kong and Taiwan were not part of China; Versace similarly faced calls for a boycott for doing the same. In 2021, China lashed out against clothing companies that had expressed concerns about forced labor in the Xinjiang cotton industry, with a particularly harsh reaction against H&M.[56] Over the past decade, dozens of celebrities and multinational corporations have apologized to China for some real or perceived offense in hopes of avoiding such punishment.[57] In 2021, the actor and wrestler John Cena, after calling Taiwan a country, apologized (in Mandarin, no less) to China.[58]

In a somewhat new development, China seems to be moving beyond trade and tourism to exploit countries' supply chain vulnerabilities. In an internal speech in April 2020, Xi Jinping emphasized that increasing the dependence of global supply chains on China could act as a key deterrent against "artificial foreign supply cuts," by which he meant efforts by the United States to restrict trade with China for strategic purposes.[59]

While Chinese leaders deny using this tactic, it is a high-level focus: Xi Jinping mentioned supply chain security and relevant diplomacy twenty times in public speeches at home and abroad within a period of two months.[60] As a result, China is very sensitive to other countries' attempts to reduce their dependence on it, repeatedly emphasizing the need to maintain the existing pattern of global supply chains and strongly opposing agendas such as "decoupling" and "de-risking" so as not to lose its advantages.[61]

The leveraging of its markets has compelled some countries to accede to its demands. South Korea, for example, promised not to deploy any new THAAD system, not to join the US missile defense system, and not to seek a military alliance between South Korea, the United States, and Japan. Evidence suggests that foreign governments take actions to prevent or punish the publication of content critical of Beijing, either at the request of Chinese representatives or to avoid tensions with a significant donor or trading partner.[62] But like the United States with its unilateral economic sanctions, China has a spotty record of success. The European Union, for example, continues to speak out against Chinese human rights abuses. China sanctioned Lithuania in response to the opening of a Taiwanese representative office in 2021, but as of January 2024, the Taiwanese office in Vilnius remained open.

From the THAAD incident with Korea to maritime disputes with Vietnam and the trade war with the United States, China understands that economic leverage does not always transfer into political power. For sanctions to change policy, the relevant interest groups in the other country must be impacted by the economic policies and have the capability to influence government decisions—conditions that are often not present.[63] Moreover, security and territorial issues often take precedence over economic ones, meaning that economic methods are less powerful in influencing states in these areas.[64] This is not to say the approach is not effective; the threat of economic punishment often keeps countries from engaging in problematic behavior in the first place.[65] In other words, economic measures may not successfully compel countries to return to Beijing's preferred policies, but the threat of such measures often deters them from taking actions Beijing might see as contrary to its core interests in the first place.

Internationalization of the Renminbi

After the end of World War II, the global economy was in shambles. Europe and much of East Asia lay in flames. The war had cost over $1 trillion, more than four times the US annual GDP at that time. The United States saw its debt levels rise to over 120 percent of GDP by 1945. The United Kingdom had it even worse—its debt peaked at over 250 percent of GDP shortly after the war.[66] World leaders, wanting to avoid another catastrophe, searched for factors that contributed to the outbreak of the war. Competing currency blocs were thought to have been one culprit, and thus President Truman concluded that promoting a common reserve currency would help to promote world peace.[67]

Other countries agreed, and in 1944 forty-four of them came together at the Bretton Woods Conference to create the postwar financial order. They established the IMF and the International Bank for Reconstruction and Development (which later became the World Bank). Wanting to avoid the competitive currency devaluations they believed had exacerbated the Great Depression, and thus the war, the countries also agreed on a system of fixed exchange rates. To anchor this system, the United States would tie its currency to the price of gold at US $35 an ounce, and other countries would peg their currencies to the dollar at a fixed price. Companies could then buy and sell goods and services using the common currency of the dollar, and central banks would keep those dollars on hand to facilitate such transactions.

For better or for worse, the United States was the only country that could provide this public good. The war had created tremendous demand for US manufactures, and enormous amounts of gold had rushed into US coffers during the war. Additionally, if the US dollar were not the reserve currency, US goods would be cheaper on the open market. Lower prices coupled with the size of the US economy would have made it almost impossible for other countries to compete, and so would hamper efforts at free trade.

To this day, the dollar remains the preferred reserve currency. It is used to settle about half of international trade, even though the United States was involved in only about 13.5 percent of world trade in 2020.[68] Indeed, in 2022, the US dollar made up about 59 percent of world central bank reserves.[69] Additionally, the US dollar's prominence is supported by the depth and liquidity of the US Treasury bond market. (Since investors believe Treasury bond transactions will continue even during major economic surprises, there is demand for US treasuries even during times of crisis.)

Chinese thinkers understand that the status of the dollar as the dominant reserve currency affords the United States several economic and geopolitical benefits—an "exorbitant privilege" (a term coined by former French president Valéry Giscard d'Estaing). This privilege bestows benefits on both the US government and the American people by enabling them to maintain high levels of consumption through cheap imported goods and cheap borrowing (i.e., the US government can run budget deficits while paying smaller amounts of interest on its debt). As one Chinese economist explains, the reserve-currency-issuing country (1) receives huge seigniorage revenues, which is the profit derived from the difference between the face value of a currency and the cost to produce it; (2) can transfer external debt and currency depreciation risks to non-issuing countries; (3) is better able to regulate its domestic economy at the cost of the long-term imbalance of international incomes and expenses; (4) can use its financial pricing power to obtain income from financial spreads, as it can set interest rates, and produce a difference between earnings and expenses on financial assets and liabilities; and (5) has an advantage in multilateral negotiations because it can use its influence over the economic and financial policy of developing countries to realize its own strategy.[70]

The dollar's dominance also gives the United States coercive options. Because most trading parties use the dollar to settle accounts and thus need access to the US financial system, the US Treasury can impose financial sanctions against a country to compel a change in behavior. By threatening to withhold access to US dollars from third parties who trade with the problematic actor, US sanctions present counterparty risk even to those not based in the United States. Additionally, the United States can coerce the Society for Worldwide Interbank Financial Telecommunication (SWIFT), a messaging network that helps banks coordinate fund transfers, to exclude targeted banks from its information system, which greatly increases their transaction costs.[71] The United States can also extract concessions by rewarding allies with vital liquidity, supplying them with cash when the dollar becomes more scarce and expensive, and denying the same to adversaries. Indeed, Chinese analysts argue that the United States' "weaponization" of the dollar, most recently against Russia for invading Ukraine, may threaten China's financial security.[72]

Leadership of the international financial system, along with possession of a popular reserve currency, was thus seen as an effective strategy that merited emulation. And as with trade, more integration into the system would be reassuring; indeed, as the following discussion highlights, many developed countries supported Chinese efforts to internationalize the RMB. China would also be able to play a more important role in global macroeconomic policy dialogue and cooperation if the RMB became a key currency.[73] The move would have domestic benefits as well: internationalizing the RMB would "help create a more balanced and fair international currency system while reducing the cost for China to raise external debt and manage the risks associated with exchange rate fluctuations."[74] As the world's top trader, China theoretically had a competitive advantage in its ability to encourage countries to adopt the RMB.[75] On top of modernizing the economy and developing a domestic market, Chinese policymakers recognized the need to optimize foreign exchange reserves through strategic allocations, which in turn helped Chinese financial institutions to expand their investments overseas.[76] This provided Chinese firms with opportunities to generate returns on their investments and diversify their portfolios, which contributes to China's economy and makes them competitive on the global stage.

Despite all these benefits, domestic factors discouraged emulation in the first decade of China's rise. After the end of the Cold War, Chinese leaders were keen to promote financial policies to support export-led growth. One of the drawbacks of the dollar's high price on the foreign exchange market is that it raises the price of importing from the United States, which hurts US exporters and American manufacturing. Consequently, China pegged the yuan to the dollar at a lower exchange rate, making its exports cheaper and helping the country's immense manufacturing base.[77] ("Yuan" and "RMB" are interchangeable terms for the same currency.) The dollar's unwavering dominance also made direct competition less attractive, especially in the 1990s and 2000s, when China's global trade position was not yet strong (in 2001, China's trade represented only 4 percent of the global total).[78]

Then the 2008 financial crisis hit, bringing a unique opportunity. Chinese strategists believed that the world's confidence in the dollar would be weakened, and major players would be more open to using the RMB.[79] The financial crisis also created an opportunity for the internationalization of the RMB and strengthened China's global influence as China became the world's second-largest economy in 2010.[80] The world's growing dependence on

China reflected a "structural weakening" of the US economy that would be accompanied by a subsequent decline of US means of controlling the global economy.[81]

Chinese leaders, hoping to gain an advantage, began to try to elevate the RMB's status, emulating the United States' strategy for financial dominance. In 2011, Chinese officials began lobbying for the RMB to be included in the IMF's SDR, an artificial currency reserve held by IMF member states that they can exchange for the component currencies, included four currencies at the time: the US dollar, the euro, the Japanese yen, and the British pound sterling.[82] Chinese leaders sought support in visits and meetings with major countries such as the United States, the United Kingdom, France, Germany, Russia, and India.[83] China argued that its economic size and recently re-formed financial system qualified the RMB for inclusion.[84] Chinese officials also argued for a new international currency system based on the SDR to re-place the dollar in transactions (an idea that subsequently went nowhere).[85]

The leaders of Great Britain, France, Germany, and the United States began to voice their support, and shortly thereafter on October 1, 2016, the IMF introduced the RMB into the SDR even though it did not objectively meet the "freely usable" standard (which means the currency is widely used to make payments for international transactions and trade in the principal exchange markets).[86] Behind that decision was a long and hard Chinese lobbying ef-fort, but the IMF also acted out of self-interest; the Fund's influence on the international monetary system would grow with the RMB's inclusion.[87]

China also emulated the US strategy of promoting its currency through the extension of swap lines—agreements that allow partner central banks to exchange their respective currencies for its partners' currency at the pre-vailing market rate. After a certain amount of time, the first bank then buys back its original currency at the original rate of exchange, regardless of how the exchange rate might have moved since then. While the central bank does have to pay a small amount of interest, the fact that the exchange rate does not change insulates the foreign central bank from exchange rate risk. While in possession of the foreign currency, the borrowing central bank can lend that currency to banks within its own country, ensuring that they have the relevant currency available to conduct transactions and pay off their foreign-currency-denominated debts.

Chinese scholars argue that the Fed's currency swap network is crucial in mitigating risks in the global dollar financing chain, functioning as a signal that bolsters international confidence and easing pressure on the foreign currency markets of emerging economies.[88] In simple terms, the fact that the Fed is willing and able to keep the money flowing even in times of crisis eases investors' risks about emerging economies having access to much-needed currency. While China had enough foreign reserves to act as a leader in financial crises, they maintain, the RMB's lesser status limits its ability to ease the short-term liquidity pressure on financial institutions. Currency swap agreements in RMB would help alleviate this problem and stimulate bilateral trade by lowering the risks and costs of using yuan in transactions. This would increase the competitiveness of China's products in both economies and enhance the stability of their financial markets.[89]

China began to pursue its own swap agreements in 2010. Exploiting gaps in the system, it pursued agreements with many countries that lacked one with the United States.[90] China now enjoys such arrangements with all countries that have such agreements with the United States save one (Mexico) as well as with an additional thirty-three countries.[91] Many of these countries import large amounts of goods from China, making access to Chinese RMB important in case the price of the dollar (the normal currency used) rises suddenly. Even though China's arrangements tend to be much smaller in scope, in 2021 the RMB became the largest swap currency at 3.47 trillion yuan.

Chinese economists were optimistic that these developments would improve its influence in global financial markets.[92] The swap arrangements would increase the RMB's use in international trade and international reserves, which Chinese scholars argue would promote the diversification of the international monetary system and challenge the US monopoly of power.[93] Developed Western economies would then be forced to consider the appeals of emerging economies and make concessions accordingly.[94]

Many believed that the RMB's inclusion in the SDR basket would encourage central banks around the world to add the yuan to their holdings, thus increasing its role as a reserve currency and Chinese financial power along with it.[95] The People's Bank concluded after the SDR inclusion that "the status of the renminbi as international currency had been preliminarily established, the convertibility of capital account of the RMB had been promoted, and the opening of financial markets had achieved remarkable results" despite China's unwillingness to allow it to be freely used.[96] Later economists argued that the internationalization of the RMB would also improve the health of China's financial institutions and would encourage enterprises to expand their operations overseas, helping China to integrate into the world economy and facilitating larger economic efforts like the BRI.[97]

But these developments had less of an impact on the internationalization of the RMB than many in China had hoped.[98] In 2022, the yuan made up just 2.76 percent of total reserves, compared to the dollar's 59.79 percent and the euro's 19.66 percent.[99] Likewise, only 3.2 percent of international trade was settled in RMB, despite China's large share of worldwide trade (China manufactures ten times more in global goods than it settles in cross-border trade in its own currency).[100] Notably, 48.6 percent of international transactions using RMB took place in Hong Kong, followed by 11.3 percent in Singapore and 5.4 percent in the United Kingdom.[101]

While China has much to gain with the successful internationalization of the RMB, additional domestic political factors have prevented the PRC from competing effectively. A currency's role in international finance has three important aspects: capital account openness (the level of restrictions on inflows and outflows of financial capital), internationalization (the extent to which it is used as a medium of exchange in transactions), and reserve holdings (whether assets in that currency are held by foreign central banks). History shows that to become a reserve currency, a country needs a very large economy compared to its peers, liquid financial markets compared to its peers, an open capital account, and a commitment to limiting fluctuations in inflation.

China possesses the first and fourth criteria, but the Party has purposely avoided the other two. The Chinese government still dominates the banking sector, and measures designed to favor that sector over other elements of the financial system have hindered China's financial development.[102] Additionally, the Chinese government, perpetually afraid of capital flight (and even more so in the COVID era), maintains a closed capital account, meaning it is difficult for investors to move money in and out of the country.

Beijing fears capital flight for a few reasons. Chinese economic managers would give up a great deal of control over China's macroeconomic situation if they allowed capital to move freely out of China. Additionally, if capital flight occurred, China's debt bubbles in areas like real estate might pop, as there would be less new investment to continue propping up those sectors. The resulting economic downturn would severely damage the Party's credibility.[103] China is trying to get around its disadvantages by taking incremental steps, such as cautiously loosening some capital restrictions. Since 2010 it has slowly opened its $13 trillion bond market, which accounts for 51 percent of all bonds issued by emerging economies, to attract foreign investors, but this move has not been enough.[104]

China does not have the competitive advantage necessary to compete directly with the dollar. Reserve currency has much to do with the maturity of one's domestic financial markets (which is why Switzerland boasts one of the largest reserve currencies in the world despite accounting for less than 1 percent of global GDP). The breadth (the availability of a range of financial instruments, including those for hedging risk), depth (the volume of financial instruments in specific markets), and liquidity (the level of turnover/trading volume) of the Chinese financial market are seriously limited compared to the United States.[105] These limitations stem in part from Chinese companies, which, in the words of economist Eswar Prasad, "suffer from weak corporate governance, limited transparency, weak auditing standards, and shoddy accounting practices."[106]

Despite these challenges, China has persisted in its attempts to internationalize the RMB. Influential players in Chinese monetary policy claim that the RMB can still gain a prominent place, that the SDR was only the first step, and that soon non-Chinese entities will be confident enough to hold RMB assets (rather than merely using RMB to settle payments).[107] Many think it is only a matter of time before the pull of the Chinese economy pushes foreign governments and commercial entities toward the RMB.[108] A key report delivered in October 2022 at the opening session of the 20th National Congress of the Communist Party of China called for efforts to "promote the internationalization of the Renminbi in an orderly way," as part of broader efforts to promote a high-standard opening up.[109] China's strategy as of 2023 consists of three prongs: encouraging more RMB payments and settlements in international trade, expanding financial opening up to provide overseas investors with more RMB-denominated assets, and strengthening international cooperation under the BRI.[110]

This optimism persists even though China under Xi Jinping has become ever more conservative on this issue, emphasizing financial security and exhibiting more caution about the depth of RMB internationalization.[111] In the eyes of the top leadership, the priority of China's financial system is to maintain a prudent monetary policy and to promote financial activities in support of the real economy, with the internationalization of the RMB a secondary priority.[112] Beijing's pursuit of such controls is firm and long-term, and it believes that the lack of strict financial regulation and excessive profit-seeking by capital are the root causes of financial crises.[113] The opening of

China's financial system will thus continue to be gradual and limited, to mitigate any financial risks.[114]

Given its inability to compete directly with the dollar, which is partly due to the need for Party control over its financial system, China seems to be moving toward an exploitation strategy—trying to internationalize the RMB but doing so in less competitive areas. China sees some opportunities in emerging economies and others that have political incentives to break free of dependency on the dollar. Zhang Yuyan, a prominent Chinese academic and former diplomat, argues that the Trump government's tariffs and Washington's use of the dollar-centric SWIFT to control international economic activities strengthened many economies' determination to end their dependence on the dollar.[115]

Subsequently, China has tried to leverage its clout in trade to enhance the status of the RMB, convincing countries, especially in the BRI, to use the RMB at least in settling their trade with China.[116] China reached an agreement with Pakistan in 2019 that the RMB will replace the dollar to "finance all future energy and transport projects" under the CPEC project.[117] In November 2022, the People's Bank of China and the State Bank of Pakistan signed an agreement to establish clearing arrangements for RMB in Pakistan.[118] Over the past year, China has reached similar agreements with Laos, Kazakhstan, and Brazil. Saudi Arabia, whose ties with the United States have been strained in recent years following the assassination of *Washington Post* columnist Jamal Khashoggi, had reportedly discussed accepting RMB for oil purchases as of 2022.[119] Additionally, at the December 2022 China-Gulf Cooperation Council summit, President Xi stated that China would encourage the use of RMB in its oil and gas trade with the Gulf nations. Finally, China has increased the use of RMB in its trade with Russia, Iran, and Myanmar over the past five years.[120]

China has also been trying to use Hong Kong to get around its issues of control. In 2022, the Hong Kong Stock Exchange (HKEX) announced it would introduce a Dual Counter Model and a Dual Counter Market Making Program, which will allow investors "to interchange securities listed in both HKD (Hong Kong dollar) and RMB counters," while the Dual Counter Market Making Program will help minimize "price discrepancies between the two counters."[121] The Dual Counter system was partly designed to mitigate the effects of a possible US delisting for Chinese firms listed on both US exchanges and the HKEX. In other words, HKEX will soon allow Hong Kong–based investors an additional opportunity to trade yuan-denominated stock.

The exploitation strategy has allowed the RMB to make a bit more headway. Between January 2020 and January 2022, for example, the RMB's share of global settlements jumped from 1.67 percent to 3.2 percent, taking it from sixth to fourth place.[122] In 2020, China settled 15 percent of its foreign trade in the currency, up from 11 percent in 2015.[123] In 2022, the total amount of cross-border RMB receipts and payments was 42 trillion yuan, representing an increase of 340 percent since 2017.[124]

In another attempt to compete where competitive forces were weaker, China established its own RMB Cross-Border Interbank Payment System (CIPS) to compete with SWIFT.[125] As of 2022, there were seventy-six direct participants in the Chinese system (institutions that maintain an account in the system), including major banks like HSBC, Standard Chartered, Citibank, and BNP Paribas. There were also 1,228 indirect participants (those that interact with the system through direct participants).[126] SWIFT connects more than 11,000 financial institutions in over 200 countries, dwarfing CIPS by a factor of ten.[127] But the number of banks processing yuan payments globally (even if not through CIPS) did grow by half between 2017 and 2020 (from 1,500 to 2,214), with most additions coming from Asia, the Middle East, and Africa.[128] Table 6.2 shows the evolving strategy of China's RMB internationalization strategy, as summarized by the deputy director of the Institute of Finance at CASS. The table demonstrates that China has consistently prioritized expanding the use of the RMB in international transactions, and that the means to do so have become increasingly diverse and comprehensive.

The solution for China may lie in an entrepreneurial approach: creating a digital RMB. This central bank digital currency (CBDC) would function as a digital equivalent of cash. It is almost like having a bank account directly with the Federal Reserve itself. CBDCs share attributes with digital payment methods such as Bitcoin, but what sets them apart is their regulation, as CBDCs are backed and overseen by a country's central bank. In 2016, the People's Bank of China established the Digital Currency Research Institute (DCRI), which has played a crucial role in China's ambition to become the first major central bank to issue a digital fiat currency.[129] Since May 2020, the Chinese central bank has experimented with a digital version of the RMB called the e-CNY.[130] Under this system, Chinese citizens can download a wallet app onto their phone and use e-CNY as payment. This arrangement lowers transaction and clearing costs but also helps the Party-state reassert control over the flow of capital and information within the economy—control

Table 6.2 Evolution of RMB Internationalization Strategy

"Old Trinity" 2009–2017	"New Trinity" 2018–2022	"New New Trinity" 2022 onward
(1) Promote RMB settlement for cross-border trade and direct investment	(1) Promote RMB invoicing in crude oil futures trading	(1) Further encourage RMB invoicing and settlement in cross-border commodity transactions
(2) Promote the development of the offshore RMB market	(2) Push for the opening of domestic financial markets to foreign institutional investors	(2) Strengthen the provision of high-quality RMB-denominated financial assets to foreign institutional investors in both the domestic and offshore markets
(3) Promote the signing of bilateral currency swap lines	(3) Promote RMB invoicing and settlement in neighboring countries (RCEP signatories) and along the Belt and Road Initiative	(3) Accelerate the construction of a cross-border RMB payment and clearing system

Source: Data from Zhang Ming [张明], "Strategic Expansion of RMB Internationalization Against the Background of New Global Changes [全球新变局背景下人民币国际化的策略扩展—从新'三位一体'到新新'三位一体']," National Institution for Finance and Development [国家金融与发展实验室], December 20, 2022, http://www.nifd.cn/Uploads/Paper/19d3ea6b-6dd0-422d-8631-a002cc65e ca9.pdf.

that had slipped away as platforms such as Alipay and WeChat facilitated massive flows of capital and data "beyond the party-state's direct line of sight."[131] The digital yuan's design offers the central bank enhanced visibility and control compared to physical cash.[132] Chinese analysts also hope that by using the e-CNY for cross-border payments instead of the US dollar, Chinese companies and their foreign customers can avoid the risk of US sanctions.[133]

While it may be too early to tell how these more exploitative and entrepreneurial approaches will pan out, it is hard to envision a future in which the RMB contends directly with the US dollar if the Party maintains its strict financial controls. Even if digital currencies rise, the dollar will remain the "foremost store of value," largely because financial assets denominated in dollars, like US government securities, are still the preferred destination for investors.[134] The digital yuan will suffer from reluctance to run business through the People's Bank, which is controlled by a Party-state that is suspicious of private financial rights.

Chinese Economic Power: A Story of Emulation and Exploitation?

Domestic economic reforms, launched under Deng Xiaoping's tutelage in 1978, were a necessary condition for China's rise. The state's stranglehold on the economy loosened, and Chinese entrepreneurship flourished. But as China shifted from its pursuit of economic development for its own sake to competing for influence with the United States, China's economic engagement took on a strategic nature. China joined international institutions like the WTO to fuel its rise and simultaneously to reassure countries of its peaceful intentions. It emulated the United States, paying lip service to the tenets of free trade even as it pursued preferential policies at home. Beijing negotiated a record number of bilateral FTAs and is currently pushing its own regional trade pacts, in contrast to the United States' inability to pen new trade deals in the region.

Nothing about this meteoric rise was guaranteed. Indeed, the past thirty years have seen numerous predictions about the demise of the Chinese economy. From the 1990s to the early 2000s, the "China collapse" theory gained traction: economists pointed to inefficient SOEs and increased competition after SOE accession, which would lead to bankruptcy and problems with the banking sector overall.[135] In the 2010s, corruption, lack of rule of law, rising wages, and large government debt caused many to worry that China's economic rise was over.[136] Other economists believed that China's economy was unlikely to collapse given its government's strong control of economic policy, property markets, and the banking system, but that a serious slowdown was inevitable.[137]

Despite all these domestic issues, China's upstart approach has afforded China a great deal of economic power, as many countries, companies, and individuals have come to depend on the Chinese market for their prosperity. China has leveraged this advantage to make economic gains, like its attempts to unseat the dollar in international finance, but also to achieve strategic victories, like the use of economic sanctions to punish countries that oppose China's political interests.

China's attempts to emulate and exploit gaps are not the whole story. In Chapter 7, I present examples of the third component of the upstart strategy—China's use of economic tools in entrepreneurial ways to compete on alternative pathways to power. The main cases, industrial policy like

Made in China 2025 and financial development assistance through policies such as BRI, mark clear attempts to gain asymmetric advantages and achieve global economic dominance. Still, as we will see, recognition of the threat has been slow and the international response insufficient, largely because of the entrepreneurial nature of these policies.

7

Entrepreneurship in Chinese Economic Policy

Before China set out to become a great power, its global economic objectives were straightforward—to build international economic relationships that would support a high growth rate at home. But by the 2000s, Beijing was considering how to use economic tools to achieve some of its broader strategic objectives.[1] For the CCP, building a "well-off" society would serve the dual purposes of maintaining power at home and creating a global power base to become a "modern great power."[2] At this point, China's economic strategy became "guided by the ambition of a great power, based on the strength of a great power, and with the fundamental goal of obtaining or maintaining the status of a great power."[3]

As described in Chapter 6, some of China's approaches emulated those of the United States, which provided the veneer of a cooperative, responsible China. Indeed, one prominent US scholar concluded in 2019 that most indicators showed China slowly but surely continuing to integrate its economy into the global order.[4] In some circles, the view persists that China is the primary beneficiary of the current international system and thus would not risk disrupting it.[5]

But one of the benefits of the upstart strategy is that China can have it both ways—it can emulate to benefit from the system, exploit gaps to get a leg up, and do things differently to create a power base independent of the United States, all while minimizing backlash. In this chapter, I show that in some cases of economic policy, entrepreneurial approaches were warranted. Chinese leaders recognized that innovation was the engine for continued economic growth, but the laissez-faire US approach could threaten Party vested interests. China's leaders instead embraced industrial policy, which includes a push to become a technological superpower. This approach leverages China's competitive advantages as a capitalist authoritarian state that can direct massive economic resources to achieve its strategic objectives. And because China is not particularly well suited to emulating the US approach to foreign development assistance, it embraced development finance assistance instead with a focus on infrastructure, which better catered to its competitive advantages.

Creating National Winners: China's Industrial Policy

Technological advancement and innovation lie at the heart of the US success story. As the United States emerged from WWII, its technological enterprise allowed for a "period of unchallenged US economic and commercial technological preeminence."[6] The federal government's unprecedented mobilization of R&D during WWII, including with the creation of the Office of Scientific Research and Development (OSRD), resulted in a more than twofold increase in spending on scientific research as compared to the prewar period. This wartime investment has been directly tied to the United States' technological dominance in the decades following the war, as US patenting in OSRD-supported areas was over 50 percent higher than in Great Britain and France by 1970.[7]

These federal investments spurred crucial innovations in nuclear weapons, missile technologies, precision munitions, computing and the internet, and stealth technologies that fueled US hard power throughout the Cold War.[8] The United States' technological enterprise was similarly central to US dominance, considering that "as much as half of post–World War II economic growth is due to R&D-fueled technological progress."[9] Of the top fifty tech companies in the world, US companies make up 85 percent of the total by market capitalization (about $15 trillion out of $17 trillion). Chinese companies, in second place, make up only 5.36 percent.[10]

The United States achieved all this with a relatively laissez-faire free market approach. It never formed a national development bank, a large state-owned equity investment fund, national indicative plans, or a Ministry of Industry. This was partly because the United States never had a need to establish a development state, but also because allowing the government to pick winners and confer unfair advantages on them is anathema to American culture. The US government is not completely uninvolved; it takes certain measures to promote economic growth and ensure American competitiveness. It does so mainly by providing tax incentives for companies to invest in R&D and making its own investments in promising technologies, especially in the defense sector (where 50–60 percent of federal research spending goes). Federal spending, however, is still far less than private sector spending; for example, in 2019 federal R&D spending was $134 billion (about half was distributed to businesses, higher education, and nonprofit institutions), whereas the private sector invested approximately $480 billion.[11]

Chinese leaders understood that innovation was necessary if China was to become a great power.[12] State media took to analyzing how a lack of technological innovation was hampering China's economic growth. Some articles pointed out that China had "dazzling" rankings in terms of GDP, foreign trade, and output of major industrial products, but it lagged far behind Western countries in terms of technological innovation.[13] Xi, for his part, believed that innovation was necessary to modernize a country with a population of more than 1 billion people, which put pressure on resources and the environment.[14] Whether in the global marketplace or on the battlefield, China would need to be at the forefront of designing, adapting, and employing new technologies against its adversaries.[15] As Xi has said, "The country is only strong when science and technology are strong."[16] He wants China to become more "competitive" and "resistant,"[17] but was concerned, as he told the Central Committee in 2015, that

China's innovation capability is not strong, the level of technology is in general not high, science and technology does not provide strong support to economic and social development, and the contribution of science and technology to economic growth is far lower than that of developed countries. This is the Achilles heel of China as an economic giant. The new technological revolution will bring more fierce technological competition, and we will be at a disadvantage in global economic competition if we fail in technology innovation.[18]

He elaborated further on the connection between innovation and great power status in a speech at a plenum conference with his colleagues in the Central Committee of the Party:

Disruptive technologies are constantly springing up, and they are reshaping the world's competitive playing field and altering the relative strength of nations. . . . China faces both historical opportunities for catching up and forbidding challenges from growing gaps. It is only by bravely setting the world trends in technological innovation that a country can gain the initiative in development and make a greater contribution to the advancement of human civilization.[19]

With these goals in mind, Xi laid out three milestones for China's innovation environment: (1) by 2020, become an "innovation-oriented" country; (2) by 2030, be ranked among the leading innovation-oriented countries; and (3) by 2050, be an established global science and technology (S&T) innovation superpower.[20]

But domestic political considerations, especially China's particular competitive advantages and the need to maintain Party control, made emulation of the United States' laissez-faire approach unattractive. The Communist Party wanted to maintain firm control over the development of the economy and the activities of its people.[21] The rise of entrepreneurs who derived their power from independent success, rather than from a Party- or state-sanctioned position, could pose a threat. Xi has recently clamped down on this entrepreneurial class; when Jack Ma complained publicly about how government regulators interfered in innovation, the initial public offering (IPO) of his Ant Group, an Alibaba affiliate, was canceled and he was forced to flee the country.[22] China is also at a disadvantage in a free market competition: the United States' democratic system of governance, coupled with its individualistic culture, encourages innovation in a way that China's communist, state-led, top-down system simply cannot.[23]

Chinese leaders knew, though, that China possessed advantages it could leverage with a different entrepreneurial approach. The country is organized well for state-directed economic initiatives. Since the government owns all of the land in China, for instance, it can sell it at preferential prices to firms in favored industries. The most innovative of its industrial policy tools are the government guidance funds (GGFs), market-oriented public-private equity funds ($820 billion dedicated by the end of 2020) that are managed professionally but controlled by the Chinese government.[24] These funds, the first of which launched in 2002, purchase stakes in promising enterprises, using their ownership position to guide the company's activities in ways that suit the government's vision.[25] The central planning approach is also integral to the communist system. Since the founding of the PRC, the CCP has issued five-year plans (FYPs) to guide the country toward goals that match the leadership's strategic vision.

To leverage these advantages and protect Party control while promoting innovation, China decided on the strategy of industrial policy. Industrial policy is "any type of selective, targeted government intervention that attempts to alter the sectoral structure of production toward sectors that are expected to offer better growth than would occur in the (non-interventionist) market equilibrium."[26] China initially did not have an industrial policy, using for the most part a light touch to encourage industries like nuclear power and civilian aircraft.[27] But in the early 2000s, under the premiership of Wen Jiabao, China began to identify and support key future industries.[28] The Medium- and Long-Term Program of Science and Technology (MLP), to which most of China's current industrial policy can trace its roots, was released in 2006. It was intended to achieve a leap in the quality of production and sustainable economic growth by relying on advancement in S&T.[29] The MLP took a "top and bottom" approach, in which the government defined some high-level objectives and combined them with funding for individual projects (which eventually resulted in the Megaprojects, rolled out in 2007–2008; thirteen are publicly known).

The 2008 financial crisis gave Chinese leaders a unique opportunity at home and abroad to take its industrial policy to the next level. Under the leadership of Hu Jintao and Wen Jiabao, a group of industrial policy advocates had come to dominate the highest levels of economic policymaking.[30] The financial crisis had hurt the Chinese economy, and Party leaders decided to enact a massive stimulus program to save China's economy. After recovery, instead of pulling back government support, they doubled down, resulting in a new wave of industrial policy in the 2009 Strategic Emerging Industries (SEI) plan. Through this plan, the government sought to promote key industries that lay at the forefront of technological innovation, including biotechnology, information technology, and new energy vehicles.[31]

When Xi Jinping rose to power in 2012, it was common knowledge that China was still behind technologically. China stood at the lower end of the value-added chain, and its advanced technology industries were underdeveloped compared to those of the United States, Japan, and Europe. A 2012 OECD report on China's place within global value chains assessed that China was heavily dependent on the import of intermediate goods, which it assembled into higher-quality products and reexported.[32] China's primary role within the global high-technology value chain was essentially that of an assembly area.

To deal with these perceived weaknesses, China launched a new wave of industrial policy in 2015. It focused on emerging technologies and placed a premium on innovation-led growth, factors that distinguished it from earlier iterations.[33] It featured several new Xi initiatives, of which Made in China 2025 is the best known. Made in China 2025 proposes a three-step strategy to turn China into a "leading manufacturing power by the year 2049" by improving or upgrading China's industrial base in ten key sectors in order to "improve its ability to innovate and grasp these cutting-edge technologies."[34] In 2016, China's leaders introduced the Innovation-Driven Development Strategy, an overarching vision for uniting China's industrial policy to promote the country's innovative capabilities. Since its introduction, those leaders have continuously emphasized innovation's centrality to China's development. Xi praised innovation as the first driving force for national development, vowing to realize autonomy and self-reliance in S&T. Li Keqiang mentioned innovation thirty-four times in his 2023 government work report, declaring that China should rely on innovation to promote the development of the real economy and gain momentum for economic growth, as well as to cope with external suppression and containment (presumably generated by the United States).[35] Table 7.1 captures the sectors the Chinese government sought to develop under each initiative.

These plans revealed the geopolitical nature of China's drive for innovation. In addition to pushing for domestic economic growth, Beijing wanted to end the country's dependence on foreign powers for access to certain technologies. Lack of innovation in these "stranglehold" technologies would hold back China's development, and foreign powers' dominance in these areas could be used to constrain China's growth.[36] In the 14th Five-Year Plan for 2021–2025, China's state planners introduced the goal of "dual circulation," according to which China relies on its large domestic market to maintain the basic functioning of its economy, while at the same time remaining connected to international markets through international trade and investment. This strategy requires that China's "domestic circulation" be immune to external fluctuations and shocks while Beijing uses "international circulation" to make itself indispensable to the outside world. As Xi Jinping explained in a speech to the CCP's Central Financial and Economic Affairs Commission in 2020, China "must tighten international production chains' dependence on China, forming powerful countermeasures and deterrent capabilities against foreigners artificially cutting off supplies."[37] The idea is that the more reliant the world is on China, the less likely countries will be to join an anti-China coalition.[38]

To develop the strategic sectors laid out in the major industrial policy drives, China has used two main tools: direct subsidies to firms and

Table 7.1 China's Major Industrial Policy Drives

Megaprojects[a]	Strategic Emerging Industries[b]	Made in China 2025[c]
1. Water pollution and treatment	*Energy conservation and environment protection*	1. New information technology
2. ULSI semiconductor manufacturing	a. Energy-efficient machinery	2. High-end numerically controlled machine tools and robots
3. Next-gen broadband wireless	b. Environment protection	3. Aerospace equipment
4. Core electronics and high-end software	c. Recycling and reutilization	4. Ocean engineering equipment and high-end vessels
5. Major new drug initiative	*Next-gen information technology*	5. High-end rail transportation equipment
6. Major infectious disease initiative	d. Next-generation internet	6. Energy-saving cars and new-energy cars
7. Genetic transformation and plant breeding	e. Core electronic components	7. Electrical equipment
8. Large passenger aircraft	f. High-end software, info services	8. Farming machines
9. High-resolution earth monitoring system	*Biotechnology*	9. New materials, such as polymers
10. Manned space flight and lunar landing	g. Biopharmaceuticals	10. Bio-medicine and high-end medical equipment
11. High-end numerically controlled machine tools	h. Biomedical engineering	
12. Large-bed oil and gas; coal gasification	i. Biological agriculture	
13. Large high-pressure nuclear reactor	j. Bio-manufacturing industry	
	Precision and high-end machinery	
	k. Commercial aircraft	
	l. Satellites and applications	
	m. Railroad, transport machinery	
	n. Marine engineering equipment	
	Intelligence manufacturing equipment	
	New energy	
	o. Wind power	
	p. Solar power	
	q. Biomass energy	
	New Materials	
	r. New materials	
	New Energy Vehicles	
	s. Electric vehicles, plug-in hybrids	

Source: Data from Barry Naughton, The Rise of China's Industrial Policy: 1978 to 2020 *(Mexico City: Catedra Mexico-China, 2021), 54–57; State Council of the People's Republic of China [*中华人民共和国国务院*], "Made in China 2025 [*中国制造2025*]," May 8, 2015, http://www.gov.cn/zhengce/content/2015-05/19/content_9784.htm; "The 13th FYP National Strategic Emerging Industry Development Plan [*十三五国家战略性新兴产业发展规划*]," State Council of the People's Republic of China [*中华人民共和国国务院*], November 29, 2016, http://www.gov.cn/zhengce/content/2016-12/19/content_5150090.htm.*

[a] Naughton, *The Rise of China's Industrial Policy*, 54–57.
[b] *The 13th FYP National Strategic Emerging Industry Development Plan* ["十三五"国家战略性新兴产业发展规划], The State Council of the People's Republic of China [中华人民共和国国务院], November 29, 2016, http://www.gov.cn/zhengce/content/2016-12/19/content_5150090.htm.
[c] The State Council of the People's Republic of China [中华人民共和国国务院], Made in China 2025, [中国制造2025] May 8, 2015, http://www.gov.cn/zhengce/content/2015-05/19/content_9784.htm.

below-market credit to SOEs. Providing direct subsidies is hardly an innovative approach, but China has employed it on a scale that is exceptional (in 2019, China spent US $53 billion compared to the United States' expenditure of $2.895 billion). The biggest beneficiaries of subsidies are firms in software, technology hardware, automobiles, transportation, and semiconductors. Still, the major difference between the approaches of the United States and China lies in the provision of below-market credit. Whereas the United States provided about $400 million in such support in 2019, China provided $74 billion.[39]

Chinese government intervention also helps to keep prices low for key commodities and inputs, which allows Chinese companies to be more competitive than their foreign counterparts. For example, lower steel prices in China (a sector dominated by SOEs) have helped Chinese wind turbine producers sell turbines at half the global average price. This, coupled with the fact that China can leverage domestic demand (it has been the largest consumer of onshore wind energy since 2011), has allowed China to dominate wind energy markets since 2021.[40]

While China's approach does not emulate that of the United States, some aspects of its approach evoke the Asian miracle economies' "catch-up" strategies, which involved developing expertise in established fields and technologies. The classic examples are the Asian Tigers: Hong Kong, Singapore, South Korea, and Taiwan. Although Chinese official media and policy documents rarely allude to following in these countries' footsteps, there is evidence that Chinese strategists have studied them.[41] But the nature and degree of Chinese intervention far supersedes these examples. In 2019, for example, the Chinese government spent 1.71 trillion yuan, or 1.73 percent of GDP, to support industries.[42] The next-highest spender as a percentage of GDP is Korea, which spent less than half as much as China at 0.67 percent of its GDP. And in nominal terms, China's $248 billion dwarfs the next-highest absolute spender, the United States, which spent only $83 billion in the same period.

Two unofficial but equally important tools unique to China's industrial policy are forced technology transfers and cyber-enabled commercial espionage. To do business in China, foreign companies must often enter joint ventures with a Chinese counterpart, and they are usually prevented from holding a controlling interest in such ventures. The Chinese government also routinely pressures foreign companies into handing over sensitive technology to the Chinese partner.[43] China allows access to its immense market based on how much technology a company is willing to share with its Chinese partners.[44] According to the Defense Innovation Unit, Chinese entities financed a notable percentage (10 to 16 percent) of all venture capital deals between 2015 and 2017, many of which came with board representation and potential technology transfer agreements.[45]

China has initiatives, like the Thousand Talents program, that not only encourage Chinese nationals with relevant expertise to return to China but also target international researchers and scientific experts who are renowned in their respective fields. To entice these individuals, attractive salaries, research funding, and other incentives are offered, with the expectation that the recipients will contribute openly or covertly to enhancing China's R&D capabilities. Accepting funding can entail contractual obligations to comply with directives from the Chinese government, which may involve engaging in illicit activities such as intellectual property theft and technology transfer to China.[46]

For decades, Chinese government and government-backed actors have hacked into companies around the world to steal sensitive technological information.[47] According to the Office of the US Trade Representative, these hacks have given China access to "a wide range of confidential business information, including trade secrets, technical data, negotiating positions, and sensitive and proprietary internal communications."[48] Despite China's repeated commitments to discontinue both tech transfers and cyber theft, such activities persist.[49] A 2013 study estimated that intellectual property theft cost the US economy over $300 billion annually, and China likely accounted for between 50 and 80 percent of that total.[50] When surveyed in 2022, American companies still ranked cyber theft as one of the five biggest challenges facing their China operations, behind US–China tensions, inconsistent regulation and enforcement, rising labor costs, and regulatory compliance risks.[51]

It is undeniable that China has achieved an impressive level of innovation thanks in part to its industrial policy. An analysis by the US think tank Information Technology and Innovation Foundation found that China had boosted its "innovation and advanced-industry capabilities" to nearly 75 percent of US levels in 2020 compared to 58 percent in 2010.[52] China is still behind the United States in eleventh place, but it has moved up from its original twenty-ninth place in 2007.[53] And while the United States remains the top destination for foreign direct investment (FDI), China's status here has improved as well, from 7 percent of the US total in 1990 to 58 percent in 2022.[54] China also publishes more scientific papers, creates more patents, and trains more scientists every year than the United States.[55] Although these comparisons are not a perfect metric, they indicate a huge improvement over the late 1990s, when China produced only 3.2 percent of the world's scientific papers and only 1.8 percent of the top-cited papers.[56] According to the Rhodium Group's annual Pathfinder Report, China's innovation system outperforms that of countries like Canada, Italy, and Spain.[57] The Global Innovation Index, an index of a country's innovation capabilities developed by the World Intellectual Property Organization, placed China as the eleventh-most-innovative country in the world in 2022, ahead of Japan and Canada.[58]

China's industrial policy has also enabled Chinese companies to dominate in key sectors. China identified solar panels, for example, as a critical technological area. Since 2000, the Chinese government has introduced more than 100 policies to support the photovoltaic industry, among them releasing export credits, increasing investment in R&D, and establishing state-sponsored laboratories in several leading companies.[59] China invested over US $50 billion in new photovoltaic capacity—ten times more than Europe—and engaged in "dumping" of exports to the United States, meaning that Chinese companies sell panels at below-market prices to drive US competitors out of business.[60] The result is Chinese dominance of this industry. The world's ten top suppliers of solar PV manufacturing equipment are all located in China, and China dominates all manufacturing stages of solar panels.[61]

China has also seen success in its concerted effort to dominate the electric vehicles (EV) industry. In the early 2000s, despite a robust auto industry, Chinese companies could not compete internationally due to "poor product quality and the failure . . . to meet safety and emissions requirements."[62] Through a combination of government support, innovation, and an enormous manufacturing base, China moved from producing 33 percent of the world's battery-electric vehicles (BEVs) in 2014 to producing 59 percent in 2021. China's production of BEVs was more than double Europe's and almost five times that of the United States.[63] Figure 7.1 shows how China has leapt ahead after starting from the same point as the United States and Europe.

China is also investing abroad to lock up key sectors of the clean-energy supply chain.[64] Take nickel as an example. China already dominates the processing of nickel, a mineral used in the production of batteries in EVs (estimates of how much of the world's processing takes place in China vary from one-third to three-quarters). Additionally, most nickel processing that takes place outside China is dominated by Chinese firms.[65] As demand

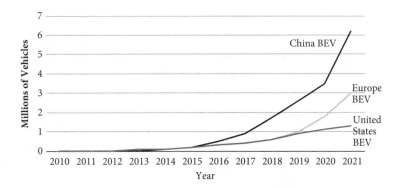

Figure 7.1 Battery-Electric Vehicle Production, 2010–2021

Source: Data from "Global Electric Car Stock, 2010–2021," International Energy Agency, May 23, 2022, https://www.iea.org/data-and-statistics/charts/global-electric-car-stock-2010–2021.

for EVs explodes over the coming decades, therefore, China has already positioned itself well for the future.

China is also giving US companies a run for their money in 5G telecommunications technology with its entrepreneurial approach to innovation. The Chinese government has been deliberate in its development of this industry; indeed, telecommunications has been featured in every major industrial policy document since 2006.[66] All of China's major telecommunications companies are state-owned, and they have been directed to invest heavily in telecommunications: $100 billion in 4G technology from 2013 to 2018, with $150 billion due to be invested in 5G technology through 2025. China has built ten times as many 5G base stations as the United States, and Chinese phones enjoyed average 5G speeds nearly four times as fast as those of the average US 5G user.[67] As a Pentagon report notes, China's first-mover advantage and aggressive pursuit of global 5G leadership "will allow China to promote its preferred standards and specifications for 5G networks and will shape the global 5G product market going forward."[68]

While China has seen great successes with its industrial policy, the state-directed approach has not been able to guarantee innovation in all sectors. China has struggled to produce state-of-the-art semiconductors, the fourth-most-traded product in the world, for which China is the largest market.[69] This is not for a lack of trying. Chinese leaders recognize that semiconductors are critical to future innovations, such as mobile devices, electric and self-driving cars, 5G internet, and AI.[70] Information technology was the first of the ten key technological areas in which Made in China 2025 outlined

China's plan to become a world leader by 2030.[71] The 13th FYP for 2016–2020 called for efforts to focus on memory boards and semiconductors, as these are areas where China is most dependent on the United States.[72] Xi even brought greater national attention to the industry when he called for the enhancement of China's "innovation engine" in 2020.[73] Washington's sanction of Huawei in 2020 (prohibiting the company from purchasing important American technology) and 2022 passage of the CHIPS and Science Act (prohibiting federally funded companies from producing advanced semiconductors in mainland China) added urgency to China's search for self-sufficiency in semiconductors.[74]

China adopted a variety of measures to support its semiconductor industry, including tax breaks, below-market land sales, and government-funded debt financing.[75] Three Chinese companies (Tsinghua Unigroup, Semiconductor Manufacturing International Corporation [SMIC], and Jiangsu Changjiang Electronic Tech [JCET]) are the largest beneficiaries in the world of government-funded debt financing, together receiving nearly $5 billion in 2014–2018. In September 2014, the Chinese government launched the National Integrated Circuit Fund, the largest and most important of the GGFs. Endowed with $21 billion in start-up capital, the fund seeks to invest in and acquire foreign integrated circuit (IC) companies. It has also used that immense sum to encourage FDI in China and joint partnerships with foreign companies.[76] In December 2022, Reuters reported that China was preparing to support its chipmaking industry with a massive $143 billion package.[77] Chinese companies have also tried to buy up foreign companies to access their proprietary technology and have even sent in spies to steal trade secrets.[78]

But for all its investment, China has so far largely failed to achieve competitiveness in this critical industry. China's share of global semiconductor sales stood at 7.6 percent in 2021, up from about 5 percent when the fund was launched, and its companies remain "notably absent" from the higher-end devices.[79] China's first successful company, SMIC, still lags behind competitors like Taiwan Semiconductor Manufacturing Company (TSMC) in producing the most advanced chips. While the United States also trails its competitors in chip production, its companies design some of the world's leading-edge computer chips and dominate the market for chipmaking software, equipment, and components.[80] Even though China is behind, the government's support of the industry coupled with its Military-Civil Fusion program has allowed Chinese companies to make progress in supercomputing and develop military-grade graphical processing unit (GPU) designs for radar and satellite applications.[81]

China has had greater success in the related industry of AI, but the results have been mixed.[82] The Chinese government believes that AI is central to the development strategies of major countries. AI is described as "the engine of a new round of industrial transformation" that will fundamentally define a country's international competitiveness.[83] Xi Jinping characterizes AI as a strategic technology that leads today's scientific revolution and a strong innovative impetus that creates spillover benefits in many other industries.[84] Chinese military experts believe that AI not only has increasing applications in military affairs but will also shift the form of future warfare.[85] In July 2017, China's State Council issued the New Generation Artificial Intelligence Development Plan (AIDP), which alongside the Made in China 2025 document forms the core of China's AI strategy, whose aim is to make China a global leader in AI technology and reduce dependence on foreign imports.[86]

China has several strengths in AI, which rests on a triad of computing power, data, and algorithms. AI engineers must design algorithms that run on extremely powerful computers to crunch massive amounts of data. Although China has struggled to produce the chips that power these algorithms, its researchers have had great success in designing algorithms and using them on huge datasets to produce effective AI models. In March 2017, Baidu established China's National Engineering Laboratory for Deep Learning Technology. Alibaba Cloud (Aliyun) is concentrating on smart cities, Tencent on medical imaging, and iFlytek on smart voice technologies. It is worth noting that these open and shared resources may also be accessible to military end users.[87]

In sum, because of China's closed political system, the US free market approach to promoting innovation was largely unavailable to Beijing. By pursuing a different pathway, China has been relatively successful in building technological and economic power despite its political limitations. China will continue with its state-driven industrial policy in its effort to become an economic and technological superpower. Over the next decade, China wants to reduce its dependence on foreign technology by advancing domestic production before eventually dominating the international market with Chinese-developed technologies. China continues to heavily invest in the manufacture of computers, communication and other electronic equipment, electrical machinery, automobiles, and general purpose and special purpose machinery, all to become a global leader in the manufacturing of high-quality and high-technology products.[88] But at the same time, the CCP is not ceding control. In March 2023, the Party created the Central Science and Technology Commission (CSTC) to guide China's innovation and dual-use technology efforts.[89]

Of course, it is possible (or likely) that if China had emulated the US approach, it would have fared even better. While China has succeeded in dominating many industries, it has underperformed in some areas. China relies on imported technologies in over thirty essential fields, such as heavy-duty gas turbines, core industrial software, and photolithography machines.[90] It appears that from the Party's perspective any marginal benefits in terms of innovation would not be worth the marginal loss in control. The Party insists on having representatives present in every company with more than fifty employees. This culture of top-down surveillance, combined with the Party's deep fear of disruptive change, likely smothers some ideas. Additionally, the Party rewards incremental progress rather than encouraging paradigm-shifting inventions, which may prevent China from making world-changing inventions.[91] The reason for control is not wholly political. Chinese leaders want to stabilize the economy, and monopolistic behavior by technology giants engenders financial risk. But the Party has also sought to reorient Chinese companies' investment and effort toward innovation areas that are more in line with the Party's strategic goals.[92]

Chinese "Foreign Aid and Development Assistance"

China's economic reach becomes vividly clear as one travels around the world, especially in Asia and Africa. Buildings in Ethiopia are covered with the signs of Chinese construction companies. The new roads in Central Asia testify to China's pervasive presence. In oil-rich countries along the Persian Gulf, Chinese-funded pipelines funnel crude to similarly financed ports, to be loaded onto tankers bound for Ningbo and Qingdao. Chinese companies have built new electric railways in two strategically located neighbors, Djibouti and Ethiopia.

On the surface, China seems to have taken a page from the US playbook. Foreign development assistance has for decades been an essential instrument of US foreign policy. From the earliest days of the Cold War, the United States used economic aid as a tool to shape the world order. The Marshall Plan, which allocated nearly $150 billion in today's money to sixteen European countries, was predicated on the idea that Europe needed substantial additional economic help to create "the political and social conditions in which free institutions [could] exist."[93] The United States has continued this tradition of promoting economic development for geopolitical motives; indeed, countries serving their two-year term on the UNSC experience an uptick in the amount of US aid they receive.[94]

US development assistance is primarily administered by USAID, which was created by the 1961 Foreign Assistance Act.[95] It covers a wide range of areas, with about a third spent on humanitarian programs, a third on health programs, a fourth on governance programs, and the remainder on administrative, agricultural, educational, and other types of programs. While these funds are spent in all corners of the globe, the bulk is dedicated to sub-Saharan Africa (31.4 percent) or Europe and Eurasia (26.3 percent).[96] While USAID upholds democratic governance and human rights as crucial to lasting development, democratization and a solid human rights record are by no means a prerequisite for receiving aid.[97]

Several factors discouraged China from emulating the US approach to building influence through development assistance. First, China had fewer economic resources than the United States. In 1994, when it established its first policy bank, Import-Export Bank, its economy was less than a tenth the size of that of the United States, and nearly two-thirds of its population still lived on less than the World Bank's poverty line of $2.15 per day.[98] Because China was operating at a competitive disadvantage, emulating the US approach was unlikely to be strategically effective or efficient.

Domestic conditions pushed China even further from emulation. Given that China was still a developing country, the idea of foreign aid was problematic at home. Critics argued that foreign aid prioritizes the welfare of foreigners over that of Chinese citizens. Even in an environment of tight media control, Chinese citizens have been known to criticize any instance of the Chinese government forgiving foreign debt and providing non-reimbursable assistance.[99] Indeed, the amount the Chinese government gives to other countries was a state secret until 2010. In 2011, China began publishing White Papers on its foreign aid and development assistance (others followed in 2014 and 2021), but Beijing keeps the specifics of its programs strictly confidential.[100]

It was also unclear whether emulating would be reassuring to the United States. The cases of the Soviet Union and later Japan demonstrate that direct competition even in development assistance can be perceived as threatening. Soviet development aid began under Khrushchev, who believed that by giving economic aid to newly independent countries, such as India, the Soviet Union could control the new country's foreign trade and thus encourage the new country to adopt socialism.[101] US analysts saw this Soviet foray into foreign aid as extremely threatening because they worried that Russia's lack of a history of colonialism in South and Southeast Asia or the Middle East gave it an advantage over the West when it came to penetrating the underdeveloped nations.[102] Similarly, in the 1980s, when Tokyo became the leading provider of aid to twenty-five nations in the developing world, many in the United States viewed Japan's aid program with suspicion.[103]

Indeed, when China did emulate a component of the US strategy by establishing its own oversight institution in the Asia Infrastructure Investment Bank in 2016, the United States viewed this action as a direct challenge to its global position.[104] The AIIB did lack some of the transparency and governance standards seen in the IMF and World Bank, but there were legitimate reasons to support it; Asian countries needed more infrastructure investment and it was better to have China spend the money through a multilateral institution.[105] But the United States refused to join because it thought the AIIB would diminish the influence of US-led institutions such as the Asian Development Bank and the World Bank and challenge American primacy in setting the rules of the "rules-based order."[106] Chinese finance minister Lou Jiwei tried to reassure the United States by arguing that the AIIB was a complement to these institutions rather than a competitor, because it focused on infrastructure rather than on social programs and general purpose loans.[107] He was unsuccessful: while most US allies joined the AIIB, which now has 106 members, the United States never did.[108]

Given that emulation would be of questionable effectiveness and was unlikely to reassure the United States, in the 2000s, China's leaders started to consider how to leverage foreign aid and development assistance differently.[109] Some sort of strategy seemed necessary, given that the provision of foreign assistance was thought to directly improve relations with other countries, encourage recipient countries to side with China in diplomatic disputes, and improve China's image across the world.[110]

Several factors shaped the contours of China's eventual approach. First, China wanted to ensure that any approach supported economic development at home (and thus would garner public support). At the time, the Party's enterprises were producing more supply than the levels of demand could justify. The Chinese government's stimulus package to boost economic activity after the 2008 financial crisis only exacerbated this issue. The country faced severe problems of overcapacity (i.e., the production of far more of a good than the market can absorb) in its heavy industry sectors like steel and concrete. But reforming those SOE-dominated sectors would be politically costly, as it would require huge layoffs. Lending money abroad to help countries pay for Chinese infrastructure was not a long-term solution, but it did provide a way to stave off these painful reforms.[111] Additionally, years of running a trade surplus with the United States had left China with massive foreign exchange reserves and not much to spend them on, allowing it to finance projects that its own companies would then implement.[112] Investing in critical infrastructure such as railways, roads, airports, and maritime corridors would enhance connectivity and thus boost China's economy.[113]

It also behooved the Party to leverage certain competitive advantages stemming from China's political and economic system. First, state-directed approaches suit China's centralized and state-dominated economic system, which is poised to coordinate large-scale investments.[114] Second, Chinese companies had the productive power and experience to build infrastructure quickly and at low cost. One McKinsey & Company analysis found that China poured 8.5 percent of its GDP into infrastructure between 1992 and 2011, exceeding the industrialized economy average of 5.0 percent.[115] The massive SOEs that were behind those investments in areas like steel, concrete, and rail combined the massive funding provided by the state with significant expertise gained through decades of the world's most intensive infrastructure projects.[116]

Lastly, Chinese leaders believed they had something to offer the developing world. From the Chinese perspective, their approach to poverty reduction has been very effective, especially at home.[117] Western aid, in contrast, is thought to be based on modernization theory, which Chinese analysts do not think accords with the real experiences and situations of developing countries.[118] Chinese thinkers believe their country is uniquely suited to provide this expertise, and the lack of emphasis on political structure and liberalization is thought to be suitable for developing countries.[119] They also suggest that China's recent experience of pulling itself out of poverty through infrastructure, investment, and heavy industry gives China an advantage over the West, where the service sector and knowledge economies now reign.[120]

The result was an entrepreneurial approach to gaining influence and power in a way that exploited the aforementioned competitive advantages and mitigated the domestic political risks. Providing development finance assistance for infrastructure, largely through BRI, would create new markets for Chinese goods and help alleviate the country's domestic overcapacity problems.[121]

China's development finance assistance is different from US official ODA, which is defined as government aid that promotes and specifically targets the economic development and welfare of developing countries.[122] In the Western context, aid refers to finance with highly concessional terms, such as zero- or low-interest loans meant for development purposes. First, Chinese "aid" is more accurately described as debt, as it usually carries higher interest rates than its Western counterparts and many of the projects China funds are not explicitly intended for development. For example, the average "grant element" (a measure that captures the generosity of lending) of a Chinese state-backed loan was only 28 percent between 2000 and 2017, compared with OECD countries' 64 percent.[123] Chinese sources recognize that the United States uses traditional ODA as the main category of aid funds, while China complements a small amount of traditional ODA with large amounts of other official flows (OOF).[124] Since the advent of the BRI, China has maintained a 31:1 ratio of loans to grants and a 9:1 ratio of OOF to ODA.[125] Between 2000 and 2017, China's ODA spending amounted to only US $101 billion, with its OOF at over $680 billion.[126]

Second, compared to Western aid, Chinese loans more often come with collateralization terms, according to which the borrowing nation puts up some sort of collateral if it cannot pay China back. For example, China can claim the revenue gained from the natural resource itself as a form of payment, as in the case of oil-rich Angola, or a port, as in the case of Sri Lanka.[127] Indeed, China intends to generate an economic return on its investments, whereas US aid programs do not include an explicit profit motive and focus more on promoting democracy, human rights, and good governance. In 2016, for instance, a Chinese official stated anonymously that China needed to fund projects that would return a profit—hardly the statement of an altruistic lender.[128] One of the main providers of Chinese state-backed financing is the Export-Import Bank, created in large part to help Chinese enterprises boost their exports abroad.

Third, China provides funding for projects that the United States does not fund. Most of China's development finance spending is directed to least developed countries (LDCs) in Africa and Asia and focuses on building infrastructure, an area in which China is competitive.[129] For example, between 2005 and 2019, China signed 544 construction contracts worth $267.7 billion with African nations, constituting one-third of the net value of China's construction projects around the world.[130] The areas the two countries fund are also different; the US State Department lists the United States' top foreign aid priorities for the 2013–2017 period as emergency response, HIV/AIDS, and government and civil society.[131] The top three priorities in the approximately $30 billion USAID budget request are areas that China is not interested in funding: fighting corruption, reinvigorating democracy and human rights, and providing tools to push back against digital repression and disinformation used by authoritarians.[132] Figure 7.2 shows how China's development financing to each region has fluctuated over the years.

Fourth, China's approach to development finance spending is distinct because it ostensibly comes with no strings attached (or at least fewer political strings). Western-led initiatives attach conditions relating to accountability and transparency and impose stricter lending standards (including debt relief and forgiveness measures). Beijing, meanwhile, places little emphasis on recipients' domestic governance, and Chinese analysts typically claim that this choice is due to respect for people's economic livelihoods.[133] Top leadership speeches and other official sources continue to emphasize that China's

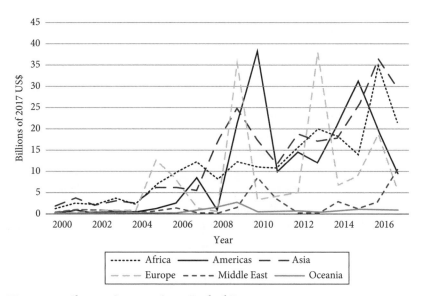

Figure 7.2 Chinese Overseas State-Backed Financing, 2000–2017

Source: Data from Samantha Custer et al., "Tracking Development Finance: An Application of AidData's TUFF 2.0 Methodology," AidData, 2021, https://www.aiddata.org/data/aiddatas-global-chinese-development-finance-dataset-version-2-0.

approach is a uniquely non-ideological way of promoting economic globalization and fostering multilateralism.[134]

Fifth, the sheer scale of China's funding puts it in a league of its own. China's foray into development finance assistance began with its 1999 Going Out policy, an explicit mandate for the PRC to invest US $3 trillion to promote Chinese investment overseas and expand its global economic influence. Since 2009, China has been the largest bilateral provider of development financing.[135] Before 2005, the United States' total development financing (ODA and OOF) dwarfed China's. But in 2009 China jumped ahead, lending over $100 billion compared to the United States' approximately $35 billion. China's state-backed financing (including both ODA and OOF) averaged about $85 billion from 2013 to 2017, meaning it outspent the United States and other major countries by a factor of two.[136] China's 2000–2018 provision of $104 billion in loans to low-income countries almost matched that of the World Bank at $106 billion.[137] China has pulled ahead in sub-Saharan Africa, lending out $66 billion to the World Bank's $62 billion. This is in large part because of Angola, which receives an outsized amount of China's aid due to its provision of oil to China.

These four components of the Chinese entrepreneurial approach to development assistance can be found in Xi Jinping's flagship BRI, launched in 2013. This was one of the first major efforts to systematically use China's newfound economic strength to build even more power and influence, especially in neighboring countries and across the developing world. The BRI seeks to connect China with the rest of the world, particularly countries in Africa and across the Eurasian landmass, to help China accomplish the dream of "great rejuvenation." The BRI's two main components are the Silk Road Economic Belt, which stretches across the Central Asian interior to terminate in the developed markets of Europe, and the Maritime Silk Road, intended to connect China via sea to critical markets in Southeast Asia, the Middle East, and Europe.[138] Beyond these two main components, the BRI includes efforts like the Digital Silk Road, which captures Chinese efforts to promote partner countries' telecommunications, computing, and other high-tech capabilities, and the Green Silk Road, a slogan intended to tie the BRI to environmentally friendly causes.

Has China's focus on development financial assistance mainly for infrastructure helped it rise to great power status? Many economists argue that the BRI has largely been a failure, associated with wasteful spending and capital flight. The program's scale has decreased dramatically over the past five years due to economic slowdown at home and pushback abroad, fueled by corruption scandals and financial difficulties in borrowing nations.

However, many critiques of China's approach are about its impact on other countries rather than on China itself. For example, economists argue that China's lending practices have contributed to debt crises in places like Sri Lanka and Zambia; forty-two countries now have levels of public debt exposure to China at more than 10 percent of GDP.[139] BRI projects seem to be the most problematic: 35 percent of the BRI infrastructure project portfolio has encountered major implementation problems, such as corruption scandals, labor violations, environmental hazards, and public protests, compared to 21 percent of the Chinese government's infrastructure portfolio outside the BRI.[140] Some places have seen a backlash against China; in many democracies the people have pushed back, leading to the election of candidates who are less enamored with Chinese aid.[141]

Even if China's assistance has led to more corruption and debt, it is less clear that this situation has reduced Chinese leverage and influence. China has successfully established itself as a financier of first resort for many low-income and middle-income countries (LMIC). Its projects provide support for its companies abroad and its attempts to internationalize the RMB.[142] For all the complaints, China has clearly identified a demand, and many countries are signing up to play a part. One analysis finds that a fully implemented BRI could reduce transport times and trade costs by 10 percent each and increase total world trade by upward of 6 percent.[143] A World Bank report similarly estimates that the initiative could raise global income by 0.7 percent by 2030 and "could contribute to lifting 7.6 million people from extreme poverty and 32 million from moderate poverty."[144] Regardless of the risks, countries are still interested in participating in the Chinese initiative. In 2022, nearly 80 percent of nations received Chinese financing (in the form of either grants or loans), and China's share of "total external debt among its 50 largest borrowers" had risen to above 40 percent on average.[145]

China may be providing aid with different goals in mind than helping other countries' economies grow. China planned to gain political support through economic assistance as an alternative to the US mode of creating alliances based on military or ideological standards, and it is undeniable that its influence has grown with its increased development financing.[146] Partner countries receiving Chinese aid must support Beijing's "One China policy" and oppose Taiwan's independence; they also tend to vote alongside Beijing in the United Nations General Assembly (UNGA). Research shows that

China allocates aid with good terms when it wants geopolitical returns, and it uses less concessional debt to finance projects it thinks will generate an economic return.[147] Chinese sources often note that the BRI, along with the AIIB, is meant to push for global rebalance and reform of the international financial order.[148] Indeed, Western countries have been reluctant to sign on to the BRI because it is obviously a tool to promote Chinese diplomatic clout.[149] The BRI, through regional integration, also helps China promote development in its western provincial regions by addressing concerns about instability and insurgency. Of the fourteen provinces in China targeted for the BRI, nine are western provincial regions.[150]

China has also used its influence with BRI countries, as well as the pull of its own economy, to influence global industrial standards in ways that enhance its companies' global competitiveness. In 2018, China launched the China Standards 2035 Plan, "aiming to create a blueprint for the Chinese government and leading tech companies to set global standards for emerging technologies, such as 5G, Internet of Things, and AI." Follow-on plans in 2021 and 2022 point to specific industries where Chinese companies should seek to promote "mutual recognition of Chinese and foreign standards" and designate specific government ministries to take charge of each effort.[151] While the United States has largely left standard setting to the commercial sector, the Chinese government ensures that its interests are represented at meetings of industry-related groups like the International Telecommunications Union.[152] Huawei, in particular, has spread its technological standards across large swaths of Eurasia and Africa by investing in 5G infrastructure, data centers, and smart cities.

China has also improved its access to the natural resources needed for its continued economic growth in part thanks to its development finance assistance strategy. It should come as no surprise that Russia, Venezuela, and Angola are the top three recipients of Chinese non-concessional financing, given that they are all major suppliers of oil to China.[153] China has been lending at relatively high interest rates of around 6 percent to resource-rich countries and then collateralizing loans with commodity receipts—if the country cannot pay, then China gets to keep whatever the resource earns via export.[154] The Maritime Silk Road and the building of commercial ports are designed to increase China's unfettered access to sea-lanes critical to China's energy imports, namely oil.[155] Notably, the first foreign port investment from the BRI was a $1.6 billion investment from Zhuhai Port Holdings in Gwadar Port (Pakistan).[156]

A decade after China became the world's number one provider of state-backed financing, the United States and its partners tried to come up with a way to compete. The first US attempt, the 2019 Blue Dot Network (BDN), brought together public, private, and civil society sectors to ensure that infrastructure projects complied with international standards of transparency, sustainability, and feasibility, thus attracting private investment to contend with Chinese state-backed financing.[157] The Biden administration's Build Back Better World (B3W) was more ambitious in its use of public funds, but both BDN and B3W failed to reach the scale of China's efforts. Moreover, although the emphasis on transparency and sustainability attracts some nations, the absence of these qualities is precisely why other countries choose to work with China in the first place.

In June 2022 the G7 rolled out the Partnership for Global Infrastructure and Investment, a repackaging of previous efforts. The participant countries hope to mobilize $600 billion for the partnership. But while the official readout expected the agreement to net over $200 billion in funding, the only specific projects listed were relatively small. The largest, a compact between Indonesia and the United States, contained only $650 million in US funding. In September 2022, the United States created the US-Pacific Partnership, which includes, among other initiatives, the promise of $810 million in funding for capacity-building programs in climate resilience, education, training for Pacific leaders, and law enforcement.[158]

China seems to be adjusting its approach in response to critiques and the new US focus. At the third Belt and Road Symposium in November 2021, Xi Jinping emphasized that future BRI projects should prioritize high-quality, "small and beautiful" projects.[159] Senior leaders are also stressing that China will promote post-pandemic economic recovery with a focus on people's livelihoods—poverty, unemployment, health, and education.[160] China seems to be pushing back against environmental complaints by committing to the Green Silk Road initiative, which includes assistance projects on climate change, clean energy, and ecological protection.[161] And China has tried to address debt-trap criticisms, for instance by forgiving in 2022 twenty-three loans to seventeen African nations.

But while Beijing is changing its approach, it is clearly not giving up on the broad strokes of its entrepreneurial approach. In 2017, the BRI was written into the CCP's charter as one of its pledges. In 2021, Xi Jinping launched the Global Development Initiative (GDI), a new effort related to the BRI.[162] Whereas the BRI was first and foremost an effort to shift China's excess supply out of the country, the GDI represents China's attempt to reshape the conversation about development writ large.[163] Hailed as the PRC's "prescription for global challenges," especially after the severe shocks brought about by the COVID-19 pandemic, GDI marks an important departure in China's approach to international development, clearly suggesting that Beijing has gained confidence on the global stage and wants to take the lead in this area.[164]

China's approach to innovation and economic ties with the developing world has diverged from the US model of free enterprise and foreign development assistance. Instead, China has tried to rely on its competitive advantages of large amounts of resources and an extensive state apparatus that has the ability and writ to allocate those resources strategically. As a result, China is becoming less reliant on the world, and the world is becoming more reliant on China. This has created unparalleled leverage for Beijing that the West is struggling to replicate. Even though the United States has found aspects of China's innovative approach to be problematic, entrepreneurship in the economic realm has not sparked the same degree of backlash as it would have in the military realm. China has also been careful to minimize threat perceptions even as its influence has grown; the fact that Latin America is not part of the BRI is a case in point.[165] China has thus been able to compete with the US global presence effectively and efficiently through the extension of its economic power.

Conclusion

Lessons for Great Power Competition

China's rise has fascinated observers for decades. Many books have been written about China's economic miracle.[1] But economic might is neither a prerequisite for great power status (as the experience of the Soviet Union testifies) nor a sufficient condition (see, for example, Japan in the 1980s). The rise to great power status requires a deliberate strategy to narrow the aspiring power's distance from the established great powers in terms of political, economic, and military power. Striving for mastery is a choice, and not all rising powers make that choice: some are happy to dominate in a narrower domain. This has clearly not been the case for China; it has employed an upstart strategy over the past thirty years to enable its rise to great power status.

By explaining how China builds power and which factors influence its choices, I provide insight into what China hopes to accomplish over the next ten years, whether Beijing will achieve its goals, and how the United States and its allies can best protect their interests. To that end, in this final chapter, I present the implications of my research for policy, offering specific and actionable recommendations for US policymakers. The upstart logic hints at what factors are likely to encourage Beijing to shift from one component of the strategy to another. I also lay out the contributions of the upstart strategy to international relations theory, which provides a framework to identify where the United States has competitive advantages and how to push the competition into these realms.

The Next Twenty Years of Chinese Strategy

Upstart provides a framework for understanding how China has managed to significantly close the gap with the United States over the past thirty years. A critical question for scholars and policymakers alike, however, is what the next thirty years will offer. The upstart framework provides a guide for analysts to interpret specific decisions by the Chinese government and understand the conditions under which China's strategy might change. What follows is a discussion of these conditions.

One of the main factors shaping Beijing's choice of components within the upstart strategy was its understanding of how the United States would interpret a particular strategy. This understanding led China to emulate when doing so would reassure the United States, and to be entrepreneurial when emulation was thought to challenge US interests too directly. The main motivation was the desire to avoid a strong response on the part of the United States.

After sidestepping the hegemon's core interests and accumulating enough power to deter or, if need be, to successfully confront the hegemon, the rising power may focus on building power in ways that more directly challenge the hegemon. Since the gap in power has narrowed between China and the United States, the inability to compete directly may become less of a consideration for Beijing. In other words, increased power may in some cases make emulation more strategically effective and efficient, so much so that its benefits outweigh the costs of a negative reaction.

For China, much of the calculation depends on Chinese leaders' perceptions of the country's relative power. On the one hand, there is still an aspirational side to China's discussion of its great power status—a related but distinct goal of becoming a "great modern socialist country," as part of Xi's China Dream of national rejuvenation and building a powerful nation. This vision includes becoming a "manufacturer of quality," a "powerful nation of science and technology," a "space power," a "country with a strong transportation network," a "maritime power," a "trader of quality," a "sports power," a "country with advanced culture," a "top performer in education," and a "talent-rich country." As Xi admits, the work is not finished. China needs sustained economic prosperity, advanced military capabilities, stable implementation of "one country, two systems," the advancement of national unification, and improvements in its innovation capability.[2]

China's elite clearly understands that China does not match US power across the board. For example, China's outward FDI per capita is far behind those of other great powers. China is still trying to build its domestic market and produce higher-value-added goods.[3] The RMB is not globalized enough to be a pricing currency or reserve currency, as it makes up only 2 percent of global cross-border payments and is not convertible (making its internationalization dependent on future financial reforms). And China is not yet a primary influencer in international trade regulations.[4] Some argue that China's ability to conduct research, propose new scientific thinking, and explore new fields is lower than that of other great powers.[5]

On the other hand, China has undoubtedly narrowed the power gap with the United States in aggregate. Thus, Chinese beliefs about whether the United States will perceive a strategy as reassuring or threatening will likely have less impact on Chinese decisions compared to the other upstart factors in the future. Given Chinese military and economic power, Chinese military strategists already believe that a preventive war would now be disastrous for the United States.[6] Perhaps more important, it now seems almost impossible to create the impression that China's rise is harmless. A consensus has grown that the West got China wrong; engagement was never going to create a China in the American image.[7] The conventional wisdom in China is that under President Trump, the United States launched a new phase of US–China relations in which the main US goal was to contain China and "win" in a competition to prevent China from matching US power.[8] Xi Jinping's often-used phrase "great changes unseen in a century" evinces a belief that the global order is undergoing a tectonic change as power shifts eastward. Whereas previously his official rhetoric refrained from overt criticism of the United States, Xi's March 2023 speech proclaimed that "Western countries—led by the US—have implemented all-round containment, encirclement and suppression against us, bringing unprecedentedly severe challenges to our country's development."[9]

But even if China grows more confident in its power, and less confident in its ability to reassure the West, the US strategic response to China may continue to shape the costs and benefits of the upstart components, and thus to influence China's choice of path. Most have accepted the reality that US policy toward China will become tougher and US attempts to counter aspects of China's rise will intensify.[10] But China will continue to try to minimize friction with the United States and other developed countries, and this should be encouraged. Moreover, the United States will still influence the existence of gaps and the strategic effectiveness and efficacy of certain approaches. For example, if Washington works to close gaps in areas where its ability to compete is weak, or if it starts to impose costs on China for its strategies (such as threatening sanctions against China for selling arms to certain countries), then exploitation may cease to be appealing. Or as Russia's relations with the United States and NATO continue to deteriorate due to Russia's invasion of Ukraine, strategies such as mediation diplomacy or the strategic partnership with Moscow may become more appealing. In other words, one takeaway of this book is that one needs a clear idea of what US strategy will look like over the next thirty years to make predictions about China.

Adherents to the emulation tradition might argue that China will start to follow in the United States' footsteps when it has the capabilities to do so. But the upstart strategy provides strong evidence against this simplistic vision of China's future. Whether improved capabilities affect China's strategy depends on the rationale behind a choice. If China eschewed emulation over the past thirty years because its leaders thought some strategies were not working well even for the United States, then Beijing is unlikely to emulate even when its ability to do so improves. In other words, China is unlikely to strive for nuclear parity with the United States, form traditional military alliances, or build an overseas basing network that facilitates foreign military interventions. If Chinese decision-makers abandon the wisdom of the upstart strategy and try to emulate anyway, as in the case of the aircraft carrier, they will likely expend many resources for little competitive gain. China is also likely to continue pursuing entrepreneurial strategies like regime neutrality, industrial policy, and digital currency even if the relative power gap narrows further, since the alternatives threaten Party control.

The area with the greatest potential for change is where China employs the same strategy but in a different competitive area, or the exploitation component of the upstart strategy. Here, China believes it does not have the competitive advantages necessary to compete directly but deems the strategy beneficial. High-level visits, arms sales, prioritizing A2/AD over power projection, gray zone tactics instead of direct military action, pushing for control over the international financial system—in these areas, China may start to compete more directly with the United States when it sees that it has a newfound power advantage. Something similar happens in the business world. Companies often start in niche markets and only directly challenge more established firms in mass markets once they have greater resources. Walmart, for example, started in small rural markets, but once it had built a strong resource base, it expanded to compete with other department stores in large urban areas.

What will happen if instead China becomes weaker over the next thirty years? Some experts argue that China has reached its peak as a rising power and faces imminent decline, raising the risk that Beijing will become more aggressive and dangerous as its window of opportunity closes.[11] But US scholars have been pointing to Chinese weaknesses for years, with some even predicting impending collapse, so it is far from certain that China's economic future will be bleak.[12] Additionally, the upstart perspective suggests that the current framing of a "peaking" China is problematic because the logic assumes that China needs the same resources as the United States to achieve what the United States achieves, and that China builds and exercises power in the same way. But China may be able to challenge the United States, and even displace it on the global stage, without the same types of power or the same amount of power. China has used the upstart strategy to compete from a weaker resource position over the past thirty years; there is no reason it cannot continue to do so. Even if China's growth stalls, Beijing will have more aggregate resources—political, military, and economic—to compete over the next twenty-five years than it had in the past thirty.

However, the *way* China competes could evolve. If the Chinese economy faces serious challenges, including weak demographics and a burgeoning debt problem, and the Chinese leadership perceives a disadvantage in resources necessary to compete, the need for strategic efficacy and Party control could wield a greater influence over the decision about which upstart component to pursue. Specifically, these factors would encourage greater reliance on entrepreneurial strategies and exploitation over emulation.

Recommendations for US Strategy

What are the implications for the current US policy debate about how to manage China's rise? Kenneth Waltz famously said that strong states can afford not to learn because only a few threats can damage them gravely, and only if those threats are carried through.[13] The rise of China is one such rare threat, and it is time for the United States to adapt. While the United States can learn from history, it finds itself in an unprecedented situation: facing a rising power that is primarily accumulating and exercising political and economic power (for now), within an institutionalized and integrated system such as the world has never before had, facing a hegemon (the United States) more constrained than previous ones, in a region (Asia) that is also rising on the whole.

The United States needs to target its approaches to build and maintain a competitive edge with its own version of an upstart strategy. Specifically, the United States and its allies should (1) avoid emulating all Chinese successes, (2) encourage more Chinese emulation where the United States and its allies maintain competitive advantages, (3) close the gaps China exploits to build power, and (4) embrace its own entrepreneurial approaches. The overall goal should be to move competition into areas where the United States has an advantage and reduce the impact of Chinese strategies where China enjoys advantages.[14]

Do not emulate all Chinese approaches. Just as emulating US successes is not always the best strategy for China, emulating China's success is not necessarily the best option for the United States. US emulation risks what the business literature calls "position stranding." This is when market leaders respond to challenges from other companies by imitating successful innovations while still pursuing a relatively consistent long-term strategy (e.g., when Apple maintained its overall positional strategy but imitated Samsung's larger screen size for new phones).[15] Such an approach often backfires. Like companies, countries that try to maintain what makes them unique while simultaneously offering what others do often end up with less at higher cost. As the competition theorist Michael Porter warns, a company should never copy another company's strategy or technology; rather, it should see how that approach can be adapted to widen what it does uniquely that is valued.[16]

The problem is that the United States does not have the same competitive advantages as China, and thus direct competition through emulation can be counterproductive. The United States is not going to maintain its position by competing in building global infrastructure, embracing state-directed industrial policies, or engaging in gray zone activities. The Chinese system is better suited for these types of control and coordination. Moreover, China may be engaging in behavior that is inconsistent with US values—from shielding autocrats from external pressure to exerting state control over key sectors of the economy. The United States needs to avoid a race to the bottom.

This discussion is not meant to support the current narrative that the Chinese system is somehow more stable, nimble, effective, and generally "better" at competing.[17] There is no doubt that the need to maintain Party control has reduced China's strategic options, often leading to suboptimal outcomes (as in the attempts to build soft power and the internationalization of the RMB), and has forced it to expend significant resources that could have been put to better use. But it is also true that Chinese leaders have often successfully adapted their approaches to leverage the strengths of their system. Regime agnosticism, training foreign law enforcement, state-directed industrial policy, development financing for politically or economically problematic infrastructure projects—these are strategies best suited to an autocratic Leninist regime.

In other words, the post–Cold War conventional wisdom that closed, communist societies cannot compete militarily or economically with liberal states is not quite accurate.[18] The US political and economic system can be a significant, perhaps decisive, advantage in great power competition *if* the United States caters to its competitive advantages. But this is a strategic choice, not a given. Instead of waiting for China to fail, the United States needs to actively succeed. In innovation, for example, a more open immigration policy that encourages skilled labor to settle in the country is an option Beijing does not have. Immigration, however, can be a strength only if the United States makes it so, by, for example, getting rid of current caps on the number of work visas given to college-educated immigrants and creating an accelerated pathway for STEM PhD graduates to gain permanent residency.[19]

Encourage Chinese emulation where beneficial. One of the main findings of my research is that the United States often enjoyed an advantage when China chose to compete directly through emulation. Additionally, China seemed more likely to move in this direction because of a desire for prestige or because doing so would significantly reduce friction not only with the United States but also with most other developed countries. Given this situation, the United States should encourage more emulation on China's part, possibly through messaging about how China cannot be considered a legitimate great power until it possesses certain capabilities or engages in certain types of activities. Indeed, although the call to be a responsible stakeholder may have been overly optimistic in its premise that China's involvement in international institutions would lead to changes in its values and interests, it did have some impact on China's allocation of resources. It would benefit the United States if more Chinese aid went to disaster relief, for example, or if the desire to dominate the international financial system pushed Beijing to float the RMB and allow for the free flow of capital in and out of the country.

This advice to encourage emulation applies to the most sensitive areas, such as overseas basing. China maintains military advantages only very close to its shores. A global military posture is expensive and can pull resources away from other conventional capabilities. It is for these reasons that China has avoided the US model for protection of its overseas interests. If, however, China felt compelled to compete directly with the United States in this way, it would be easier for the United States to prevail in the overall military competition with China.

Lastly, there are some areas where Chinese emulation enhances Chinese influence and power, but the United States should encourage it anyway because of positive externalities for other aspects of US interests. For example, Chinese involvement in a North Korea contingency would reduce the likelihood of nuclear use on the peninsula.[20] China is also in a unique position to encourage Russia to come to the negotiating table to end the war in Ukraine. Concessions will have to be made to China, and probably to Russia if the talks that emerge are to have any hope of ending in a settlement. China will have to prove its value to Ukraine too—which may mean a greater economic presence for Beijing in postwar reconstruction. But for all its problems, an active Chinese role looks like our best bet for peace in Ukraine.

Fill the gaps. One way China builds power is through exploiting the gaps in US strategy and the international order. Whether it is selling drones, engaging in diplomatic outreach to developing countries, developing A2/AD capabilities that target US bases, or stealing foreign technology to support its industrial policy, China sees an opening and exploits it. The best way forward for the United States is to close these gaps.

One area that deserves particular attention is the rules-based international order. Scholars project a confidence that the US-led world order is all-encompassing and durable.[21] But what China discovered was that some parts of the world were largely outside the system and consequently were not benefiting from it. These included unsavory regimes the United States has little engagement with and parts of the world the United States had neglected. Moreover, Chinese strategists argue for bolstering China's international voice and influence in international institutions that the West abandoned, especially during the Trump administration.[22] The United States needs to be more present diplomatically and economically, in ways that leverage US competitive advantages. For example, the Biden administration's Indo-Pacific Economic Framework would greatly increase its attractiveness if it offered signatories preferential access to the US market.[23]

The WTO provides a good example of an institution that needs revisiting. The WTO's roots date back to WWII and its aftermath, an era when the United States represented half of global economic output and most of the free world depended on aid from Washington. The most recent bout of negotiation, the Doha Round, was over a decade ago (and it failed). The organization's last true success came in the 1994 Uruguay Round, before China had become a member. China has exploited this lack of consensus to avoid punishment for violating WTO accession agreements and to achieve its four broad trade priorities: "pushing for indigenous innovation, driving self-sufficiency, enhancing national security, and market reform and opening."[24] Notably, the term "state-owned enterprise" is entirely absent from the framework negotiated in Uruguay in 1994, effectively exempting a huge portion of the Chinese economy from WTO rules regarding tariffs, intellectual property, and a host of critical trade issues.[25]

To counter this situation, the United States should put more pressure on China to meet its obligations under its accession agreement, ideally along with other G7 countries that could encourage states targeted with Chinese economic coercion to bring a case to the WTO.[26] At the very least, this would make the exploitation less strategically effective and efficient. But to do so, the United States needs to strengthen, not weaken, the organization. President Trump's approach—refusing to appoint new members to the body's highest court, effectively shutting it down—only enhanced China's ability to exploit the uncertainty.

In the military realm, the way to close gaps is to reduce vulnerabilities to create deterrence by resiliency. Similar to deterrence by punishment, deterrence by resiliency is primarily concerned with how to shape an adversary's perceptions of the deterrer's capabilities. But unlike deterrence by punishment, the goal is not to create fear of retaliation but rather to encourage the perception that disruptive events would have little effect. Believing that attempts to impose costs will be of limited benefit, the adversary is less likely to pursue such a path. The concept is related to deterrence by denial but differs in that a country is not preventing the successful execution of military operations. Operational-level actions will succeed, but deterrence by resiliency shows that this success will not translate into the attainment of strategic-level objectives, as previously thought.

The term "resiliency" is used here to refer to a state's ability to both absorb and deflect costs at a given level of violence. Resiliency, then, is about signaling to China that the benefits of a particular military action will be less than China believes them to be. This can be because countries have viable alternatives, redundancy, or improved defenses. For example, it is hard to deter China from attacking space assets because the operational benefits are so high and the costs so low. In this case, increasing defenses is not possible. But the United States can take several actions to show that, in reality, such an attack would not greatly affect US military operations. Perhaps the United States can launch new satellites into orbit more quickly than it did previously; perhaps it has placed several constellations to enhance redundancy or has signed agreements with other countries to be able to quickly substitute national assets with theirs.[27] The same goes for US basing in Asia. The more sites from which the United States can operate, and the more capable the US force posture is of adapting to changing circumstances, the less attractive it becomes to launch missile strikes on US bases.

The United States should also invest time and resources in areas that lack a clear, strong international consensus on norms. Cyber, AI, and counterspace weapons are areas where the United States would benefit from establishing clear limits. US-China cyber relations have deteriorated as China has blocked US-led norm-building efforts within the UN Group of Governmental Experts (GGE) and, since 2014, has hosted a rival annual World Internet Conference in Wuzhen.[28] Despite early success under the Obama administration in establishing a "common understanding on cyberespionage" and an agreement not to "conduct or knowingly support cyber-enabled theft of intellectual property," Chinese cyberespionage and malicious activity across cyberspace have played an increasingly large role in tensions, with no comprehensive agreement in sight.[29] While the UN GGE did develop a set of norms for cyberspace in 2015 that were agreed to and formalized by all UN member states in 2021 as a part of the Open-Ended Working Group, these norms remain largely voluntary, unenforced, and unimplemented.[30]

Establishing norms for counterspace weapons, including direct-ascent anti-satellite missile systems, shows more promise of cooperation considering China's long-standing opposition to the militarization of space—including with its 2008 Draft Treaty on the Prevention of the Placement of Weapons in Outer Space, the Threat or Use of Force Against Outer Space Objects—and the 2022 US moratorium on anti-satellite weapons testing.[31] AI also seems promising; while it is a bit too early to tell, this research suggests that China's approach to regulation of AI will depend on which aspects of AI it believes constrain the United States and which will provide China with military advantages. In general, China sees great promise in using AI for military purposes. A 2017 State Council document claims that China must "seize the major strategic opportunities for the development of artificial intelligence [and] build China's first-mover advantage in the development of artificial intelligence" to lead the world in AI by 2030.[32] This, in turn, would give the PLA a substantial advantage over its adversaries with less ability to utilize information.[33]

Pursue entrepreneurial approaches. The United States needs to rethink the ways it builds and exercises power to be competitive in the twenty-first century. In business, "the leader establishes the competitive status quo within its industry" but will likely experience decline if it "do[es] not attempt to disrupt the status quo."[34] But established powers often have trouble doing new things, even when they face a challenge for power from below. Like industry leaders, great powers often have less incentive to innovate because of their dominance.[35] Rather than decline while clinging to the strategies that originally made them powerful, leaders in the international system must "recognize that they must be close to ruthless in cannibalizing their current products and processes just when they are most lucrative, and begin the search, over and over."[36]

The only way the United States can maintain its position relative to China is to take entrepreneurial actions of its own. This means deliberately considering whether it is time for a change in US practices. Should the United States consider enhancing its engagement with problematic countries instead of cutting off diplomatic relations? Should the United States take a position on the territorial disputes in the South China Sea? How can the US defense industry be restructured to allow for the mass production of the munitions needed for possible contingencies in Asia? Is it time to share technologies or capabilities with our allies, as in the recent AUKUS deal? Success requires new approaches that are more than just variations on an old theme. This includes pursuing new policies that reduce the effectiveness and efficacy of Chinese entrepreneurial approaches. For example, the United States could push to establish a new international regime to monitor and regulate internal security cooperation between states.

In the nuclear realm, my research suggests that China is not striving for parity—and the Chinese logic holds that once a retaliatory capability threshold is met, marginal increases in nuclear weapons thereafter have no strategic significance. Whether the United States has eighteen times more nuclear weapons or six times more, the nuclear balance has the same impact on conflict dynamics. The real problem is the atrophy of the United States' conventional deterrent in the Indo-Pacific, which has opened the possibility that Beijing may use force to gain control over Taiwan. As Chapters 4 and 5 suggest, these conventional challenges are real and difficult to remedy. Thus, a more innovative approach to arms control might be warranted. Specifically, I recommend that the United States consider asymmetric arms control arrangements, agreeing to reductions in US theater missile defense capabilities or even in the number of nuclear warheads in exchange for demobilization of certain types and numbers of Chinese conventional missiles.

This approach would reduce the A2/AD threat against US military forces and have negligible strategic impact on the nuclear balance of power—but China might agree to it given its own concerns about the survivability of its second-strike capability.

On the South China Sea, the US approach has been insufficient to counter China's consolidation of control over these waterways. The United States should consider expanding its operations to include escorting fishing and oil exploration vessels for allies and partners who lack the necessary naval or coast guard forces. The United States could specify that its defense commitments to countries in the region extend to protection of those countries' rights within their EEZs. Similarly, it should signal that if China takes aggressive moves in the region, the United States will reconsider its neutral diplomatic position regarding the sovereignty of disputed islands.

Meanwhile, the United States should lead a massive diplomatic effort to get claimants in Southeast Asia to an agreement about the islands' sovereignty and the rights granted by those islands, refraining from any unilateral changes to the status quo. Once the claimants have reached a shared understanding, they should ask the international community to help them enforce this agreement against China. Washington could then set up multiple levers of pressure in the economic and diplomatic spheres to punish Chinese non-compliance. Policies could include expelling China from international organizations, implementing economic sanctions, and further restricting export of technology to China.

In the matter of deterring economic warfare, the United States needs to reconceptualize its alliances. To many players in Asia, the most likely threat from China is not one of invasion and occupation. China restricts freedom of action, or the ability of allies to do what is in their best interest, through a combination of economic, political, and military means. The Chinese have shown themselves more than willing to use their economy as a tool of statecraft. The United States and its allies should follow suit. China's bullying of smaller economies like Lithuania and Australia cannot be tolerated, and when China uses boycotts or tariffs to damage such countries, the United States and other G7 countries should fill the gap. Some analysts have suggested that the United States should buy up any product that China boycotts—for example, by maintaining a "Strategic Shiraz Reserve," in reference to the Australian wine on which China passed tariffs after a diplomatic dispute.[37] Jokes aside, the idea is not far off the mark. But potentially more powerful is the threat of collective response not only to military attacks but to economic ones as well.

If China restricts tourism to punish a country, the United States and its allies should do the same to China. The United States should run simulations and "war games" to determine how best to coordinate actions across domains and countries to deter China from using economic punishment.

I have written extensively elsewhere about how to enhance deterrence over the Taiwan Strait, but entrepreneurial approaches are needed here more than ever.[38] The key strategic goal would be to destroy China's ability to transport, land, and sustain an invasion force on Taiwan. With this in mind, the allies should invest in anti-ship missiles, submarines, and undersea mines. The United States also needs to invest in its bomber fleet to deliver more fire-power to the Strait, and the Departments of State and Defense should re-double their efforts to secure more access, basing, and overflight rights in regional countries. The recent US-Philippines agreement to provide more basing on a rotational basis for US forces is a promising development.[39]

Appropriations reform, to accelerate production and delivery of munitions to US forces as well as to partners like Taiwan, is crucial; if a war broke out in Asia today, the United States would run out of munitions in a matter of days. To address this looming munitions shortage, experts rec-ommend moving away from single-year defense appropriations to approve multiyear contracts.[40] But perhaps something more drastic is needed—such as a rethinking of the public-private partnership between defense contractors and the US government. For example, one of the main issues is insufficient skilled labor; recruiting and retaining workers is more challenging when un-employment rates are low and workforce participation rates are already high. The United States could consider establishing a new reserve force of skilled labor that surges to work with defense contractors when needed.

Resiliency also extends to economic policies. The United States has been engaging in innovative thinking about how to prevent China from obtaining US technology. In the words of National Security Advisor Jake Sullivan:

> On export controls, we have to revisit the longstanding premise of maintaining "relative" advantages over competitors in certain key technologies. We previously maintained a "sliding scale" approach that said we need to stay only a couple of generations ahead. That is not the stra-tegic environment we are in today. Given the foundational nature of certain technologies, such as advanced logic and memory chips, we must maintain as large of a lead as possible.[41]

In October 2022, the Commerce Department's Bureau of Industry and Security passed new measures to prevent the flow of technologies critical to China's AI endeavors. In the same year, US Congress passed the CHIPS and Science Act, which increases federal funding for scientific R&D, allocates $52 billion to support the semiconductor industry, and contains other provisions geared toward competition with China. The act provides billions for the Pentagon to fund semiconductor research and millions for the Department of State to coordinate with allies who have key roles in supply chains. It aims to leverage private sector strengths by providing tax incentives for advanced manufacturing as well. In early 2023, the Biden administration achieved another win by convincing Japan and the Netherlands, each of which plays a critical role in the worldwide semiconductor supply chain, to adopt similar export control measures.

The United States needs a strategy to engage with the rest of the world—to cultivate and value the expertise necessary to understand each unique situation and what it demands. This is especially true of the developing world, which the United States has ignored for far too long. Being the external security partner of choice is no longer sufficient. One thing is certain: the United States needs to commit more funds than China does to its relationship with developing countries, with a focus on areas in which the United States enjoys competitive advantages. The United States can expand its efforts in medical fields, but also in education and technical training for interested countries. Additionally, Washington should take a page out of China's playbook and stop tying development assistance so closely to political reform. If the United States and others continue to tie aid to such reform, we know that many countries will fly to China's "no strings attached" investment. This is not to say the United States should abandon its policy of promoting good governance and democratic norms, but simply that we should play the long game and engage with these countries to promote better practices step-by-step over longer periods of time.

Likewise, the United States should engage more with authoritarian regimes that it considers repugnant. When the United States has a problem with a country, it should enhance its in-country presence and engagement, not close embassies and cut off ties.[42] To treat talking as a reward only reduces US influence in such countries and creates situations where Washington needs Beijing's help to solve the world's most important issues. In more general terms, the United States needs to assess whether practices that served US purposes in the past are the best ways forward for protecting US security and interests. Bureaucracies need to adjust, to reward those who experiment and propose agile policies instead of following the de facto preference for the status quo.

At the risk of stating the obvious, competition—even when it is zero-sum—can push all countries to be the best versions of themselves. Striving for technological innovation, global economic development, institutional growth and reform, and even military buildups can lead to a more peaceful, prosperous, and sustainable world. It can give small and medium-sized countries more freedom to pursue the policies that are best for their people and compel US and Chinese leaders to create the best possible future for everyone.[43] Chinese leaders will always want to make China the most powerful country possible—attempting to convince them otherwise would be a fool's errand. But the United States can ensure that its approach to this new world, one in which it is no longer the sole superpower, makes it a better version of itself at home and abroad. And even though China is unlikely to emulate the US approach wholesale, the United States can make some pathways to power more appealing than others. Despite China's newfound position and power, the United States and its rules-based international order can not only survive but thrive over the next thirty years. We just need to find our own upstart strategy and create the right mix of emulation, exploitation, and entrepreneurship.

Understanding China and the Challenge of Its Rise

This in-depth look at how China builds power offers some broader insights into power and the international system. First, why have some rising powers succeeded in their bid for hegemony, while others have not? I provide a preliminary answer to this question before proposing some future avenues of research. The key, I suggest, is the mixture of emulation, entrepreneurship, and exploitation. If countries emulate when the conditions are not right, their attempts prove costly, not only in terms of what they achieve for the resources expended but also in terms of the great power response. The correct mix is likely to vary from country to country and time period to time period. Domestic politics shape the costs and benefits of the three upstart components. When the rising power has a system similar to the established great power's, emulation might be more effective and reassuring. But when countries are vastly different, the opposite is likely true. Perhaps

Japan's biggest mistake during its late nineteenth-century and early twentieth-century rise was that it "deliberately emulated Western political institutions, social customs, economic practices, and military techniques."[44] Unsurprisingly, China's entrepreneurship and exploitation—gray zone activities, A2/AD, industrial policy, development financing, regime neutrality— have accumulated more power than emulative attempts.

The best balance between emulation, exploitation, and entrepreneurship is also likely to vary by country, as well as throughout history as the nature of power and the international order evolve. The implication for scholars is clear: research that looks at how countries have successfully bid for great power status in the past—Great Britain, France, the Soviet Union, the United States—has limited utility in understanding future great powers. The upstart theory suggests ample theoretical and empirical reasons to expect China's case to be different.[45]

The nature of the international system itself may be a factor that determines whether countries can rise successfully. In other words, certain world orders might be more conducive to the rise of new powers. The contemporary liberal order, for example, may be an ideal system for promoting a country's rise while delaying countervailing actions, for two reasons. First, the system, with its emphasis on globalization and multilateralism, has created unprecedented opportunities to accumulate power peacefully (i.e., in a reassuring manner). And all nations can reap these benefits. As a result, China could accumulate power without triggering heightened threat perceptions in the United States—imagine how differently the United States would have responded to a Chinese NATO compared to the BRI. Second, while a declining hegemon once had the option to launch a preventive war against a challenger, current norms and institutional constraints mean this option is no longer viable. As John Ikenberry argues, the United States has set up an institutionally based international order in which its power is constrained in exchange for the consensus of the weaker powers.[46] These points suggest that more research needs to focus on additional ways the international system shapes the costs and benefits of different approaches in great power competition.

Why do great powers often fail to counter challenges before the power gap is closed? Most scholarship in international relations turns to the strategies and decisions of the great power to explain how the rising power manages to reach a certain level of power.[47] Specifically, it advances three explanations: the great power may make imprudent choices, may accept its decline, or may cooperate with one rising power to confront a different, more threatening rising power.

This book offers a different explanation, one that better accounts for the active role the rising power plays in shaping the great power's response. As I have shown, Chinese leaders explicitly considered how the United States was likely to perceive and react to a given strategy, and they prioritized approaches that would discourage or at least delay US responses that could thwart, undermine, or delay its rise. The upstart strategy is designed partly to reassure the great power and avoid posing a direct threat. In other words, great powers are not failing to respond in isolation. Instead, rising powers might be designing strategies to encourage delayed responses to their accumulation of power.

This research also encourages scholars to rethink the concept of revisionism. Many scholars and strategists have concerned themselves with how to characterize Chinese intentions.[48] This book moves away from treating intentions as objective facts to be deciphered and presents a potentially unpopular interpretation: perceptions of intentions are subjective. Use of force can support the status quo or deviate from it; changing the international order can contribute to peace (as when the United States set up a network of international institutions after WWII) or undermine it. The United States might see emulation as threatening, and thus revisionist, as would be the case if China followed the US example of a global basing network. Or emulation can be reassuring, and thus seen as status quo behavior, when it is in line with US preferences, such as Chinese contributions to HADRs or UNPKOs. China understands that to a degree, the United States defines what is threatening or reassuring. To rise successfully, China had to take that factor into account when deciding on the best way to accumulate power in a specific realm. In other words, it is not only Chinese behavior that shapes perceptions of intentions, but also perceptions of intentions that shape Chinese behavior.

I also provide a clear articulation of the multitude of ways US strategy impacts Chinese strategy. Other China specialists have recognized pieces of the puzzle.[49] When Chinese leaders make decisions, they take into account US perceptions, the existence of gaps, and domestic political considerations. But it would be an oversimplification, and empirically inaccurate, to argue that one of these factors alone shapes China's diplomatic, economic, or military strategy. The upstart strategy zooms out to show how these factors interact with perceptions of the effectiveness of US strategies to shape Chinese leaders' choice of pathway to power.

The result is a more dynamic picture of Chinese grand strategy, one that China's leaders are constantly recalibrating. While specific upstart policies change over time with changing conditions, China's desire for great power status remains constant. In China's lexicon, over the past thirty years it has achieved a great deal of "strategic space," or comprehensive national power to deter external interference, especially from US attempts to counter its trajectory.[50] In all the assessments and recalibrations, Chinese behavior, discourse, and capabilities show that US strategy is the primary determinant of China's approaches. In other words, the United States has not been an enemy per se over the past thirty years but has been the standard, defining what is considered entrepreneurial, an exploitable blind spot, or worthy of emulation through its practice and strategy. Through this unique position, the United States has the opportunity to influence China's future, and with that, to ensure a brighter future for the whole world.

Notes

Introduction

1. See comments quoted from Li Ruihan, former Politburo Standing Committee member and chairman of the People's Consultative Conference, in Zong Hairen [宗海仁], *China's Leaders: The Fourth Generation* [中国掌舵者：第四代] (New York: Mirror Books [明镜出版社], 2002), 123–124; Jiang Zemin [江泽民], *The Selected Works of Jiang Zemin, Volume 3* [江泽民文选(第三卷)] (Beijing: People's Publishing House [人民出版社], 2006), 578–585.

2. For a perspective from a high-ranking diplomat in the Hu Jintao administration on needing to avoid upsetting the United States while China developed, see Dai Bingguo [戴秉国], *Strategic Dialogues: Dai Binguo's Memoirs* [战略对话：戴秉国回忆录] (Beijing: People's Publishing House [人民出版社], 2016), 75. For references to national humiliation and building a stronger China in official rhetoric, see Jiang Zemin [江泽民], "Accelerating the Reform, the Opening to the Outside World and the Drive for Modernization, so as to Achieve Greater Successes in Building Socialism with Chinese Characteristics [加快改革开放和现代化建设步伐 夺取有中国特色社会主义事业的更大胜利]," 14th Party Congress Political Report, Beijing, October 12, 1992; Hu Jintao [胡锦涛], "Firmly March on the Path of Socialism with Chinese Characteristics and Strive to Complete the Building of a Moderately Prosperous Society in All Respects [坚定不移沿着中国特色社会主义道路前进 为全面建成小康社会而奋斗]," 18th Party Congress Political Report, Beijing, November 8, 2012; Xi Jinping [习近平], "Secure a Decisive Victory in Building a Moderately Prosperous Society in All Respects and Strive for the Great Success of Socialism with Chinese Characteristics for a New Era [决胜全面建设小康社会 夺取新时代中国特色社会主义伟大胜利]," 19th Party Congress Political Report, Beijing, October 18, 2017.

3. For example, this point was emphasized particularly by former premier Zhu Rongji when he was working to enable China's joining of the WTO in 2001. See Zhu Rongji [朱镕基], *Zhu Rongji Meets the Press* [朱镕基答记者问] (Beijing: People's Publishing House [人民出版社], 2009), 254.

4. "Asia Power Index 2021: Diplomatic Influence," Lowy Institute, https://power.lowyinstitute.org/compare/?countries=united-states,china.

5. Jim Garamone, "China's Capabilities Growth Shows Why U.S. Sees Nation as Pacing Challenge," Department of Defense News, October 27, 2021, https://www.defense.gov/News/News-Stories/Article/Article/2824060/chinas-capabilities-growth-shows-why-us-sees-nation-as-pacing-challenge/.

6. Thomas J. Shattuck, "Assessing One Year of PLA Air Incursions into Taiwan's ADIZ," *Global Taiwan Brief* 6, no. 20 (2021): 14–17.

7. "Full Text of the Report to the 20th National Congress of the Communist Party of China," Ministry of Foreign Affairs of the People's Republic of China [中华人民共和国外交部], October 25, 2022, https://www.fmprc.gov.cn/eng/zxxx_662805/202210/t20221025_10791908.html.

8. "Upstart," *Oxford English Dictionary* online, https://www.oed.com/view/Entry/220 196, accessed May 20, 2023.

9. "Upstart," *Britannica Dictionary*, https://www.britannica.com/dictionary/upstart, accessed May 20, 2023.

10. Andrew Hill and Stephen Gerras, "Systems of Denial: Strategic Resistance to Military Innovation," *Naval War College Review* 69, no. 1 (Winter 2016): 110. See also Clayton Christensen, *The Innovator's Dilemma: The Revolutionary Book That Will Change the Way You Do Business* (New York: Harper Business Books, 2011).

11. Pepsi, for instance, was able to exploit Coke's blind spot in the US domestic market, as the latter had begun to concentrate primarily on foreign markets based on the mistaken belief that the US soft drink market had little room left for growth. Curtis M. Grimm, Hun Lee, and Ken G. Smith, *Strategy as Action: Competitive Dynamics and Competitive Advantage* (Oxford: Oxford University Press, 2006), 115–119.

12. New market entrants such as Under Armour and Wal-Mart gained market share by doing things differently. Grimm, Lee, and Smith, *Strategy as Action*, 113–114.

13. Grimm, Lee, and Smith, *Strategy as Action*, 194.

14. For example, Quibi, an app that aimed to deliver high-quality short-form content to users, failed to disrupt its competitors, such as TikTok and YouTube, and collapsed after less than a year despite raising nearly $2 billion in funding. Dade Hayes, Jill Goldsmith, Dominic Patten, "Quibi to Shut Down, Ending $2B Streaming Experiment," *Deadline*, October 21, 2020, https://deadline.com/2020/10/quibi-to-shut-down-ending-2b-streaming-experiment-1234601356/.

15. M. Taylor Fravel, for example, splits China's strategy into the pre- and post-1993 periods in his book on Chinese military strategy. M. Taylor Fravel, *Active Defense: China's Military Strategy Since 1949* (Princeton, NJ: Princeton University Press, 2019), 182–216. Avery Goldstein, in his assessment of Chinese grand strategy, puts the beginning of China's deliberate efforts to rise to great power status in 1996, when the Chinese leader Jiang Zemin began to pursue the rejuvenation of the Chinese nation. Avery Goldstein, "China's Grand Strategy Under Xi Jinping: Reassurance, Reform, and Resistance," *International Security* 45, no. 1 (2020): 164–201. Rush Doshi argues that China's grand strategy to displace the United States has consisted of three stages, the first of which started in 1989 with the goal of "quietly blunt[ing]" American power over China. Rush Doshi, *The Long Game: China's Grand Strategy and the Displacement of American Order* (New York: Oxford University Press, 2021).

16. Wang Lisheng [王立胜], "Deng Xiaoping's Grasping of the 'Important Period of Strategic Opportunity' and His Thought [邓小平对'重要战略机遇期'的把握及其思想]," *Literature of Chinese Communist Party* [党的文献], no. 4 (2006): 41–42.

17. " 'China's Rise' Has Become a Buzzword in the World Again, Foreign Media Comment at Great Length ['中国崛起'再成世界流行语 境外媒体评论连篇累牍]," *China*

Daily [中国日报], February 26, 2008, http://www.chinadaily.com.cn/hqzg/2008-02/26/content_6484556.htm.

18. Theo Farrell, "Improving in War: Military Adaptation and the British in Helmand Province, Afghanistan, 2006–2009," *Journal of Strategic Studies* 38, no. 4 (2015): 570.

19. These datasets can be found at www.orianaskylarmastro.com/upstart.

20. The full appendix of Chinese sources can be found at www.orianaskylarmastro.com/upstart.

21. Robert A. Dahl, "The Concept of Power," *Behavioral Science* 2, no. 3 (1957): 202; Michael Beckley, *Unrivaled: Why America Will Remain the World's Sole Superpower* (Ithaca, NY: Cornell University Press, 2018).

22. For example, see Yuan Peng [袁鹏], "The Coronavirus Pandemic and the Great Changes Unseen in a Century [新冠疫情与百年变局]," *Contemporary International Relations* [现代国际关系], no. 5 (2020): 1–6.

23. David A. Baldwin, *Power and International Relations* (Princeton, NJ: Princeton University Press, 2016), 174.

24. Kenneth Waltz, "The Emerging Structure of International Politics," *International Security* 18, no. 2 (Autumn 1993): 50; Hans Morgenthau, *Politics Among Nations: The Struggle for Power and Peace* (New York: McGraw-Hill, 1993), 72.

25. Yan Xuetong [阎学通] et al., "A Conversation by Writing on the 'Rise of Powers and China's Choices' ['大国崛起与中国的选择'笔谈]," *Social Sciences in China* [中国社会科学], no. 5 (2005): 58. To be considered "rising," a country has to have the ambition to influence the world. Men Honghua [门洪华], "The Rise of China and Changes in the Global Order [中国崛起与国际秩序变革]," *Quarterly Journal of International Politics* [国际政治科学], no. 1 (2016): 73.

26. "Military and Security Developments Involving the People's Republic of China 2020," US Department of Defense, 2020, i, https://media.defense.gov/2020/Sep/01/2002488689/-1/-1/1/2020-DOD-CHINA-MILITARY-POWER-REPORT-FINAL.PDF.

27. Paul Kennedy, *The Rise and Fall of the Great Powers: Economic Change and Military Conflict from 1500 to 2000* (New York: Random House, 1987), 539; Jack S. Levy, *War in the Modern Great Power System: 1495–1975* (Lexington: University Press of Kentucky, 1983), 15–16; Baldwin, *Power and International Relations*, 175; John Mearsheimer, *The Tragedy of Great Power Politics* (New York: W. W. Norton, 2001), 5.

28. "Military and Security Developments Involving the People's Republic of China 2020," ii.

29. Robert Gilpin, *War and Change in World Politics* (Cambridge: Cambridge University Press, 1981), 215–216; Daniel Deudney, "Hegemony, Nuclear Weapons, and Liberal Hegemony," in *Power, Order, and Change in World Politics*, ed. G. John Ikenberry (Cambridge: Cambridge University Press, 2014), 203.

30. Hans M. Kristensen and Matt Korda, "Status of World Nuclear Forces," Federation of American Scientists, May 2021, https://fas.org/issues/nuclear-weapons/status-world-nuclear-forces/.

31. A. F. K. Organski and Jacek Kugler, *The War Ledger* (Chicago: University of Chicago Press, 1980); Therese Anders, Christopher J. Fariss, and Jonathan N. Markowitz, "Bread Before Guns or Butter: Introducing Surplus Domestic Product (SDP),"

International Studies Quarterly 64, no. 2 (2020): 392–405; Jacek Kugler and William Domke, "Comparing the Strength of Nations," *Comparative Political Studies* 19, no. 1 (1986): 39–69.

32. "Are Patents Indicative of Chinese Innovation?," ChinaPower, February 15, 2016, https://chinapower.csis.org/patents/; Central Intelligence Agency, "China," *The World Factbook* (Washington, DC: Government Printing Office, 2021); "Literacy Rate, Adult Total (% of People Ages 15 and Above)—China," World Bank, https://data.worldbank.org/indicator/SE.ADT.LITR.ZS?locations=CN, accessed January 19, 2024.

33. "Thucydides's Trap Case File: 16. 1990s–Present—United Kingdom and France vs. Germany—NO WAR," Harvard Kennedy School Belfer Center for Science and International Affairs, March 17, 2017, https://www.belfercenter.org/thucydides-trap/case-file.

34. "Can India Become a Great Power?," *The Economist*, March 30, 2013, https://www.economist.com/leaders/2013/03/30/can-india-become-a-great-power.

35. Gian Luca Gardini, "Brazil: What Rise of What Power?," *Bulletin of Latin American Research* 35, no. 1 (2016): 5.

36. Manjari Chatterjee Miller, *Why Nations Rise: Narratives and the Path to Great Power* (New York: Oxford University Press, 2021), 10.

37. Hu Angang [胡鞍钢] et al., "The Rise and Decline of Great Power and China's Opportunity: Assessment of Comprehensive National Power [大国兴衰与中国机遇 : 国家综合国力评估]," *Economic Heralds* [经济导刊], no. 3 (2017): 14–25. See also Hu Angang [胡鞍钢] et al., "Assessment of China's and the US's Comprehensive National Power (1990–2013) [对中美综合国力的评估(1990–2013)]," *Journal of Tsinghua University* [清华大学学报], no. 1 (2015): 26–39. For other early studies of CNP, see Zhao Xuebo [赵雪波], "Analysis of the Components of Comprehensive National Power [综合国力构成要素辨析]," *World Economy and Politics* [世界经济与政治], no. 5 (2001); Wang Ling [王玲], "Measuring Comprehensive National Power [关于综合国力的测度]," *World Economy and Politics* [世界经济与政治], no. 6 (2006): 45–51. This last assessment by Wang Ling cites 2003 results from the Chinese Academy of Sciences Sustainable Development Strategy Study Group that ranked the United States as number one in power and China as number seven.

38. Wang Jisi [王缉思], "Is China the Second Greatest Power in the World? [中国是世界第二强国吗?]," China.com.cn [中国网], April 14, 2011, http://opinion.china.com.cn/opinion_94_14694.html; Fu Ying [傅莹], "Is China a Great Power? [中国是强国吗?]," Ministry of Foreign Affairs of the People's Republic of China [中华人民共和国外交部], May 7, 2009, https://www.fmprc.gov.cn/web/gjhdq_676201/gj_676203/oz_678770/1206_679906/ywfc_679928/200905/t20090507_9355291.shtml.

39. Yan Xuetong, "The Rise of China and Its Power Status," *Chinese Journal of International Politics* 1, no. 1 (2006): 21, 30; Wang Yi [王毅], "Write a Marvelous Chapter on Great Power Diplomacy with Chinese Characteristics [谱写中国特色大国外交的时代华章]," State Council of the People's Republic of China [中华人民共和国中央人民政府], September 23, 2019, http://www.gov.cn/guowuyuan/2019-09/23/content_5432243.htm; "What Should a Great Power Look like? President Xi Will Tell You [大国

应该是什么样子？习近平主席告诉你]," CCTV.com [央视网], April 20, 2021, https://news.cctv.com/2021/04/20/ARTIzqlZxTBV8rJrva0YxANX210420.shtml; "2018, These Great Power Projects Make Me Proud [2018, 这些大国重器让我骄傲]," *People's Daily* [人民日报], December 26, 2018, https://baijiahao.baidu.com/s?id=1620878036385131751&wfr=spider&for=pc.

40. "Yang Jiechi Elucidates China's Stances in the Opening Remark of the China–US High-Level Strategic Talks [杨洁篪在中美高层战略对话开场白中阐明中方有关立场]," Xinhua.com [新华网], March 19, 2021, http://www.xinhuanet.com/world/2023/19/c_1127230729.htm.

41. For a broader discussion about how to best conceptualize revisionism, see Oriana Skylar Mastro, "Understanding the Challenge of China's Rise: Fixing Conceptual Confusion About Intentions," *Journal of Chinese Political Science* 27, no. 3 (2022): 585–600.

Chapter 1

1. Statistic calculated from Graham Allison, *Destined for War: Can America and China Escape Thucydides's Trap?* (Melbourne: Scribe Publications, 2018).

2. Allison, *Destined for War*.

3. Michael Beckley and Hal Brands, *Danger Zone: The Coming Conflict with China* (New York: W. W. Norton, 2022).

4. Kenneth N. Waltz, *Theory of International Politics* (Reading, MA: Addison-Wesley, 1979), 127–128.

5. Niccolò Machiavelli, *The Prince*, trans. Tim Parks (New York: Penguin, 2009), 59.

6. Barry R. Posen, "Nationalism, the Mass Army and Military Power," *International Security* 18, no. 2 (Fall 1993): 80–124; Scott Sagan, "Why Do States Build Nuclear Weapons? Three Models in Search of a Bomb," *International Security* 21, no. 3 (Winter 1996): 54–86.

7. Aidan Powers-Riggs, "Covid-19 Is Proving a Boon for Digital Authoritarianism," Center for Strategic and International Studies, August 17, 2020, https://www.csis.org/blogs/new-perspectives-asia/covid-19-proving-boon-digital-authoritarianism.

8. Steve Wood, "Prestige in World Politics: History, Theory, Expression," *International Politics* 50, no. 3 (May 2013): 388; Rohan Mukherjee, "Rising Powers and the Quest for Status in International Security Regimes" (PhD dissertation, Princeton University, 2016), 140.

9. Nick Smith, "Grand Delusions: The Psychology of Aircraft Carriers," *Harvard International Review* 24, no. 3 (Fall 2002): 7–8; Lilach Gilady, *The Price of Prestige: Conspicuous Consumption in International Relations* (Chicago: University of Chicago Press, 2018); Michelle Murray, "Identity, Insecurity, and Great Power Politics: The Tragedy of German Naval Ambition Before the First World War," *Security Studies* 19, no. 4 (2010): 675; Joslyn N. Barnhart, "Prestige, Humiliation and International Politics" (PhD dissertation, UCLA, 2013).

10. William C. Wohlforth et al., "Moral Authority and Status in International Relations: Good States and the Social Dimension of Status Seeking," *Review of International Studies* 44, no. 3 (2017): 527, 532.

11. Raymond Kuo, *Following the Leader: International Order, Alliance Strategies, and Emulation* (Stanford, CA: Stanford University Press, 2021), 33.

12. Alastair Iain Johnston, *Social States: China in International Institutions, 1980–2000* (Princeton, NJ: Princeton University Press, 2007), 23.

13. Heather Berry, Mauro Guillen, and Arun Hendi, "Is There Convergence Across Countries? A Spatial Approach," *Journal of International Business Studies* (2014): 387–404, https://www.ncbi.nlm.nih.gov/pmc/articles/PMC4286895/#R6.

14. Clark Kerr, Frederick Harbison, John Dunlop, and Charles Myers, "Industrialism and Industrial Man," *International Labour Review* 71, no. 3 (1955): 236–251; Frank Dobbin, Beth Simmons, and Geoffrey Garrett, "The Global Diffusion of Public Policies: Social Construction, Coercion, Competition, or Learning?," *Annual Review of Sociology* 33 (2007): 449–472; Simone Polillo and Mauro F. Guillén, "Globalization Pressures and the State: The Worldwide Spread of Central Bank Independence," *American Journal of Sociology* 110, no. 6 (2005): 1764–1802; Klaus Weber, Gerald F. Davis, and Michael Lounsbury, "Policy as Myth and Ceremony? The Global Spread of Stock Exchanges, 1980–2005," *Academy of Management Journal* 52, no. 6 (2009): 1319–1347.

15. David Strang and Stephen Meyer, "Institutional Conditions for Diffusion," *Theory and Society* 22, no. 4 (August 1993): 487–511.

16. Paul J. DiMaggio and Walter W. Powell, "The Iron Cage Revisited: Institutional Isomorphism and Collective Rationality in Organizational Fields," *American Sociological Review* 48, no. 2 (April 1983): 147–160.

17. Johnston, *Social States*, 45–46.

18. Amitav Acharya, "How Ideas Spread: Whose Norms Matter? Norm Localization and Institutional Change in Asian Regionalism," *International Organization* 58, no. 2 (2004): 239–275.

19. "Roman Aqueducts," National Geographic, September 29, 2022, https://education.nationalgeographic.org/resource/roman-aqueducts/.

20. Manousos E. Kambouri, *The Rise of Persia and the First Greco-Persian Wars: The Expansion of the Achaemenid Empire and the Battle of Marathon* (Yorkshire, UK: Pen and Sword Military, 2022).

21. Nicola Di Cosmo, *Ancient China and Its Enemies: The Rise of Nomadic Power in East Asian History* (Cambridge: Cambridge University Press, 2002), https://doi.org/10.1017/CBO9780511511967.

22. Alexander Anievas and Kerem Nişancıoğlu, "How Did the West Usurp the Rest? Origins of the Great Divergence over the 'Longue Durée,'" *Comparative Studies in Society and History* 59, no. 1 (2017): 34–67, http://www.jstor.org/stable/26293559.

23. "Part I: Expansion and Conflict," in *The Cambridge History of Communism*, ed. N. Naimark, S. Pons, and S. Quinn-Judge (Cambridge: Cambridge University Press, 2017), 13–314.

24. To be sure, some may maintain that the United States protects its interests via permanent occupation—consider, for instance, Puerto Rico or the Philippines (hence the American Anti-Imperialist League). Indeed, the extent to which the United States' foreign behavior constitutes imperialism is a hotly contested matter, one that falls well outside the scope of this writing. Michael Gerson and Alison Lawler Russell, "American Grand Strategy and Seapower," CNA Analysis and Solutions, November 2011, https://www.cna.org/archive/CNA_Files/pdf/d0025988.a2.pdf.

25. Geoffrey L. Herrera and Thomas G. Mahnken, "Military Diffusion in Nineteenth Century Europe: The Napoleonic and Prussian Military Systems," in *The Diffusion of Military Technology and Ideas*, ed. Emily Goldman and Leslie Eliason (Stanford, CA: Stanford University Press, 2003), 205–242.

26. "The Naval Race Between Britain and Germany before the First World War," Imperial War Museums, n.d., https://www.iwm.org.uk/history/the-naval-race-between-britain-and-germany-before-the-first-world-war, accessed June 2, 2023; John D. Maurer, "The Anglo-German Naval Rivalry and Informal Arms Control, 1912–1914," *Journal of Conflict Resolution* 36, no. 2 (1992): 284–285.

27. Deborah Welch Larson and Alexei Shevchenko, "Status Seekers: Chinese and Russian Responses to U.S. Primacy," *International Security* 34, no. 4 (2010): 78.

28. Larson and Shevchenko, "Status Seekers," 82.

29. The "international order" is best understood as "the emergent property of the interactions of multiple state and nonstate actors" across different domains (military, human rights, trade, environment, information, etc.). Alastair Iain Johnston, "China in a World of Orders: Rethinking Compliance and Challenge in Beijing's International Relations," *International Security* 44, no. 2 (2019): 12.

30. In addition to the actions of competitors, Porter argues that there are five forces that impact the degree of competitiveness within an industry, and thus the prospects for profitability: the bargaining power of buyers, the bargaining power of suppliers, the threat of new entrants, the threat of substitute products or services, and rivalry among existing competitors. Michael E. Porter, *Competitive Strategy: Techniques for Analyzing Industries and Competitors* (New York: Free Press, 1980).

31. Stacie E. Goddard, "Brokering Change: Networks and Entrepreneurs in International Politics," *International Theory* 1, no. 2 (2009): 250.

32. In contrast, Yu-Ming Liou, Paul Musgrave, and J. Furman Daniel argue that rising states will typically choose to imitate the hegemonic state's military innovations and strategies rather than investing heavily in their own military innovations because of the lower risk of destabilization. Yu-Ming Liou, Paul Musgrave, and J. Furman Daniel III, "The Imitation Game: Why Don't Rising Powers Innovate Their Militaries More?," *Washington Quarterly* 38, no. 3 (Fall 2015): 157–174.

33. Curtis M. Grimm, Hun Lee, and Ken G. Smith, *Strategy as Action: Competitive Dynamics and Competitive Advantage* (Oxford: Oxford University Press, 2006), 103. In political science, the concept has mainly been used in political analysis to understand the motivations of non-state actors that serve as norm entrepreneurs, political entrepreneurs, and brokers. For a thorough review of the concept of entrepreneurship across disciplines, see Goddard, "Brokering Change."

34. The causal relationship between entrepreneurship and innovation is still a matter of debate. See, for example, Alexander Brem, "Linking Innovation and Entrepreneurship: Literature Overview and Introduction of a Process-Oriented Framework," *International Journal of Entrepreneurship and Innovation Management* 14, no. 1 (June 2011): 6–35.

35. Definition inspired by Goddard, "Brokering Change," 251.

36. G. John Ikenberry, *After Victory: Institutions, Strategic Restraint, and the Rebuilding of Order After Major Wars* (Princeton, NJ: Princeton University Press, 2001).

37. Margaret MacMillan, *The War That Ended Peace: How Europe Abandoned Peace for the First World War* (London: Profile Books, 2013), 38.

38. For more on China's emulation of other countries, see William H. Overholt, *China's Crisis of Success* (Cambridge: Cambridge University Press, 2017), 7–45.

39. Yan Xuetong [阎学通], "Yan Xuetong: The Overall 'Periphery' Is More Important than the United States [阎学通：整体的'周边'比美国更重要]," Carnegie Endowment for International Peace, January 13, 2015, https://carnegieendowment.org/2015/01/13/zh-pub-57696.

40. Sun Xuefeng [孙学峰], "Strategic Choice and the Success or Failure of Great Power Rise [战略选择与大国崛起成败]," in *The Rise of China and Its Strategy* [中国崛起及其战略], ed. Yan Xuetong [阎学通] and Sun Xuefeng [孙学峰] (Beijing: Peking University Press [北京大学出版社], 2015), 43–45; Sun Xuefeng [孙学峰], "Strategic Choices for Solving the Rising Dilemma [缓解崛起困境的战略选择]," in *The Dilemma of China's Rise: Theoretical Reflections and Strategic Choices* [中国崛起困境：理论思考与战略选择], ed. Sun Xuefeng [孙学峰] (Beijing: Social Sciences Academic Press [社会科学文献出版社], 2011), 24.

41. Sun, "Strategic Choices for Solving the Rising Dilemma," 33–34.

42. Liu Zhongmin [刘中民], "Thoughts on Sea Power and the Rise of a Great Power [关于海权与大国崛起问题的若干思考]," *World Economics and Politics* [世界经济与政治], no. 12 (2007): 10–13.

43. Li Qiang [李强], "Peaceful Rise and the Choice of China's Developmental Strategy [和平崛起与中国发展战略的选择]," *Social Sciences in China* [中国社会科学]," Aisixiang.com [爱思想], November 29, 2011, https://www.aisixiang.com/data/6547.html.

44. Ren Tianyou [任天佑], *Road to Reform Strengthening the Military* [问道改革强军] (Beijing: National Defense University Press [国防大学出版社], 2015), 32.

45. Fu Ying [傅莹], "Sino-American Relations After the Coronavirus [新冠疫情后的中美关系]," *China-US Focus* [中美聚焦], June 26, 2020, http://cn.chinausfocus.com/foreign-policy/20200629/41939.html.

46. Sun, "Strategic Choice and the Success or Failure of Great Power Rise," 43–45; Yan, "Yan Xuetong: The Overall 'Periphery' Is More Important than the United States."

47. Hu Jintao [胡锦涛], "Coordinate Both Domestic and International Situations and Improve the Level of Diplomatic Work [统筹国内国际两个大局，提高外交工作能力水平]," in *Selected Writings of Hu Jintao, Volume III* [胡锦涛文选(第三卷)], ed. CPC Editorial Committee [中共中央文献编辑委员会] (Beijing: People's Publishing House [人民出版社], 2016), 236; Jiang Zemin [江泽民], "Jiang Zemin: The

International Situation and Military Strategic Policy [江泽民：国际形势和军事战略方针]," *Reform Data* [中国改革信息库], January 13, 1993, http://www.reformdata.org/1993/0113/5616.shtml.

48. Jiang Zemin [江泽民], *Jiang Zemin on Socialism with Chinese Characteristics (Special Excerpts)* [江泽民论有中国特色社会主义(专题摘编)] (Beijing: Central Party Literature Press [中央文献出版社], 2002), 527–528; Yan, "Yan Xuetong: The Overall 'Periphery' Is More Important than the United States."

49. Hu Jintao [胡锦涛], "Integrating Both the Domestic and International Imperatives, Improving the Capability of Diplomatic Work [统筹国内国际两个大局，提高外交工作能力水平]," in *Selected Writings of Hu Jintao, Volume III* [胡锦涛文选(第三卷)], ed. CPC Editorial Committee [中共中央文献编辑委员会] (Beijing: People's Publishing House [人民出版社], 2016), 236.

50. Jiang Zemin [江泽民], *The Selected Works of Jiang Zemin, Volume III* [江泽民文选(第三卷)] (Beijing: People's Publishing House [人民出版社], 2006), 542; Tao Chun [陶春], "Seize the Important Period of Strategic Opportunity of Our Nation's Development with Determination [牢牢把握国家发展重要战略机遇期]," *Study Times* [学习时报], December 4, 2012, http://theory.people.com.cn/n/2012/1204/c49150-19785409.html; Zhu Feng [朱锋], "The Period of Strategic Opportunity in China's Next Ten Years: Must We Make New Choices? [中国未来十年的战略机遇期：我们必须做出新的选择吗?]," *Journal of International Studies* [国际政治研究], no. 2 (2014): 10.

51. Evan S. Medeiros, *China's International Behavior: Activism, Opportunism, and Diversification* (Santa Monica, CA: RAND, 2009), 57.

52. Joseph A. Schumpeter, *Capitalism, Socialism and Democracy* (New York: HarperCollins, 1962), 105.

53. Robert Jervis, "Hypotheses on Misperception," *World Politics* 20, no. 3 (April 1968): 454–479.

54. Grimm, Lee, and Smith, *Strategy as Action*, 194.

55. Grimm, Lee, and Smith, *Strategy as Action*, 119.

56. Jack S. Levy, "Prospect Theory and International Relations: Theoretical Applications and Analytical Problems," *Political Psychology* 13, no. 2 (June 1992): 283–310.

57. Randall Schweller, *Unanswered Threats: Political Constraints on the Balance of Power* (Princeton, NJ: Princeton University Press, 2008), 21.

58. Medeiros, *China's International Behavior*, 56.

59. Efficiency is the "balance between economy in terms of resources such as time, money, space, or materials, and the achievement of an organization's goals and objectives." "Efficiency," in *QFinance: The Ultimate Resource*, 5th ed., ed. Qatar Financial Center (London: A. & C. Black, 2014).

60. Andy Marshall argues that efficiency and effectiveness are key if the United States is to prevail against another country with commensurate resources. Andy W. Marshall, *Long-Term Competition with the Soviets: A Framework for Strategic Analysis* (Santa Monica, CA: RAND Corporation, 1972), viii–x.

61. Aaron L. Friedberg, *In the Shadow of the Garrison State: America's Anti-Statism and Its Cold War Grand Strategy* (Princeton, NJ: Princeton University Press, 2000), 333.

62. Michael Beckley, *Unrivaled: Why America Will Remain the World's Sole Superpower* (Ithaca, NY: Cornell University Press, 2018).

63. Stephen G. Brooks and William C. Wohlforth, "Power, Globalization, and the End of the Cold War: Reevaluating a Landmark Case for Ideas," *International Security* 25, no. 3 (Winter 2000): 22.

64. Richard N. Foster, *Innovation: The Attacker's Advantage* (New York: Summit Books, 1986); Michael Porter, *Competitive Advantage: Creating and Sustaining Superior Performance* (Berkeley: University of California Press, 1985).

65. A clear illustration is the rise of Microsoft as a personal computing hegemon in the 1980s despite the earlier dominance of IBM. Grimm, Lee, and Smith, *Strategy as Action*, 83–84. See also Stephen Young, Chun-Hua Huang, and Michael McDermott, "Internationalization and Competitive Catch-up Processes: Case Study Evidence on Chinese Multinational Enterprises," *Management International Review* 36, no. 4 (1996): 295–314.

66. Philippe Aghion, Stefan Bechtold, Lea Cassar, and Holger Herz, "The Causal Effects of Competition on Innovation: Experimental Evidence," *Journal of Law, Economics, and Organization* 34, no. 2 (May 2018): 163.

67. Grimm, Lee, and Smith, *Strategy as Action*, 103.

68. Peter Liberman, "The Spoils of Conquest," *International Security* 18, no. 2 (1993): 126; Stephen G. Brooks, "The Globalization of Production and the Changing Benefits of Conquest," *Journal of Conflict Resolution* 43, no. 5 (October 1999): 646–670.

69. Eric Lipton, "Faced with Evolving Threats, U.S. Navy Struggles to Change," *New York Times*, September 4, 2023, https://www.nytimes.com/2023/09/04/us/politics/us-navy-ships.html.

70. For example, Mancur Olson, in *The Rise and Decline of Nations: Economic Growth, Stagflation, and Social Rigidities* (New Haven, CT: Yale University Press, 1985), argues that the accumulation of interest groups and the rent-seeking behavior they engage in will, over time, lead to economic stagnation and decline. Likewise, Douglass North, in *Institutions, Institutional Change and Economic Performance* (Cambridge: Cambridge University Press, 1990), emphasizes the role of institutions in shaping economic development and suggests that institutional rigidity can contribute to a country's decline.

71. Zhang Ruizhuang [张睿壮], "Where Is the City upon the Hill Today? [山巅之城今安在]," People.cn [人民网], October 16, 2016, http://opinion.people.com.cn/n1/2016/1016/c1003-28781314.html; Liang Yabin [梁亚滨], "The Cost of Hegemony—An Analysis of the Cause of the Financial Crisis from the Perspective of US Decline [霸权的代价—从美国霸权衰落分析美国金融危机的起因]," *Pacific Journal* [太平洋学报], no. 5 (2010): 30–40; Liang Yabin [梁亚滨], "From Stakeholder to Strategic Assurance: The Sino-US Relationship during the Decline of the US [从利益攸关方到战略再保证：霸权衰落下的中美关系]," *Contemporary Asia-Pacific* [当代亚太], no. 3 (2010): 22–40.

72. Liu Jianfei [刘建飞], "Meddling with Everything, Leave a Mess Everywhere: The Mismatch Between Ends and Means [四处插手反而留下烂摊子，目标与现实之

间存在差距]," People.cn [人民网], October 16, 2016, http://opinion.people.com.cn/n1/2016/1016/c1003-28781317.html.

73. Liu, "Meddling with Everything, Leave a Mess Everywhere"; Lin Ziheng [林子恒], "Xi Jinping: World Political Parties Should Coordinate to Address Challenges [习近平：全球各政党应开展协作应对挑战]," *Zaobao* [联合早报], December 2, 2017, http://www.zaobao.com.sg/special/report/politic/cnpol/story20171202-815500.

74. Hal Brands, "Democracy vs. Authoritarianism: How Ideology Shapes Great-Power Conflict," *Survival* 60, no. 5 (2018): 63.

75. Rebecca Friedman Lissner and Mira Rapp-Hooper, "The Day After Trump: American Strategy for a New International Order," *Washington Quarterly* 41, no. 1 (2018): 7–25.

76. Dan Reiter and Allan C. Stam, *Democracies at War* (Princeton, NJ: Princeton University Press, 2002), https://press.princeton.edu/books/paperback/9780691089492/democracies-at-war.

77. Stephen G. Brooks and William C. Wohlforth, "The Rise and Fall of the Great Powers in the Twenty-First Century: China's Rise and the Fate of America's Global Position," *International Security* 40, no. 3 (2016): 7–53.

78. Erik Gartzke and Kristian Skrede Gleditsch, "Why Democracies May Actually Be Less Reliable Allies," *American Journal of Political Science* 48, no. 4 (2004): 775–795; Stephen M. Walt, "America's Polarization Is a Foreign Policy Problem, Too," *Foreign Policy*, March 11, 2019, http://foreignpolicy.com/2019/03/11/americas-polarization-is-a-foreign-policy-problem-too/; Brands, "Democracy vs. Authoritarianism"; Rachel Kleinfeld, "Do Authoritarian or Democratic Countries Handle Pandemics Better?," Carnegie Endowment for International Peace, March 31, 2020, https://carnegieendowment.org/2020/03/31/do-authoritarian-or-democratic-countries-handle-pandemics-better-pub-81404.

79. Ian Bremmer, "How China's Economy Is Poised to Win the Future," *Time*, November 2, 2017, https://time.com/5006971/how-chinas-economy-is-poised-to-win-the-future/.

80. Michael J. Mazarr et al., "Understanding the Emerging Era of International Competition," RAND Corporation, 2018, 12, https://www.rand.org/pubs/research_reports/RR2726.html.

81. Porter, *Competitive Advantage*. Unlike competitive advantage, comparative advantage does not necessarily signify differentiation; it refers to a relative measure of efficiency in production. David Ricardo, *On Principles of Political Economy and Taxation* (London: John Murray, 1817).

82. Deborah Avant, *Political Institutions and Military Change: Lessons from Peripheral Wars* (Ithaca, NY: Cornell University Press, 1994).

83. Strang and Meyer, "Institutional Conditions for Diffusion"; David Strang and Sarah A. Soule, "Diffusion in Organizations and Social Movements: From Hybrid Corn to Poison Pills," *Annual Review of Sociology* 24 (1998): 265–290.

84. "Party, Government, Military, Civilians, Academia; East, West, South, North, Center, Party Is the Leader of All [党政军民学，东西南北中，党是领导一切的]," People.cn [人民网], February 14, 2022, http://dangjian.people.com.cn/n1/2022/0214/c117092-32351226.html.

85. Gao Yu [高瑜], "Xi Jinping the Man [男儿习近平]," Deutsche Welle Chinese Website [德国之声中文网], January 26, 2013, https://www.dw.com/zh/男儿习近平/a-16549520.

86. CPC History and Literature Research Institute [中共中央党史和文献研究院] ed., *Excerpts from Xi Jinping's Statements on the Concept of Comprehensive National Security* [习近平关于总体国家安全观论述摘编] (Beijing: Central Party Literature Press [中央文献出版社], 2018), 33–34.

87. Ikenberry, *After Victory*, 23.

88. Goddard argues that if a rising power's claims are inconsistent with prevailing norms and rules, then great powers are more likely to see its actions as threatening. Stacie E. Goddard, *When Right Makes Might* (Ithaca, NY: Cornell University Press, 2018), 2.

89. Mazarr et al., "Understanding the Emerging Era of International Competition," 16.

90. Porter, *Competitive Strategy*, 59.

91. The fixed costs of a particular strategy are those that do not change in relation to the "output" of the activity, whereas variable costs are those that "vary with the quantity of output produced." N. Greg Mankiw, *Principles of Economics* (Mason, OH: South-Western, 2007), 275–277.

92. Johnston's chart on the number of reports on China's Cooperative Actions shows how the 70 percent of cooperative reports can be thought to overshadow the 30 percent of non-cooperative reports. Johnston, "China in a World of Orders," 15.

93. James G. March and Johan P. Olsen, "The Institutional Dynamics of International Political Orders," *International Organization* 52, no. 4 (Autumn 1998): 943–944.

94. Johnston, "China in a World of Orders," 12.

95. This argument is inspired by a critique of modernization theory: Suzanne Berger and Ronald Dore, *National Diversity and Global Capitalism* (Ithaca, NY: Cornell University Press, 1996).

96. Wang Yizhou [王逸舟] et al., eds., *Report on Global Politics and Security (2010)* [全球政治与安全报告（2010）] (Beijing: Social Sciences Literature Press [社会科学文献出版社], 2009), 274–275.

97. He Fang [何方], "Is It Multipolarity or 'One Superpower, Several Great Powers' [是多极化还是"一超多强"]," *World Affairs* [国际政治], no. 17 (1998): 20–22; Du Xiaoqiang [杜小强], "New Investigations into the Multipolarization of the International Strategic Landscape [国际战略格局多极化新探]," *World Economy and Politics* [世界经济与政治], no. 4 (1987): 1–7; Wu Guifu [武桂馥], "The Competition Between the US, Japan, and Western Europe and the Multipolar Trends of the Global Landscape [美、日、西欧竞争与世界格局的多极化趋势]," *Future and Development* [未来与发展], no. 6 (1990): 16–19.

98. Avery Goldstein, *Rising to the Challenge: China's Grand Strategy and International Security* (Stanford, CA: Stanford University Press, 2005), 133.

99. Liu Huaqing [刘华清], *Memoirs of Liu Huaqing* [刘华清回忆录] (Beijing: PLA Publishing House [解放军出版社], 2004), 637.

100. Social identity theory posits three ways in which individuals, groups, or states seek to join higher-status groups: social mobility, wherein status-seekers "emulate a higher status group"; social competition, wherein status-seekers "compete with

[the higher status group] for preeminence"; and social creativity, wherein the status-seeker "establish[es] excellence in a different area." Deborah Welch Larson and Alexei Shevchenko, "Russia Says No: Power, Status, and Emotions in Foreign Policy," *Communist and Post-Communist Studies* 47, no. 3–4 (2014): 269–279. My argument is similar, but there are two key differences. First, my theory focuses on how rising powers build power, not status for its own sake. Second, rising power strategies will have all three of these components, though in a unique combination. Specifically, all rising powers are competing with the incumbent great power, and they will do so partly through emulation, but most critically through creative approaches. The entrepreneurial approach, however, is also about how they build power, in that they may seek excellence in the same areas as the great power, but in different ways.

101. For example, see Li Zhaolong [李朝龙] et al., eds., *A Review of Major Military Reforms in the Major Powers Since the 20th Century* [二十世纪以来世界主要国家重大军事改革述评] (Beijing: National Defense University Press [国防大学出版社], 2015).

102. John Lewis Gaddis, *Strategies of Containment: A Critical Appraisal of American National Security Policy During the Cold War* (Oxford: Oxford University Press, 2005), 60.

103. Gaddis, *Strategies of Containment*, 94–95.

104. Gaddis, *Strategies of Containment*, 60, 145, 159.

105. There is a nascent literature that evaluates rising power strategies as well. For example, David M. Edelstein, *Over the Horizon: Time, Uncertainty, and the Rise of Great Powers* (Ithaca, NY: Cornell University Press, 2017); Joshua R. Itzkowitz Shifrinson, *Rising Titans, Falling Giants* (Ithaca, NY: Cornell University Press, 2018).

106. This is the dominant policy narrative. See Kurt M. Campbell and Ely Ratner, "The China Reckoning: How Beijing Defied American Expectations," *Foreign Affairs*, March–April 2018; "How the West Got China Wrong," *The Economist*, March 1, 2018, https://www.economist.com/leaders/2018/03/01/how-the-west-got-china-wrong?gclid=CjwKCAjwrdmhBhBBEiwA4Hx5gz0uYyzm5oNCLtqUmF7loJt7oF2FdwW3wnabdGcpqw7lklhYFVnXnxoC-0IQAvD_BwE&gclsrc=aw.ds.

Chapter 2

1. In 1989, China participated in 37 intergovernmental organizations and 677 international non-governmental organizations. In 2022, the numbers were 743 and 4,803, respectively. Union of International Associations, *Yearbook of International Organizations (1990/1991)*; Union of International Associations, *Yearbook of International Organizations (2021/2022)*.

2. Niu Jun [牛军], "Cycle: China-US Relations and the Evolution of the Asia-Pacific Order (1978–2018)" [轮回：中美关系与亚太秩序演变 (1978–2018)]," *Chinese Journal of American Studies* [美国研究], no. 6 (2018): 9–25.

3. "Asia Power Index 2021: Diplomatic Influence," Lowy Institute, https://power.lowyinstitute.org/explore/diplomatic-influence/.

4. Jim Richardson, "To Win Friends and Influence People, America Should Learn from the CCP," *Foreign Policy*, July 22, 2021; Nahal Toosi, "'Frustrated and Powerless': In Fight with China for Global Influence, Diplomacy Is America's Biggest Weakness," Politico, October 23, 2022, https://www.politico.com/news/2022/10/23/china-diplomacy-panama-00062828.

5. Peter Wallensteen and Isak Svensson, "Talking Peace: International Mediation in Armed Conflicts," *Journal of Peace Research* 51, no. 2 (2014): 315–237; Kyle Beardsley, "Agreement Without Peace? International Mediation and Time Inconsistency Problems," *American Journal of Political Science* 52, no. 4 (2008): 723–740.

6. Patrick M. Regan et al., "Diplomatic Interventions and Civil War: A New Dataset," *Journal of Peace Research* 46, no. 1 (2009): 135–146.

7. "George Mitchell: Building Peace in Northern Ireland," United States Institute of Peace, 2011, https://www.usip.org/public-education-new/george-mitchell-building-peace-northern-ireland; "Camp David Accords and the Arab-Israeli Peace Process," Office of the Historian, Foreign Service Institute, United States Department of State, https://history.state.gov/milestones/1977-1980/camp-david#:~:text=In%20the%20end%2C%20while%20the,Gaza%20and%20the%20West%20Bank.

8. Fu Yuhong [富育红], "The Major Opportunities and Challenges China Faces After the US Withdrawal from Afghanistan [美国撤军阿富汗后中国面临的机遇与挑战]," *International Relations Studies* [国际关系研究], no. 5 (2014): 81–92.

9. Yan Xuetong [阎学通], "From Keeping a Low Profile to Striving for Achievement [从韬光养晦到奋发有为]," *Chinese Journal of International Politics* [国际政治科学], no. 4 (2014): 1–35; Men Honghua [门洪华] and Zhong Feiteng [钟飞腾], "Studies on China's Overseas Interests: Past, Present and Prospects [中国海外利益研究的历程、现状与前瞻]," *Foreign Affairs Review* [外交评论], no. 5 (2009): 58.

10. Edward Wong, "U.S. Officials Repeatedly Urged China to Help Avert War in Ukraine," *New York Times*, February 25, 2022, https://www.nytimes.com/2022/02/25/us/politics/us-china-russia-ukraine.html.

11. Dai Bingguo [戴秉国], *Strategic Dialogues: Dai Bingguo's Memoirs* [战略对话：戴秉国回忆录] (Beijing: People's Publishing House [人民出版社], 2016), 217.

12. Cheng Xin [成欣] and Wang Huihui [王慧慧], "Promoting the Resumption of Diplomatic Relations Between Saudi Arabia and Iran Shows China's Leadership as a Major Power [促成沙特、伊朗复交展现中国大国担当]," *People's Daily* [人民日报], March 14, 2023, http://paper.people.com.cn/rmrbhwb/html/2023-03/14/content_25970291.htm. Zhang Zhiyong [张智勇], "China's Efforts to Mediate Ukraine Crisis in the Spotlight [中国斡旋乌克兰危机的努力备受瞩目]," *Guangming Daily* [光明日报], March 20, 2022, https://epaper.gmw.cn/gmrb/html/2022-03/20/nw.D110000gmrb_20220320_1-08.htm.

13. "China Will Set Up a Preparatory Office for the International Organization for Mediation in the Hong Kong Special Administrative Region [中方将在香港特区设立国际调解院筹备办公室]," Ministry of Foreign Affairs of the People's Republic of China [中华人民共和国外交部], November 1, 2022, https://www.mfa.gov.cn/web/wjbxw_673019/202211/t20221101_10795358.shtml.

14. For the appendix on Chinese mediation activities, please go to www.orianaskylarmas
tro.com/upstart.

15. Zha Daojiong [查道炯], "China's Oil Interests in Africa: A Topic of International Politics   [中国在非洲的石油利益：国际政治课题]," *International Politics Quarterly* [国际政治研究], no. 4 (July 2006): 53–67.

16. For the appendix on Chinese mediation activities, please go to www.orianaskylarmas
tro.com/upstart.

17. Yee Nee Lee, "Trump Says China Has Been 'a Big Help' in US Dealings with North Korea," CNBC, February 28, 2019, www.cnbc.com/2019/02/28/trump-says-china-
has-been-a-big-help-in-us-dealings-with-north-korea.html.

18. I-wei Jennifer Chang, "China and Yemen's Forgotten War," United States Institute of Peace, January 16, 2018, https://www.usip.org/publications/2018/01/china-and-yem
ens-forgotten-war.

19. Li Zhaoxing [李肇星], *Untold Stories of My Diplomatic Life* [说不尽的外交] (Beijing: CITIC Publishing House [中信出版社], 2014), 113.

20. Li, *Untold Stories of My Diplomatic Life*, 113.

21. Shi Jiangtao, "Israel-Gaza Crisis an Opportunity for China to Position Itself as Peace Broker," *South China Morning Post*, May 22, 2021, https://www.scmp.com/news/
china/diplomacy/article/3134478/israel-gaza-crisis-opportunity-china-position-its
elf-peace; "The Latest: China Calls for UN Council Action, Slams US," Associated Press, May 15, 2021, https://apnews.com/article/middle-east-a240cfbb37bc3662a
98d20e92bd38069.

22. Oriana Skylar Mastro, "Noninterference in Contemporary Chinese Foreign Policy: Fact or Fiction?," in *China and International Security: History, Strategy, and 21st Century Policy*, ed. Donovan Chau and Thomas Kane (Santa Barbara, CA: Praeger, 2014), 2:95–114; Wang Meng [王猛], "Darfur Crisis: The Challenge to and Juncture of Changes in China's Foreign Policy [达尔富尔危机：中国外交转型的挑战与契机]," *World Economy and Politics* [世界经济与政治], no. 6 (2005): 38; An Huihou [安惠侯], "Non-Interference Must Be Insisted Upon [坚持不干涉内政原则不动摇]," *Jiefang Daily* [解放日报], December 10, 2013.

23. Cheng Qian, "The Culture of China's Mediation in Regional and International Affairs," *Conflict Resolution Quarterly* 28, no. 1 (2010): 53–65; Wang Yizhou [王逸舟], *A Wise and Benevolent Power: Creative Involvement in a Nutshell* [仁志大国：创造性介入概说] (Beijing: Peking University Press [北京大学出版社], 2018).

24. Wang Jisi [王缉思], "Wang Jisi: 'Marching Westward': The Rebalancing of China's Geostrategy [王缉思：'西进'，中国地缘战略再平衡], Aisixiang.com [爱思想], October 19, 2012, https://www.aisixiang.com/data/58232.html.

25. Robert O. Keohane, "The Demand for International Regimes," *International Organization* 36, no. 2 (Spring 1982): 325–355.

26. G. John Ikenberry, "Institutions, Strategic Restraint, and the Persistence of American Postwar Order," *International Security* 23, no. 3 (Winter 1998–1999): 43–78.

27. "National Security Strategy," White House, March 1990, https://nssarchive.us/wp-
content/uploads/2020/04/1990.pdf.

28. "Assessment of Member States' Advances to the Working Capital Fund for 2022 and Contributions to the United Nations Regular Budget for 2022," United Nations Secretariat, January 4, 2022, http://undocs.org/en/ST/ADM/SER.B/1038; "How We Are Funded," United Nations Peacekeeping, https://peacekeeping.un.org/en/how-we-are-funded, accessed November 15, 2022.

29. Dai, *Strategic Dialogues*, 121–122.

30. "Revenue by Government Donor," United Nations Chief Executive Board, https://unsceb.org/fs-revenue-government-donor, accessed September 14, 2022.

31. Ann Kent, "China's Participation in International Organisations," in *Power and Responsibility in Chinese Foreign Policy*, ed. Yongjin Zhang and Greg Austin (Canberra: Australia National University Press, 2013), 132–166.

32. Wang Yizhou [王逸舟], *Global Politics and Chinese Diplomacy* [全球政治和中国外交] (Beijing: World Affairs Press [世界知识出版社], 2003), 143.

33. Tang Yongsheng [唐永胜], ed., *On National Competitive Strategy* [国家竞争战略论] (Beijing: Current Affairs Press [时事出版社], 2018), 241.

34. Wang, *Global Politics and Chinese Diplomacy*, 51–52.

35. Dataset constructed in conjunction with Texas A&M University's Economic Statecraft Program. It can be found at www.orianaskylarmastro.com/upstart.

36. "What Are UN Specialized Agencies, and How Many Are There?," United Nations, accessed January 19, 2024, https://ask.un.org/faq/140935.

37. Lily Kuo, "China Is Set to Dominate the Deep Sea and Its Wealth of Rare Metals," *Washington Post*, October 19, 2023, https://www.washingtonpost.com/world/interactive/2023/china-deep-sea-mining-military-renewable-energy/.

38. Colum Lynch and Robbie Gramer, "Outfoxed and Outgunned: How China Routed the U.S. in a U.N. Agency," *Foreign Policy*, October 23, 2019, https://foreignpolicy.com/2019/10/23/china-united-states-fao-kevin-moley/.

39. "China's Meng Hongwei Elected President of INTERPOL," INTERPOL, November 10, 2016, https://www.interpol.int/en/News-and-Events/News/2016/China-s-Meng-Hongwei-elected-President-of-INTERPOL.

40. Mikko Huotari et al., "China's Emergence as a Global Security Actor: Strategies for Europe," *MERICS*, July 2017, 39.

41. While China was reelected in 2020, the number of countries that voted for it decreased by forty-one. See Sophie Richardson, "China Grudgingly Gets UN Rights Body Seat," Human Rights Watch, October 13, 2020, https://www.hrw.org/news/2020/10/13/china-grudgingly-gets-un-rights-body-seat#.

42. Li, *Untold Stories of My Diplomatic Life*, 237–238.

43. Andréa Worden, "China at the UN Human Rights Council: Conjuring a 'Community of Shared Future for Humankind'?," in *An Emerging China-Centric World Order: China's Vision for a New World Order in Practice*, ed. Nadège Rolland (Seattle: National Bureau of Asian Research, 2020), 33–48.

44. "A/HRC/51/L.6 Vote Item 2—40th Meeting, 51st Regular Session Human Rights Council," United Nations Human Rights Council, October 6, 2022, https://media.un.org/en/asset/k1w/k1w9tube8v.

45. Kelley E. Currie, "How to Stop China Killing Human Rights at the U.N.," *Foreign Policy*, November 9, 2022, https://foreignpolicy.com/2022/11/09/china-human-rig hts-un-xinjiang-resolution-international-system/.

46. Rana Siu Inboden, "China and the International Human Rights Regime: 1982–2011" (PhD dissertation, Oxford University, 2014), 9, https://ethos.bl.uk/OrderDetails. do;jsessionid=3AC660B99F42571C5775F3F23B4AB665?uin=uk.bl.ethos.686939, quoted in Ted Piccone, "China's Long Game on Human Rights at the United Nations," Brookings Institution, September 2018, 2, https://www.brookings.edu/wp-content/ uploads/2018/09/FP_20181009_china_human_rights.pdf.

47. Culture (in places that find it appealing), political values (when the country lives up to them at home and abroad), and foreign policies (when they are seen as legitimate and having moral authority) are the main sources of soft power. Joseph S. Nye Jr., "The Limits of Chinese Soft Power," Project Syndicate, July 10, 2015, https://www.proj ect-syndicate.org/commentary/china-civil-society-nationalism-soft-power-by-jos eph-s--nye-2015-07.

48. Joseph S. Nye Jr., "Soft Power," *Foreign Policy*, no. 80 (1990): 153–171.

49. Justina Crabtree, "'China Is Everywhere' in Africa's Rising Technology Industry," CNBC, July 28, 2017, https://www.cnbc.com/2017/07/28/china-is-everywhere-in-africas-rising-technology-industry.html.

50. Samantha Custer et al., *Influencing the Narrative: How the Chinese Government Mobilizes Students and Media to Burnish Its Image* (Williamsburg, VA: AidData at William & Mary, 2019), 27.

51. "The Interpretation of the 17th National Congress of China's Communist Party: Improve the Nation's Cultural Soft Power [党的十七大报告解读：提高国家的文化软实力]," Xinhua.com [新华网], December 28, 2007, http://www.gov.cn/ jrzg/2007-12/28/content_845741.htm.

52. "The Interpretation of the 17th National Congress of China's Communist Party: Improve the Nation's Cultural Soft Power." Many leadership statements also focused on the cultural aspect. See Liu Yunshan [刘云山], "Cultural Practitioners Should Spread Positive Energy and Build Soft Power [文化工作者要传播正能量，建设软实力]," People.cn [人民网], February 1, 2013, http://politics.people.com.cn/ n/2013/0201/c70731-20407850.html.

53. "Bo Xilai: Advanced Culture Is the Backbone of Social Progress [薄熙来：先进文化是社会进步的主心骨]," Federation of Literary and Art Circles of the Hong Kong SAR [香港特别行政区文学艺术界联合会], http://www.xgwl.hk/hk/?action-viewn ews-itemid-275.

54. "China Lacks Initiative in the Global Community, There Is a Need to Strengthen Soft Power [中国缺乏国际话语权 需增强软实力]," *China Gate* [热点论坛], December 24, 2009, https://m.wenxuecity.com/bbs/military/623477.html.

55. Guo Linxia [国林霞], "Analysis of China's Current Soft Power [中国软实力现状分析]," *The Contemporary World* [当代世界], no. 3 (March 5, 2007): 37–39; Chen Yugang [陈玉刚], "An Attempt to Illustrate China's Soft Power Construction in Globalization [试论全球化背景下中国软实力的构建]," *International Review* [国际观察], no. 2 (March 5, 2007): 40; Yan Xuetong [阎学通], "The Core of Soft Power

Is Political Capability [软实力的核心是政治实力]," *Century Journal* [世纪行], no. 6 (June 15, 2007): 42–43.

56. Joseph S. Nye Jr., Elizabeth Economy, and David Shambaugh, "Is China's Soft Power Strategy Working?," ChinaPower, February 27, 2016, http://chinapower.csis.org/is-chinas-soft-power-strategy-working/.

57. Rachelle Peterson, "Outsourced to China: Confucius Institutes and Soft Power in American Higher Education," National Association of Scholars, April 5, 2017, https://www.nas.org/reports/outsourced-to-china/full-report#ConfuciusInstitutesWorldwide.

58. "China Is Spending Billions to Make the World Love It," *The Economist*, March 23, 2017, https://www.economist.com/china/2017/03/23/china-is-spending-billions-to-make-the-world-love-it; CNN Press Room, "CNN Worldwide Fact Sheet," February 2023, https://cnnpressroom.blogs.cnn.com/cnn-fact-sheet/; "Overseas Branches [派驻国外分支机构]," Xinhua News Agency [新华社], http://www.xinhuanet.com/xhsld/2021-02/09/c_1211019859.htm.

59. Paul Mozur, "Live from America's Capital, a TV Station Run by China's Communist Party," *New York Times*, February 28, 2019, https://www.nytimes.com/2019/02/28/business/cctv-china-usa-propaganda.html; James Griffiths, "Trump Is Right That China Uses Its Media to Influence Foreign Opinion, but So Does Washington," CNN, September 30, 2018, https://www.cnn.com/2018/09/29/politics/china-media-influence-intl/index.html; Samantha Custer et al., "Ties That Bind: Quantifying China's Public Diplomacy and Its 'Good Neighbor' Effect," AidData at William & Mary, July 27, 2018, https://www.aiddata.org/publications/ties-that-bind.

60. "Xi Jinping Attends the Central Conference on Work Relating to Foreign Affairs and Makes Important Remarks [习近平出席中央外事工作会议并发表重要讲话]," Xinhuanet.com [新华网], November 29, 2014, http://www.xinhuanet.com/politics/2014-11/29/c_1113457723.htm. Such rhetoric continued through Xi's tenure. See "General Secretary Xi Jinping Speaks About International Communication [习近平总书记这样谈国际传播]," Wenming.cn [中国文明网], August 16, 2021, http://www.wenming.cn/ll_pd/ll_xgzt/202108/t20210816_6143596.shtml.

61. "General Secretary Xi Jinping Speaks About International Communication."

62. "World Soft Power Index 2023," Indian Strategic Studies Forum, 2023, https://issf.org.in/.

63. Laura Silver, Kat Devlin, and Christine Huang, "Unfavorable Views of China Reach Historic Highs in Many Countries," Pew Research Center, October 6, 2020, https://www.pewresearch.org/global/2020/10/06/unfavorable-views-of-china-reach-historic-highs-in-many-countries/.

64. Megan Brennan, "Record-Low 15% of Americans View China Favorably," Gallup, March 7, 2023, https://news.gallup.com/poll/471551/record-low-americans-view-china-favorably.aspx.

65. Laura Silver, Christine Huang, and Laura Clancy, "How Global Public Opinion of China Has Shifted in the Xi Era," Pew Research Center, September 28, 2022, https://www.pewresearch.org/global/2022/09/28/how-global-public-opinion-of-china-has-shifted-in-the-xi-era/.

66. Sharon Seah et al., *The State of Southeast Asia: 2021* (Singapore: ISEAS–Yusof Ishak Institute, 2021).

67. Around a quarter of the entries at Cannes in 2018 were from China, but China had only nine winners. "China Brands Go Global," R3, October 21, 2019, https://rthree.com/insights/china-brands-go-global/.

68. "At Home with External Propaganda," China Media Project, December 8, 2021, https://chinamediaproject.org/2021/12/08/at-home-with-external-propaganda/.

69. Nicole Talmacs, "Africa and Africans in *Wolf Warrior 2*: Narratives of Trust, Patriotism and Rationalized Racism Among Chinese University Students," *Journal of Asian and African Studies* 55, no. 8 (2020): 1230–1245.

70. Marty Swant, "The 2020 World's Most Valuable Brands," *Forbes*, July 24, 2020, https://www.forbes.com/the-worlds-most-valuable-brands/.

71. Kathryn Virzi and Carol Parrington, "Identifying Factors That Hinder the Acceptance of Chinese Brands Among US Consumers," *OALib*, no. 6 (July 2019): 1–12.

72. Caroline Gray et al., "Caught in the Middle: Views of US-China Competition Across Asia," Eurasia Group Foundation, June 2023, https://egfound.org/wp-content/uploads/2023/06/Caught-in-the-Middle.pdf.

73. Joshua Kurlantzick, *Charm Offensive: How China's Soft Power Is Transforming the World* (New Haven, CT: Yale University Press, 2007), 11.

74. Lee Edwards, "Confucius Institutes: China's Trojan Horse," Heritage Foundation, March 27, 2021, https://www.heritage.org/homeland-security/commentary/confucius-institutes-chinas-trojan-horse.

75. "How Many Confucius Institutes Are in the United States?," National Association of Scholars, June 22, 2023, https://www.nas.org/blogs/article/how_many_confucius_institutes_are_in_the_united_states; Sarah Cook, "Beijing's Global Megaphone," Freedom House, January 11, 2020, https://freedomhouse.org/report/special-report/2020/beijings-global-megaphone.

76. "China's Confucius Institutes: An Inquiry by the Conservative Party Human Rights Commission," Conservative Party Human Rights Commission, February 2019, https://web.archive.org/web/20191016144832/http://www.conservativehumanrights.com/news/2019/CPHRC_Confucius_Institutes_report_FEBRUARY_2019.pdf.

77. Dov S. Zakheim, "Time to Shut Down All Confucius Institutes—Whatever They Might Be Called," *The Hill*, November 11, 2022, https://thehill.com/opinion/national-security/3729453-time-to-shut-down-all-confucius-institutes-whatever-they-might-be-called/.

78. Li Mingjiang, "China Debates Soft Power," in *Chinese Scholars and Foreign Policy*, ed. Huiyin Feng, Kai He, and Yan Xuetong (New York: Routledge, 2020), 45.

79. Fu Ying [傅莹], "Sino-American Relations After COVID-19 [新冠疫情后的中美关系]," *China-US Focus* [中美聚焦], June 26, 2020, http://cn.chinausfocus.com/foreign-policy/20200629/41939.html.

80. Data generated using *People's Daily*'s Graphic and Textual Database [人民日报图文数据库], available via http://data.people.com.cn/rmrb, accessed December 16, 2022.

81. "China's Economy and the Beijing Olympics," *Congressional Research Service*, August 6, 2008, https://www.everycrsreport.com/reports/RS22936.html; Nye, Economy, and Shambaugh, "Is China's Soft Power Strategy Working?"

82. For Xi's views on soft power, see "Xi Jinping Talks About the Nation's Cultural Soft Power: Strengthens Chinese People's Confidence and Integrity [习近平谈国家文化软实力：增强做中国人的骨气和底气]," People.com.cn [中国共产党新闻网], June 25, 2015, http://cpc.people.com.cn/xuexi/n/2015/0625/c385474-27204268.html; Bai Guolong [白国龙] et al., "Whether It Is Hard or Soft Power, Both Rely on Talents' Abilities—Xi Jinping's Important Speech at the Meeting of the Chinese Academy of Sciences and the Chinese Academy of Engineering Attracted Huge Resonation [实力、软实力，归根到底要靠人才实力—习近平总书记在两院院士大会上的重要讲话引起热烈反响之四]," Youth.cn [中国青年网], June 1, 2018, http://news.youth.cn/sz/201806/t20180601_11634058.htm; Fan Zhou [范周] and Zhou Jie [周洁], "Study on China's Cultural Soft Power Construction Under the 'One Belt, One Road' Strategic Background ['一带一路'战略背景下的中国文化软实力建设研究]," *Tongji University Journal Social Science Section* [同济大学学报社会科学版] 27, no. 5 (November 14, 2016): 45; Hu Jian [胡键], "'One Belt, One Road' and China's Rise in Soft Power] ['一带一路'与中国软实力的提升]," *Journal of Social Sciences* [社会科学], no. 1 (January 10, 2020): 18.

83. Custer et al., *Influencing the Narrative*, 23.

84. Erich Schwartzel, "How China Captured Hollywood," *The Atlantic*, February 8, 2022, https://www.theatlantic.com/international/archive/2022/02/china-captured-hollywood/621618/.

85. Yao Wen, "Branding and Legitimation: China's Party Diplomacy amid the COVID-19 Pandemic," *China Review* 21, no. 1 (February 2021): 55–89.

86. Timothy D. Hoyt, *Military Industry and Regional Defense Policy: India, Iraq and Israel* (New York: Routledge, 2011), 56; Keith Krause, "Military Statecraft: Power and Influence in Soviet and American Arms Transfer Relationships," *International Studies Quarterly* 35, no. 3 (1991): 313–336.

87. "U.S. Arms Sales and Defense Trade," US Department of State, January 20, 2021, https://www.state.gov/u-s-arms-sales-and-defense-trade/.

88. Aaron Mehta, "US Increases Dominance of Global Arms Exports," *Defense News*, March 15, 2021, https://www.defensenews.com/global/2021/03/15/us-increases-dominance-of-global-arms-exports/.

89. "U.S. Arms Transfers Increased by 2.8 Percent in FY 2020 to $175.08 Billion," US Department of State, January 20, 2020, https://www.state.gov/u-s-arms-transfers-increased-by-2-8-percent-in-fy-2020-to-175-08-billion/.

90. "Fiscal Year 2021 U.S. Arms Transfers and Defense Trade," US Department of State, December 22, 2021, https://www.state.gov/fiscal-year-2021-u-s-arms-transfers-and-defense-trade/.

91. William D. Hartung, Christina Arabia, and Elias Yousif, "The Trump Effect: Trends in Major U.S. Arms Sales 2019," Center for International Policy, May 2020, https://securityassistance.org/publications/the-trump-effect-trends-in-major-arms-sales-in-2019/; William D. Young and Elias Yousif, "US Arms Sales Trends: 2020 and

Beyond from Trump to Biden," *Security Assistance Monitor*, April 2021, https://sec urityassistance.org/publications/u-s-arms-sales-trends-2020-and-beyond-from-trump-to-buden/.

92. "US Arms Sales to Taiwan," Forum on the Arms Trade, https://www.forumarmstr ade.org/ustaiwan.html.

93. Andrew J. Pierre, "Arms Sales: The New Diplomacy," *Foreign Affairs* 60, no. 2 (Winter, 1981): 267.

94. Zhang Qingmin [张清敏], "The Formation and Evolution of American Policy on Transfer of Conventional Weapons (1947–1992) [美国常规武器转让政策的形成与转变 (1947–1992)]," *Chinese Journal of American Studies* [美国研究] 23, no. 3 (2009): 73–91.

95. Zhang, "The Formation and Evolution of American Policy on Transfer of Conventional Weapons," 88; Li Chen [李晨], "The US Sold Arms to Saudi Arabia, Where Did the 100 Billion Protection Fee Go? [美国向沙特出售千亿武器'保护费'花哪了?]," 81.cn [中国军网], May 22, 2017, http://www.81.cn/gjzx/2017-05/22/content_7612637.htm.

96. These sources point out that most recently the United States is pursuing such a strategy to deal with competition in the South China Sea. See Zhao Yi [赵毅], "The Current Military Presence of USA in Southeast Asia [当前美国在东南亚的军事存在探析]," *Southeast Asian Studies* [东南亚研究], no. 5 (2014): 64; Zhai Kun [翟崑] and Song Qirun [宋清润], "The Development of US-Thailand Maritime Security Cooperation and Its Motivation [美泰海洋安全合作的演变及动因]," *Pacific Journal* [太平洋学报] 27, no. 1 (2019): 16–17.

97. But it is also pointed out that this strategy entails the downsides of possibly fueling regional conflicts and equipping potential future enemies. For some representative Chinese sources on the United States' arms sales, see Qi Haixia [漆海霞] and Zhou Jiaren [周建仁], "Arms Sales and US Strategic Deployment in the Asia-Pacific [军售与美国亚太地区战略布局]," *Chinese Social Science* [中国社会科学], no. 5 (2015): 161–162; Jiao Shixin [焦世新], "The Asia-Pacific Rebalancing and the Adjustment of US Policy Towards the South China Sea ['亚太再平衡'与美国对南海政策的调整]," *American Studies* [美国研究] 30, no. 6 (2016): 83–86; Zhang Shirong [张仕荣], "The US's Asia-Pacific Rebalance Strategy and Its Impact on China–US Relations [美国'亚太再平衡战略'及对中美关系的影响]," *Contemporary World and Socialism* [当代世界与社会主义], no. 4 (2012): 30–32.

98. Sidhant Sibal, "Several Countries Concerned over Faulty Chinese Military Equipment," WION, November 7, 2020, https://www.wionews.com/world/several-countries-concerned-over-faulty-chinese-military-equipment-341382.

99. Sixty-six percent of offers in 2019 were of aircraft. Hartung, Arabia, and Yousif, "The Trump Effect," 6.

100. Zhou Jiaren [周建仁], "Coping with America's Alliance Strategy Within the Context of the Rebalancing to Asia and the Pacific [同盟理论与美国'重返亚太'同盟战略应对]," *Contemporary Asia-Pacific* [当代亚太], no. 4 (2015): 34; Qi Haixia [漆海霞], "View Partial Feature of the US's Strategic Shift to the East from Arms Sales [从军售看美国战略重心东易的局部特征]," *Journal of University of International*

Relations [国际关系学院学报], no. 4 (2012); Qi and Zhou, "Arms Sales and US Strategic Deployment in the Asia-Pacific"; Jiao, "The Asia-Pacific Rebalancing and the Adjustment of US Policy Towards the South China Sea."

101. Data generated using Stockholm International Peace Research Institute's Arms Transfers Database, available via https://www.sipri.org/databases/armstransfers. The United States recorded 14.515 billion trend-indicator value (TIV) in 2022, while China recorded a total of 2.017 billion TIV.

102. A. Trevor Thrall and Jordan Cohen, "Explaining U.S. Arms Sales," Cato Institute, June 18, 2020, https://www.cato.org/blog/explaining-us-arms-sales; "SIPRI Arms Transfers Database," Stockholm International Peace Research Institute, https://www.sipri.org/databases/armstransfers.

103. "Congressional Research Service Reports on Conventional Weapons Systems," Congressional Research Service, https://sgp.fas.org/crs/weapons/index.html. The values of the arms transfers are adjusted to the USD values in 2022 for comparison.

104. "Comparison: China-US, Global Arms Trade Data," Lowy Institute Asia Power Index, 2023, https://power.lowyinstitute.org/data/defence-networks/global-arms-transfers/arms-export-partnerships/.

105. "China Spreads Its Tentacles with Arms Exports," ANI News, February 25, 2021, https://www.aninews.in/news/world/asia/china-spreads-its-tentacles-with-arms-exports20210225132552.

106. "Why China's Submarine Deal with Bangladesh Matters," *The Diplomat*, January 20, 2017, https://thediplomat.com/2017/01/why-chinas-submarine-deal-with-banglad esh-matters/.

107. "World Development Indicators—GDP Per Capita (Current US$)," World Bank, https://data.worldbank.org/indicator/NY.GDP.PCAP.CD, accessed June 9, 2023.

108. Nilotpal Bhattacharjee, "China's Warning to Bangladesh on the Quad," *The Diplomat*, May 18, 2021, https://thediplomat.com/2021/05/chinas-warning-to-ban gladesh-on-the-quad/.

109. "Embargoed and Sanctioned Countries," University of Pittsburgh Office of Trade Compliance, https://www.tradecompliance.pitt.edu/embargoed-and-sanctioned-countries, accessed June 7, 2023.

110. Marwaan Macan-Markar, "Myanmar Embraces Russian Arms to Offset China's Influence," Nikkei Asia, February 9, 2021, https://asia.nikkei.com/Spotlight/Myan mar-Coup/Myanmar-embraces-Russian-arms-to-offset-China-s-influence.

111. ChinaPower Team, "How Dominant Is China in the Global Arms Trade?," ChinaPower, April 26, 2018, http://chinapower.csis.org/china-global-arms-trade/.

112. In 1991, the George H. W. Bush administration enacted sanctions against China, accusing Beijing of transferring missile technology to Pakistan. After Beijing pledged to abide by the MTCR, the administration lifted those sanctions. However, the US government has since accused Beijing of violating that pledge— China maintains at best what could be called a "spotty" record when it comes to the MTCR pledge. Paula A. DeSutter, "China's Record of Proliferation Activities," US State Department, July 24, 2003, https://2001-2009.state.gov/t/vci/rls/rm/24518.htm.

113. Daryl G. Kimball, "U.S. Aims to Expand Drone Sales," Arms Control Association, July/August 2020, https://www.armscontrol.org/act/2020-07/news/us-aims-exp and-drone-sales.

114. ChinaPower Team, "How Dominant Is China in the Global Arms Trade?"; Ergen Hu [胡尔根], "China's CASC Rainbow Exports to More than a Dozen Countries with More than 200 Orders in a Year [中国彩虹无人机出口十多国家 年交付200余架]," Huanqiu.com [环球网], January 13, 2017, https://mil.huanqiu.com/article/9CaKrnJZIdj.

115. ChinaPower Team, "Drone Transfers Data," ChinaPower, https://chinapower.csis.org/data/sipri-drones-transfer-data/, accessed December 6, 2022.

116. ChinaPower Team, "Is China at the Forefront of Drone Technology," ChinaPower, May 29, 2018, https://chinapower.csis.org/china-drones-unmanned-technology/.

117. "SIPRI Arms Transfers Database," Stockholm International Peace Research Institute, https://www.sipri.org/databases/armstransfers.

118. Oil data from "Customs Statistics Online Query Platform [海关统计数据在线查询平台]," General Administration of Customs of the People's Republic of China [中华人民共和国海关总署], http://stats.customs.gov.cn/, accessed June 7, 2023. Data on arms transfers from "SIPRI Arms Transfers Database."

119. Shi Lei [石磊], "Military Partnership Between the United States and South America After the Cold War [冷战后美国与南美洲国家的军事合作]," *Latin American Studies* [拉丁美洲研究] 38, no. 3 (2016); ChinaPower Team, "How Dominant Is China in the Global Arms Trade?"

120. Zhao Jiandong [赵建东], "US Media: China's Arms Exports Have Unique Advantages [美媒：中国武器出口具有独特优势]," Huanqiu.com [环球网], October 12, 2022, https://oversea.huanqiu.com/article/4A22gvyepsX.

121. Guo Xiaobin [郭晓兵], "US Arms Sales: The 'Political Scheme' Behind the 'Business Plan' [美国军售：'生意经'背后的'政治账']," *PLA Daily* [解放军报], December 17, 2020.

122. "The Fear of No War: US Arms Sales Grow Against the Odds, Who is a Better War Dealer Than the US [唯恐天下无战！美国军售逆势增长 战争贩子舍美其谁？]," CCTV News [央视新闻], March 17, 2022, https://news.cctv.com/2022/03/17/ARTIoIchOyZfAbMyTDpdDYH9220317.shtml; Sun Ding [孙丁], "US Arms Sales Grow Against the Odds, Exporting Unrest and Harming the World [美国军售逆势增长输出动乱危害世界]," Xinhua News Agency [新华社], March 15, 2022, http://www.news.cn/world/2022-03/15/c_1128473330.htm.

123. 22 CFR § 126.1, "Prohibited Exports, Imports, and Sales to or from Certain Countries."

124. "Arms Embargoes," SIPRI, https://www.sipri.org/databases/embargoes.

125. "EU Arms Embargo on China," SIPRI, November 20, 2012, https://www.sipri.org/databases/embargoes/eu_arms_embargoes/china.

126. Ni Ligang [倪利刚], "China Squeezed Out Russia and Suddenly Second in the World in Arms Sales? [中国挤掉俄罗斯 突然'军售世界第二'了?]," iFeng [凤凰网], December 12, 2020, https://news.ifeng.com/c/829COcWfjZC; Tang Yihong [唐宜红] and Qi Xianguo [齐先国], "Changes in Global Arms Trade Policy and Its Lesson to China [全球军品贸易政策变迁及对我国的启示]," *International Trade* [国际贸易], no. 2 (2015): 30.

127. Hans J. Morgenthau, "Diplomacy," *Yale Law Journal* 55, no. 5 (August 1946): 1067.

128. "1996, Bringing-In and Going-Out Strategy [1996, '引进来'和'走出去'战略]," Xinhua News Agency [新华社], December 8, 2021, http://www.news.cn/politics/2021-12/08/c_1211478976.htm.

129. ChinaPower Team, "What Do Overseas Visits Reveal About China's Foreign Policy Priorities?," ChinaPower, March 29, 2021, https://chinapower.csis.org/diplomatic-visits/.

130. China has 27 regional embassies, 179 global embassies, and 48 second-tier regional consulates, while the United States has 26, 178, and 28, respectively. "Lowy Institute Asia Power Index 2023 Edition," Lowy Institute, 2023, https://power.lowyinstitute.org/data/diplomatic-influence/diplomatic-network/.

131. Yan Xuetong [阎学通], "Yan Xuetong: The Overall 'Periphery' Is More Important than the United States [阎学通：整体的'周边'比美国更重要]," *Global Times* [环球时报], January 13, 2015, http://opinion.huanqiu.com/1152/2015-01/5392162.html.

132. Abdi Latif Dahir, "The Reason American Presidents Keep Visiting the Same African Countries," Quartz, October 9, 2018, https://qz.com/africa/1417273/the-reason-american-presidents-keep-visiting-the-same-few-african-countries/.

133. Kemi Lijadu, "Chinese Leaders Visit Africa More Often than You Think and Not Always the Places You Expect," Quartz, July 26, 2018, https://qz.com/africa/1335418/chinese-leaders-visit-africa-more-often-than-you-think-and-not-always-the-places-you-expect/.

134. "Travels of Barack Obama," Office of the Historian, US Department of State, https://history.state.gov/departmenthistory/travels/president/obama-barack; "Travels of Donald J. Trump," Office of the Historian, US Department of State, https://history.state.gov/departmenthistory/travels/president/trump-donald-j.

135. ChinaPower Team, "What Do Overseas Visits Reveal About China's Foreign Policy Priorities?"

136. Wilder Alejandro Sanchez, "No US President Has Ever Visited Central Asia. Biden Can Change That," *World Politics Review*, April 9, 2021, https://www.worldpoliticsreview.com/articles/29559/no-u-s-president-has-ever-visited-central-asia-biden-can-change-that; ChinaPower Team, "What Do Overseas Visits Reveal About China's Foreign Policy Priorities?"

137. ChinaPower Team, "What Do Overseas Visits Reveal About China's Foreign Policy Priorities?"; Diplomatic Agenda, Ministry of Foreign Affairs of the People's Republic of China [中华人民共和国外交部], https://www.fmprc.gov.cn/mfa_eng/wjdt_665385/wsrc_665395/.

138. ChinaPower Team, "What Do Overseas Visits Reveal About China's Foreign Policy Priorities?"

139. Richard R. Verma, "Remarks to the Foreign Policy for America 2023 Leadership Summit," US Department of State, June 12, 2023, https://www.state.gov/remarks-to-the-foreign-policy-for-america-2023-leadership-summit/.

140. Neil Thomas, "Far More World Leaders Visit China than America," *The Interpreter*, July 28, 2021, https://www.lowyinstitute.org/the-interpreter/far-more-world-leaders-visit-china-america.

141. ChinaPower Team, "What Do Overseas Visits Reveal About China's Foreign Policy Priorities?"

142. Yang Jiechi [杨洁篪], "Continue to Create New Prospects for Foreign Work Under the Guidance of General Secretary Xi Jinping's Diplomatic Thoughts [在习近平总书记外交思想指导下不断开创对外工作新局面]," Ministry of Foreign Affairs of the People's Republic of China [中华人民共和国外交部], January 14, 2017, https://www.mfa.gov.cn/web/gjhdq_676201/gjhdqzz_681964/sgwyh_682446/zyjh_682456/201701/t20170114_9385067.shtml.

143. Wang Jisi [王缉思], "Wang Jisi: 'Marching Westward': The Rebalancing of China's Geostrategy [王缉思：'西进'，中国地缘战略再平衡], Huanqiu.com [环球网], October 17, 2012, http://opinion.huanqiu.com/opinion_world/2012-10/3193760.html.

144. China's list of peripheral countries includes Russia, Japan, North Korea, South Korea, Mongolia, ASEAN nations, India, Pakistan, and Central Asian countries. See "China's Relations with Peripheral Countries [中国与周边国家的关系]," Gov.cn [中国政府网], June 30, 2005, https://www.gov.cn/test/2005-06/30/content_11177.htm. See also Yan, "Yan Xuetong: The Overall 'Periphery' Is More Important than the United States."

145. Li, *Untold Stories of My Diplomatic Life*, 185.

146. Roderick Kefferpütz, "Big Fish in Small Ponds: China's Subnational Diplomacy in Europe," *MERICS*, November 18, 2021, https://merics.org/en/report/big-fish-small-ponds-chinas-subnational-diplomacy-europe.

147. Sun Cheng [孙承], "China 'Surrounds Cities with Rural Areas' and Uses Local Governments in Western Countries to Oppose Countries' Policies Toward China [中国'以农村包围城市'，利用西方国家地方政府对抗各国对华政策]," Voice of America, December 8, 2021, https://www.voachinese.com/a/china-subnational-diplomacy-20211207/6343105.html; Chen Xiang [陈翔] and Wei Hong [韦红], "China's Local Diplomacy Under the Perspective of 'One Belt, One Road' ['一带一路'建设视野下的中国地方外交]," *International Review* [国际观察] 6, no. 35.

148. Emily de La Bruyère and Nathan Picarsic, "All Over the Map," Foundation for the Defense of Democracies, November 15, 2021, https://www.fdd.org/analysis/2021/11/15/all-over-the-map/.

149. Salvatore Babones, "A House Divided: The AFRB and China's Subnational Diplomacy in Australia," Analysis Paper 17, Centre for Independent Studies, November 2020, 3, https://www.cis.org.au/publications/analysis-papers/a-house-divided-the-afrb-and-chinas-subnational-diplomacy-in-australia/.

150. Reuters Staff, "U.S. Designates Chinese Body a Foreign Mission, Quits Local Cooperation Agreement," Reuters, October 28, 2020, https://www.reuters.com/article/us-usa-china-pompeo/u-s-designates-chinese-body-a-foreign-mission-quits-local-cooperation-agreement-idUSKBN27D305.

151. "Safeguarding Our Future: Protecting Government and Business Leaders at the U.S. State and Local Level from People's Republic of China (PRC) Influence Operations," National Counterintelligence and Security Center, July 2022, https://www.dni.gov/files/NCSC/documents/SafeguardingOurFuture/PRC_Subnational_Influence-06-July-2022.pdf.

152. Custer et al., *Ties That Bind*, 23.

153. ChinaPower Team, "How Is China Bolstering Its Military Diplomatic Relations?," ChinaPower, October 27, 2017, https://chinapower.csis.org/china-military-diplomacy/.

154. Larry Hanauer and Lyle J. Morris, "China in Africa: Implications of a Deepening Relationship," RAND Corporation, 2014, 3, https://www.rand.org/pubs/research_briefs/RB9760.html.

155. Dai Bingguo [戴秉国], "Remarks by Dai Bingguo at Center for Strategic and International Studies," Embassy of the People's Republic of China in Georgia [中华人民共和国驻格鲁吉亚大使馆], July 6, 2016, http://ge.china-embassy.gov.cn/eng/xwdt/201607/t20160706_1056446.htm.

Chapter 3

1. "Deng Xiaoping's Speech at the Sixth Special Session of the UN General Assembly [邓小平在联大第六届特别会议上的发言]," Communist Party Network [共产党员网], delivered April 11, 1974, https://news.12371.cn/2015/09/28/ARTI1443384874163974.shtml?ticket=.

2. Yang Jiemian [杨洁勉], "70 Years of Chinese Diplomacy: Innovative Practices and Theory Building [中国外交70年：实践创新和理论建设]," *China International Studies* [中国国际问题研究], no. 5 (2019): 6–19.

3. Secretariat of the Center for the Study of Xi Jinping's Diplomatic Thought [习近平外交思想研究中心秘书处], "Constructing a Unique Style of Chinese Diplomacy: Meaning and Paths to Realization [塑造中国外交独特风范：内涵与实践路径]," *International Studies* [国际问题研究], no. 6 (2021): 10.

4. Secretariat of the Center for the Study of Xi Jinping's Diplomatic Thought, "Constructing a Unique Style of Chinese Diplomacy," 10.

5. Derek Scissors, "China's Overseas Investment Starts the Long Climb Back," American Enterprise Institute, 2021, https://www.aei.org/research-products/report/chinas-overseas-investment-starts-the-long-climb-back/.

6. Lindsey W. Ford and James Goldgeier, "Retooling America's Alliances to Manage the China Challenge," Brookings Institution, 2021, https://www.brookings.edu/research/retooling-americas-alliances-to-manage-the-china-challenge/.

7. Harry Bliss and Bruce Russett, "Democratic Trading Partners: The Liberal Connection, 1962–1989," *Journal of Politics* 60, no. 4 (1998): 1126–1147; Mira Rapp-Hooper, *Shields of the Republic* (Cambridge, MA: Harvard University Press, 2020); G. John Ikenberry, "Liberalism and Empire: Logics of Order in the American Unipolar Age," *Review of International Studies* 30, no. 4 (2004): 609–630. For a review of all US alliance commitments, see Brett Leeds et al., "Alliance Treaty Obligations and Provisions, 1815–1944," *International Interactions* 28, no. 3 (2002): 237–260.

8. Rapp-Hooper, *Shields of the Republic*; Fareed Zakaria, *The Post-American World* (New York: W. W. Norton, 2007), 178.

9. For some representative sources, see Xu Jin [徐进], "The Cause of Contemporary China's Aversion to Alliances [当代中国拒斥同盟心理的由来]," *International Economic Review* [国际经济评论], no. 5 (2015): 143–154; Su Xiaohui [苏晓晖], "Chinese Diplomacy 'Finds Partners Not Allies' [中国外交'结伴而不结盟']," *People's Daily Global Edition* [人民日报海外版], January 2, 2015; Ling Shengli [凌胜利], "Why Doesn't China Set Up Alliances? [中国为什么不结盟?]," *Foreign Affairs Review* [外交评论], no. 3 (2013): 20–33.

10. Sun Degang [孙德刚], "On 'Quasi-Alliance' Strategy [论'准联盟'战略]," *World Economics and Politics* [世界经济与政治], no. 2 (2011): 55–79.

11. Adam P. Liff, "China and the US Alliance System," *China Quarterly*, no. 233 (2018): 156–157.

12. Ling Shengli [凌胜利], "Can China Form Alliances? [中国可以结盟吗?]," *Friends of the Leader* [领导之友], no. 1 (2012): 52–53.

13. Zhang Bowen [张博文], "Will China Abandon the 'Non-Alliance' Policy? [中国会放弃'不结盟'政策吗?]," *Global Prospect* [国际展望], no. 10 (2000): 17–18; Yan Xuetong [阎学通], "Is Russia Reliable [俄罗斯可靠吗?]," *International Economic Review* [国际经济评论], no. 3 (2012): 21–25.

14. "Why Is the Sino-Russian Relationship So Good but Still Not Allied [中俄关系这么好，为啥不结盟]," *Xinhua News Agency* [新华社], March 22, 2023, http://www.news.cn/world/2023-03/22/c_1211740381.htm.

15. Sun Ru [孙茹], "Building Partnership Network: An Upgrade of China's Non-Alliance Policies [构建伙伴关系网：中国不结盟政策的升级版]," *World Affairs* [世界知识], no. 6 (2015): 58–60. For an assessment of the debate among Chinese scholars, see Liu Ruonan and Liu Feng, "Contending Ideas on China's Non-Alliance Strategy," *Chinese Journal of International Politics* 10, no. 2 (2017): 151–171.

16. Dai Weilai [戴维来], "Initial Discussion on Medium-Power Nations' Global Leadership [中等强国的国际领导权问题初探]," *Forum of World Economics and Politics* [世界经济与政治论坛], no. 2 (2016): 58; Guo Shuyong [郭树勇], "The Leadership in Global Governance and China's Role [全球治理领导权问题与中国的角色定位]," *People's Forum* [人民论坛], no. 14 (2017): 25–36; Zhou Jianren [周建仁], "Theories of Alliance Formation: A Review and Considerations for Chinese Policy [联盟形成理论：评估及对中国的政策启示]," *Contemporary Asia-Pacific* [当代亚太], no. 3 (2012): 61.

17. The United States leads the world in nominal GDP, and seven of the other top ten countries are US allies.

18. Sun Ru [孙茹], "Building a Partnership Network: An Upgrade of China's Non-Alliance Policies [构建伙伴关系网：中国不结盟政策的升级版]," *World Affairs* [世界知识], no. 6 (2015): 58–60; Li Ziguo, "An Evolving Partnership," *Beijing Review*, October 16, 2014, http://www.bjreview.com.cn/world/txt/2014-10/13/content_644116_2.htm.

19. Sheng Ping [盛平] and Wang Zaixin [王再兴], *Chronology of Hu Yaobang's Thought 1975–1989* [胡耀邦思想年谱, 1975–1989] (Hong Kong: Taide Times Publishing House [泰德时代出版社], 2007); Song Yimin [宋以敏], "Hu Yaobang Made Corrections on China's Foreign Relations [胡耀邦在对外关系上的拨乱反正]," *Yanhuang Chunqiu* [炎黄春秋], no. 5 (2013); Sun Degang [孙德刚], "On 'Quasi-Alliance' Strategy [论'准联盟'战略]," *World Economics and Politics* [世界经济与政治], no. 2 (2011): 55–79.

20. Hu Jintao [胡锦涛], *Hu Jintao's Selected Work (Volume I)* [胡锦涛文选(第一卷)] (Beijing: Military Science Publishing House [人民出版社], 2016), 188; Yu Ruidong [余瑞冬], "Full Text of Hu Jintao's Speech at SCO Moscow Summit [胡锦涛在上海合作组织莫斯科峰会上讲话全文]," Xinhua.com [新华网], May 30, 2003, https://www.chinanews.com/n/2003-05-30/26/308504.html; Nie Lubin, "Hu Jintao Illustrates the Five Big Achievements of the SCO [胡锦涛阐述上合组织五大成就]," Huanqiu.com [环球网], June 6, 2012, https://m.huanqiu.com/article/9CaKrnJvHYC.

21. Zhang Hongliang [张宏良], "How to View Qin Gang and Wang Yi's 'Three-Noes' [如何看待秦刚的'三不原则' 和王毅的'三无原则']," Fuxing Net [复兴网], January 14, 2023, https://www.mzfxw.com/e/action/ShowInfo.php?classid=12&id=171317.

22. Ling, "Why Doesn't China Set Up Alliances?"; Wang Fan [王帆], "Alliance Management Theory and Dilemma [联盟管理论与联盟管理困境]," *Chinese Journal of European Studies* [欧洲研究], no. 4 (2006): 111–125; Zhang Yunling [张蕴岭], "Overestimate One's Own Power, Abducted by Extremist Opinions—Two Risks in the Process of a Great Power's Rise [高估自己的力量，被极端舆论绑架 大国崛起过程中的两大风险]," *People's Forum* [人民论坛], no. 4 (2013): 50–51.

23. Lei Yu, "China's Strategic Partnership with Latin America: A Fulcrum in China's Rise," *International Affairs* 91, no. 5 (2015): 1054.

24. Lucyna Czechowska et al., *States, International Organizations and Strategic Partnerships* (Cheltenham, UK: Edward Elgar, 2019), 19; Thomas S. Wilkins, "Russo–Chinese Strategic Partnership: A New Form of Security Cooperation?," *Contemporary Security Policy* 29, no. 2 (2008): 358–383, https://doi.org/10.1080/13523260802284365.

25. Georg Strüver, "China's Partnership Diplomacy: International Alignment Based on Interests or Ideology," *Chinese Journal of International Politics* 10, no. 1 (2017): 31–65; Dai Zheng [戴正] and Zheng Xianwu [郑先武], "The Evolution of Alliance Theory—Its Mirroring Effect on the Chinese Thinking of International Relations [同盟理论的演进过程—兼论其对中国国际关系理念的镜鉴作用]," *Guangxi Social Sciences* [广西社会科学], no. 12 (2019): 73–79.

26. "Speech by H. E. Wen Jiabao, Premier of the State Council of the People's Republic of China," Mission of the People's Republic of China to the European Union, May 12, 2004, http://www.chinamission.be/eng/zt/t101949.htm.

27. Deng Yong, "Remolding Great Power Politics: China's Strategic Partnerships with Russia, the European Union, and India," *Journal of Strategic Studies* 30, no. 4–5 (2007): 863.

28. Wang Yi [王毅], "Insist on Correct View of Righteousness and Benefits, Actively Play the Role of Responsible Great Powers: Deeply Comprehend the Spirit of Comrade Xi Jinping's Important Speech on Diplomatic Work [人民日报：坚持正确义利观　积极发挥负责任大国作用：深刻领会习近平同志关于外交工作的重要讲话精神]," People.cn [人民网], September 10, 2013; "China's Peripheral Diplomacy: Advancing Grand Strategy [中国周边外交：推进大战略]," Xinhua.com [新华网], October 26, 2013, http://news.sina.com.cn/o/2013-10-26/201028540080.shtml; "Yang Jiechi: Promote the Construction of a Community of Shared Future for Mankind [杨洁篪：推动构建人类命运共同体]," CPC News [中国共产党新闻网], November 19, 2017, http://cpc.people.com.cn/n1/2017/1119/c64094-29654801.html.

29. Han Zhen and Mihaela Papa, "Alliances in Chinese International Relations: Are They Ending or Rejuvenating?," *Asian Security* 17, no. 2 (2020): 7.

30. Evan S. Medeiros, *China's International Behavior: Activism, Opportunism, and Diversification* (Santa Monica, CA: RAND, 2009), 82; see online appendix at www.orianaskylarmastro.com/upstart.

31. Full dataset can be found at www.orianaskylarmastro.com/upstart.

32. Han and Papa, "Alliances in Chinese International Relations."

33. Yan Xuetong [阎学通], "Yan Xuetong: The Overall 'Periphery' Is More Important than the United States [阎学通：整体的'周边'比美国更重要]," *Global Times* [环球时报], January 13, 2015, http://opinion.huanqiu.com/1152/2015-01/5392162.html.

34. China has formed bilateral strategic partnerships with forty developing nations. Of all covered in these deals, eighty-nine are developing. Full appendix available online at www.orianaskylarmastro.com/upstart.

35. Hua Yisheng [华益声], "'One Belt, One Road' Is a Blessing for World Peace [一带一路是世界和平稳定之福]," *People's Daily* [人民日报], May 18, 2017; Su Xiaohui [苏晓晖], "A New Model of International Relations Is Needed Under the New Historical Conditions [新的历史条件下需要新型国际关系]," *People's Daily Global Edition* [人民日报海外版], April 29, 2015; "Yang Jiechi: Promote the Construction of a Community of Shared Future for Mankind."

36. Lei Yu, "China's Strategic Partnership with Latin America: A Fulcrum in China's Rise," *International Affairs* 91, no. 5 (2015): 1047–1048; Sun Ru [孙茹], "Building Partnership Network: An Upgrade of China's Non-Alliance Policies [构建伙伴关系网：中国不结盟政策的升级版]," *World Affairs* [世界知识], no. 6 (2015): 58–60.

37. Sun Degang, "China's Partnership Diplomacy in the Middle East," The Asia Dialogue, March 24, 2020, https://theasiadialogue.com/2020/03/24/chinas-partnership-diplomacy-in-the-middle-east/.

38. Strüver, "China's Partnership Diplomacy," 55.

39. Ling, "Why Doesn't China Set Up Alliances?," 24, 28, 32–33.

40. The goal is to "seek common ground on major issues while shelving differences on the minor ones" [求同存异]. Zhou Hong [周弘] and Jin Ling [金玲], "Seventy Years of China-Europe Relations: The Formation of Multi-Facet Partnership [中欧关系70年：多领域伙伴关系的发展]," *Chinese Journal of European Studies* [欧洲研究] 37, no. 5 (2019): 1–15.

41. Twenty-six of the 64 countries with which China has signed bilateral strategic partnerships scored as "free" on Freedom House's Freedom in the World index. Of all the countries covered, 48 of 128 scored as "free" or up. See appendix on China's strategic partnerships online at www.orianaskylarmastro.com/upstart.

42. Jin Canrong [金灿荣] et al., "The Rise of Middle Powers and the New Focus of Chinese Diplomacy [中等强国崛起与中国外交的新着力点]," *Contemporary International Relations* [现代国际关系], no. 8 (2010): 1–6.

43. Cheng Xin [成欣] and Wang Huihui [王慧慧], "Promoting the Resumption of Diplomatic Relations Between Saudi Arabia and Iran Shows China's Leadership as a Major Power [促成沙特、伊朗复交展现中国大国担当]," *People's Daily* [人民日报], March 14, 2023, http://paper.people.com.cn/rmrbhwb/html/2023-03/14/content_25970291.htm.

44. Wang Jianwei, "China: A Challenge or Opportunity for the United States?," *Journal of East Asian Studies* 3, no. 2 (2003): 293–333; "President Jiang Zemin and U.S. President Bush Met with Press," Embassy of the People's Republic of China in the Independent State of Papua New Guinea, October 19, 2001, http://pg.china-embassy.gov.cn/eng/zt/fk/200110/t20011019_980230.htm.

45. "Remarks by President Obama and President Xi Jinping of the People's Republic of China," White House, June 7, 2013, https://sunnylands.org/article/remarks-by-president-obama-and-president-xi-jinping-of-the-peoples-republic-of-china/.

46. Stephen M. Walt, "The Sunnylands Summit Won't Stop Sino-American Rivalry," *Foreign Policy*, June 5, 2013, https://foreignpolicy.com/2013/06/05/the-sunnylands-summit-wont-stop-sino-american-rivalry/.

47. Michael J. Green, *By More than Providence: Grand Strategy and American Power in the Asia Pacific Since 1783* (New York: Columbia University Press, 2017), 526–527.

48. Adam P. Liff, "China and the US Alliance System," *China Quarterly*, no. 233 (March 2018): 156–157.

49. Shen Zhihua [沈志华], "From Xibaipo to Moscow: Mao Zedong's Announcement of 'Leaning to One Side'—Rediscussions on the Background and Basis of Sino-Soviet Alliance [从西柏坡到莫斯科：毛泽东宣布向苏联'一边倒'—关于中苏同盟建立之背景和基础的再讨论]," *CCP Party History* [中共党史研究], no. 4 (2009): 14–33; Wu Juan [武娟], "China's Diplomatic Policy Is Independent and Sovereign, an Actual Non-Alliance [中国的对外政策是独立自主的，是真正的不结盟]," People.cn [人民网], September 12, 2017, http://cpc.people.com.cn/n1/2017/0912/c69113-29529025.html; John Garver, *China's Quest: A History of the Foreign Relations of the People's Republic of China* (Oxford: Oxford University Press, 2016), 114–116.

50. R. Clarke Cooper, "America as the Security Partner of Choice: Highlights of 2019 and a Look Ahead to 2020," US Department of State, January 15, 2020, https://2017-2021.

state.gov/america-as-the-security-partner-of-choice-highlights-of-2019-and-a-look-ahead-to-2020/; Donald J. Trump, "National Security Strategy of the United States 2017," White House, December 2017, https://trumpwhitehouse.archives.gov/wp-content/uploads/2017/12/NSS-Final-12-18-2017-0905.pdf; Carla Babb, "US Wants to Remain 'Partner of Choice' in South America," Voice of America, August 13, 2018, https://www.voanews.com/americas/us-wants-remain-partner-choice-south-america.

51. Charles Hooper, "Defense Security Cooperation Agency Chief on the Value of Partnerships," *Defense News*, December 4, 2019, https://www.defensenews.com/outlook/2019/12/02/defense-security-cooperation-agency-chief-on-the-value-of-partnerships/.

52. Susan B. Epstein and Liana W. Rosen, "U.S. Security Assistance and Security Cooperation Programs: Overview of Funding Trends," Congressional Research Service, February 1, 2018, https://crsreports.congress.gov/product/pdf/R/R45091/3.

53. Epstein and Rosen, "U.S. Security Assistance and Security Cooperation Programs."

54. "International Military Training and Education Programs," Defense Security Cooperation Agency, https://www.dsca.mil/50th-anniversary/international-military-and-education-programs, accessed June 14, 2023.

55. Alexandra Gheciu, "Security Institutions as Agents of Socialization? NATO and the 'New Europe,'" *International Organization* 59, no. 4 (2005): 973–1012.

56. "China's National Defense in the New Era," State Council Information Office of the People's Republic of China, July 2019, https://www.andrewerickson.com/2019/07/full-text-of-defense-white-paper-chinas-national-defense-in-the-new-era-english-chinese-versions/; "Key NATO and Allied Exercises in 2019," North Atlantic Treaty Organization, February 2019, https://www.nato.int/nato_static_fl2014/assets/pdf/pdf_2019_02/1902-factsheet_exercises_en.pdf.

57. ChinaPower Team, "How Is China Bolstering Its Military Diplomatic Relations?," ChinaPower, October 27, 2017, https://chinapower.csis.org/china-military-diplomacy/.

58. Jonah Victor, "China's Security Assistance in Global Competition," in *The PLA Beyond Borders: Chinese Military Operations in Regional and Global Context*, ed. Joel Wuthnow et al. (Washington, DC: National Defense University Press, 2021), 281.

59. Most of these are non-combat, often multilateral international exercises. ChinaPower Team, "How Is China Bolstering Its Military Diplomatic Relations?"

60. Kyuri Park, "Ripe for Cooperation or Rivalry? Commerce, Realpolitik, and War Memory in Contemporary Sino-Japanese Relations," *Asian Security* 4, no. 2 (2008): 18.

61. "From 2003 to 2017, China loaned $2.53 billion to eight African countries explicitly for military and national defense purposes" compared to the United States' "$753 million in foreign military financing to African countries, with only $15.4 million for military construction projects." Victor, "China's Security Assistance in Global Competition," 285.

62. Jessica Chen Weiss, "A World Safe for Autocracy? China's Rise and the Future of Global Politics," *Foreign Affairs* 98, no. 4 (2019); Adrian Zenz, "China's Domestic Security Spending: An Analysis of Available Data," *China Brief* 18, no. 4 (2018); Josh Chin, "China Spends More on Domestic Security as Xi's Powers Grow," *Wall Street Journal*, March 6, 2018, https://www.wsj.com/articles/china-spends-more-on-domestic-security-as-xis-powers-grow-1520358522.

63. "The New Big Brother—China and Digital Authoritarianism," United States Senate Foreign Relations Committee Staff Report, July 21, 2020, 7.

64. Amy Qin, "Chinese City Uses Facial Recognition to Shame Pajama Wearers," *New York Times*, January 21, 2020, https://www.nytimes.com/2020/01/21/business/china-pajamas-facial-recognition.html.

65. Lin Chunyin [林春茵] and Peng Lifang [彭莉芳], "Learning Kungfu, Studying the Goose Step, and Speak in Chinese—Many Foreign Police Now Have Their 'Chinese Shifu' [学功夫踢正步说中文，好多外国警察有了'中国师傅']," China News Service [中国新闻社], February 27, 2019, https://www.chinanews.com.cn/m/sh/2019/02-27/8766233.shtml; Sun Wenyu, "PLA's Goose-Stepping Highlight of Qatari National Day Military Parade," People.cn, December 20, 2017, http://en.people.cn/n3/2017/1220/c90000-9306770.html.

66. The complete dataset can be found at www.orianaskylarmastro.com/upstart. Exact numbers are not reported. Data is gleaned from technical studies such as the following: Zhong Sheng [钟声], Liu Jianchang [刘建昌], and Zhang Ling [张玲], "On the Experiences and Inspirations from the Overseas Police Training in China: A Case Study of Overseas Police Training Practice in Guangxi Police Academy [外警培训的经验和启示：以广西警察学院外警培训实践为例]," *Journal of Guangxi Police Higher Occupation School* [广西警官高等专科学校学报], no. 6 (December 1, 2016): 100; Yin Bo [尹波], "The Current Needs, Problems and Perfection of the Foreign Police Training Work in China [当前我国外警培训工作的需求，问题与完善]," *Journal of Liaoning Police Academy* [辽宁警察学院学报], no. 5 (2020): 81–85.

67. "China to Build Asia's Largest UN Police Training Center," *People's Daily Online*, August 20, 2002, http://en.people.cn/200208/20/eng20020820_101732.shtml.

68. "About the Center [中心概况]," China Peacekeeping Police Training Center [中国维和警察培训中心], http://39.100.105.116/pages/overview/about.html.

69. "The 2019 Foreign Police Training Working Session Was Held in Our School [我校召开2019年外警培训工作会议]," People's Public Security University of China [中国人民公安大学], May 16, 2019, http://www.ppsuc.edu.cn/info/1016/7469.htm.

70. Ge Tailiang [戈太亮] and Wang Lu [王露], "Zhenjiang Police Hosted Foreign Training Program for the First Time [镇江警方首次承接公安部外警培训项目]," Jschina.com.cn [中国江苏网], October 25, 2018, https://baijiahao.baidu.com/s?id=1615260178350728242&wfr=spider&for=pc; Zhang Weihua [张卫华], "Experts from the International Cooperation Bureau of the Ministry of Public Security Came to Our School and Led the Foreign Police Training [公安部国际合作局专家到我院指导外警培训工作]," Henan Police College [河南警察学院], October 18, 2017, https://pxb.hnp.edu.cn/info/1056/1352.htm; "Vice President Hu Chuanping

and Others Participated in the National Public Security Forum on Foreign Police Training [胡传平副院长一行参加全国公安机关外警培训工作座谈会]," Railway Police College [铁道警察学院], April 17, 2018, http://www.rpc.edu.cn/info/1020/2841.htm.

71. "Friendship on the Sea: Coast Guard Law Opened up a New Chapter for Law Enforcement Cooperation [宗海谊：《海警法》开启海上执法合作新篇章]," Huanqiu.com [环球网], April 29, 2020, https://baijiahao.baidu.com/s?id=169832302 1814705096&wfr=spider&for=pc.

72. "Chinese, Philippine Coast Guards Hold Joint Exercise to Achieve Interoperability at Sea," China Military [中国军网], January 16, 2020, http://eng.chinamil.com.cn/view/2020-01/16/content_9718789.htm.

73. "CCG 'Haijing 3306' Debuts at International Multilateral Exercise and Returns Triumphantly ['中国海警3306船'首秀国际多方演习后凯旋]," Chinanews.com [中国新闻网], June 25, 2015, https://www.chinanews.com.cn/gn/2015/06-25/7366312.shtml.

74. Zhao Lei [赵磊] and Su Hongfeng [苏红锋], "China Coast Guard Visits South Korea for the First Time and Conducts Joint Maritime Exercise [中国海警首次访韩并与韩海警开展海上联演]," *China Daily* [中国日报], June 18, 2016, https://china.chinadaily.com.cn/2016-06/18/content_25757883.htm.

75. Liu Xiaolin [刘晓林] and Zhang Yiqi [张一琪], "Four Days and Three Nights, Experience Mekong River Patrol [四天三夜, 亲历湄公河巡航]," *People's Daily* [人民日报], May 5, 2018, http://world.people.com.cn/GB/n1/2018/0505/c1002-29966381.html; "China-Laos-Myanmar-Thailand Mekong River Joint Patrol Command Center Established in Yunnan [中老缅泰湄公河联合巡逻执法联合指挥部在云南成立]," Xinhua News Agency [新华社], December 9, 2011, http://www.gov.cn/jrzg/2011-12/09/content_2016216.htm.

76. Deng Yanyan [邓彦妍], Jin Jijian [金继坚], and Dong Guiying [董桂英], "The 100th China-Laos-Myanmar-Thailand Joint Patrol on the Mekong River Was Officially Launched [第100次中老缅泰湄公河联合巡逻执法行动正式启动]," Yunnan TV [云南电视台], December 10, 2020, https://baijiahao.baidu.com/s?id=168566514765 0095474&wfr=spider&for=pc.

77. Alina Polyakova and Chris Meserole, "Exporting Digital Authoritarianism," Brookings Institution, August 2019, 6.

78. Margaret Roberts, *Censored: Distraction and Diversion Inside China's Great Firewall* (Princeton, NJ: Princeton University Press, 2018).

79. Connor Fiddler, "The 3 Pillars of Chinese Foreign Policy: The State, the Party, the People," *The Diplomat*, February 3, 2021, https://thediplomat.com/2021/02/the-3-pillars-of-chinese-foreign-policy-the-state-the-party-the-people/.

80. Polyakova and Meserole, "Exporting Digital Authoritarianism." We do not have details about the content of the training, but we know that many officials return home to implement cybersecurity laws similar to those of China. "The New Big Brother," 31.

81. Adrian Shahbaz, Allie Funk, and Kian Vesteinsson, "Freedom on the Net 2022: Countering an Authoritarian Overhaul of the Internet," Freedom House, 2022.

82. Aidan Powers-Riggs, "Covid-19 Is Proving a Boon for Digital Authoritarianism," Center for Strategic and International Studies, August 17, 2020, https://www.csis. org/blogs/new-perspectives-asia/covid-19-proving-boon-digital-authoritarianism.

83. Katherine Atha et al., "China's Smart Cities Development," SOSi International, January 2020, https://www.uscc.gov/sites/default/files/China_Smart_Cities_Deve lopment.pdf.

84. Sheena Chestnut Greitens, "Dealing with Demand for China's Global Surveillance Exports," Brookings Institution, April 2020, 2; Steven Feldstein, "The Global Expansion of AI Surveillance," Carnegie Endowment for International Peace, 2019.

85. Feldstein, "The Global Expansion of AI Surveillance," 1.

86. Feldstein, "The Global Expansion of AI Surveillance," 2.

87. Greitens, "Dealing with Demand for China's Global Surveillance Exports," 6.

88. Elly Cosgrove, "One Billion Surveillance Cameras Will Be Watching Around the World in 2021, a New Study Says," CNBC, December 6, 2019, https://www.cnbc. com/2019/12/06/one-billion-surveillance-cameras-will-be-watching-globally-in- 2021.html..

89. Ross Andersen, "The Panopticon Is Already Here: China's Artificial Intelligence Surveillance State Goes Global," *The Atlantic*, September 2020; Feldstein, "The Global Expansion of AI Surveillance," 2.

90. "The New Big Brother," 27.

91. Cheng Jie [程结] and Ouyang Xu [欧阳旭], "Research on Cross-Cultural Communication of Foreign Police Training Under the Perspective of 'One Belt, One Road' ['一带一路'视阈下外警培训跨文化交流研究]," *Journal of Liaoning Public Security and Judiciary Officials* [辽宁公安司法管理干部学院学报], no. 2 (2019): 36.

92. "US Report Accuses China of Digital Authoritarianism," BBC News, July 21, 2020, https://www.bbc.com/news/technology-53490042.

93. Marian L. Lawson and Susan B. Epstein, "Democracy Promotion: An Objective of U.S. Foreign Assistance," Congressional Research Service, January 4, 2017, https:// www.everycrsreport.com/files/20190104_R44858_aaa79dc011a9a071c15be af4bcb8e1accefc564c.pdf; Peter M. Haas and John A. Hird, eds., *Controversies in Globalization: Contending Approaches to International Relations* (Los Angeles: CQ Press, 2012), 491.

94. Scholars have amplified the message. See Thomas Carothers, "Democracy Promotion Under Clinton," *Washington Quarterly* 18, no. 4 (1995): 13–25. Michael McFaul and Francis Fukuyama posit that every US enemy has been either an autocracy or a political movement built upon undemocratic ideals. Francis Fukuyama and Michael McFaul, "Should Democracy Be Promoted or Demoted?," *Washington Quarterly* 31, no. 1 (2007): 23–45. Americans also view democracy promotion as cultural and an inherent moral obligation; even the founding fathers argued in support of US democracy promotion abroad as part of the United States' destiny. See Tony Smith, *America's Mission* (Princeton, NJ: Princeton University Press, 2012). The benefits of promoting democracy are prominent in every US National Security Strategy of this period. See for example, Bill Clinton, "A National Security Strategy

of Engagement and Enlargement," White House, February 1996, https://fas.org/ spp/military/docops/national/1996stra.htm; Barack Obama, "National Security Strategy," White House, May 2010, https://obamawhitehouse.archives.gov/sites/ default/files/rss_viewer/national_security_strategy.pdf, 37. "Free governments do not oppress their people or attack other free nations. Peace and international stability are most reliably built on a foundation of freedom." George W. Bush, "National Security Strategy of the United States of America 2002," White House, September 2002, https://2009-2017.state.gov/documents/organization/63562.pdf.

95. These include the Afghanistan Security Forces Fund (ASFF), Coalition Readiness Support Program (CRSP), DoD Regional Centers for Security Studies, Foreign Security Forces: Authority to Build Capacity—Section 333, Global Security Contingency Fund (GSCF) (Section 1207), Humanitarian Assistance, Indo-Pacific Maritime Security Initiative (MSI), Mine Action (MA) Programs, Regional Defense Combating Terrorism and Irregular Warfare Fellowship Program (CTFP), Service-Sponsored Activities, and "Miscellaneous, DoD/DOS Non-Security Assistance" and "Non-Security Assistance, Unified Command." See "Fiscal Year (FY) 2021 President's Budget: Justification for Security Cooperation Program and Activity Funding," Office of the Secretary of Defense, April 2020.

96. Dov H. Levin, "Partisan Electoral Interventions by the Great Powers: Introducing the PEIG Dataset," *Conflict Management and Peace Science* 36, no. 1 (2019): 88–106.

97. Monica Duffy Toft, "Why Is America Addicted to Foreign Interventions?," *National Interest*, December 10, 2017, https://nationalinterest.org/feature/why-america-addicted-foreign-interventions-23582; James Meernik, "United States Military Intervention and the Promotion of Democracy," *Journal of Peace Research* 33, no. 4 (1996): 391–402.

98. Steven Finkel, Anibal Perez-Linan, and Mitchell Seligson, "The Effects of U.S. Foreign Assistance on Democracy Building, 1990–2003," *World Politics* 59, no. 3 (2007): 404–438.

99. Lawson and Epstein, "Democracy Promotion."

100. In 2017, seventy-one countries incurred net declines compared to thirty-five that made gains. This marked the twelfth consecutive year in which declines outnumbered improvements. See Michael J. Abramowitz, "Freedom in the World, 2018," Freedom House, February 5, 2018, https://freedomhouse.org/report/free dom-world/2018/democracy-crisis; "Democracy in Retreat," Freedom House, 2019, https://freedomhouse.org/report/freedom-world/2019/democracy-retreat.

101. Larry Diamond, "Facing Up to the Democratic Recession," *Journal of Democracy* 26, no. 1 (2015): 142.

102. Chen Ling and Barry Naughton, "A Dynamic China Model: The Co-Evolution of Economics and Politics in China," *Journal of Contemporary China* 26, no. 103 (2017): 18–34. See this source for an extensive history and analysis of how it has adapted since 1992.

103. Zhao Suisheng, "The China Model: Can It Replace the Western Model of Modernization?," *Journal of Contemporary China* 19, no. 65 (2010): 1; Joseph Fewsmith, "Debating 'the China Model,'" *China Leadership Monitor*, no. 35 (2011): 7.

104. For one of the earliest views of the term "China model," see Rowan Callick, "How Long Can Economic Freedom and Political Repression Coexist? Rowan Callick Examines Beijing's Sinister Policy Formulation," *The American*, November 13, 2007, http://www.american.com/archive/2007/november-december-magazinecontents/the-china-model.

105. Gary S. Becker, "Democracy or Autocracy: Which Is Better for Economic Growth?," Hoover Institution, October 10, 2010, https://www.hoover.org/research/democracy-or-autocracy-which-better-economic-growth.

106. The European Union is counted as one partner. The two non-democracies are Hong Kong and Vietnam. "Democracy Index 2020," Economist Intelligence Unit, https://www.eiu.com/n/campaigns/democracy-index-2020/; Feng Zhongping and Huang Jing, "China's Strategic Partnership Diplomacy: Engaging with a Changing World," European Strategic Partnerships Observatory, Working Paper, June 2014, https://www.files.ethz.ch/isn/181324/China%E2%80%99s%20strategic%20partnership%20diplomacy_%20engaging%20with%20a%20changing%20world%20.pdf.

107. Andrew J. Nathan, "China's Challenge," *Journal of Democracy* 26, no. 1 (2015): 157.

108. Luo Yanhua [罗艳华], "The Strategic Means and Realistic Dilemma of U.S. Democratic Export [美国民主输出的战略手段与现实困境]," *People's Forum* [人民论坛], no. 35 (2021): 40–43.

109. Zhao Qizheng [赵启正], "How to Approach the China Model of Development? [如何看待中国发展模式？]," State Council Information Office [国务院新闻办公室], March 2, 2010, http://www.scio.gov.cn/ztk/xwfb/jjfyr/21/mtbd/Document/558321/558321.htm; Zhang Yesui [张业遂], "Zhang Yesui Responds to the Question of Whether China Exports Its Model Because It Wants to Change the World Order [中国向外输出中国模式是要改变国际秩序？张业遂回应]," China News [中国新闻网], March 4, 2018, http://www.chinanews.com/gn/2018/03-04/8459318.shtml.

110. Su Changhe [苏长和], "China Will Not Export Its Model, the China Model Is Also Not Easy for Others to Follow [中国模式不会出口，别人也不易学]," Aisixiang.com [爱思想], January 31, 2021, https://www.aisixiang.com/data/89824.html.

111. Barry Naughton, "China's Distinctive System: Can It Be a Model for Others?," *Journal of Contemporary China* 19, no. 65 (2010): 437–460; Wade Shepard, "Why China's Development Model Won't Work in Africa," *Forbes*, October 31, 2019, https://www.forbes.com/sites/wadeshepard/2019/10/31/why-chinas-development-model-wont-work-in-africa/?sh=5e1e6a8257af; Yuen Yuen Ang, "The Real China Model: It's Not What You Think It Is," *Foreign Affairs*, June 29, 2018, https://www.foreignaffairs.com/articles/asia/2018-06-29/real-china-model.

112. Seva Gunitsky, "Democracy's Future: Riding the Hegemonic Wave," *Washington Quarterly* 41, no. 2 (2018): 115–135.

113. Ya Mei, "Full Text of President Xi's Speech at Opening of Belt and Road Forum," Xinhua.com, May 14, 2017, http://www.xinhuanet.com/english/2017-05/14/c_136282982.htm.

114. Wang Xiangping, "An Analysis of the Chinese Communist Party Leaders' Discourse on the China Model [解析中共领导人关于'中国模式'的论述]," CPC News [中国

共产党新闻网], October 9, 2013, http://theory.people.com.cn/n/2013/1009/c83 867-23139105-8.html.

115. "Xi Jinping: 'China Does Not Import Foreign Models, and Does Not Export China Model' [习近平：'中国不输入外国模式，也不输出中国模式']," RFI [法国国际 广播电台], January 12, 2017, https://www.rfi.fr/cn/%E4%B8%AD%E5%9B%BD/ 20171201-%E4%B9%A0%E8%BF%91%E5%B9%B3%E4%B8%AD%E5%9B%BD %E4%B8%8D%E8%BE%93%E5%85%A5%E5%A4%96%E5%9B%BD%E6%A8 %A1%E5%BC%8F%EF%BC%8C%E4%B9%9F%E4%B8%8D%E8%BE%93%E5%8 7%BA%E4%B8%AD%E5%9B%BD%E6%A8%A1%E5%BC%8F.

116. Cheng Cheng, "China Will Not 'Export' Chinese Model: Xi," Xinhua.com [新华 网], December 1, 2017, http://www.xinhuanet.com/english/2017-12/01/c_136793 833.htm; Shi Zhiyu [石之瑜], "What Is the China Model That the West Has Been Opposing To? [西方反对的是什么中国模式]," Zaobao [联合早报], November 7, 2017, http://www.haozaobao.com/mon/keji/20171107/40997_2.html.

117. "Will China 'Export Its Values?' [中国会搞'文化输出'吗？]," *People's Daily* [人民日 报], November 14, 2013, http://theory.people.com.cn/n/2013/1114/c371516-23543 735-2.html; Qi Peiyu [祁培育], "Foreign Ministry: China Has Never 'Exported' the China Mode, and Has Never Asked Other Countries to 'Replicate Its Homework' [外交部：中国从不'输出'中国模式，也从未要求'抄中国作业']," State Council of the People's Republic of China [中华人民共和国中央人民政府], April 10, 2020, http://www.gov.cn/xinwen/2020-04/10/content_5500781.htm.

118. Secretariat of the Center for the Study of Xi Jinping's Diplomatic Thought [习 近平外交思想研究中心秘书处], "Constructing a Unique Style of Chinese Diplomacy: Meaning and Paths to Realization [塑造中国外交独特风范：内涵与 实践路径]," *International Studies* [国际问题研究], no. 6 (2021): 10.

119. Joshua Cooper Ramo, *The Beijing Consensus* (London: Foreign Policy Centre, 2004), 4.

120. Garver, *China's Quest*, 380.

121. David Dollar, "Seven Years into China's Belt and Road," Brookings Institution, October 1, 2020, https://www.brookings.edu/blog/order-from-chaos/2020/10/01/ seven-years-into-chinas-belt-and-road/.

122. There are a few cases in which China issued no comment, particularly in cases of very small island nations. In the case of democratic elections that have not been free and fair, China has also offered its congratulations to the winner.

123. Raymond Zhong, "China Congratulates Biden on Presidential Victory," *New York Times*, November 13, 2020, https://www.nytimes.com/2020/11/13/world/asia/ china-congratulations-biden.html.

124. Richard Wike and Janell Fetterolf, "Global Public Opinion in an Era of Democratic Anxiety," Pew Research Center, December 7, 2021, https://www.pewresearch.org/ global/2021/12/07/global-public-opinion-in-an-era-of-democratic-anxiety/.

125. Nathan, "China's Challenge," 158.

126. Garver, *China's Quest*, 477–480.

127. Nathan, "China's Challenge," 158.

128. Sophie Richardson, "China's Influence on the Global Human Rights System," Human Rights Watch, September 14, 2020, https://www.hrw.org/news/2020/09/14/chinas-influence-global-human-rights-system.

129. Lindsey W. Ford, "Refocusing the China Debate: American Allies and the Question of US-China 'Decoupling,'" Brookings Institution, February 7, 2020, https://www.brookings.edu/blog/order-from-chaos/2020/02/07/refocusing-the-china-debate-american-allies-and-the-question-of-us-china-decoupling/.

130. Steven Lee Myers, "An Alliance of Autocracies? China Wants to Lead a New World Order," *New York Times*, March 29, 2021, https://www.nytimes.com/2021/03/29/world/asia/china-us-russia.html.

131. "China's Warning to Biden," *Wall Street Journal*, March 21, 2021, https://www.wsj.com/articles/chinas-warning-to-biden-11616360915.

132. "Full Text: The Report on Human Rights Violations in the United States in 2020," Xinhua.com [新华网], March 24, 2021, http://www.xinhuanet.com/english/2021-03/24/c_139832301.htm.

133. Yuan Peng, president of the China Institutes of Contemporary International Relations, a government think tank, quoted in Myers, "An Alliance of Autocracies?"

134. "CCP Buys Media Influence by Paying Millions to US Dailies, Magazines: Report," *Times of India*, July 4, 2021, https://timesofindia.indiatimes.com/world/china/ccp-buys-media-influence-by-paying-millions-to-us-dailies-magazines-report/articleshow/84109897.cms.

135. Matt Schrader, "Friends and Enemies: A Framework for Understanding Chinese Political Interference in Democratic Countries," German Marshall Fund Alliance for Securing Democracy, April 2020.

136. Sarah Cook, "The Globalization of China's Media Controls: Key Trends from 2018," *The Diplomat*, December 15, 2018, https://thediplomat.com/2018/12/the-globalization-of-chinas-media-controls-key-trends-from-2018/.

137. Renée Diresta et al., "Telling China's Story: The Chinese Communist Party's Campaign to Shape Global Narratives," Stanford Internet Observatory, 12, https://purl.stanford.edu/pf306sw8941.

138. "Beijing's Global Media Influence 2022," Freedom House, https://freedomhouse.org/report/beijing-global-media-influence/2022/authoritarian-expansion-power-democratic-resilience.

139. Jonathan E. Hillman, "Corruption Flows Along China's Belt and Road," Center for Strategic and International Studies, January 18, 2019, https://www.csis.org/analysis/corruption-flows-along-chinas-belt-and-road.

140. Schrader, "Friends and Enemies."

141. Diresta et al., "Telling China's Story," 7. For a comprehensive review of Chinese influence activities in a number of countries, especially key liberal democracies, see Larry Diamond and Orville Schell, eds., *China's Influence and American Interests* (Stanford, CA: Hoover Institution Press, 2018), 145–186; Anne-Marie Brady, "Magic Weapons: China's Political Influence Activities Under Xi Jinping," Wilson Center, September 18, 2017, https://www.wilsoncenter.org/article/magic-weapons-chinas-political-influence-activities-under-xi-jinping.

142. Schrader, "Friends and Enemies."

143. See Appendix 1, "Chinese Influence Operations Bureaucracy," in Diamond and Schell, eds., *China's Influence and American Interests*, 151–163.

144. "SPJ Code of Ethics, Society of Professional Journalists," revised September 6, 2014, https://www.spj.org/ethicscode.asp.

145. "China Publishes Revised Code of Ethics for Journalists," Xinhua, December 15, 2019, https://www.chinadaily.com.cn/a/201912/15/WS5df63766a310cf3e3557e 3b7.html.

146. Kurt M. Campbell and Jake Sullivan, "Competition Without Catastrophe: How America Can Both Challenge and Coexist with China," *Foreign Affairs* 98, no. 5 (2019).

147. Mark Hannah and Caroline Gray, "Global Views of American Democracy," Eurasia Group Foundation, March 31, 2020, https://egfound.org/2020/03/modeling-democracy/.

148. Lawson and Epstein, "Democracy Promotion," 20.

149. John Dotson, "The CCP's Renewed Focus on Ideological Indoctrination, Part 1: The 2019 Guidelines for 'Patriotic Education,'" Jamestown Foundation, December 10, 2019, https://jamestown.org/program/the-ccps-renewed-focus-on-ideological-ind octrination-part-1-the-2019-guidelines-for-patriotic-education/; John Dotson, "The CCP's Renewed Focus on Ideological Conditioning, Part 2: The New Five-Year Plan for Training Party Cadres," Jamestown Foundation, December 31, 2019, https://jamestown.org/program/the-ccps-renewed-focus-on-ideological-condition ing-part-2-the-new-five-year-plan-for-training-party-cadres/.

150. Abby Johnston and Catherine Trautwein, "What Is the China Model? Understanding the Country's State-Led Economic Model," *Frontline*, PBS, May 17, 2019, https:// www.pbs.org/wgbh/frontline/article/china-trade-war-trump-tariff/.

151. Maya Wang, "China's Techno-Authoritarianism Has Gone Global," *Foreign Affairs*, April 8, 2021, https://www.foreignaffairs.com/articles/china/2021-04-08/chinas-tec hno-authoritarianism-has-gone-global. As of 2020, Beijing reportedly had 1.15 million closed-circuit television surveillance cameras installed to observe a population of roughly 20 million. Matthew Keegan, "The Most Surveilled Cities in the World," *US News*, August 14, 2020, www.usnews.com/news/cities/articles/2020-08-14/the-top-10-most-surveilled-cities-in-the-world.

152. Yang Yuan, "China Stifles Foreign Internet to Control Coronavirus Coverage," *Financial Times*, February 17. 2020, https://www.ft.com/content/0aa9c0ec-517a-11ea-8841-482eed0038b1.

153. "Two Arrested and 13 Charged in Three Separate Cases for Alleged Participation in Malign Schemes in the United States on Behalf of the Government of the People's Republic of China," US Department of Justice Office of Public Affairs, October 24, 2022, https://www.justice.gov/opa/pr/two-arrested-and-13-charged-three-separ ate-cases-alleged-participation-malign-schemes-united.

154. "MEPs Refuse Any Agreement with China Whilst Sanctions Are in Place," European Parliament, May 20, 2021, https://www.europarl.europa.eu/news/en/press-room/

20210517IPR04123/meps-refuse-any-agreement-with-china-whilst-sancti ons-are-in-place.

155. Liang Shengwen [梁生文], "A New Political Party System Contributes Chinese Wisdom to the Development of World Party Politics-International Online [新型政党制度为世界政党政治发展贡献中国智慧]," *CRJ Online* [国际在线], March 8, 2018, http://news.cri.cn/20180308/962b9850-3a41-45ac-57c0-a4afdaa2d9e4. html; "How China's Communist Party Trains Foreign Politicians," *The Economist*, December 10, 2020, https://www.economist.com/china/2020/12/10/how-chinas-communist-party-trains-foreign-politicians.

156. "Xi Jinping: Fully Confident to Provide a Chinese Solution for Mankind's Exploration of a Better Social System [习近平：完全有信心为人类对更好社会制度的探索提供中国方案]," *The Paper* [澎湃新闻], July 1, 2016, https://www. thepaper.cn/newsDetail_forward_1492012; "Full Text of Xi Jinping's Report at 19th CPC National Congress," *China Daily*, November 4, 2017, https://www.chinadaily. com.cn/china/19thcpcnationalcongress/2017-11/04/content_34115212.htm.

157. Seva Gunitsky, *Aftershocks: Great Powers and Domestic Reforms in the Twentieth Century* (Princeton: Princeton University Press, 2017).

158. Evan S. Medeiros and Taylor Fravel, "China's New Diplomacy," *Foreign Affairs* 82, no. 6 (2003): 22–35, 23.

159. "Liu Xiaoming, Ambassador to the UK: The Reason There Is 'Wolf Warrior' Is Because There Are 'Wolves' in the World [驻英大使刘晓明：之所以有'战狼' 是因为这个世界有'狼']," CCTV.com [央视新闻], May 25, 2020, http://m.news.cctv. com/2020/05/24/ARTI8BYmADeqivsgNvMiMRF4200524.shtml.

160. Zhu Zhiqun, "Interpreting China's 'Wolf-Warrior Diplomacy,'" *The Diplomat*, May 15, 2020, https://thediplomat.com/2020/05/interpreting-chinas-wolf-warrior-diplomacy/.

161. "The Glorious Course of China's Cross-Century Diplomacy (Abstract) [中国跨世纪外交的光辉历程(摘要)]," Ministry of Foreign Affairs of the People's Republic of China [中华人民共和国外交部], October 17, 2002, https://www.mfa.gov.cn/web/ ziliao_674904/zt_674979/ywzt_675099/zt2002_675989/2319_676055/200210/ t20021017_7965253.shtml.

162. Xi Jinping [习近平], "Xi Urges Breaking New Ground in Major Country Diplomacy with Chinese Characteristics [努力开创中国特色大国外交新局面]," Xinhua. com [新华网], June 22, 2018, http://www.xinhuanet.com/politics/2018-06/23/c_ 1123025806.htm; Wang Yi [王毅], "Speech by Minister Wang Yi at the Luncheon of the Second World Peace Forum [王毅部长在第二届世界和平论坛午餐会上的演讲]," Ministry of Foreign Affairs of the People's Republic of China [中华人民共和国外交部], June 27, 2013, https://www.mfa.gov.cn/web/wjbzhd/201306/t20130627 _349225.shtml.

163. "The Enrichment and Development of the Theoretical and Practical Innovations of Major-Country Diplomacy with Chinese Characteristics (People's Opinion) [丰富发展了中国特色大国外交理论和实践创新成果（人民观点）]," People.cn [人民网], October 11, 2022, http://theory.people.com.cn/n1/2022/1011/c40531-32542 668.html.

Chapter 4

1. Valerie Insinna, "A US Air Force War Game Shows What the Service Needs to Hold Off—or Win Against—China in 2030," *Defense News*, April 12, 2021, https://www.defensenews.com/training-sim/2021/04/12/a-us-air-force-war-game-shows-what-the-service-needs-to-hold-off-or-win-against-china-in-2030/.

2. "A Conversation with US Indo-Pacific Command's Adm. Philip Davidson," American Enterprise Institute event, March 4, 2021, https://www.aei.org/events/a-conversation-with-us-indo-pacific-commands-adm-philip-davidson/.

3. The rationale behind China's anti-ship ballistic missile program, for example, highlights the need to target US carriers, avoid the humiliation of 1996, and "reunify" with Taiwan. Liu Min [刘敏], "Can the US Stop China's ASBMs? [美军能拦截中国反舰弹道导弹吗？]," *The Paper* [澎湃新闻], October 27, 2020, https://www.thepaper.cn/newsDetail_forward_9745432.

4. Lu Jun [陆军], "What Is the Real Informatized War—Reflections on the Pattern of Future Wars [什么是真正的信息化战争—对未来战争形态的思考]," *PLA Daily* [解放军报], January 12, 2017, http://www.xinhuanet.com//mil/2017-01/12/c_129443322_2.htm

5. Ren Tianyou [任天佑], *Road to Reform Strengthening the Military* [问道改革强军] (Beijing: National Defense University Press [国防大学出版社], 2015).

6. Hu Jintao [胡锦涛], "Building a Consolidated National Defense and a Strong Military That Is Commensurate with National Security and Development Interests [建设与国家安全和发展利益相适应的巩固国防和强大军队]," in *Selected Writings of Hu Jintao, Volume III* [胡锦涛文选，第三卷], ed. CPC Editorial Committee [中共中央文献编辑委员会] (Beijing: People's Publishing House [人民出版社], 2016), 37.

7. Zheng Bijian, "China's 'Peaceful Rise' to Great-Power Status," *Foreign Affairs*, September 2005, https://www.foreignaffairs.com/articles/asia/2005-09-01/chinas-peaceful-rise-great-power-status. The concept was later revised to peaceful development.

8. Robert B. Zoellick, "Whither China: From Membership to Responsibility?," Remarks to the National Committee on US–China Relations, September 21, 2005, https://2001-2009.state.gov/s/d/former/zoellick/rem/53682.htm.

9. David Shambaugh, *China Goes Global: The Partial Power* (New York: Oxford University Press, 2013), 217.

10. Hu Jintao [胡锦涛], "Integrating Both the Domestic and International Imperatives, Improving the Capability of Diplomatic Work [统筹国内国际两个大局，提高外交工作能力水平]," in *Selected Writings of Hu Jintao*, 236–238.

11. Hu Jintao [胡锦涛], "Integrating Both the Domestic and International Imperatives, Improving the Capability of Diplomatic Work [统筹国内国际两个大局，提高外交工作能力水平]," in *Selected Writings of Hu Jintao*, 236–238.

12. Luo Jianbo [罗建波], "What Kind of Great Power Responsibility Should China Assume [中国应该承担什么样的大国责任]," *Xuexi Daily* [学习时报], September 15, 2014, http://theory.people.com.cn/n/2014/0915/c40531-25660831.html. See also Xu Jin [徐进], "How China Should Fulfill Its International Responsibilities [中国应

该如何履行国际责任]," *China Daily*, October 11, 2014, https://column.chinadaily.com.cn/a/201410/11/WS5bed2437a3101a87ca93e050.html.

13. Xiao Tianliang [肖天亮], ed., *Science of Military Strategy* [战略学] (Beijing: National Defense University Press [国防大学出版社], 2015), 297.

14. Hu Erjie [胡二杰], "UN Peacekeeping Operations and China's National Image Building [联合国维和行动与中国国家形象建设]," *Quarterly Journal of Public Diplomacy* [公共外交季刊], no. 3 (2017): 92–99.

15. Alan J. Vick et al., *Preparing the U.S. Air Force for Military Operations Other than War* (Santa Monica, CA: RAND Corporation, 1972).

16. James Siebens and Ryan Lucas, *Military Operations Other than War in China's Foreign Policy* (Washington, DC: Stimson Center, 2022).

17. Meng Wenting [孟文婷], "Literature Review on China's Participation in UN Peacekeeping Operations [中国参与联合国维和行动的研究述评]," *Journal of International Studies* [国际政治研究], no. 4 (2017): 92–94.

18. Hu, "UN Peacekeeping Operations and China's National Image Building," 92–99.

19. Tang Hao [唐昊], "Strategic Considerations on China's Protection on Overseas Interests [关于中国海外利益保护的战略思考]," *Contemporary International Relations* [现代国际关系], no. 6 (2011): 4–5; Oriana Skylar Mastro, "China Can't Stay Home," *National Interest*, no. 135 (January/February 2015): 38–45.

20. Mastro, "China Can't Stay Home," 39–40.

21. Mastro, "China Can't Stay Home," 41.

22. "The Diversified Employment of China's Armed Forces," State Council Information Office, April 2013, http://english.www.gov.cn/archive/white_paper/2014/08/23/content_281474982986506.htm.

23. Tuan Vu, "The PLAN's Anti-Piracy Missions in the Gulf of Aden, Africa," *Journal of Military and Strategic Studies* 20, no. 1 (2019): 226–233; "United Nations Documents on Piracy," United Nations Division for Ocean Affairs and the Law of the Sea, May 24, 2012, https://www.un.org/depts/los/piracy/piracy_documents.htm.

24. "China's 41st Naval Escort Taskforce Sets Off for Gulf of Aden," Chinese Ministry of Defense, May 19, 2022, http://eng.mod.gov.cn/news/2022-05/19/content_4911166.htm; "10 Years of China's Gulf of Aden Journey: A Global Player with More Responsibility," CGTN, December 27, 2018, https://news.cgtn.com/news/3d3d774e32456a4e31457a6333566d54/share_p.html.

25. Wang Hairong [王海荣], "Forging the Shield of Peace: China Accelerates Modernization of National Defense and Military Through Reforms [铸造和平之盾: 中国通过改革加快国防和军队现代化建设]," *Beijing Review* [北京周报], August 12, 2022.

26. "Troop and Police Contributors," United Nations Peacekeeping, https://peacekeeping.un.org/en/troop-and-police-contributors, accessed June 26, 2023.

27. Daniel M. Hartnett, "China's First Deployment of Combat Forces to a UN Peacekeeping Mission—South Sudan," US-China Economic and Security Review Commission, March 13, 2012, https://www.uscc.gov/sites/default/files/Research/MEMO-PLA-PKO_final_0.pdf.

28. State Council Information Office of the People's Republic of China [中华人民共和国国务院新闻办公室], "The Diversified Employment of China's Armed Forces [中国武装力量的多样化运用]," April 2013, https://www.gov.cn/zhengce/2013-04/16/content_2618550.htm.

29. See "Documentary of China's Evacuation of Overseas Chinese from Yemen [中国从也门撤侨纪实]," *People's Daily Online* [人民网], April 17, 2015, http://politics.people.com.cn/n/2015/0407/c70731-26809482.html.

30. "Most of the Chinese Citizens in Sudan Have Been Evacuated in Batches, Orderly and Safely [大部分在苏丹中国公民已分批、有序、安全撤离]," Ministry of Foreign Affairs of the People's Republic of China [中华共人民共和国外交部], April 26, 2023, https://www.mfa.gov.cn/wjbzwfwpt/kzx/tzgg/202304/t20230426_11066274.html.

31. For the full dataset, see www.orianaskylarmastro.com/upstart.

32. Matthew Southerland, "The Chinese Military's Role in Overseas Humanitarian Assistance and Disaster Relief: Contributions and Concerns," US-China Economic and Security Review Commission, July 11, 2019, 2, https://www.uscc.gov/research/chinese-militarys-role-overseas-humanitarian-assistance-and-disaster-relief-contributions.

33. Tang Yongsheng [唐永胜], "China and UN Peacekeeping Operations [中国与联合国维和行动]," *World Economics and Politics* [世界经济与政治], no. 9 (2002): 42.

34. Joel Wuthnow, "PLA Operation Lessons from UN Peacekeeping," in *The PLA Beyond Borders: Chinese Military Operations in Regional and Global Context*, ed. Joel Wuthnow et al. (Washington, DC: National Defense University Press, 2021), 236.

35. Lv You [吕游], "Research on Building Up the Support Capability of Military Airlifting in Overseas Non-War Military Actions [涉外非战争军事行动航空运输保障能力建设研究]," *Traffic Engineering and Technology for National Defense* [国防交通工程与技术], no. 6 (2015): 1; Tan Wenhu [谈文虎], "Diversified Military Tasks Draw Innovations in Military Training [多样化军事任务牵引军事训练创新]," *PLA Daily* [解放军报], July 1, 2008.

36. Southerland, "The Chinese Military's Role in Overseas Humanitarian Assistance and Disaster Relief," 4–5.

37. Zhang Xin [张鑫], "China: The PLA's Logistical Base in Djibouti Is a Decision Made by Friendly Consultation Between China and Djibouti [中方：解放军驻吉布提保障基地系中吉两国友好协商作出的决定]," *Global Times* [环球时报], July 12, 2017, https://world.huanqiu.com/article/9CaKrnK41VZ.

38. Tang Yongsheng [唐永胜], ed., *On National Competitive Strategy* [国家竞争战略论] (Beijing: Current Affairs Press [时事出版社], 2018), 241–242.

39. Liu Wanli [刘万利], "Put the People First, Diplomacy for the People [以人为本 外交为民]," *People's Daily Online* [人民网], April 7, 2014, http://military.people.com.cn/n/2015/0407/c172467-26804330.html.

40. Ren Huai [任怀], "This Is Our Home Country That You Can Always Trust [这就是祖国，你永远可以相信她]," *People's Daily* [人民日报], May 7, 2023, http://world.people.com.cn/n1/2023/0507/c1002-32680345.html.

41. Data taken from IMDB's Box Office Mojo, https://www.boxofficemojo.com/release/rl4093871617/, accessed July 28, 2023.

42. In 2012, their behavior improved, with China starting to escort all merchant ships, regardless of nationality. Vu, "The PLAN's Anti-Piracy Missions in the Gulf of Aden, Africa," 230.

43. "How We Are Funded," UN Peacekeeping, https://peacekeeping.un.org/en/how-we-are-funded, accessed June 26, 2023; "UN Document A/67/224/Add. 1: Scale of Assessments for the Apportionment of the Expenses of the United Nations Peacekeeping Operations," United Nations General Assembly, December 27, 2015, https://documents-dds-ny.un.org/doc/UNDOC/GEN/N12/665/78/PDF/N1266578.pdf?OpenElement.

44. "Troop and Police Contributors," United Nations Peacekeeping, downloaded June 26, 2023, https://peacekeeping.un.org/en/troop-and-police-contributors; "China Takes First Step in $1 Billion Pledge to U.N. to Fund Peace, Development," *Reuters*, May 6, 2016, https://www.reuters.com/article/us-china-un-idUSKCN0XX1YI/.

45. See appendix on China's HADR activities at www.orianaskylarmastro.com/upstart.

46. Southerland, "The Chinese Military's Role in Overseas Humanitarian Assistance and Disaster Relief," 6, 10; "Ebola: From Recovery to Self-Reliance," USAID, https://2017-2020.usaid.gov/ebola, accessed August 4, 2023.

47. Evan S. Medeiros, *Reluctant Restraint: The Evolution of China's Nonproliferation Policies and Practices, 1980–2004* (Stanford, CA: Stanford University Press, 2007).

48. Alastair Iain Johnston, *Social States: China in International Institutions, 1980–2000*, Vol. 108 (Princeton: Princeton University Press, 2008), xxi.

49. "China in the Nuclear Suppliers Group (NSG)," US Department of State Archive, May 18, 2004, https://2001-2009.state.gov/t/isn/rls/rm/32570.htm.

50. These seventeen treaties are: the Comprehensive Test Ban Treaty, the Partial Nuclear Test Ban Treaty, the Convention on Nuclear Safety, the London Convention on Nuclear Dumping, the Convention on Assistance in Case of Nuclear Accident, the Convention on Early Notification of Nuclear Accident, the Convention on the Physical Protection of Nuclear Material, the International Convention on the Suppression of Acts of Nuclear Terrorism, the Nuclear Non-Proliferation Treaty, the Biological Weapons Convention, the Chemical Weapons Convention, the Arms Trade Treaty, the Convention on Certain Conventional Weapons, the Environmental Modification Techniques Treaty, the Outer Space Treaty, the Seabed Arms Control Treaty, and the Antarctic Treaty.

51. Jeff Abramson and Greg Webb, "U.S. to Quit Arms Trade Treaty," Arms Control Association, May 2019, https://www.armscontrol.org/act/2019-05/news/us-quit-arms-trade-treaty.

52. Xu Nengwu [徐能武] and Long Kun [龙坤], "Practical Arguments, Theoretical Logic, and Engagement Strategies for Arms Control in Space [太空军备控制的现实争辩、理论逻辑和参与策略]," *International Outlook* [国际展望], 6 (2021): 65, 73.

53. Tang Yongsheng [唐永胜], ed., *On National Competitive Strategy* [国家竞争战略论] (Beijing: Current Affairs Press [时事出版社], 2018), 241–242.

54. State Council Information Office of the People's Republic of China [中华人民共和国国务院新闻办公室], "China's National Defense in 2010 [2010年中国的国防]," March 31, 2011, http://www.gov.cn/zhengce/2011-03/31/content_2618567.htm; "Statement by H. E. Amb. Li Song on Nuclear Non-Proliferation at the Tenth NPT Review Conference," Ministry of Foreign Affairs of the People's Republic of China [中华人民共和国外交部], August 10, 2022, https://www.fmprc.gov.cn/eng/wjb_663 304/zzjg_663340/jks_665232/kjfywj_665252/202208/t20220810_10738694.html.

55. Medeiros, *Reluctant Restraint*.

56. Johnston, *Social States*, xxvi.

57. Fan Jishe [樊吉社], "China-US Arms Control: Cooperation and Divergence, Motivations and Trends [中美军控_合作与分歧、动因与走势]," *International Economic Review* [国际经济评论], 5 (2001): 41.

58. Xin Yi [忻怿], "From Resistance to Participation: China–US Nuclear Dialogue (1976–1992) [由抵制到参与:中美核军控对话(1976–1992)]," *Military History Studies* [军事历史研究], no. 5 (2018): 55–70.

59. Gao Wanglai [高望来], "New Security Doctrine and China's Participation in the Arms Control System [新安全观与中国参与军控体系的实践]," *Social Sciences* [社会科学], no. 4 (2014): 29–36.

60. Yang Wenjing [杨文静], "China's Integration into International Regimes and the US Factors [中国融入国际机制与美国因素]," *Contemporary International Relations* [现代国际关系], no. 10 (2004): 29–35.

61. "The Hague Code of Conduct (HCOC)," Center for Arms Control and Non-Proliferation, https://armscontrolcenter.org/wp-content/uploads/2019/12/HCOC-new.pdf, accessed July 29, 2023.

62. Alastair Iain Johnston, "China in a World of Orders: Rethinking Compliance and Challenge in Beijing's International Relations," *International Security* 44, no. 2 (2019): 9–60.

63. Shirley A. Kan, "China and Proliferation of Weapons of Mass Destruction and Missiles: Policy Issues," Congressional Research Service, January 5, 2015.

64. Yin Chengde [尹承德], "New START Treaty and the Dream of Nuclear-Weapon-Free World [美俄核裁军条约与无核世界神话]," *International Studies* [国际问题研究], no. 4 (2010): 11–18.

65. Steven Jiang and Ben Westcott, "China Says It Won't Join Nuclear Talks Until the US Reduces Its Arsenal," CNN, July 8, 2020, https://www.cnn.com/2020/07/08/asia/china-us-nuclear-treaty-intl-hnk/index.html.

66. Academy of Military Science, Military Strategy Research Center [军事科学院军事战略研究部], ed., *Science of Military Strategy* [战略学] (Beijing: Military Science Press [军事科学出版社], 2013), 177.

67. "Editorial: On China-Related Nuclear Arms Control Issues, the US Side Should Not Forcefully Lead the Rhythm [社评：关于涉华核军控问题，美方莫强带节奏]," *Global Times* [环球时报], November 18, 2021, https://opinion.huanqiu.com/article/45dYHEuRtod.

68. "The First Gulf War," Office of the Historian, US Department of State, https://history.state.gov/departmenthistory/short-history/firstgulf, accessed January 19, 2024.

69. Jiang Zemin [江泽民], "On Military Strategic Guidelines and National Defense Technology [关于军事战略方针和国防科技问题]," in *Selected Writings of Jiang Zemin, Volume I* [江泽民文选，第一卷] (Beijing: People's Publishing House [人民出版社], 2006), 142–147.

70. Zhang Wannian Writing Group [张万年写作组], *Biography of Zhang Wannian, Volume II* [张万年传(下)] (Beijing: PLA Publishing House [解放军出版社], 2011), 62; Liu Huaqing [刘华清], "Unswervingly Advance Along the Road of Building a Modern Army with Chinese Characteristics [坚定不移地沿着建设有中国特色现代化军队的道路前进]," *PLA Daily* [解放军报], August 6, 1993.

71. Zhang Wannian Writing Group, *Biography of Zhang Wannian, Volume II*, 63.

72. Liu, "Unswervingly Advance Along the Road of Building a Modern Army with Chinese Characteristics."

73. He Zhu [荷竹], *Experts Evaluate the Iraq War* [专家评说伊拉克战争] (Beijing: Military Science Press [军事科学出版社], 2004), 147–148; PLA Academy of Military Sciences [军事科学院军事历史研究部], *The Complete History of the Gulf War* [海湾战争全史] (Beijing: PLA Publishing House [解放军出版社], 2000), 458; Jiang Zemin [江泽民], *Selected Writings of Jiang Zemin, Volume III* [江泽民文选，第三卷] (Beijing: People's Publishing House [人民出版社], 2006), 359–360.

74. Li Chenggang [李成刚], "Local Wars After the End of the Cold War—Gulf War [冷战结束后的局部战争—海湾战争]," *Military History* [军事史林], no. 2 (2021): 17–29.

75. Zhang Zhen [张震], *Zhang Zhen's Memoir, Volume II* [张震回忆录（下）] (Beijing: PLA Publishing House [解放军出版社], 2003), 363; He, *Experts Evaluate the Iraq War*, 151.

76. Jiang, "The International Situation and Military Strategic Guidelines [国际形势和军事战略方针]," in *Selected Writings of Jiang Zemin, Volume III*, 278–294; Bai Ruixue [白瑞雪], Xiong Zhengyan [熊争艳], and Li Zhihui [李志辉], "China's Active Defense Military Strategic Guidelines Have Undergone Many Adjustments [中国积极防御军事战略方针历经多次调整]," *People's Daily Online* [人民网], May 26, 2015, http://military.people.com.cn/n/2015/0526/c172467-27057937.html.

77. Bai, Xiong, and Li, "China's Active Defense Military Strategic Guidelines Have Undergone Many Adjustments"; M. Taylor Fravel, *Active Defense: China's Military Strategy since 1949* (Princeton: Princeton University Press, 2019), 218.

78. Bai, Xiong, and Li, "China's Active Defense Military Strategic Guidelines Have Undergone Many Adjustments."

79. Jiang Zemin [江泽民], *The Selected Works of Jiang Zemin, Volume III* [江泽民文选(第三卷)] (Beijing: People's Publishing House [人民出版社], 2006), 359–360.

80. "China's National Defence in 2004 [2004年中国的国防]," State Council Information Office of the People's Republic of China [中华人民共和国国务院新闻办公室], May 27, 2005, http://www.gov.cn/zhengce/2005-05/27/content_2615731.htm.

81. Tan, "Diversified Military Tasks Draw Innovations in Military Training"; Liu, "Unswervingly Advance Along the Road of Building a Modern Army with Chinese Characteristics"; Tan Wenhu [谈文虎], "Diversified Military Tasks Draw

Innovations in Military Training [多样化军事任务牵引军事训练创新]," *PLA Daily* [解放军报], July 1, 2008.

82. For some examples of how the services worked to meet these goals, see Second Artillery Political Department [第二炮兵政治部], *Glorious Era: Reflecting on the Second Artillery's Development and Advances During the Period of Reform and Opening* [辉煌年代：回顾在改革开放中发展前进的第二炮兵] (Beijing: CCP Central Committee Literature Publishing House [中央文献出版社], 2008), 534–538; "Navy Commander: China's Five Major Naval Services Are Transforming to Information Technology [海军司令员：中国海军5大兵种正向信息化转型]," Xinhua News [新华社], April 15, 2009, http://mil.news.sina.com.cn/2009-04-15/1834548881.html; Li Zhihui [李志晖] et al., "Chinese Navy Launches Strategic Transformation [中国海军启动战略转型]," Xinhua News [新华社], May 26, 2015, http://www.xinhuanet.com/politics/2015-05/26/c_1115408221.htm; Zhang Li [张力], "Chinese Air Force's Strategic Transformation: From Zero to 'Integrating Aviation and Space Power, and Strike and Defense Capabilities' [中国空军战略转型历程:从零到空天一体攻防兼备]," *News China* [中国新闻周刊], November 12, 2014, http://news.sina.com.cn/c/2014-11-12/170731133436.shtml.

83. Xi Jinping [习近平], "Secure a Decisive Victory in Building a Moderately Prosperous Society in All Respects and Strive for the Great Success of Socialism with Chinese Characteristics for a New Era—Delivered at the 19th National Congress of the Communist Party of China [决胜全面建成小康社会 夺取新时代中国特色社会主义伟大胜利—在中国共产党第十九次全国代表大会上的报告]," State Council of the People's Republic of China [中华人民共和国中央人民政府], October 18, 2017, https://www.gov.cn/zhuanti/2017-10/27/content_5234876.htm.

84. Chen Jiesheng [陈杰生] et al., *Strategic Conception of Space Military Utilization* [太空军事运用战略构想] (Beijing: National Defense Industry Press [国防工业出版社], 2021).

85. Li Daguang [李大光], "On Space Control [试论制天权]," *Journal of the Academy of Equipment Command and Technology* [装备指挥技术学院学报] 15, no. 3 (June 2004): 55–60.

86. Chang Xianqi [常显奇], "Space Strategy and National Security [空间战略与国家安全]," *Chinese Military Sciences* [中国军事科学], no. 1 (2002): 12.

87. Chang Xianqi [常显奇], "Space Strength and the New Revolution in Military Affairs [空间力量与新军事变革]," *Chinese Military Sciences* [中国军事科学], no. 3 (2003): 59.

88. Zhu Tingchang [朱听昌] and Liu Jing [刘菁], "Vying for Space Supremacy: The Development and Influence of America's 'High Frontier' Strategy [争夺制天权：美国'高边疆'战略的发展历程及其影响]," *Military History Studies* [军事历史研究], no. 3 (2004): 115–126.

89. "Aerospace Science and Technology Group Released the 'Blue Book on China's Aerospace Science and Technology Activities (2021)' [航天集团发布'中国航天科技活动蓝皮书（2021年）']," China Aerospace Science and Technology Corporation [中国航天科技集团有限公司], February 11, 2022; ChinaPower

Team, "How Is China Advancing Its Space Launch Capabilities?," ChinaPower, November 5, 2019, https://chinapower.csis.org/china-space-launch/.

90. ChinaPower Team, "How Is China Advancing Its Space Launch Capabilities?"

91. William J. Broad, "How Space Became the Next 'Great Power' Contest Between the U.S. and China," *New York Times*, January 24, 2021, https://www.nytimes.com/2021/01/24/us/politics/trump-biden-pentagon-space-missiles-satellite.html; Peter Wood, Alex Stone, and Taylor E. Lee, *China's Ground Segment: Building the Pillars of a Great Space Power* (Montgomery, AL: China Aerospace Studies Institute, 2021).

92. "Two Chinese Missiles Failed to Launch in 1996 GPS Suspected to Be Tampered with by the US Military [96年我2枚导弹发射失败 GPS疑被美军做手脚]," *Global Times* [环球时报], December 30, 2012, https://mil.huanqiu.com/article/9CaKrnJypD4; Liu Jingfeng [刘景丰], "A Brief History of Beidou: Understanding the 26-Year Growth Path of the Domestic Navigation System [北斗简史：一文读懂国产导航的26年成长路]," *The Paper* [澎湃], June 24, 2020, https://m.thepaper.cn/baijiahao_7979721.

93. "UCS Satellite Database," Union of Concerned Scientists, January 1, 2023, https://www.ucsusa.org/resources/satellite-database.

94. ChinaPower Team, "How Is China Advancing Its Space Launch Capabilities?"

95. Jia Huajie [贾华杰] et al., "Network-centric Warfare and Its New Technologies [网络中心战及其新技术]," *Defense Science and Technology* [国防科技] 32.04 (2011): 44.

96. Ashley Townshend, Brendan Thomas-Noone, and Matilda Steward, "Averting Crisis: American Strategy, Military Spending and Collective Defence in the Indo-Pacific," United States Study Centre, August 19, 2019, https://www.ussc.edu.au/analysis/averting-crisis-american-strategy-military-spending-and-collective-defence-in-the-indo-pacific.

97. "World Fleet Statistics 1999," Lloyd's Register Foundation, 2000.

98. Ronald O'Rourke, "China Naval Modernization: Implications for U.S. Navy Capabilities—Background and Issues for Congress," Congressional Research Service, May 25, 2023, https://crsreports.congress.gov/product/pdf/RL/RL33153/267.

99. James R. Holmes and Toshi Yoshihara, *Red Star over the Pacific*, 2nd ed. (Annapolis: US Naval Institute Press, 2018), 156–157.

100. Jiang, *The Selected Works of Jiang Zemin, Volume III*, 542.

101. Zhu Feng [朱锋], "The Period of Strategic Opportunity in China's Next Ten Years: Do We Have to Make Different Choices? [中国未来十年的战略机遇期:我们必须做出新的选择吗?]," *Journal of International Studies* [国际政治研究], no. 2 (2014).

102. Han Weifeng [韩卫锋] et al., *Practical Military Reform* [实战化的军事改革] (Beijing: PLA Press [解放军出版社], 2015).

103. "General Secretary Xi Jinping Discusses How to Understand and Take Advantage of the Important Period of Strategic Opportunity [习近平总书记谈如何认识和把握重要战略机遇期]," *Qiushi* [求是网], September 5, 2022, http://www.qstheory.cn/zhuanqu/2022-09/05/c_1128976641.htm.

104. "The Maritime Strategy, 1984," in John B. Hattendorf and Peter M. Swartz, *U.S. Naval Strategy in the 1980s: Selected Documents* (Newport, RI: Naval War College Press, 2008).

105. "US Aircraft Carrier Commander Asserts Freedom to Navigate the South China Sea," Radio Free Asia, September 13, 2021, https://www.rfa.org/english/news/china/usa-southchinasea-09132021185504.html.

106. For a discussion of the role that carriers play in US strategy, see Michael E. O'Hanlon, "The Future of the Aircraft Carrier and the Carrier Air Wing," *Joint Forces Quarterly* 90, no. 3 (2018): 16–23.

107. For a good review of the debate over the carrier's utility, see Robert C. Rubel, "The Future of the Future of Aircraft Carriers," *Naval War College Review* 64, no. 4 (2011): 1–16.

108. Ronald O'Rourke, "Navy *Ford* (CVN-78) Class Aircraft Carrier Program: Background and Issues for Congress," Congressional Research Service, March 27, 2023, https://crsreports.congress.gov/product/pdf/RS/RS20643.

109. Liu Huaqing [刘华清], *Memoirs of Liu Huaqing* [刘华清回忆录] (Beijing: PLA Publishing House [解放军出版社], 2004), 478.

110. Liu, *Memoirs of Liu Huaqing*, 480.

111. Ye Zicheng [叶自成], "China's Sea Power Must Be Subordinate to Its Land Power [中国海权须从属于陆权]," *International Herald Leader* [国际先驱导报], March 2, 2007, http://news.sina.com.cn/c/2007-03-02/101312410732.shtml.

112. Cheng Gang [程刚] and Zhang Mian [张勉], "Why China Did Not Build Aircraft Carrier [中国为何不造航母]," *Party Forum* [党政论坛], no. 1 (2003): 24.

113. "The Significance of the *Varyag* Aircraft Carrier to China's National Strategy Is Something That Cannot Be Purchased with Money [瓦良格号航母对中国意义国家战略金钱买不来]," Sina.com [新浪军事], March 24, 2015, http://mil.news.sina.com.cn/2015-03-24/1058825518.html; *Liu Huaqing Chronicles, Volume 3* [刘华清年谱(下卷)] (Beijing: PLA Publishing House [解放军出版社], 2016), 1195.

114. "China's First Aircraft Carrier *Liaoning* Formally Enters Service [中国首艘航空母舰"辽宁舰"正式交接入列]," China News [中国新闻网], September 25, 2012, https://www.chinanews.com.cn/mil/2012/09-25/4209663.shtml.; Xiong Songce [熊崧策], "The *Varyag* That Came All This Distance [不远万里来到中国的'瓦良格'号]," *Science and Technology Review* [科技导报] 30, no. 5 (2012).

115. Liu Zhaohui [刘朝晖], "What Is the Status of China's Aircraft Carrier Development [中国航母发展到什么地位了]," *Xinmin Weekly* [新民周刊], June 18, 2021, https://m.xinminweekly.com.cn/content/16015.html.

116. "China's 048 Aircraft Carrier Project Is Revealed: Building 10 Carriers by the Nation's 100th Anniversary [中国"048航母建造工程"曝光 建国百年将有10艘]," iFeng [凤凰网], January 17, 2017, http://imil.ifeng.com/50587137/news.shtml?srctag=pc2m&back&back.

117. For example, see Lara Seligman, "Nothing Projects Power Like an Aircraft Carrier. Does the Pentagon Think Otherwise?," *Foreign Policy*, March 1, 2019, https://foreignpolicy.com/2019/03/01/nothing-projects-power-like-an-aircraft-carrier-does-the-pentagon-think-otherwise-mattis-military-uss-truman/.

118. "Military and Security Developments Involving the People's Republic of China 2022," US Department of Defense, November 2022, https://media.defense.gov/2022/Nov/29/2003122279/-1/-1/1/2022-MILITARY-AND-SECURITY-DEVELOPMENTS-INVOLVING-THE-PEOPLES-REPUBLIC-OF-CHINA.PDF.

119. Rush Doshi, *The Long Game: China's Grand Strategy and the Displacement of American Order* (New York: Oxford University Press, 2021), 207.

120. Robbie Gramer and Jack Detsch, "China Eyes Pacific Supremacy with New Carrier," *Foreign Policy*, July 15, 2021, https://foreignpolicy.com/2021/07/15/china-aircraft-carrier-pacific-security/.

121. "Nuclear Submarines and Aircraft Carriers," United States Environmental Protection Agency, updated July 14, 2022, https://www.epa.gov/radtown/nuclear-submarines-and-aircraft-carriers; ChinaPower Team, "What Do We Know (So Far) About China's Second Aircraft Carrier?," ChinaPower, April 22, 2017, https://chinapower.csis.org/china-aircraft-carrier-type-001a/. ChinaPower Team, "How Does China's First Aircraft Carrier Stack Up?," ChinaPower, December 9, 2015, https://chinapower.csis.org/aircraft-carrier/. More bullish Chinese assessments claim the *Fujian* is getting close to US carrier capabilities.

122. "Navy Aircraft Carriers: Cost-Effectiveness of Conventionally and Nuclear-Powered Carriers," Government Accountability Office, National Security and International Affairs Division, August 1998, https://www.govinfo.gov/content/pkg/GAOREPORTS-NSIAD-98-1/html/GAOREPORTS-NSIAD-98-1.htm.

123. David Axe, "Why China Is Relentlessly Pursuing Nuclear Aircraft Carriers," *National Interest*, January 27, 2022, https://nationalinterest.org/blog/reboot/why-china-relentlessly-pursuing-nuclear-aircraft-carriers-200024.

124. Jun Wu [军武], "What Difficulties Does China Face in Building a Giant Nuclear-Powered Aircraft Carrier [中国要造巨型核动力航母还面临哪些难关]," *Life and Disaster* [生命与灾害], no. 3 (2022).

125. Jun Wu [军武], "How Will China's Aircraft Carrier Fleet Develop in the Future [中国海军航母舰队，未来会向哪方面发展]," *Life and Disaster* [生命与灾害], no. 12 (2021).

126. "China's Next Aircraft-Carrier Will Be Its Biggest," *The Economist*, July 3, 2021, https://www.economist.com/china/2021/07/03/chinas-next-aircraft-carrier-will-be-its-biggest.

127. "The *Liaoning* Carrier Launched and Recovered 200 Aircraft in Just 10 Days, Japan Is Anxious [辽宁舰舰载机10天起降超200次　日本很焦虑]," CCTV [央视网], May 18, 2022, https://v.cctv.com/2022/05/18/VIDENeVqD9AIz565aPRmSz1x220518.shtml.

128. Chad Peltier, "China's Logistics Capabilities for Expeditionary Operations," US-China Economic and Security Review Commission, April 15, 2020, available at https://www.uscc.gov/research/chinas-logistics-capabilities-expeditionary-operations.

129. "The Significance of the *Varyag* Aircraft Carrier."

130. Li Gang, "China Refitting Aircraft Carrier Body for Research, Training," Xinhua News, July 27, 2011, https://web.archive.org/web/20140104005718/http://eng.mod.

gov.cn/TopNews/2011-07/27/content_4284108.htm; "Beijing Says Liaoning Is Now a 'Combat Carrier,'" *Asia Times*, April 25, 2019, https://asiatimes.com/2019/04/beij ing-says-liaoning-is-now-a-combat-carrier/.

131. Ni Guanghui [倪光辉], "Domestic-Made Aircraft Carrier, Expanding China's New Blue Ocean [国产航母开拓中国新蓝海]," People.cn [人民网], April 27, 2017, http://opinion.people.com.cn/n1/2017/0427/c1003-29238768.html; Yang Zhen [杨 震] and Cai Liang [蔡亮], "On Aircraft Carriers and China's Seapower [论航空母舰 与中国海权]," *Contemporary World* [当代世界], no. 8 (2017): 42–45.

132. Zhong Sheng [钟声], "No One Has the Rights to Judge Our Development of Aircraft Carriers [对我发展航母说三道四没资格]," Huanqiu.com [环球网], September 29, 2012, https://mil.huanqiu.com/article/9CaKrnJxfDm; "China Aircraft Carrier: Sailing from Today to the Future [中国航母: 从今天驶向未来]," *PLA Daily* [解放军报], September 26, 2012, http://mil.news.sina.com.cn/2012-09-26/ 0639702133.html.

133. "Premier Zhou: I Cannot Be Resigned to the Fact I Haven't Seen the Aircraft Carrier [周总理：看不到航母我不甘心啊！]," State Administration of Science, Technology and Industry for National Defense, PRC [国家国防科技工业局], September 29, 2013, http://gfplatform.cnsa.gov.cn/n6909/n7005/c39340/cont ent.html.

134. "Chinese Aircraft Carrier Under Construction, Will Not Enter Other Countries [中 国航母在建 不会驶入他国]," *Hong Kong Business Report* [香港商报], June 7, 2011, quoted in Adam Liff, "Shadowing the Hegemon? Great Power Norms, Socialization, and the Military Trajectories of Rising Powers" (PhD dissertation, Princeton University, June 2014).

135. Liu, *Memoirs of Liu Huaqing*, 477–479.

136. "Stories of Aircraft Carrier *Liaoning*," CCTV, August 26, 2017, available at https:// www.youtube.com/watch?v=vzQ_I_aVusA.

137. Liu, *Memoirs of Liu Huaqing*, 479.

138. "Aircraft Carrier Made in China," CCTV Voice of China, June 17, 2017, https:// youtu.be/XsrdFSqOWB8; "People's Navy Pursues Its Dream for 70 Years: Reviewing the Past Life of the First Aircraft Carrier *Liaoning*!," CCTV National Memories, April 24, 2019, https://youtu.be/Q__lvdZd3DM.

139. Li Longyi [李龙伊], "The First Aircraft Carrier (New China's 'Firsts' Chapter of National Defense) [第一艘航空母舰（新中国的'第一'·国防篇）]," People.cn [人 民网], October 7, 2019, http://politics.people.com.cn/n1/2019/1007/c1001-31385 573.html; Liu, *Memoirs of Liu Huaqing*, 479.

140. Wang Hongliang [王宏亮], "Toward the Deep Blue: What the *Fujian* Could Do in the Long Term (2/2) [走向深蓝：福建舰的远期愿景（下）]," *The Paper* [澎湃新 闻], July 14, 2022, https://www.thepaper.cn/newsDetail_forward_18978204.

141. Jake Wilson, "China's Domestic Aircraft Carrier Program: Modernization and Challenges," *Wild Blue Yonder*, November 12, 2021, https://www.airuniversity. af.edu/Wild-Blue-Yonder/Article-Display/Article/2842336/chinas-domestic-aircr aft-carrier-program-modernization-and-challenges/.

142. *Military Balance 2001* (London: International Institute for Strategic Studies, 2001), 333–335.

143. "Trends in World Military Expenditure, 2022," Stockholm International Peace Research Institute, April 2023, https://www.sipri.org/sites/default/files/2023-04/230 4_fs_milex_2022.pdf.

144. Xue Zhiliang [薛志亮], "Beware of Strategic Disruptive Mistakes [谨防战略性颠覆性错误]," *PLA Daily* [解放军报], January 30, 2018, http://m.xinhuanet.com/mil/2018-01/30/c_129801390.htm.

145. Zuo Fengrong [左凤荣], "Causes and Consequences of the Soviet Union's Path to the Arms Race [苏联走上军备竞赛之路的原因与后果]," *Heilongjiang Social Sciences* [黑龙江社会科学], no. 5 (2001): 33–36; Han Yichen [韩奕琛], "How the Soviet Union Was Dragged Down by the United States [苏联是如何被美国拖垮的]," *Lingdao Wencui* [领导文萃], no. 18 (2016): 113.

146. Zuo Fengrong [左凤荣], "Lessons from the Soviet Union on the Issue of Civil-Military Integration [苏联在军民融合问题上的教训]," *Exploration and Free Views* [探索与争鸣], no. 8 (2020): 133–141.

147. "To Jointly Create the Glorious Achievement of the Complete Reunification of the Motherland and the Great Rejuvenation of the Nation [共同创造祖国完全统一、民族伟大复兴的光荣伟业]," *People's Daily* [人民日报], October 12, 2021, http://opinion.people.com.cn/n1/2021/1012/c1003-32250220.html.

148. Jiang Zemin [江泽民], "Revisiting and Summarizing the Work of the Central Military Committee in the Last Ten Years [十年来军委工作的回顾和总结]," in *The Selected Works of Jiang Zemin, Volume II* [江泽民文选, 第二卷] (Beijing: People's Publishing House [人民出版社], 2006), 461.

149. For example, see "Missiles Expert: Develop What the Enemy Fears, Put the Target Firmly on the Achilles Heel of Our Strongest Foes [导弹专家: 敌人怕啥发展啥 瞄准强敌死穴打]," Huanqiu.com [环球网], February 28, 2015, https://www.gfbzb. gov.cn/zbbm/gfzs/201502/20150228/1430988518.html; Tian Yuanfa [田元发], "One Cannot Chart New Paths When Following Others' Footsteps [踩着别人的脚印走不出新路]," *PLA Daily* [解放军报], March 1, 2017, http://military.people. com.cn/n1/2017/0301/c1011-29115671.html; "Striving to Realize Higher Quality and More Efficient Sustainable Development [努力实现更高质量更高效益更可持续的发展]," State Administration for Science, Technology and Industry for National Defense [国家国防科技工业局], July 31, 2017, http://www.sastind.gov. cn/n152/n6759499/n6759501/c6793977/content.html; Zhang Wannian [张万年], *Zhang Wannian Military Writings* [张万年军事文选] (Beijing: PLA Publishing House [解放军出版社], 2008), 732.

150. Zhang Wannian Writing Group [张万年写作组], *Biography of Zhang Wannian, Volume II* [张万年传(下)] (Beijing: People's Liberation Army Publishing House [解放军出版社], 2011), 63.

151. Eric Heginbotham et al., *The US-China Military Scorecard: Forces, Geography, and the Evolving Balance of Power, 1996–2017* (Santa Monica, CA: RAND, 2015).

152. ChinaPower Team, "Does China's J-20 Rival Other Stealth Fighters?," ChinaPower, February 23, 2018, https://chinapower.csis.org/china-chengdu-j-20/.

153. "Military and Security Developments Involving the People's Republic of China 2022," 81–82.

154. In a RAND simulation of an attack on Kadena, 36 Chinese missiles closed the runways for 4 days, scaling up to 43 days of closure if 274 missiles were to be used. The study also noted that the "DF-21C-class missile could carry hundreds of submunitions, blanketing hundreds of square feet so that every aircraft parked in the area would have a high probability of being damaged." With just 108 missiles, China could shut down the airfield for a week and, with a high probability of success, destroy every fighter on the base. Heginbotham et al., *The US-China Military Scorecard*, 60.

155. "The Five Chinese Weapons That the US Army Is Most Afraid Of: DF-21D Is the First [美军最害怕的5款中国武器 DF-21D导弹居首]," *China Military* [中国军网], May 8, 2014, http://www.81.cn/bqtd/2014-05/08/content_5895795.htm; "The Vulnerability of America's Asia-Pacific Bases Is Revealed: 34 Chinese Missiles Can Overwhelm Kadena [美亚太基地弱点被曝光：中国34枚导弹可瘫痪嘉纳]," Xilu.com [西陆网], March 5, 2016, http://junshi.xilu.com/20160305/100001000 0933219.html; "US Experts Simulate Chinese Missile Surprise Attack on US Pacific Base: Warships in Port Wiped Out [美国专家模拟中国导弹奇袭美军太平洋基地：港内军舰覆灭]," iFeng [凤凰网], July 12, 2017, http://inews.ifeng.com/51419 992/news.shtml?&back; Ge Tengfei and Chen Xi, "An Analysis of the United States' Deterrence by Denial Strategy Against China," *Journal of International Security Studies*, September 16, 2022, available at https://interpret.csis.org/translations/an-analysis-of-the-united-states-deterrence-by-denial-strategy-against-china/.

156. "Military and Security Developments Involving the People's Republic of China 2005," US Department of Defense, 2005, 45, available at http://www.andrewerick son.com/wp-content/uploads/2015/11/DoD_China-Report_2005.pdf; "Military and Security Developments Involving the People's Republic of China 2022," 167.

157. "Military and Security Developments Involving the People's Republic of China 2010," US Department of Defense, 2010, 66, available at http://www.andrewerick son.com/wp-content/uploads/2015/11/DoD_China-Report_2010.pdf; "Military and Security Developments Involving the People's Republic of China 2022," 167.

158. David Webb, "Dong Feng-16 (CSS-11)," Missile Defense Advocacy Online, February 2017, https://missiledefenseadvocacy.org/missile-threat-and-proliferation/todays-missile-threat/china/dong-feng-16/; "DF-15," *Missile Threat*, Center for Strategic and International Studies, August 5, 2021, https://missilethreat.csis.org/missile/df-15-css-6/.

159. Chen Haidong [陈海东] et al., "Study for the Guidance Scheme of Reentry Vehicles Attacking Slowly Moving Targets [再入飞行器攻击慢速活动目标的制导方案研究]," *Missiles and Space Vehicles* [导弹与航天运载技术], no. 6 (2000): 6–9.

160. "F-35C Combat Radius Lightning Flash Fact," Defense Visual Information Distribution Service, May 10, 2022, https://www.dvidshub.net/video/846199/f-35c-combat-radius-lightning-flash-fact#:~:text=The%20F%2D35C%20has%20a,19%2C200%20lb%20internal%20fuel%20capacity; "DF-21 (CSS-5)," *Missile*

Threat, Center for Strategic and International Studies, updated March 28, 2022, https://missilethreat.csis.org/missile/df-21/.

161. "Military and Security Developments Involving the People's Republic of China 2022," viii; Eric Heginbotham et al., *The US-China Military Scorecard*, 170.

162. "A Constructive Year for Chinese Base Building," Asia Maritime Transparency Initiative, December 14, 2017, https://amti.csis.org/constructive-year-chinese-building/

163. Lonnie Henley, "PLA Operational Concepts and Centers of Gravity in a Taiwan Conflict," Testimony Before the US-China Economic and Security Review Commission Hearing on Cross-Strait Deterrence, February 18, 2021, https://www.uscc.gov/sites/default/files/2021-02/Lonnie_Henley_Testimony.pdf.

164. "Military and Security Developments Involving the People's Republic of China 2022," 61.

165. Kris Osborn, "Could the US Military Gain Air Supremacy in a War with China?," *National Interest*, November 8, 2021, https://nationalinterest.org/blog/buzz/could-us-military-gain-air-supremacy-war-china-195867.

166. Jin Lin [金霖], "From the United States Air Force's 'Crushing Victory' (Continued) [从美国空军'惨胜'说开去（续）]," Grandview Institution [国观智库], April 26, 2021, https://www.grandviewcn.com/shishipinglun/590.html.

167. Timothy A. Walton and Bryan Clark, "Resilient Aerial Refueling: Safeguarding the US Military's Global Reach," Hudson Institute, November 2021, 29, https://s3.amazonaws.com/media.hudson.org/Walton%20Clark_Resilient%20Aerial%20Refueling.pdf.

168. Wei Chengxi [魏晨曦], "Space War and Its Operational Environment [太空战及其作战环境]," *Aerospace China* [中国航天], no. 10 (2001): 40; Zhang Yuliang [张玉良] et al., eds., *The Science of Campaigns* [战役学] (Beijing: National Defense University Press [国防大学出版社], 2006): 87.

169. Yu Jixun [于际训], *The Science of Second Artillery Campaigns* [第二炮兵战役学] (Beijing: PLA Publishing House [解放军出版社], 2004), 341; Huang Zhicheng [黄志澄], "Thinking and Knowledge About Space War [关于太空战的认知与思考]," *Aerospace International* [国际太空], no. 6 (2003): 10–15; Tan Heyi [谈何易] and Zhang Ke [张珂], *Network Electronic Warfare* [网电战] (Beijing: Publishing House of Electronics Industry [电子工业出版社], 2019). .

170. Zhang Yan [张岩], *Theory of Strategic Deterrence* [战略威慑论] (Beijing: Social Sciences Literature Press [社会科学文献出版社], 2018), 97–98.

171. David Talbot, "How Technology Failed in Iraq," *MIT Technology Review*, November 1, 2004, https://www.technologyreview.com/2004/11/01/232152/how-technology-failed-in-iraq/.

172. Yu, *The Science of Second Artillery Campaigns*, 341.

173. Long Kun [龙坤] and Zhu Qichao [朱启超], "Algorithmic Warfare: Concept, Characteristics and Implications ['算法战争' 的概念、特点与影响]," *National Defense Science and Technology* [国防科技] 38, no. 6 (2017): 41.

174. Dai Yifang [戴怡芳], ed., *Reflections and Prospects for Military Studies* [军事学研究回顾与展望] (Beijing: Military Sciences Press [军事科学出版社], 1995), 94.

175. "Cyber Capabilities and National Power: A Net Assessment," International Institute for Strategic Studies, June 28, 2021, https://www.iiss.org/blogs/research-paper/2021/06/cyber-capabilities-national-power.

176. Omer Yoacimik and Vivek Ganti, "DDoS Attack Trends for Q4 2021," *i*, January 10, 2022, https://blog.cloudflare.com/ddos-attack-trends-for-2021-q4/. In its 2021 annual report, cybersecurity firm CrowdStrike found that Chinese state-affiliated hacker groups were responsible for 67 percent of intrusions in the year leading up to June 2021. "Nowhere to Hide: 2021 Threat Hunting Report," CrowdStrike, June 2021, https://go.crowdstrike.com/rs/281-OBQ-266/images/Report2021Threat Hunting.pdf.

177. "China and Russia Jointly Submitted the Draft Treaty on PPWT to the Conference on Disarmament," Ministry of Foreign Affairs of the People's Republic of China, February 2, 2008, https://www.fmprc.gov.cn/mfa_eng/wjb_663304/zzjg_663340/jks_665232/jkxw_665234/200802/t20080212_599177.html.

178. Todd Harrison, "International Perspectives on Space Weapons," Center for Strategic and International Studies, May 27, 2020, https://www.csis.org/analysis/internatio nal-perspectives-space-weapons.

179. Xi Jinping, "Remarks at the Opening Ceremony of the Second World Internet Conference," Ministry of Foreign Affairs of the People's Republic of China, December 16, 2015, https://www.fmprc.gov.cn/eng/wjdt_665385/zyjh_665391/201 512/t20151224_678467.html.

180. The predicted cost of a DF-21D is reported here as the approximate per-unit cost for the United States to produce a similar missile, because China does not publish missile costs. Jacob Cohn et al., "Leveling the Playing Field: Reintroducing US Theater-Range Missiles in a Post-INF World," Center for Strategic and Budgetary Assessments, 2019, https://csbaonline.org/uploads/documents/Leveling_the_Playing_Field_web_Final_1.pdf; Ronald O'Rourke, "Navy *Ford* (CVN-78) Class Aircraft Carrier Program: Background and Issues for Congress," Congressional Research Service, April 28, 2022, https://sgp.fas.org/crs/weapons/RS20643.pdf; "F-16 Fighting Falcon," United States Air Force, accessed July 6, 2022, https://www.af.mil/About-Us/Fact-Sheets/Display/Article/104505/f-16-fighting-falcon/. The average anti-air missile test costs approximately $2 million, which is the benchmark used in the text.

181. James Mattis, "Summary of the 2018 National Defense Strategy of the United States of America: Sharpening the American Military's Competitive Edge," US Department of Defense, January 21, 2018, https://dod.defense.gov/Portals/1/Documents/pubs/2018-National-Defense-Strategy-Summary.pdf.

182. Graham Allison and Jonah Glick-Unterman, "The Great Military Rivalry: China vs the US," Belfer Center for Science and International Affairs, December 16, 2021, https://www.belfercenter.org/publication/great-military-rivalry-china-vs-us.

183. Liu, *Memoirs of Liu Huaqing*, 637.

184. Dai Yifang [戴怡芳], ed., *Reflections and Prospects for Military Studies* [军事学研究回顾与展望] (Beijing: Military Sciences Press [军事科学出版社], 1995), 34.

Chapter 5

1. Daron Acemoglu et al., "A Dynamic Theory of Resource Wars," *Quarterly Journal of Economics* 127, no. 1 (2012): 283–331.

2. "NSC 68: United States Objectives and Programs for National Security," National Security Council, April 14, 1950, available at https://irp.fas.org/offdocs/nsc-hst/nsc-68.htm.

3. Bill Clinton, "1999 National Security Strategy," White House, December 2, 1999, https://clintonwhitehouse4.archives.gov/media/pdf/nssr-1299.pdf.

4. "National Defense Strategy of the United States of America," US Department of Defense, March 2005, 5, https://history.defense.gov/Portals/70/Documents/nds/2005_NDS.pdf?ver=tFA4Qqo94ZB0x_S6uL0QEg%3d%3d; "Sustaining US Global Leadership: Priorities for 21st Century Defense," US Department of Defense, January 2012, https://nssarchive.us/wp-content/uploads/2020/04/defense_strategic_guidance.pdf; "Summary of the 2018 National Defense Strategy," US Department of Defense, January 2018, https://nssarchive.us/wp-content/uploads/2020/04/2018_NDS.pdf; "2022 National Defense Strategy," US Department of Defense, October 27, 2022, 1, https://media.defense.gov/2022/Oct/27/2003103845/-1/-1/1/2022-NATIONAL-DEFENSE-STRATEGY-NPR-MDR.PDF.

5. Joseph R. Biden, "2022 National Security Strategy," White House, October 12, 2022, https://www.whitehouse.gov/wp-content/uploads/2022/10/Biden-Harris-Administrations-National-Security-Strategy-10.2022.pdf.

6. Lu Nanquan [陆南泉], "Deng Xiaoping's Theories on the Soviet Union's Socialist Model [邓小平对苏联社会主义模式的论述]," Eeo.com.cn [经济观察网], August 18, 2014, http://www.eeo.com.cn/2014/0818/265117.shtml.

7. Zhang Yunling [张蕴岭], "The Comprehensive Security Concept and Reflecting on China's Security [综合安全观及对我国安全的思考]," *Contemporary Asia-Pacific* [当代亚太], no. 1 (2000): 13; Liu Yong [刘勇], "The US and Japan Have Massively Increased Their Military Spending. It Is Self-Evident Who They Are Targeting. How Should China Avoid Falling into an Arms Race? [美日大举增加军费，针对谁不言而喻，中国该如何避免陷入军备竞赛]," NetEase News [网易新闻], December 19, 2022, https://www.163.com/dy/article/HOVB3ABH0552UZ8P.html; Feng Yaren [冯亚仁] et al., "US Spurs Arms Race Around China [美在中国周边刺激军备竞赛]," *Global Times* [环球时报], March 13, 2023, https://world.huanqiu.com/article/4C50rIqXCAx.

8. Jiang Zemin [江泽民], *Jiang Zemin on Socialism with Chinese Characteristics (Special Excerpts)* [江泽民论有中国特色社会主义(专题摘编)] (Beijing: Central Party Literature Press [中央文献出版社], 2002).

9. "China Began New Military Reform [中国开始新军事变革]," State Council of the People's Republic of China [中华人民共和国中央人民政府], http://www.gov.cn/test/2005-06/28/content_10531.htm; "Deng Xiaoping's Theories on Military Construction in the New Era [邓小平新时期军队建设思想]," International College of Defense Studies, PLA National Defense University [中国人民解放军国防大学国际防务学院], December 4, 2020, http://www.cdsndu.org/index.php/zgjswha/40.html.

10. Marina Rudyak, "The CMP Dictionary: Modernization," China Media Project, May 2, 2023, https://chinamediaproject.org/the_ccp_dictionary/modernization/.

11. The PLAN had commissioned at most four *Jin*-class nuclear missile submarines in 2010, but the submarines suffered from reactor problems and were not yet operational. See Bernard Cole, *The Great Wall at Sea: China's Navy in the Twenty-First Century* (Annapolis: US Naval Institute Press, 2011), 97, 109.

12. James R. Holmes and Toshi Yoshihara, *Red Star over the Pacific*, 2nd ed. (Annapolis: US Naval Institute Press, 2018); Ronald O'Rourke, "China Naval Modernization: Implications for U.S. Navy Capabilities—Background and Issues for Congress," Congressional Research Service, May 25, 2023, https://crsreports.congress.gov/product/pdf/RL/RL33153/267.

13. Andrew Salerno-Garthwaite, "J-20 Chengdu: Mighty Dragon in the Heart of China's Military Modernisation," Airforce Technology, September 14, 2022, https://www.airforce-technology.com/features/j-20-and-chinas-military-modernisation/; "Air Force F-22 Fighter Program," Congressional Research Service, July 11, 2013, 5, https://www.everycrsreport.com/files/20130711_RL31673_c70b986e6de321f9f00ccbb5173d56d3fc781d1a.pdf.

14. Taken from J. David Singer, Stuart Bremer, and John Stuckey, "Capability Distribution, Uncertainty, and Major Power War, 1820–1965," in Bruce Russett, ed., *Peace, War, and Numbers*, Correlates of War National Material Capabilities, Vol. 6 (Beverly Hills, CA: Sage Publishing, 1972): 19–48.

15. Singer, Bremer, and Stuckey, "Capability Distribution, Uncertainty, and Major Power War."

16. ChinaPower Team, "What Does China Really Spend on Its Military?," ChinaPower, December 28, 2015, updated May 27, 2021; "SIPRI Military Expenditure Database," Stockholm International Peace Research Institute, https://www.sipri.org/databases/milex, accessed August 25, 2023.

17. M. Taylor Fravel, *Active Defense: China's Military Strategy Since 1949* (Princeton, NJ: Princeton University Press, 2019), 205.

18. John A. Vasquez, "Why Do Neighbors Fight? Proximity, Interaction, or Territoriality," *Journal of Peace Research* 32, no. 3 (1995): 284.

19. Anthony J. Blinken, "Sixth Anniversary of the Philippines-China South China Sea Arbitral Tribunal Ruling," US Department of State, July 11, 2022, https://www.state.gov/sixth-anniversary-of-the-philippines-south-china-sea-arbitral-tribunal-ruling/.

20. "Why the South China Sea Has Once Again Become a Stage for Great Power Competition [南海缘何再度成为大国角逐的舞台]," National Institute for South China Sea Studies [中国南海研究所], February 27, 2021, http://www.nanhai.org.cn/review_c/528.html.

21. Liu Yijian [刘一建], Shi Ping [时平], and Feng Liang [冯梁], *On the History of China's Sea Power* [中华海权史论] (Beijing: National University of Defense Press [国防大学出版社], 2000).

22. Michael Mazarr, "Mastering the Gray Zone: Understanding a Changing of Conflict," United States Army War College, December 2015, 58, https://publications.armywar college.edu/pubs/2372.pdf.

23. ChinaPower Team, "Are Maritime Law Enforcement Forces Destabilizing Asia?," ChinaPower, August 18, 2016, https://chinapower.csis.org/maritime-forces-destab ilizing-asia/.

24. Bonny Lin et al., "Countering China's Coercion Against U.S. Allies and Partners in the Indo-Pacific," in *Competition in the Gray Zone* (Santa Monica, CA: RAND Corporation, 2022), https://www.rand.org/pubs/research_reports/RRA594-1.html.

25. They describe "gray zone activities" as a Western concept whose purpose is to attack and manipulate public opinion on China's legitimate strategic and diplomatic actions. See, for example, Chinese Academy of Social Sciences, "One Belt, One Road" Research Center [中国社会科学院"一带一路"研究中心], "Great Attention Should Be Paid to the Strategic Games and Contests Between Major Powers in the 'Gray Zone' [应高度重视大国在'灰色地带'的战略博弈与较量]," *Friends of Party Members and Cadres* [党员干部之友], no. 4 (2022): 40–41; Shen Zhixiong [沈志雄], "Gray Zones and China–US Strategic Competition ['灰色地带'与中美战略竞争]," *World Affairs*, no. 11 (2019): 17–19.

26. Huang Zongding [黃宗鼎], "China's Maritime Militia Under Xi Jinping [習近平主政之下的中國海上民兵]," *Defense Security Biweekly* [國防安全雙週報], June 11, 2019, https://indsr.org.tw/respublicationcon?uid=12&resid=704&pid=2564.

27. Gregory B. Poling and Harrison Pretat, "Pulling Back the Curtain on China's Maritime Militia," Center for Strategic and International Studies, November 18, 2021, https://www.csis.org/analysis/pulling-back-curtain-chinas-maritime-militia.

28. Andrew S. Erickson, "Shining a Spotlight: Revealing China's Maritime Militia to Deter Its Use," *National Interest*, November 25, 2018, https://nationalinterest. org/feature/shining-spotlight-revealing-china%E2%80%99s-maritime-mili tia-deter-its-use-36842.

29. ChinaPower Team, "Are Maritime Law Enforcement Forces Destabilizing Asia?"; *Military Balance 2022* (London: International Institute for Strategic Studies, 2022), 238.

30. Central Intelligence Agency, "The United Front in Communist China," May 1957, xi, 1.

31. "The 2003 Political Work Guidelines of the People's Liberation Army [中国人民解放军政治工作条例(2003)]," Reform Data [中国改革信息库], December 5, 2003, http://www.reformdata.org/2003/1205/4925.shtml.

32. Li Mingjun [李明峻], "Legal Warfare [法律战]," *New Century Think Tank Forum* [新世纪智库论坛], no. 43 (2008): 51–52.

33. Fan Gaoyue [樊高月], "Public Opinion Warfare, Psychological Warfare, and Legal Warfare to Accelerate the Victory of the War [舆论战、心理战、法律战三大战法加速战争胜利]," March 8, 2005, Sina News [新浪网], http://news.sina.com.cn/o/2005-03-08/10245297499s.shtml.

34. "Mao Zedong Values the Importance of the Battlefield of Public Opinion, Emphasizing Holding Pamphlets in the Left Hand and Guns and Bullets in the Right

Hand [毛泽东重视舆论战场 强调左手拿传单右手拿枪弹]," *China News* [中国新闻网], September 13, 2010, https://www.chinanews.com.cn/cul/2010/09-13/2528 710.shtml.

35. Peng Dunwen [彭敦文], "Contemporary Value of Mao Zedong's 'On Protracted War' [毛泽东'论持久战'的当代价值]," *People's Forum* [人民论坛], no. 28 (2020): 80–81; Wang Wen [王文], "US-China Competition in the Next Five Years [未来五年的中美博弈]," *China Business Journal* [中国经营网], January 19, 2021, http://www.cb.com. cn/index/show/zl/cv/cv13454491859/p/s.html. See also Deng Yuwen [邓聿文], "Guest Remarks: Protracted Warfare Between the CCP and the US [客座评论：中共对美的持久战]," Deutsche Welle Chinese website [德国之声中文网], October 25, 2020, https://www.dw.com/zh/%E5%AE%A2%E5%BA%A7%E8%AF%84%E8%AE %BA%E4%B8%AD%E5%85%B1%E5%AF%B9%E7%BE%8E%E7%9A%84%E6 %8C%81%E4%B9%85%E6%88%98/a-55370231; and "Six Advantages of China and the US in Their Great Power Competition [中美深度博弈下，中国和美国的各六大优势]," Guancha.cn [观察者网], August 1, 2020, https://user.guancha.cn/main/ content?id=358564&page=2.

36. Peter Mattis, "China's Three Warfares in Perspective," *War on the Rocks*, January 30, 2018, https://warontherocks.com/2018/01/chinas-three-warfares-perspective/.

37. Zhang Yuliang [张玉良] et al., ed., *The Science of Campaigns* [战役学] (Beijing: PLA National Defense University Press [国防大学出版社], 2006), 203, 206.

38. Clint Watts, *Messing with the Enemy: Surviving in a Social Media World of Hackers, Terrorist, Russians, and Fake News* (Sydney: HarperCollins, 2019), 301.

39. Fan, "Public Opinion Warfare, Psychological Warfare, and Legal Warfare to Accelerate the Victory of the War"; Xiao Tianliang [肖天亮], *Science of Military Strategy* [战略学] (Beijing: Military Sciences Press [军事科学出版社], 2015).

40. Oriana Skylar Mastro, "How China Is Bending the Rules in the South China Sea," *The Interpreter*, February 17, 2021, https://www.lowyinstitute.org/the-interpreter/how- china-bending-rules-south-china-sea.

41. "Foreign Ministry Spokesperson Lu Kang's Remarks on Statement by Spokesperson of US State Department on South China Sea Arbitration Ruling," Ministry of Foreign Affairs of the People's Republic of China, July 12, 2016, https://www.fmprc.gov.cn/ mfa_eng/xwfw_665399/s2510_665401/2535_665405/201607/t20160713_696 684.html.

42. Mazarr, "Mastering the Gray Zone," 72.

43. Kapil Bhatia, "Coercive Gradualism Through Gray Zone Statecraft in the South China Seas: China's Strategy and Potential U.S. Options," *Joint Forces Quarterly* 91, no. 4 (2018): 24–33.

44. Michael Green et al., "Countering Coercion in Maritime Asia: The Theory and Practice of Gray Zone Deterrence," Center for Strategic and International Studies, May 9, 2017.

45. Alastair Iain Johnston, *Cultural Realism: Strategic Culture and Grand Strategy in Chinese History* (Princeton, NJ: Princeton University Press, 1998), 248–250, 99–102.

46. Johnston, *Cultural Realism*, 103.

47. Bonny Lin et al., "Competition in the Gray Zone: Countering China's Coercion Against US Allies and Partners in the Indo-Pacific," RAND Corporation, 2022, https://www.rand.org/pubs/research_reports/RRA594-1.html.

48. Mazarr, "Mastering the Gray Zone," 88.

49. Michael Green, "The Legacy of Obama's 'Pivot' to Asia," *Foreign Policy*, September 3, 2016, https://foreignpolicy.com/2016/09/03/the-legacy-of-obamas-pivot-to-asia/.

50. Harry S. Truman, "The President's News Conference, November 30, 1950," in *Public Papers of the Presidents of the United States: Harry S. Truman, 1950* (Washington, DC: US Government Print Office, 1965), 724–728.

51. "Memorandum of Discussion at a Special Meeting of the National Security Council on Tuesday, March 31, 1953," in *Foreign Relations of the United States, 1952–1954, Korea, Volume XV, Part 1* (Washington: US Government Printing Office, 1984), 826.

52. "142. Memorandum of a Conversation Between the Secretary of State and Senator Walter George, Department of State, Washington, March 7, 1955," in *Foreign Relations of the United States, 1955–1957, China, Volume II* (Washington, DC: US Government Printing Office, 1986), 337.

53. Shen Zhihua [沈志华], "Aid and Restriction: The USSR and the Development of Atomic Weapons in China (1949–1960) [援助与限制:苏联与中国的核武器研制 (1949–1960)]," *Historical Research* [历史研究], no. 3 (2004): 491.

54. *The Chronicles of Zhou Enlai's Life, 1949–1976* [周恩来年谱, 1949–1976] (Beijing: Central Party Literature Press [中央文献出版社], 1997), 445.

55. *The Chronicles of Mao Zedong's Life, 1949–1976, Volume II* [毛泽东年谱, 1949–1976 (第二卷)] (Beijing: Central Party Literature Press [中央文献出版社], 2013), 567.

56. *The Chronicles of Mao Zedong's Life, 1949–1976, Volume IV* [毛泽东年谱, 1949–1976 (第四卷)] (Beijing: Central Party Literature Press [中央文献出版社], 2013), 386, 467.

57. *The Chronicles of Deng Xiaoping's Life, 1975–1997, Volume I* [邓小平年谱(上册)] (Beijing: Central Party Literature Press [中央文献出版社], 2004), 308.

58. M. Taylor Fravel and Evan S. Medeiros, "China's Search for Assured Retaliation: The Evolution of Chinese Nuclear Strategy and Force Structure," *International Security* 35, no. 2 (2010): 87.

59. "Nonstrategic Nuclear Weapons," Congressional Research Service, July 15, 2021, https://fas.org/sgp/crs/nuke/RL32572.pdf.

60. For example, Jiang Zemin highlighted China's limited resources and the importance of developing conventional capabilities in Jiang Zemin [江泽民], *The Selected Works of Jiang Zemin, Volume I* [江泽民文选(第三卷)] (Beijing: People's Publishing House [人民出版社], 2006), 74–79; *Volume II*, 269–270, 458.

61. Shou Xiaosong [寿晓松], *The Science of Military Strategy* [战略学] (Beijing: Military Sciences Press [军事科学出版社], 2013); Li Tilin [李体林], "Creative Development of the Nuclear Strategic Theory of China Since the Reform and Opening-Up [改革开放以来中国核战略理论的发展]," *China Military Science* [中国军事科学], no. 6 (2008): 42.

62. General Office of the Central Military Commission [中央军委办公厅], ed., *Selection of Deng Xiaoping's Expositions on Army Building in the New Period* [邓小平关于新军队建设论述选编] (Beijing: Bayi Publishing House [八一出版社], 1993), 44–45.

63. Headquarters of the Second Artillery [第二炮兵司令部], *The Science of Military Strategy of the Second Artillery* [第二炮兵战略学] (Beijing: Lantian Press [蓝天出版社], 1996), 83–85.

64. "SIPRI Military Expenditure Database"; Stephen I. Schwartz, *Atomic Audit: The Costs and Consequences of US Nuclear Weapons Since 1940* (Washington, DC: Brookings Institution Press, 1998).

65. "Projected Costs of U.S. Nuclear Forces, 2021 to 2030," Congressional Budget Office, May 2021, https://www.cbo.gov/publication/57240.

66. "Global Nuclear Stockpiles, 1945–1996," Brookings Institution, August 1998, https://web.archive.org/web/20160513152457/http://www.brookings.edu/about/projects/archive/nucweapons/stockpile.

67. Schwartz, "The Hidden Costs of Our Nuclear Arsenal." For the costs of different delivery systems, see "Average Unit Acquisition Costs for Strategic Nuclear Delivery Vehicles," Brookings Institution, 1998, https://www.brookings.edu/average-unit-acquisition-costs-for-strategic-nuclear-delivery-vehicles/.

68. Hans M. Kristensen, Matt Korda, and Eliana Reynolds, "Chinese Nuclear Weapons, 2023," *Bulletin of the Atomic Scientists* 79, no. 2 (2023): 108–133.

69. Hans M. Kristensen and Matt Korda, "Nuclear Notebook: United States Nuclear Weapons, 2023," *Federation of Atomic Scientists* 79, no. 1 (2023): 29.

70. Fravel and Medeiros, "China's Search for Assured Retaliation," 49–50.

71. "China's National Defense in 2006 [2006年中国的国防]," State Council Information Office of the People's Republic of China [中华人民共和国国务院新闻办公室], December 2006, http://www.gov.cn/zwgk/2006-12/29/content_486759.htm.

72. Shou Xiaosong [寿晓松], *The Science of Military Strategy* [战略学] (Beijing: Military Sciences Press [军事科学出版社], 2013), 173, argues that China's limited arsenal initially created the necessity for a no-first-use pledge. This commitment to a minimal deterrence with a no-first-use pledge has been communicated explicitly in its 2006, 2008, 2010, and 2013 white papers.

73. Wu Chunsi [吴莼思], "Nuclear Security Summit, Global Nuclear Order and the Role of China [核安全峰会、全球核秩序建设与中国角色]," *International Security Research* [国际安全研究] 33, no. 2 (2015): 56–57.

74. David J. Trachtenberg, "US Extended Deterrence: How Much Strategic Force Is Too Little?," *Strategic Studies Quarterly* 6, no. 2 (2012): 68.

75. "China's National Defense in 2008 [2008年中国的国防]," State Council Information Office of the People's Republic of China [中华人民共和国国务院新闻办公室], January 2009, http://www.gov.cn/zwgk/2009-01/20/content_1210224.htm.

76. "Nuclear Posture Review Report," US Department of Defense, April 2010, https://dod.defense.gov/Portals/1/features/defenseReviews/NPR/2010_Nuclear_Posture_Review_Report.pdf; "The Bush Doctrine," Carnegie Endowment for International Peace, October 7, 2002, https://carnegieendowment.org/2002/10/07/bush-doctrine-pub-1088.

77. "Nuclear Posture Review," US Department of Defense, February 2018, 21, https://media.defense.gov/2018/Feb/02/2001872886/-1/-1/1/2018-NUCLEAR-POSTURE-REVIEW-FINAL-REPORT.PDF.

78. William Burr, "The 'Launch on Warning' Nuclear Strategy and Its Insider Critics," George Washington University National Security Archive, June 11, 2019, https://nsarchive.gwu.edu/briefing-book/nuclear-vault/2019-06-11/launch-warning-nuclear-strategy-its-insider-critics.

79. "Military and Security Developments Involving the People's Republic of China 2022," 95; "Frequently Asked Questions About Hair-Trigger Alert," Union of Concerned Scientists, January 15, 2015, https://www.ucsusa.org/resources/frequently-asked-questions-about-hair-trigger-alert.

80. "Fact Sheet: China's Nuclear Inventory," Arms Control Association, April 2, 2020, https://armscontrolcenter.org/fact-sheet-chinas-nuclear-arsenal/.

81. "Military and Security Developments Involving the People's Republic of China 2022," 99; "Chinese Ballistic Missile Early Warning," Global Security, May 3, 2020, https://www.globalsecurity.org/space/world/china/warning.htm; Peter Wood et al., "China's Ground Segment: Building the Pillars of a Great Space Power," China Aerospace Studies Institute, September 2020, https://www.airuniversity.af.edu/Portals/10/CASI/documents/Research/Space/2021-03-01%20Chinas%20Ground%20Segment.pdf?ver=z4ogY_MrxaDurwVt-R9J6w%3d%3d.

82. Cameron M. Keys, "FY2024 Defense Budget Request: Space-Based Satellite Programs," Congressional Research Service, June 13, 2023, https://crsreports.congress.gov/product/pdf/IN/IN12176.

83. About 43 percent of the Russian force is land-based. See ChinaPower Team, "How Is China Modernizing Its Nuclear Forces?," ChinaPower, updated October 28, 2020, https://chinapower.csis.org/china-nuclear-weapons/.

84. "Military and Security Developments Involving the People's Republic of China 2022," 60.

85. Yu Jixun [于际训], *The Science of Second Artillery Campaigns* [第二炮兵战役学] (Beijing: PLA Publishing House [解放军出版社], 2004), 42–43.

86. Gerald C. Brown, "Understanding the Risks and Realities of China's Nuclear Forces," Arms Control Association, June 2021, https://www.armscontrol.org/act/2021-06/features/understanding-risks-realities-chinas-nuclear-forces.

87. "Missiles of the United States," *Missile Threat*, Center for Strategic and International Studies, March 3, 2021, https://missilethreat.csis.org/country/united-states/.

88. Kristensen, Korda, and Reynolds, "Chinese Nuclear Weapons, 2023," 109.

89. "Military and Security Developments Involving the People's Republic of China 2020," 55.

90. Zhang Jiadong [张家栋], "Why Would America Hype Up 'China's Hypersonic Weapon'? [美国为何热炒'中国高超音速武器']," *Global Times* [环球时报], October 22, 2021, https://opinion.huanqiu.com/article/45GcOxgUZmq.

91. Matt Korda and Hans M. Kristensen, "China Is Building a Second Nuclear Missile Silo Field," *Federation of American Scientists*, July 26, 2021, https://fas.org/publication/china-is-building-a-second-nuclear-missile-silo-field/.

92. Robert S. Norris and Hans M. Kristensen, "Global Nuclear Weapons Inventories, 1945–2010," *Bulletin of the Atomic Scientists* 66, no. 4 (July 2010): 77–83.

93. Exact estimates of the size of the US nuclear arsenal vary slightly across sources. Most accounts refer back to two authoritative sources: an estimate of 5,800 from Hans M. Kristensen, "World Nuclear Forces," Stockholm International Peace Research Institute, 2020, https://sipri.org/yearbook/2020/10, and one of 5,244 from Hans M. Kristensen and Matt Korda, "Status of World Nuclear Forces," Federation of American Scientists, March 2023, https://fas.org/initiative/status-world-nuclear-forces/. Analysts agree that there are about 3,800 active warheads in the military stockpile but put the number of retired warheads awaiting dismantlement between 1,750 and 2,000, which explains the variance in the total number.

94. Kristensen and Korda, "Status of World Nuclear Forces."

95. Eric Heginbotham et al., "The U.S.-China Military Scorecard," RAND Corporation, 2015, https://www.rand.org/content/dam/rand/pubs/research_reports/RR300/RR392/RAND_RR392.pdf.

96. "2023 Report on the Military and Security Developments Involving the People's Republic of China," U.S. Department of Defense, 2023. https://media.defense.gov/2023/Oct/19/2003323409/-1/-1/1/2023-MILITARY-AND-SECURITY-DEVELOPMENTS-INVOLVING-THE-PEOPLES-REPUBLIC-OF-CHINA.PDF; Heginbotham et al., *The US-China Military Scorecard*.

97. Jessie Yeung, "China Claims Successful Anti-Ballistic Missile Interceptor Test," CNN, 2022, https://www.cnn.com/2022/06/19/china/china-anti-ballistic-missile-test-intl-hnk/index.html.

98. Anthony H. Cordesman and Joseph Kendall, "Chinese Space Strategy and Developments," in *Chinese Strategy and Military Modernization in 2016: A Comparative Analysis* (Washington, DC: Center for Strategic and International Studies, 2016), 427–453.

99. Headquarters of the Second Artillery, *The Science of Military Strategy of the Second Artillery*, 112–117, 152–161.

100. "U.S. Experts: America Expands Network of Missile Defense in Asia, Targeting North Korea Explicitly and China Implicitly [美专家: 美扩展亚洲导弹防御网明指朝鲜暗指中国]," iFeng News [凤凰网], August 24, 2012, http://phtv.ifeng.com/program/comment/detail_2012_08/24/17064804_0.shtml; "U.S. Attempts to Increase Deployment of 'Territorial Defense Radars' in Asia-Pacific; Sharp Comment: This Is Planting Mines for Regional Security [美国欲在亚太增加部署'国土防御雷达' 锐评: 这是借机为地区安全埋雷]," 81.cn [中国军网], March 15, 2019, http://www.81.cn/gjzx/2019-03/15/content_9451030.htm.

101. All statistics taken from "Trade Statistics by Country/Region," World Integrated Trade Solution, accessed December 15, 2022, https://wits.worldbank.org/countrystats.aspx?lang=en.

102. "General Profile: China," UNCTADSTAT, October 20, 2022, https://unctadstat.unctad.org/CountryProfile/GeneralProfile/en-GB/156/index.html; "General Profile: United States," UNCTADSTAT, October 20, 2022, https://unctadstat.unctad.org/CountryProfile/GeneralProfile/en-GB/842/index.html.

103. ChinaPower Team, "How Is China Feeding Its Population of 1.4 Billion?," ChinaPower, January 25, 2017, updated August 26, 2020, https://chinapower.csis. org/china-food-security/.

104. Zheng Xin, "China's Oil Dependence on Imports Sees Drop," State Council of the People's Republic of China, February 24, 2022, http://english.www.gov.cn/news/ topnews/202202/24/content_WS6216e221c6d09c94e48a569e.html.

105. "2021 Customs Statistics Online Data Query Platform—Integrated Circuits [2021年海关统计数据在线查询平台—集成电路]," General Administration of Customs of the PRC [中华人民共和海关总署], http://stats.customs.gov.cn/, accessed July 5, 2023.

106. "International Tourism, Number of Departures—China," World Bank, undated, accessed November 29, 2023, https://data.worldbank.org/indicator/ST.INT. DPRT?locations=CN.

107. The above represents 2017 numbers. For more specifics, see Paul Nantulya, "Chinese Security Contractors in Africa," Carnegie Endowment for International Peace, October 8, 2020, https://carnegieendowment.org/2020/10/08/chinese-secur ity-contractors-in-africa-pub-82916; "Chinese Workers in Africa," China Africa Research Initiative, January 2022, http://www.sais-cari.org/data-chinese-workers- in-africa;

108. Research Group of International Investment [国际投资研究室], *Country-Risk Rating of Overseas Investment from China (2020)* [中国海外投资国家风险评级 (2020)] (Beijing: Institute of World Economics and Politics, Chinese Academy of Social Sciences [世界经济与政治研究所, 中国社会科学院], 2020).

109. Research Group of International Investment [国际投资研究室], *Country-Risk Rating of Overseas Investment from China (2018)* [中国海外投资国家风险评级 (2018)] (Beijing: Institute of World Economics and Politics, Chinese Academy of Social Sciences [世界经济与政治研究所, 中国社会科学院], 2018); Research Group of International Investment [国际投资研究室], *Country-Risk Rating of Overseas Investment from China (2021)* [中国海外投资国家风险评级 (2021)] (Beijing: Institute of World Economics and Politics, Chinese Academy of Social Sciences [世界经济与政治研究所, 中国社会科学院], 2021).

110. "The Ministry of Commerce Holds Regular Press Conference on December 2, 2015 [商务部召开例行新闻发布会 (2015年12月2日)]," Ministry of Commerce of the People's Republic of China [中华人民共和国商务部], December 2, 2015, http:// www.mofcom.gov.cn/article/ae/slfw/201512/20151201199367.shtml.

111. Wang Duanyong, "The Safety of Chinese Citizens Abroad: A Quantitative Interpretation of the Special Notices for Chinese Citizens Abroad," *Journal of Current Chinese Affairs* 42, no. 1 (2013): 167–198; Xia Liping [夏莉萍], "Effectiveness Evaluation and Improvement Direction of the Construction of China's Consular Protection Mechanism [中国领事保护机制建设的成效评估与改进方向]," *International Forum* [国际论坛], no. 1 (2023): 54–68.

112. Paul Nantulya, "Chinese Security Contractors in Africa," Carnegie Endowment for International Peace, October 8, 2020, https://carnegieendowment.org/2020/10/08/ chinese-security-contractors-in-africa-pub-82916.

113. "Foreign Media: Li Keqiang's Africa Tour Brings a 'Chinese Whirlwind' [外媒: 李克强非洲行掀起 '中国旋风']," CPC News [中国共产党新闻网], May 14, 2014, http://cpc.people.com.cn/n/2014/0514/c64095-25016609.html.

114. "Reading the Chinese Diplomacy Key Words of Wang Yi's Trip to Africa [解读王毅非洲之行的中国外交关键词]," Xinhua.com [新华网], December 4, 2021, http://www.news.cn/world/2021-12/04/c_1211474100.htm.

115. Timothy Heath, "China's Pursuit of Overseas Security," RAND Corporation, 2018, ix–x, https://www.rand.org/pubs/research_reports/RR2271.html.

116. Heath, "China's Pursuit of Overseas Security," ix–x.

117. "Quadrennial Defense Review," Historical Office of the Secretary of Defense, https://history.defense.gov/Historical-Sources/Quadrennial-Defense-Review/.

118. "Summary of the National Defense Strategy of the United States of America," US Department of Defense, https://dod.defense.gov/Portals/1/Documents/pubs/2018-National-Defense-Strategy-Summary.pdf.

119. Joshua Dewberry, "Air Force Unveils New Mission Statement," Air Force news release, April 8, 2021, https://www.af.mil/News/Article-Display/Article/2565837/air-force-unveils-new-mission-statement/.

120. Daniel Immerwahr, *How to Hide an Empire: A History of the Greater United States* (New York: Farrar, Straus and Giroux, 2019), 516.

121. "Military and Civilian Personnel by Service/Agency by State/Country, September 2022 and September 2008," DMDC, accessed July 5, 2023, https://dwp.dmdc.osd.mil/dwp/app/dod-data-reports/workforce-reports.

122. Michael J. Lostumbo et al., "Overseas Basing of U.S. Military Forces: An Assessment of Relative Costs and Strategic Benefits," RAND Corporation, 2013, 20–30, https://www.rand.org/pubs/research_reports/RR201.html.

123. Angela O'Mahony et al., "U.S. Presence and the Incidence of Conflict," RAND Corporation, 2018, 11, https://www.rand.org/pubs/research_reports/RR1906.html; Lustumbo et al., "Overseas Basing of U.S. Military Forces," 8.

124. "Operation and Maintenance Overview Fiscal Year 2022 Budget Request," Office of the Secretary of Defense, August 2021, 187–190, 267–269, https://comptroller.defense.gov/Portals/45/Documents/defbudget/FY2022/FY2022_OM_Overview.pdf.

125. Jennifer Kavanagh et al., "Characteristics of Successful U.S. Military Interventions," RAND Corporation, 2019, 30–32, https://www.rand.org/pubs/research_reports/RR3062.html; Jennifer Kavanagh et al., "The Past, Present, and Future of U.S. Ground Interventions," RAND Corporation, 2017, 17, https://www.rand.org/pubs/research_reports/RR1831.html. Note that these numbers do not include covert or civilian interventions. Between 1947 and 1989, the United States attempted seventy-two regime change interventions, sixty-six of which were covert operations. Lindsey A. O'Rourke, "The U.S. Tried to Change Other Countries' Governments 72 Times During the Cold War," *Washington Post*, December 23, 2021.

126. "Costs of War Summary of Findings," Watson Institute for International and Public Affairs, https://watson.brown.edu/costsofwar/papers/summary.

127. "SIPRI Military Expenditure Database," Stockholm International Peace Research Institute, https://www.sipri.org/databases/milex.

128. Xi Jinping [习近平], *Edited Selections of Xi Jinping's Comments on the Comprehensive National Security Concept* [习近平关于总体国家安全观论述摘编] (Beijing: Central Party Literature Press [中央文献出版社], 2018), 26–27, 40–47, 55.

129. Zhen Bingxi [甄炳禧], "Is the 21st Century the Century of the US or the Century of China? Analysis on the Shift in the Sino-US Balance of Power: A Global Perspective [21世纪:美国世纪还是中国世纪—全球视野下的中美实力对比变化分析]," *Frontiers* [学术前沿], no. 21 (2015): 55.

130. Fu Ying [傅莹] and Wu Shicun [吴士存], "The Situation in the South China Sea and the Controversy over the Spratly Islands: A Look Back at History and Realistic Assessments [南海局势及南沙群岛争议: 历史回顾与现实思考]," Xinhua.com [新华网], May 12, 2016, http://www.xinhuanet.com/world/2016-05/12/c_128977 813.htm.

131. Heath, "China's Pursuit of Overseas Security."

132. Deng Xiaoping [邓小平], *The Selected Works of Deng Xiaoping, Volume III* [邓小平文选(第三卷)] (Beijing: People's Publishing House [人民出版社], 1994), 49, 88, 363.

133. Mao Zedong [毛泽东], "Mao Zedong and Others Send a Telegram Congratulating the 24th Anniversary of the Independence of the Democratic Republic of Vietnam [毛泽东等祝贺越南民主共和国独立二十四周年的电报]," in *The Manuscripts of Mao Zedong Since the Establishment of the PRC, Volume XIII* [建国以来毛泽东文稿(第十三册)] (Beijing: Central Party Literature Press [中央文献出版社], 1998), 64; Li Qingsi [李庆四], "Twenty Years of the US in Afghanistan—with a Wave They Leave a Mess Behind [美国在阿富汗的20年：挥一挥衣袖，留下了一地鸡毛]," Guangming [光明网], September 15, 2021, https://theory.gmw.cn/2021-09/15/content_35164733.htm.

134. Wang Jisi [王缉思], "The Historical Lessons of the Soviet-US Rivalry and China's Rise to Power [苏美争霸的历史教训和中国的崛起道路]," Cfisnet.com [国际网], May 12, 2015, http://comment.cfisnet.com/2015/0512/1301371.html.

135. "Constitution of People's Republic of China [中华人民共和国宪法]," http://www.spp.gov.cn/spp/xf/201801/t20180131_363386.shtml; Xi Jinping [习近平], "Establish a Comprehensive Well-Off Society, Seize the Great Victory of Socialism with Chinese Characteristics in the New Era—Report at the 19th National Congress of the Communist Party of China [决胜全面建成小康社会，夺取新时代中国特色社会主义伟大胜利—在中国共产党第十九次全国代表大会上的报告]," Xinhua.com[新华网],October 27, 2017, http://www.xinhuanet.com/politics/19cpcnc/2017-10/27/c_1121867 529.htm.

136. Bi Wenbo [毕文波], "On China's Military Strategic Thought in the New Period [论中国新时期军事战略思维]," *Military History Research* [军事历史研究], no. 2 (2004): 55.

137. Isaac B. Kardon, "China's Overseas Base, Places, and Far Seas Logistics," in *The PLA Beyond Borders: Chinese Military Operations in Regional and Global Context*, ed. Joel Wuthnow et al. (Washington, DC: National Defense University Press, 2021), 92, 75.

138. "The Chinese Military Has Always Been a Staunch Force in Safeguarding World Peace [中国军队始终是维护世界和平的坚定力量]," Ministry of Defense of the People's Republic of China [中华人民共和国国防部], January 10, 2023, http://www.mod.gov.cn/gfbw/jmsd/4930331.html; "Is the Djibouti Military Base the First Step for Overseas Expansion? The Ministry of Foreign Affairs Responded [吉布提军事基地是海外扩张第一步？外交部回应]," *China.com* [中华网], July 12, 2017, https://3g.china.com/act/news/10000159/20170712/30960936.html.

139. Richard Gowan, "China's Pragmatic Approach to UN Peacekeeping," Brookings Institution, September 14, 2020, https://www.brookings.edu/articles/chinas-pragmatic-approach-to-un-peacekeeping/.

140. Heath, "China's Pursuit of Overseas Security," 28–32.

141. *Military Balance 2022*, 261; Mikko Huotari et al., "China's Emergence as a Global Security Actor," Mercator Institute for China Studies, July 2017, 59, https://merics.org/sites/default/files/2020-04/China%27s%20Emergence%20as%20a%20Global%20Security%20Actor.pdf.

142. Huotari et al., "China's Emergence as a Global Security Actor," 58.

143. Heath, "China's Pursuit of Overseas Security."

144. Task Force 88, which was formed from the Pakistani Navy in 2016, is composed of approximately 400 marines specializing in port defense, outfitted with gunboats, frigates, fast-attack craft, aircraft, and drones. Siegfried Wolf, "The Growing Security Dimension of the China-Pakistan Economic Corridor," Italian Institute for International Political Studies, March 10, 2020, https://www.ispionline.it/en/pubblicazione/growing-security-dimension-china-pakistan-economic-corridor-25316.

145. "China May Deploy Marines to Gwadar Port," *Maritime Executive*, March 17, 2017, https://www.maritime-executive.com/article/china-may-deploy-marines-to-gwadar-port; "Pakistan Military Raises New Security Division: Report," *Times of Islamabad*, October 15, 2019, https://timesofislamabad.com/15-Oct-2019/pakistan-military-raises-new-security-division-report.

146. "Timeline: China-Myanmar Relations," *The Irawaddy*, January 13, 2020, https://www.irrawaddy.com/specials/timeline-china-myanmar-relations.html.

147. "China, Ethiopia Ink Accord on Establishing Security Safeguarding Mechanism for Major Projects Under BRI," Xinhua, March 7, 2021, http://www.xinhuanet.com/english/2021-03/07/c_139792150.htm.

148. Andrea Ghiselli, "Continuity and Change in China's Strategy to Protect Overseas Interests," War on the Rocks, August 4, 2021, https://warontherocks.com/2021/08/continuity-and-change-in-chinas-strategy-to-protect-overseas-interests/.

149. Vladimir Fyodorov, "Chinese Weapons to Help Nigeria Fight Terrorism [中国武器助尼日利亚反恐]," Sputnik [俄罗斯卫星通讯社], April 10, 2020, https://sputniknews.cn/20200410/1031194430.html.

150. Heath, "China's Pursuit of Overseas Security," 23.

151. "National Public Security Work Conference Held in Beijing on International Cooperation Work [全国公安国际合作工作会议在京召开]," Xinhua.com [新华网], February 7, 2017, http://www.xinhuanet.com/politics/2017-02/07/c_1120426453.htm.

152. Shi Yang [石杨], "Raise High the Flag of Mutually Beneficial Cooperation, Protect Security and Development Interests, the MPS Is Succeeding in Its International Cooperation Efforts [高举合作共赢旗帜, 维护安全发展利益, 公安国际合作工作成果丰硕]," Ministry of Public Security of the People's Republic of China [中华人民共和国公安部], February 9, 2017, https://www.mps.gov.cn/n2253534/n2253535/c5629811/content.html.

153. "China and the Interpol Begin 'One Belt, One Road' Security Cooperation [中国与国际刑警组织开展'一带一路'安保合作]," Ministry of Public Security of the People's Republic of China [中华人民共和国公安部], May 13, 2017, https://www.mps.gov.cn/n2253534/n2253535/c5697574/content.html.

154. Yuan Meng [袁猛], "Nie Furu Attends the Global Police Summit in South Korea [聂福如赴韩国出席国际警察峰会]," Ministry of Public Security of the People's Republic of China [中华人民共和国公安部], October 24, 2019, https://www.mps.gov.cn/n2253534/n2253535/c7268106/content.html; "Previous Event, International Police Summit in Seoul, 2019," International Police Summit, https://ips2021.kr/eng/sub01/event.html.

155. An agreement was also reached with France but was aborted. Thomas Eder, Bertram Lang, and Moritz Rudolf, "China's Global Law Enforcement Drive," Mercator Institute for China Studies, January 18, 2017, 2, https://merics.org/sites/default/files/2020-05/China%27s%20global%20law%20enforcement%20drive.pdf; Lindsey Ford, "Extending the Long Arm of the Law: China's International Law Enforcement Drive," Brookings Institution, January 15, 2021, https://www.brookings.edu/blog/order-from-chaos/2021/01/15/extending-the-long-arm-of-the-law-chinas-international-law-enforcement-drive/.

156. "Two Arrested for Operating Illegal Overseas Police Station of the Chinese Government," US Department of Justice, April 17, 2023, https://www.justice.gov/opa/pr/two-arrested-operating-illegal-overseas-police-station-chinese-government.

157. "110 Overseas: Chinese Transnational Policing Gone Wild," Safeguard Defenders, September 12, 2022; Yuan Yang, "China's Offshore 'Police Service Stations' Spark European Alarm," *Financial Times*, November 14, 2022, https://www.ft.com/content/147ce066-cc5b-4af6-98cd-9ba39eb29829; "Ministry of Public Security: The Number of Telecom and Network Fraud Cases Dropped Year-on-Year for Nine Consecutive Months [公安部: 电信网络诈骗例案数9个月同比下降]," China News [中国新闻网], April 14, 2022, https://www.chinanews.com.cn/cj/2022/04-14/9728557.shtml.

158. Du Maozhi [杜懋之] and Yang Li [杨莉], "The Evolution of Chinese Overseas Counter-Terrorism Strategy [中国海外反恐战略的演进]," *Social Sciences International* [国外社会与科学], no. 2 (2017): 155–157.

159. Giulia Sciorati, "Not a Military Base: Why Did China Commit to an Outpost in Tajikistan?," Italian Institute for International Political Studies, November 2, 2021, https://www.ispionline.it/en/pubblicazione/not-military-base-why-did-china-commit-outpost-tajikistan-32177.

160. Joel Wuthnow, "China's Other Army: The People's Armed Police," *China Strategic Perspectives*, no. 14 (April 2019): 30.

161. Matthew Southerland, Will Green, and Sierra Janik, "The Shanghai Cooperation Organization: A Testbed for Chinese Power Projection," US-China Economic and Security Review Commission, November 12, 2020, https://www.uscc.gov/sites/defa ult/files/2020-11/Shanghai_Cooperation_Organization-Testbed_for_Chinese_P ower_Projection.pdf.

162. Max Markusen, "A Stealth Industry: The Quiet Expansion of Chinese Private Security Companies," Center for International and Strategic Studies, January 2022, https://csis-website-prod.s3.amazonaws.com/s3fs-public/publication/220112_ Markusen_StealthIndustry_ChinesePSCs.pdf?VersionId=agENkxBjcx0dJsycS rvu_Y_AmBObnHNk.

163. Paul Goble, "Beijing Expanding Size and Role of Its 'Private' Military Companies in Central Asia," Jamestown Foundation, July 20, 2021, https://jamestown.org/prog ram/beijing-expanding-size-and-role-of-its-private-military-companies-in-cent ral-asia/; Meia Nouwens, "Guardians of the Belt and Road," International Institute for Strategic Studies, August 17, 2018, https://www.iiss.org/blogs/research-paper/ 2018/08/guardians-belt-and-road.

164. Sergey Sukhankin, "Chinese Private Security Contractors: New Trends and Future Prospects," *China Brief* 20, no. 9 (2020).

165. Courtney Weinbaum et al., "China's Weapons Exports and Private Security Contractors," RAND Corporation, 2022, https://www.rand.org/pubs/tools/TLA2 045-1.html.

166. Nantulya, "Chinese Security Contractors in Africa"; "About Us [关于我们]," DeWei Security Service [德威安保], http://www.dewesecurity.com/gywm.

167. Lucy Best, "What Motivates Chinese Peacekeeping?," Council on Foreign Relations, January 7, 2020, https://www.cfr.org/blog/what-motivates-chinese-peacekeeping.

168. Joel Wuthnow, "PLA Operation Lessons from UN Peacekeeping," in *The PLA Beyond Borders: Chinese Military Operations in Regional and Global Context*, ed. Joel Wuthnow et al. (Washington, DC: National Defense University Press, 2021), 252.

169. Lucy Poni, "South Sudan Opposition Against UNMISS Guarding Oil Facilities," VOA News, May 29, 2014, https://www.voanews.com/a/south-sudan-opposition- against-unmiss-guarding-oil-facilities/1925529.html; Okech Francis, "China Gets a Sixth of South Sudan Oil Output to Build Highways," *Bloomberg*, April 5, 2019, https://www.bloombergquint.com/global-economics/china-gets-a-sixth-of-south- sudan-oil-output-to-build-highways#:~:text=(Bloomberg)%20%2D%2D%20So uth%20Sudan%20tripled,nation's%20biggest%20infrastructure%2Ddevelopm ent%20project.

170. John Hudson, Ellen Nakashima, and Liz Sly, "Buildup Resumed at Suspected Chinese Military Site in UAE, Leak Says," *Washington Post*, April 26, 2023, https://www.was hingtonpost.com/national-security/2023/04/26/chinese-military-base-uae/.

171. Liang Fang [梁芳], "What Are the Risks to the 'Maritime Silk Road' Sea-Lanes? [今日'海上丝绸之路'通道风险有多大？]," *Defense Reference* [国防参考], March 13, 2015, http://www.81.cn/jwgd/2015-02/11/content_6351319.htm.

172. Pan Shanju [潘珊菊], "Released White Paper on China's Military Strategy Is the First to Put Forward 'Overseas Interests Area,' Struggle for Rights Will Persist [国防白皮书首提海外利益攸关区 维权斗争将长期存在]," *Jinghua Times* [京华时报], May 27, 2015, http://military.people.com.cn/n/2015/0527/c1011-27061467.html.

173. "China's National Defense in the New Era," State Council Information Office of the People's Republic of China, July 24, 2019, http://www.chinadaily.com.cn/specials/whitepaperonnationaldefenseinnewera.pdf.

174. Isaac B. Kardon and Wendy Leutert, "Pier Competitor: China's Power Position in Global Ports," *International Security* 46, no. 4 (Spring 2022): 9–47, 12.

175. Umesh Moramudali, "The Hambantota Port Deal: Myths and Realities," *The Diplomat*, January 1, 2020, https://thediplomat.com/2020/01/the-hambantota-port-deal-myths-and-realities/.

176. Jennifer Hillman and David Sacks, "How the US Should Respond to China's Belt and Road," Council on Foreign Relations, March 2021, https://www.cfr.org/report/chinas-belt-and-road-implications-for-the-united-states/.

177. Every Chinese white paper issued from 1995 to 2019 has opposed overseas basing.

178. Li Jian [李剑], Chen Wenwen [陈文文], and Jin Jing [金晶], "Indian Ocean Seapower Structure and the Expansion of China's Sea Power into the Indian Ocean [印度洋海权格局与中国海权的印度洋拓展]," *Pacific Journal* [太平洋学报] 22, no. 5 (2014); Andrew Scobell, David Lai, and Roy Kamphausen, eds., *Chinese Lessons from Other People's Wars* (Carlisle, PA: Strategic Studies Institute, 2011).

179. Zheng Chongwei [郑崇伟], Gao Zhansheng [高占胜], and Gao Chengzhi [高成志], "The Strategy of Maritime Silk Road in the 21st Century: Construction of Strategic Strong Points [经略21世纪海上丝路: 战略支撑点的构建]," in *Proceedings from the 8th Maritime Power Strategy Forum* [第八届海洋强国战略论坛文集], October 21, 2016; Li Qingsi [李庆四] and Chen Chunyu [陈春雨], "Analysis of China's Overseas Port Chain Basing Strategy [试析中国的海外港链基地战略]," *Area Studies and Global Development* [区域与全球发展] 3, no. 2 (2019): 131–132.

180. Li and Chen, "Analysis of China's Overseas Port Chain Basing Strategy."

181. Liang, "What Are the Risks to the 'Maritime Silk Road' Sea-Lanes?"; Li Jian [李剑], Chen Wenwen [陈文文], and Jin Jing [金晶], "Overall Situation of Sea Power in the Indian Ocean and the Expansion in the Indian Ocean of Chinese Seapower [印度洋海权格局与中国海权的印度洋扩展]," *Pacific Journal [太平洋学报]* 22, no. 5 (2014), 74–75.

182. Li, Chen, and Jin, "Overall Situation of Sea Power in the Indian Ocean," 75.

183. Isaac Kardon, "China's Military Diplomacy and Overseas Security Activities," Carnegie Endowment for International Peace, January 26, 2023.

184. John Mearsheimer, *The Tragedy of Great Power Conflicts* (New York: W. W. Norton, 2001), 213.

185. Rush Doshi, *The Long Game: China's Grand Strategy and the Displacement of American Order* (New York: Oxford University Press, 2021), 645–646.

186. *Military Balance 2018* (London, UK: International Institute for Strategic Studies, 2018), 209.

187. "Military Transport Aircraft Strength by Country," *Global Firepower*, 2022, https://www.globalfirepower.com/aircraft-total-transports.php.

188. Dingding Chen, "China Is No International Security Free Rider," *The Diplomat*, August 13, 2014, https://thediplomat.com/2014/08/china-is-no-international-security-free-rider/.

189. Yan Xuetong [阎学通], "Yan Xuetong: The Overall 'Periphery' Is More Important than the United States [阎学通：整体的'周边'比美国更重要]," Carnegie Endowment for International Peace, January 13, 2015, https://carnegieendowment.org/2015/01/13/zh-pub-57696.

Chapter 6

1. "GDP per Capita (Current US$) | Data," World Bank, 2015, https://data.worldbank.org/indicator/NY.GDP.PCAP.CD; "Overview of the Food and Agriculture Situation in China," in *Innovation, Agricultural Productivity and Sustainability in China* (Paris, France: Organization for Economic Cooperation and Development, 2018).

2. UN Comtrade Database, https://comtradeplus.un.org/, accessed April 6, 2023.

3. "China: A Development Partner to the Pacific Region," Ministry of Foreign Affairs of the People's Republic of China, March 11, 2022, https://www.fmprc.gov.cn/mfa_eng/wjb_663304/zwjg_665342/zwbd_665378/202203/t20220311_10650946.html; "World Integrated Trade Solution," World Bank, https://wits.worldbank.org/Default.aspx?lang=en#, accessed April 19, 2023.

4. China likely owns more, but it can be difficult to track, especially if procured through third parties. These holdings demonstrate the interconnectivity of the economies but do not give China significant leverage over the United States as long as US debt remains a highly desired asset. "Table 5: Major Foreign Holders of Treasury Securities," US Department of the Treasury, undated, https://ticdata.treasury.gov/resource-center/data-chart-center/tic/Documents/slt_table5.html, accessed November 29, 2023; Brad W. Setser, "A Bit More on Chinese, Belgian and Saudi Custodial Holdings," Council on Foreign Relations, June 20, 2016, https://www.cfr.org/blog/bit-more-chinese-belgian-and-saudi-custodial-holdings.

5. "International Trade in Goods and Services," US Department of Commerce, Bureau of Economic Analysis, https://www.bea.gov/data/intl-trade-investment/international-trade-goods-and-services, accessed July 25, 2023.

6. Edgar Crammond, "The Economic Relations of the British and German Empires," *Journal of the Royal Statistical Society* 77, no. 8 (1914): 777–824.

7. "U.S. Direct Investment Abroad: Balance of Payments and Direct Investment Position Data," US Department of Commerce, Bureau of Economic Analysis, https://www.bea.gov/international/di1usdbal, accessed July 25, 2023; Derek Scissors, "China's Global Investment Tracker," American Enterprise Institute, July 24, 2023, https://www.aei.org/research-products/report/chinas-global-investment-surges-finally/.

8. Scott L. Kastner and Margaret M. Pearson, "Exploring the Parameters of China's Economic Influence," *Studies in Comparative International Development* 56, no. 1 (March 2021): 18–44, https://doi.org/10.1007/s12116-021-09318-9.

9. Wang Jisi, "The Plot Against China? How Beijing Sees the New Washington Consensus," *Foreign Affairs*, June 22, 2021, https://www.foreignaffairs.com/print/node/1127545; "GDP (Current $)—China," World Bank, https://data.worldbank.org/indicator/NY.GDP.MKTP.CD?locations=CN, accessed March 31, 2023.

10. "Increasingly Negative Evaluations of China Across Advanced Economies," Pew Research Center, October 5, 2020, https://www.pewresearch.org/global/wp-content/uploads/sites/2/2020/10/PG_2020.10.06_Global-Views-China_0-01.png.

11. "America's Economic Outperformance Is a Marvel to Behold," *The Economist*, April 13, 2023, https://www.economist.com/briefing/2023/04/13/from-strength-to-strength.

12. G. John Ikenberry, "American Power and the Empire of Capitalist Democracy," *Review of International Studies* 27 (December 2001): 191–212.

13. Pan Yichen [潘怡辰], Yuan Bo [袁波], and Wang Qingchen [王清晨], "Interpretation of 'The 20th Anniversary of China's Free Trade Zone Construction and RCEP Implementation Progress Report' ["中国自由贸易区建设20周年暨RCEP实施进展报告"解读]," *Foreign Investment in China* [中国外资], no. 23 (2022): 14.

14. Jiang Hong [江虹], "The Economic Advantages of Building the Sino-ASEAN Free Trade Zone [建立中国—东盟自由贸易区的经济效益分析]," *International Trade Journal* [国际贸易问题], no. 4 (2005): 52.

15. He Ping [贺平], "China's Economic Diplomacy in 70 Years: Overall Evolution, Strategic Intentions and Contributory Factors [70年中国经济外交的整体演变、战略意图和影响因素]," *World Economic Studies* [世界经济研究], no. 11 (2019): 9; Peng Xingzhi [彭兴智] and Zhang Lixiang [张礼祥], "A Study on Measures of the Construction of the Hainan Free Trade Port Promoting Regional Economic Cooperation in the South China Sea [海南自由贸易港建设推动南海区域经济合作的策略研究]," *International Trade* [国际贸易], no. 1 (2023): 3–10.

16. Sun Xue [孙雪], Chou Huafei [仇华飞], "Interests, Relative Strength, and Strategic Choices of China's Economic Diplomacy [利益、相对实力与中国经济外交的策略选择]," *Journal of International Relations* [国际关系研究], no. 1 (2019): 127–141.

17. James Reilley, "China's Economic Statecraft: Turning Wealth into Power," Lowy Institute, November 2013.

18. Li Wei [李巍] and Sun Yi [孙忆], "Understanding China's Economic Diplomacy [理解中国经济外交]," *Foreign Affairs Review* [外交评论], no. 4 (2014): 1–24.

19. Liu Guangxi [刘光溪], "Analysis of the Cost of China's Pending Accession to the 'Economic UN' [简析我国加入'经济联合国'久拖不决的代价]," *International Trade* [国际贸易], no. 1 (1998): 6–9.

20. Long Yongtu [龙永图], "The Core Interest of China's Accession to WTO and Existing Problems [中国入世的核心利益及发展中存在的问题]," *International Economic Review* [国际经济评论], no. 5 (2011): 17.

21. Zhu Rongji [朱镕基], *Zhu Rongji Meets the Press* [朱镕基答记者问] (Beijing: People's Press [人民出版社], 2009), 105.

22. Aaron L. Friedberg, *Getting China Wrong* (Cambridge, UK: Polity Press, 2022), 23–46.

23. Shivshankar Menon, "How China Bucked Western Expectations and What It Means for World Order," Brookings Institution, March 10, 2016, https://www.brookings.edu/articles/how-china-bucked-western-expectations-and-what-it-means-for-world-order/; Hui Feng, *The Politics of China's Accession to the World Trade Organization* (London: Routledge, 2006), 91–92.

24. Joo-Youn Jung, "Retreat of the State? Restructuring the Chinese Central Bureaucracies in the Era of Economic Globalization," *China Review* 8, no. 1 (Spring 2008): 105–125.

25. Zhang Yi [章冀], "Research on the Comparative Advantages of China's Foreign Trade Under the New Environment of International Trade [国际贸易新环境下中国外贸比较优势研究]," *China Circulation Economy* [全国流通经济], no. 32 (2020): 18–20.

26. Wayne Morrison, "China's Economic Rise: History, Trends, Challenges, and Implications for the United States," Congressional Research Service, February 5, 2018, 18.

27. "GDP Growth (Annual %)," World Bank, https://data.worldbank.org/indicator/NY.GDP.MKTP.KD.ZG, accessed July 25, 2023.

28. The PRC gained China's seat in the IMF and World Bank in 1980 after the normalization of relations with the United States.

29. "China Signed Its First FTA with a Developed Country," Chinese Ministry of Commerce, April 10, 2008, http://fta.mofcom.gov.cn/enarticle/enrelease/200911/1699_1.html; "China-Singaporean FTA Signed in Beijing," Chinese Ministry of Commerce, October 29, 2008, http://fta.mofcom.gov.cn/enarticle/chinasingaporeen/chinasingaporeennews/200910/51186_1.html; Song Guoyou [宋国友], "Global FTA Competition and China's Strategic Choices [全球自由贸易协定竞争与中国的战略选择]," *Contemporary International Relations* [现代国际关系], no. 5 (2013): 30–35.

30. Jiang, "The Economic Advantages of Building the Sino-ASEAN Free Trade Zone," 50.

31. Zhang Yunling [张蕴岭], "RCEP Is a Good Platform [RCEP是个好平台]," *World Affairs* [世界知识], no. 16 (2019): 72.

32. Wang Yizhou [王逸舟], *Global Politics and Chinese Diplomacy* [全球政治和中国外交] (Beijing: World Knowledge Press [世界知识出版社], 2003), 143.

33. See database on China's leadership positions in international institutions.

34. The author was talking about APEC, but this applies to China's approach more broadly. Wang Yusheng [王嵎生], "Personally Experiencing APEC: A Chinese Official's Observations and Experiences [亲历APEC：一个中国高官的体察]" (Beijing: World Knowledge Press [世界知识出版社], 2000), 117, 155, 173–176.

35. Li Wei and Sun Yi, "Understanding China's Economic Diplomacy."

36. Feng Yanli [冯颜利] and Liao Xiaoming [廖小明], "Being Good at Grasping China's Development Opportunities Brought About by Global Financial Crisis and Economic Crisis [要善于把握全球金融危机与经济危机给中国发展带来的机遇]," *Journal of China University of Mining and Technology (Social Sciences)* [中国矿业大学学报(社会科学版)], no. 1 (2014): 5–14.

37. Ma Hongfan [马洪范], "Trump's 'America First Strategy' Will Bring China New Chances [特朗普'美国优先'战略带给中国新机遇]," *Fiscal Science* [财政科学], no. 3 (2017): 126–130.

38. Michael J. Green, *By More than Providence: Grand Strategy and American Power in the Asia Pacific Since 1783* (New York: Columbia University Press, 2017), 535–539.

39. Xi Jinping [习近平], "Keynote Speech at the Opening Ceremony of the World Economic Forum Annual Meeting 2017 [在世界经济论坛2017年年会开幕式上的主旨演讲]," Xinhua, January 17, 2017, http://www.xinhuanet.com/politics/2017-01/18/c_1120331545.htm.

40. Yuan Peng [袁鹏], "The Coronavirus Pandemic and the Great Changes Unseen in a Century [新冠疫情与百年变局]," *Contemporary International Relations* [现代国际关系], no. 5 (2020).

41. "A World Divided: Russia, China and the West," Bennett Institute for Public Policy, October 20, 2022, 18, https://www.bennettinstitute.cam.ac.uk/wp-content/uploads/2023/01/A_World_Divided.pdf.

42. Data on China's free trade agreements taken from "China Free Trade Network," Chinese Ministry of Commerce, http://fta.mofcom.gov.cn/english/fta_qianshu.shtml, accessed January 25, 2024; US data taken from "Free Trade Agreements," Office of the US Trade Representative, https://ustr.gov/trade-agreements/free-trade-agreements, accessed January 25, 2024.

43. Peter A. Petri and Michael Plummer, "RCEP: A New Trade Agreement That Will Shape Global Economics and Politics," Brookings Institution, November 16, 2020, https://www.brookings.edu/articles/rcep-a-new-trade-agreement-that-will-shape-global-economics-and-politics/; "A New Centre of Gravity: The Regional Comprehensive Economic Partnership and Its Trade Effects," UNCTAD, December 15, 2021, https://unctad.org/system/files/official-document/ditcinf2021d5_en_0.pdf.

44. Jill Jermano, "Economic and Financial Sanctions in U.S. National Security Strategy," *PRISM* 7, no. 4 (2018): 64–73.

45. Data taken from Center for a New American Security's Sanctions by the Numbers project, https://www.cnas.org/sanctions-by-the-numbers, accessed November 29, 2023. Data on the Biden administration's sanctions following Russia's invasion from Emily Kilcrease, Jason Bartlett, and Mason Wong, "Sanctions by the Numbers: Economic Measures Against Russia Following Its 2022 Invasion of Ukraine," Center for a New American Security, June 16, 2022, https://www.cnas.org/publications/reports/sanctions-by-the-numbers-economic-measures-against-russia-following-its-2021-invasion-of-ukraine.

46. "Treasury Sanctions Impede Russian Access to Battlefield Supplies and Target Revenue Generators," US Treasury Department, July 20, 2023, https://home.treasury.gov/news/press-releases/jy1636.

47. For a discussion of the logic behind the strategy, see Bai Lianlei [白联磊], "Why China Is Reluctant in Using Economic Sanctions [中国为何不愿使用经济制裁]," *Fudan International Relations Review* [复旦国际关系评论], no. 18 (2016): 150–166.

48. James Reilly, "China's Unilateral Sanctions," *Washington Quarterly* 35, no. 4 (2012): 121–133.

49. "Foreign Ministry Spokesperson Hua Chunying's Regular Press Conference on March 25, 2021," Ministry of Foreign Affairs of the People's Republic of China, March

25, 2021, https://www.fmprc.gov.cn/mfa_eng/xwfw_665399/s2510_665401/2511_665403/202103/t20210325_9170713.html.

50. Victor Cha, "How to Stop Chinese Coercion: The Case for Collective Resilience," *Foreign Affairs*, December 14, 2022, https://www.foreignaffairs.com/world/how-stop-china-coercion-collective-resilience-victor-cha.

51. Marcin Szczepański, "China's Economic Coercion: Evolution, Characteristics and Countermeasures," European Parliamentary Research Service, 2022, 5–6, https://www.europarl.europa.eu/RegData/etudes/BRIE/2022/738219/EPRS_BRI(2022)738219_EN.pdf.

52. Ethan Meick and Nargiza Salidjanova, "China's Response to U.S.-South Korean Missile Defense System Deployment and Its Implications," US-China Economic and Security Review Commission, July 26, 2017, https://www.uscc.gov/sites/default/files/Research/Report_China%27s%20Response%20to%20THAAD%20Deployment%20and%20its%20Implications.pdf.

53. "Tourism Statistics," Ministry of Transportation and Communications of the Republic of China, https://admin.taiwan.net.tw/English/FileUploadCategoryList E003130.aspx?CategoryID=b54db814-c958-4618-9392-03a00f709e7a&appname= FileUploadCategoryListE003130, accessed March 31, 2023.

54. Laura He, "China Suspends Business Ties with NBA's Houston Rockets over Hong Kong Tweet," CNN Business, October 7, 2019, https://www.cnn.com/2019/10/07/business/houston-rockets-nba-china-daryl-morey/index.html; Owen Poindexter, "Silver: China Blackout Cost NBA 'Hundreds of Millions,'" Front Office Sports, June 6, 2022, https://frontofficesports.com/silver-china-blackout-cost-nba-hundreds-of-millions/.

55. Viking Bohman and Hillevi Pårup, "Purchasing with the Party: Chinese Consumer Boycotts of Foreign Companies, 2008–2021," *Swedish National China Center*, no. 2 (2022): 2.

56. Vanessa Friedman and Elizabeth Paton, "What Is Going on with China, Cotton and All of These Clothing Brands?," *New York Times*, March 29, 2021, https://www.nytimes.com/2021/03/29/style/china-cotton-uyghur-hm-nike.html.

57. Josh Horwitz, "A 16-Year-Old Pop Star Was Forced to Apologize to China for Waving Taiwan's Flag," Quartz, January 16, 2016, https://qz.com/596261/a-16-year-old-pop-star-was-forced-to-apologize-to-china-for-waving-taiwans-flag; Lucas Niewenhuis, "All the International Brands That Have Apologized to China," SupChina, October 25, 2019, https://signal.supchina.com/all-the-international-brands-that-have-apologized-to-china/.

58. Daniel Victor, "John Cena Apologizes to China for Calling Taiwan a Country," *New York Times*, May 25, 2021, https://www.nytimes.com/2021/05/25/world/asia/john-cena-taiwan-apology.html.

59. Xi Jinping [习近平], "Xi Jinping: Several Major Issues in the National Medium- and Long-Term Economic and Social Development Strategy [习近平: 国家中长期经济社会发展战略若干重大问题]," Qiushi [求是], November 3, 2020, http://www.qstheory.cn/zhuanqu/2020-11/03/c_1126690768.htm.

60. "Wen Jiabao: China Regulates and Controls Rare Earth but Never Blocks It [温家宝:中国对稀土加以管理和控制　但决不封锁]," China News [中国新闻网], October 7, 2010, https://www.chinanews.com.cn/cj/2010/10-07/2570433.shtml; Li Yu [李煜], "Xi Jinping Mentioned Supply Chains 20 Times in His Supply Chain Diplomacy Around the 20th National Congress of the CCP [二十大前后，习近平的"供应链外交"20次谈供应链]," CN156.com [第一物流网], November 18, 2022, http://www.cn156.com/cms/scm/111512.html.

61. Ren Hongbin [任鸿斌], "Working Together to Maintain the Security and Stability of the Global Industrial Chain Supply Chain [携手维护全球产业链供应链安全稳定]," Chinese People's Institute of Foreign Affairs [中国人民外交学会], http://www.cpifa.org/cms/book/225; Wei Jianhua [魏建华] et al., "From 'Decoupling' from China to 'De-risking'—Reveal the 'Risk Control' Lies of US 'Political Crooks' [从对华'脱钩'到'去风险'——起底美'政治骗子'的'风控'谎言]," Xinhua News Agency [新华网], July 5, 2023, http://www.news.cn/world/2023-07/05/c_1129733026.htm.

62. Jonas Gamso, "Is China Exporting Media Censorship? China's Rise, Media Freedoms, and Democracy," *European Journal of International Relations* 27, no. 3 (May 22, 2021): 135406612110157, https://doi.org/10.1177/13540661211015722.

63. Li Xiangyang [李向阳], "The Idea, Organization and Implementation Mechanisms of Economic Diplomacy with Chinese Characteristics: On the Economic Diplomatic Attributes of 'One Belt, One Road' [中国特色经济外交的理念、组织机制与实施机制——兼论"一带一路"的经济外交属性]," *World Economics and Politics* [世界经济与政治], no. 3 (2021): 28.

64. Li, "The Idea, Organization and Implementation Mechanisms of Economic Diplomacy with Chinese Characteristics," 30.

65. Peter Harrell et al., "China's Use of Coercive Economic Measures," Center for a New American Security, June 2018, 31, https://www.cnas.org/publications/reports/chinas-use-of-coercive-economic-measures.

66. "Economic Consequences of War on the US Economy," Institute for Economics and Peace, https://www.economicsandpeace.org/wp-content/uploads/2015/06/The-Economic-Consequences-of-War-on-US-Economy_0.pdf; "Post–World War II Debt Reduction," Office for Budget Responsibility, July 2013, https://obr.uk/box/post-world-war-ii-debt-reduction/.

67. Michael D. Bordo, "The Bretton Woods International Monetary System: A Historical Overview," in *A Retrospective on the Bretton Woods System: Lessons for International Monetary Reform*, ed. Michael D. Bordo and Barry Eichengreen (Chicago: University of Chicago Press, 1993), 3–108.

68. "World Trade Summary 2020 Data," World Integrated Trade Solution, undated, https://wits.worldbank.org/countryprofile/en/country/wld/year/ltst/summary; Rebecca M. Nelson and Martin A. Weiss, "The US Dollar as the World's Dominant Reserve Currency," Congressional Research Service, September 15, 2022, https://crsreports.congress.gov/product/pdf/IF/IF11707#:~:text=Because%20many%20central%20banks%20and,rates)%20than%20it%20would%20otherwise, accessed January 19, 2024.

69. Nelson and Weiss, "The US Dollar as the World's Dominant Reserve Currency."

70. Li Huifen [李惠芬], "The Operation and Reforms of the US Dollar's Reserve Currency System [美元储备货币体系的运行及其变革]," *Productivity Research* [生产力研究], no. 16 (2009): 44. See also Gu Yue [顾月], Wang Ruicong [王瑞聪], and Zhu Qin [朱沁], "Pros and Cons of RMB Internationalization [人民币国际化的利与弊]," *Modern Business* [现代商业], no. 36 (2020): 67.

71. Emily Jin, "Why China's CIPS Matters (and Not for the Reasons You Think)," *Lawfare*, April 5, 2022, https://www.lawfareblog.com/why-chinas-cips-matters-and-not-reasons-you-think.

72. Zhang Ming [张明], "Strategic Expansion of RMB Internationalization Against the Background of New Global Changes [全球新变局背景下人民币国际化的策略扩展—从新'三位一体'到新新'三位一体']," National Institution for Finance and Development [国家金融与发展实验室], December 20, 2022, http://www.nifd.cn/Uploads/Paper/19d3ea6b-6dd0-422d-8631-a002cc65eca9.pdf; "Foreign Minister Qin Gang Meets the Press," Ministry of Foreign Affairs of the People's Republic of China, March 7, 2023, https://www.fmprc.gov.cn/mfa_eng/zxxx_662805/202303/t20230307_11037190.html.

73. Gu Yue [顾月], Wang Ruicong [王瑞聪], and Zhu Qin [朱沁], "Pros and Cons of RMB Internationalization [人民币国际化的利与弊]," *Modern Business* [现代商业], no. 36 (2020): 66.

74. Zhou Lanxu, "RMB Internationalization Gets More Attention," *China Daily* [中国日报], December 28, 2022, https://global.chinadaily.com.cn/a/202212/28/WS63aba467a31057c47eba68f9.html.

75. ChinaPower Team, "Is China the World's Top Trader?," ChinaPower, March 28, 2019, https://chinapower.csis.org/trade-partner/.

76. Feng and Liao, "Being Good at Grasping China's Development Opportunities Brought About by Global Financial Crisis and Economic Crisis."

77. In 2005, under pressure from trading partners, China allowed its currency to appreciate against the dollar and other currencies. The yuan appreciated until 2008, when China reinstated the peg following the global financial crisis. After two years, China again allowed the yuan to "float," that is, investors could buy and sell it on the open market at the price they saw fit. However, this is a "managed float" system, meaning China does not allow the rate to change too drastically on a given day.

78. "Trade Data," UN Comtrade Database, https://comtradeplus.un.org/TradeFlow?Frequency=A&Flows=X&CommodityCodes=TOTAL&Partners=0&Reporters=all&period=2022&AggregateBy=none&BreakdownMode=plus, accessed July 24, 2023.

79. Jiang Mengying [蒋梦莹], "Yi Gang: RMB's Path to SDR Is Also China's Path to Economic Reform and Opening Up [易纲: 人民币加入SDR之路也是中国经济改革开放之路]," *The Paper* [澎湃新闻], December 21, 2017, https://www.thepaper.cn/newsDetail_forward_1914606.

80. Peng Bingqi [彭冰琪], "A Brief Discussion on China's Opportunities After the Financial Crisis [浅议后金融危机的中国机遇]," *Modern Economic Information* [现代经济信息], no. 21 (2013): 5.

81. Yuan Peng [袁鹏], "Financial Crisis and US Economic Hegemony: An Interpretation of History and Politics [金融危机与美国经济霸权：历史与政治的解读]," *Contemporary International Relations* [现代国际关系], no. 5 (2009): 3–5.

82. Zhou Xiaochuan, "Reform the International Monetary System," speech delivered March 23, 2009, https://www.bis.org/review/r090402c.pdf.

83. "International Monetary System Reform and RMB Officially Joining in SDR [国际货币体系改革与人民币正式加入SDR——人民币加入SDR系列文章之一]," Xinhua.com [新华网], September 21, 2016, http://www.pbc.gov.cn/goutongjiaoliu/113456/113469/3145762/index.html.

84. "China's Financial Reform and Opening-Up in RMB Joining SDR: Series on RMB Joining SDR No. 4 [人民币加入SDR过程中的中国金融改革和开放—人民币加入SDR系列文章之四]," Xinhua.com [新华网], September 26, 2016, http://www.pbc.gov.cn/goutongjiaoliu/113456/113469/3149490/index.html.

85. "Member Newsletter, 2009 Issue 2 [会员通讯2009第二期]," China Center for International Economic Exchanges [中国国际经济交流中心], June 3, 2009, http://www.cciee.org.cn/Detail.aspx?newsId=58&TId=106; Zhou, "Reform the International Monetary System."

86. "Q and A on 2015 SDR Review: IMF's Executive Board Completes Review of SDR Basket, Includes Chinese Renminbi," International Monetary Fund, November 30, 2015, https://www.imf.org/external/np/exr/faq/sdrfaq.htm#four.

87. Jue Wang, "China-IMF Collaboration: Toward the Leadership in Global Monetary Governance," *Chinese Political Science Review*, no. 3 (2018): 75–76.

88. Zhang Ce [张策], He Qing [何青], and Tang Bowen [唐博文], "Who Will Ultimately Benefit from the RMB Currency Swap Agreements? A Bilateral Trade Perspective [人民币货币互换协议，谁最终获益？—基于双边贸易的视角]," International Currency Institute of the Renmin University of China [中国人民大学国际货币研究所], http://www.imi.ruc.edu.cn/docs/2020-12/357eec6ffcc84c519909cd7cf81bf632.pdf.

89. Zhang, He, and Tang, "Who Will Ultimately Benefit from the RMB Currency Swap Agreements?"

90. See online appendix of its swap agreements at www.orianaskylarmastro.com/upstart.

91. Zhou, "RMB Internationalization Gets More Attention."

92. Yuan Man [袁满] and Han Xiao [韩笑], "Zhou Xiaochuan on RMB Joining SDR: Historical Development of Opening-Up [周小川谈人民币入篮SDR：对外开放进程的历史性进展]," *Caijing* [财经], October 9, 2017, https://finance.sina.cn/2017-10-10/detail-ifymrcmm9684931.d.html.

93. "What Does It Mean That the 'Scale of RMB Exchange Is Already the Largest in the World'? [人民币在全球的'互换规模已是第一'意味着什么？]," Sina Finance [新浪财经], March 16, 2021, https://finance.sina.com.cn/money/forex/forexroll/2021-03-17/doc-ikkntiam3169592.shtml.

94. Xu Mingqi [徐明棋], "Central Bank Currency Swaps: Impact on the International Monetary System [央行货币互换：对国际货币体系的影响]," *Social Sciences* [社会科学], no. 3 (2016): 64.

95. "The Impacts and Implications of RMB Joining SDR: Series on RMB Joining SDR No. 5 [人民币加入SDR的影响和意义—人民币加入SDR系列文章之五]," Xinhua.com [新华网], September 27, 2016, http://www.pbc.gov.cn/goutongjiao liu/113456/113469/3150428/index.html; People's Bank of China [中国人民银行], *2016 RMB Internationalization Report* [2016年人民币国际化报告], July 2016, 43.

96. People's Bank of China [中国人民银行], *2019 RMB Internationalization Report* [2019年人民币国际化报告], August 2019, 71–72.

97. Gu Yue [顾月], Wang Ruicong [王瑞聪], and Zhu Qin [朱沁], "Pros and Cons of RMB Internationalization [人民币国际化的利与弊]," *Modern Business* [现代商业], no. 36 (2020): 66; Zhu Sichang [朱四畅], "Importance of RMB Internationalization [人民币国际化的重要性]," *Fortune Today* [今日财富], no. 16 (2019): 215; Yu Xugang [余旭港], "Research on the Impact of RMB Internationalization on 'One Belt, One Road'—Based on the Perspective of the Impact of Exchange Rate on Export Trade [人民币国际化对'一带一路'的影响研究—基于汇率对出口贸易影响的视角]," *National Economic Circulation* [全国流通经济], no. 22 (2018): 4.

98. Cao Yuanzheng [曹远征], "China's Reform and Opening Up in Dynamic Evolutions [动态演进的中国改革开放]," BOCI Group [中银国际], 2017, https://www.bocigr oup.com/wap/Inner/NewsDetail/2079.

99. "Official Foreign Exchange Reserves (COFER)," International Monetary Fund, https://data.imf.org/?sk=E6A5F467-C14B-4AA8-9F6D-5A09EC4E62A4, accessed November 29, 2023.

100. Joe Guastella and Ken DeWoskin, "China Dispatch: Can the RMB Achieve Global Currency Status?," Deloitte and *Wall Street Journal*, May 9, 2022, https://deloitte.wsj. com/cfo/china-dispatch-can-the-rmb-achieve-global-currency-status-01652106 334. .

101. "2022 Renminbi Internationalization Report [2022 年人民币国际化报告]," People's Bank of China [中国人民银行], September 24, 2022, http://www.gov.cn/ xinwen/2022-09/24/content_5711660.htm.

102. Eswar S. Prasad, *The Dollar Trap: How the U.S. Dollar Tightened Its Grip on Global Finance* (Princeton, NJ: Princeton University Press, 2014), 240–241.

103. For more Chinese thinking on the trade-offs and the need for a strong government, see Zhang Liqing [张礼卿], Chen Weidong [陈卫东], and Xiao Geng [肖耿], "Further Promoting RMB Internationalization in an Orderly Manner [如何进一步有序推进人民币国际化？]," *International Economic Review* [国际经济评论], no. 3 (2023): 38–50; Zhang Huimin [张慧敏], "The Practical Significance and Advancement Path of RMB Internationalization [人民币国际化的现实意义与推进路径]," *Northern Economy* [北方经济], no. 11 (2020): 75; Shao Yutong [邵雨桐], "Research on the Role of RMB Internationalization in Promoting International Trade under 'One Belt, One Road' ['一带一路'倡议下人民币国际化对国际贸易的支撑作用研究], *China Journal of Commerce* [中国商论], no. 3 (2023): 61–63.

104. "China Wants to Make the Yuan a Central-Bank Favourite," *The Economist*, May 7, 2020, https://www.economist.com/special-report/2020/05/07/china-wants-to-make-the-yuan-a-central-bank-favourite.

105. Prasad, *The Dollar Trap*, 268.

106. Eswar Prasad, *Gaining Currency: The Rise of the Renminbi* (Oxford: Oxford University Press, 2017), 132.

107. Huang Yiping [黄益平], "The Past, Present, and Prospective of RMB Internationalization [人民币国际化的历史、现在和未来]," *Caixin* [财新], December 29, 2022, https://opinion.caixin.com/2022-12-29/101983326.html.

108. He Liping [贺力平], Zhao Xueyan [赵雪燕] and Wang Jia [王佳], "On the Relation Between Economic Scale and Currency's International Position: An Interpretation of Determination of the US Dollar as an International Reserve Currency [经济规模与货币国际地位的关系—兼论美元国际储备货币地位的决定]," *Academic Research* [学术研究], no. 8 (2018): 95–105; Gao Haihong [高海红], "The Deep Conflict of the US Dollar's Reserve Status [美元储备地位的深层次矛盾]," *China Finance* [中国金融], no. 4 (2022): 83–84.

109. Xi Jinping, "20th Party Congress Work Report," October 16, 2022, https://www.fmprc.gov.cn/eng/zxxx_662805/202210/t20221025_10791908.html.

110. Zhou, "RMB Internationalization Gets More Attention."

111. People's Bank of China [中国人民银行], *2021 RMB Internationalization Report* [2021年人民币国际化报告], September 2021, 4–5.

112. Yi Gang [易纲], "Report by the State Council on the Financial Work [国务院关于金融工作情况的报告]," October 29, 2022, https://www.safe.gov.cn/hainan/2022/1109/1686.html.

113. Xi Jinping [习近平], "Keynote Speech on the Opening Ceremony of the World Economic Forum Annual Meeting 2017 [在世界经济论坛2017年年会开幕式上的主旨演讲]," Xinhua News Agency [新华社], January 18, 2017, http://www.xinhuanet.com/politics/2017-01/18/c_1120331545.htm.

114. Xi Jinping [习近平], "Speech at the Meeting with Hong Kong and Macau Visiting Missions to the 40 Years Anniversary Celebration of China's Reform and Opening Up [会见香港澳门各界庆祝国家改革开放40周年访问团时的讲话]," *People's Daily* [人民日报], November 12, 2018, https://www.gov.cn/gongbao/content/2018/content_5343727.htm.

115. Zhang Yuyan [张宇燕], "Understanding the Great Changes Unseen in a Century [理解百年未有之大变局]," *International Economic Review* [国际经济评论], no. 5 (2019): 14.

116. Tu Yonghong [涂永红], "Promoting RMB Internationalization in an Orderly Manner [有序推进人民币国际化]," *Economic Daily* [经济日报], December 16, 2022, http://finance.people.com.cn/n1/2022/1216/c1004-32588241.html.

117. Muhammad Tayyab Safdar and Joshua Zabin, "Pakistan and the Belt and Road: New Horizons for a Globalized RMB," *The Diplomat*, September 4, 2020, https://thediplomat.com/2020/09/pakistan-and-the-belt-and-road-new-horizons-for-a-globalized-rmb/.

118. "PBC and SBP Sign MOU on Establishing RMB Clearing Arrangements in Pakistan," People's Bank of China, November 2, 2022, http://www.pbc.gov.cn/en/3688110/3688172/4437084/4700940/index.html.

119. Summer Said and Stephen Kalin, "Saudi Arabia Considers Accepting Yuan Instead of Dollars for Chinese Oil Sales," *Wall Street Journal*, March 15, 2022, https://www.

wsj.com/articles/saudi-arabia-considers-accepting-yuan-instead-of-dollars-for-chinese-oil-sales-11647351541.

120. Maha Kamel and Hongying Wang, "Petro-RMB? The Oil Trade and the Internationalization of the Renminbi,'" *International Affairs* 95, no. 5 (2019): 1131–1148; John Geddie, "Myanmar Seeks Closer China Ties with Renminbi Trade Project," Reuters, December 22, 2021, https://www.reuters.com/markets/currenc ies/myanmar-says-accept-renminbi-settlements-stresses-china-ties-2021-12-22/.

121. "HKEX to Introduce HKD-RMB Dual Counter Model and Dual Counter Market Making Programme in Hong Kong Securities Market," HKEX, December 13, 2022, https://www.hkex.com.hk/News/News-Release/2022/221213news?sc_lang=en.

122. Guastella and DeWoskin, "China Dispatch: Can the RMB Achieve Global Currency Status?"

123. "China Wants to Make the Yuan a Central-Bank Favourite," *The Economist*, May 7, 2020. https://www.economist.com/special-report/2020/05/07/china-wants-to-make-the-yuan-a-central-bank-favourite. For more detailed statistics on Chinese foreign trade, see: People's Bank of China [中国人民银行], *2022 Renminbi Internationalization Report* ['2022 年人民币国际化报告'], September 24, 2022, http://www.gov.cn/xinwen/2022-09/24/content_5711660.htm.

124. "China Expands Cross-Border RMB Use," State Council Information Office of the People's Republic of China [中华人民共和国国务院新闻办公室], March 6, 2023, http://english.scio.gov.cn/pressroom/2023-03/06/content_85146981.htm#:~:text=China's%20cross%2Dborder%20receipts%20and,to%20a%20press%20confere nce%20Friday.

125. Li Ruohan [李若菡] and Cai Hongbo [蔡宏波], "Lessons on National Financial Security Drawn from the US and Western Sanctions for the Russia-Ukraine Crisis [俄乌冲突美西方对俄金融制裁对我国金融安全的启示]," January 15, 2023, https://www.gmw.cn/xueshu/2023-01/15/content_36304300.htm.

126. Barry Eichengreen, "Sanctions, SWIFT, and China's Cross-Border Interbank Payments System," Center for Strategic and International Studies, May 20, 2022, https://www.csis.org/analysis/sanctions-swift-and-chinas-cross-border-interbank-payments-system.

127. "Compliance," Society for Worldwide Interbank Financial Transactions, https://www.swift.com/about-us/legal/compliance-0/swift-and-sanctions#how-is-swift-governed?, accessed February 21, 2023.

128. "China Wants to Make the Yuan a Central-Bank Favourite."

129. "Knowledge Base: Digital Currency Research Institute (数字货币研究所) of the People's Bank of China—DigiChina," DigiChina, June 8, 2022, https://digichina.stanford.edu/work/knowledge-base-digital-currency-research-institute-of-the-peoples-bank-of-china/.

130. "The Digital Yuan Offers China a Way to Dodge the Dollar," *The Economist*, September 5, 2022, https://www.economist.com/finance-and-economics/2022/09/05/the-digital-yuan-offers-china-a-way-to-dodge-the-dollar.

131. Darrell Duffie and Elizabeth Economy, *Digital Currencies: The US, China, and the World at a Crossroads* (Stanford, CA: Hoover Institution Press, 2022), 38.

132. "Lexicon: 'Controllable Anonymity' or 'Managed Anonymity' (可控匿名) and China's Digital Yuan," DigiChina, March 8, 2022, https://digichina.stanford.edu/work/lexicon-controllable-anonymity-or-managed-anonymity-and-chinas-digital-yuan/.

133. Pang Dongmei [庞冬梅], "The Value, Challenges and System Construction of Developing Digital RMB Cross-Border Transactions [发展数字人民币跨境交易的价值，挑战及制度构建]," *Shanghai Law Journal* [上海法学研究], no. 5 (2022): 271.

134. Prasad, *The Dollar Trap*, xvii.

135. Nicholas R. Lardy, *China's Unfinished Economic Revolution* (Washington, DC: Brookings Institution Press, 1998); Gordon Chang, *The Coming Collapse of China* (New York: Random House, 2001).

136. James R. Gorrie, *The China Crisis: How China's Economic Collapse Will Lead to a Global Depression* (Hoboken, NJ: John Wiley & Sons, 2013).

137. Simon X. B. Zhao et al., "How Big Is China's Real Estate Bubble and Why Hasn't It Burst Yet?," *Land Use Policy* 64 (2017): 153–162; Xu Jianguo, "China: Collapse of Threat?," *New Zealand International Review* 36, no. 6 (2011): 13–16.

Chapter 7

1. Chang Lulu [常璐璐] and Chen Zhimin [陈志敏], "The Use of Attractive Economic Power in Chinese Diplomacy [吸引性经济权力在中国外交中的运用]," *Foreign Affairs Review* [外交评论], no. 3 (2014): 1–16; Dou Xiaobo [窦晓博], "Economic Diplomacy and Chinese Soft Power [经济外交与中国软实力]," *Theory Research* [学理论], no. 26 (2012): 6.

2. Wang Changlin [王昌林], "The Main Process, Important Role, Valuable Experience and Suggestions of the Formulation and Implementation of the Five-Year Plan (Plan) for National Economic And Social Development [国民经济和社会发展五年规划（计划）制定和实施的主要历程、重要作用、宝贵经验与建议]," The National People's Congress of the People's Republic of China [全国人民代表大会], October 20, 2020, https://www.ndrc.gov.cn/wsdwhfz/202010/t20201021_1248571.html.

3. Li Xiangyang [李向阳], "The Idea, Organization and Implementation Mechanisms of Economic Diplomacy with Chinese Characteristics: On the Economic Diplomatic Attributes of BRI [中国特色经济外交的理念、组织机制与实施机制——兼论'一带一路'的经济外交属性]," World Economics and Politics [世界经济与政治], no. 3 (2021): 28.

4. Alastair Iain Johnston, "China in a World of Orders: Rethinking Compliance and Challenge in Beijing's International Relations," *International Security* 44, no. 2 (2019): 9–60.

5. See, for example, Stephen M. Walt, "China Wants a 'Rules-Based International Order,' Too," *Foreign Policy*, March 31, 2018, https://foreignpolicy.com/2021/03/31/china-wants-a-rules-based-international-order-too/.

6. National Academy of Engineering, *Mastering a New Role: Shaping Technology Policy for National Economic Performance* (Washington, DC: National Academies Press, 1993), 7.

7. Lauri Scherer, "World War II R&D Spending Catalyzed Post-War Innovation Hubs," *NBER Digest*, no. 9 (2020): 2.

8. Mick Ryan, "An Evolving Twentieth-Century Profession: Technology After World War II," Modern War Institute, July 1, 2021, https://mwi.westpoint.edu/an-evolving-twentieth-century-profession-technology-after-world-war-ii/.

9. "American Competitiveness Initiative," Domestic Policy Council, Office of Science and Technology Policy, February 2006, https://georgewbush-whitehouse.archives.gov/stateoftheunion/2006/aci/aci06-booklet.pdf.

10. "Largest Tech Companies by Market Cap," Companiesmarketcap.com, https://companiesmarketcap.com/tech/largest-tech-companies-by-market-cap/, accessed August 4, 2023.

11. "U.S. R&D Expenditures, by Performing Sector and Source of Funds: 2010–20," National Center for Science and Engineering Statistics, June 1, 2022, https://ncses.nsf.gov/pubs/nsf22330#:~:text=New%20data%20from%20the%20National,in%202019%20(table%201).

12. "Xi Jinping on Vigorously Promoting Scientific and Technological Innovation [习近平谈大力推进科技创新]," Xinhua.com [新华网], September 29, 2021, http://www.xinhuanet.com/politics/leaders/2021-09/29/c_1127917942.htm; "Introduction to Main Chapters of Xi Jinping's *On Self-Reliance and Self-Improvement in Science and Technology* [习近平同志"论科技自立自强"主要篇目介绍]," State Council of the People's Republic of China [中华人民共和国中央人民政府], May 28, 2023, https://www.gov.cn/yaowen/liebiao/202305/content_6883464.htm?eqid=d8b7a77c009f46fd00000003647cb09b.

13. Huang Ning [黄宁], "Is China's Technological Opening Lagging Behind Economic Opening? [中国的科技开放落后于经济开放吗?]," *China Scitechnology Think Tank* [科技中国], no. 11 (2020): 29–32.

14. "The Political Bureau of the CPC Central Committee Held Its Ninth Collective Study Session, Chaired by Xi Jinping [中共中央政治局举行第九次集体学习 习近平主持]," Xinhua News Agency [新华社], October 1, 2013, https://www.gov.cn/ldhd/2013-10/01/content_2499370.htm.

15. "Xi Jinping: Accelerate the Construction of an S&T Great Power to Achieve High-Level S&T Self-Reliance and Self-Improvement [习近平：加快建设科技强国 实现高水平科技自立自强]," State Council of the People's Republic of China [中华人民共和国中央人民政府], April 30, 2022, https://www.gov.cn/xinwen/2022-04/30/content_5688265.htm.

16. "Introduction to Main Chapters of Xi Jinping's *On Self-Reliance and Self-Improvement in Science and Technology* [习近平同志"论科技自立自强"主要篇目介绍]."

17. "Watch Xi Jinping's Important Speeches to Understand the 'Big Circulation' and 'Dual Circulation' [看习近平这几次重要讲话，弄懂"大循环""双循环"]," Xinhua.com [新华网], September 5, 2020, http://www.xinhuanet.com/politics/xxjxs/2020-09/05/c_1126455277.htm.

18. Xi Jinping [习近平], "Remarks on the Second Plenary Session of the Fifth Plenary Session of the 18th Central Committee of the Party [在党的十八届五中全会第二次全体会议上的讲话]," *CPC News* [中国共产党新闻网], January 1, 2016, http://cpc.people.com.cn/n1/2016/0101/c64094-28002398.html.

19. "Outline of the National Innovation-Driven Development Strategy," Central Committee of the Chinese Communist Party and the State Council of the People's Republic of China, May 19, 2016, trans. Georgetown Center for Security and Emerging Technology, https://cset.georgetown.edu/publication/outline-of-the-national-innovation-driven-development-strategy/.

20. "Outline of the National Innovation-Driven Development Strategy."

21. For instance, Ant Financial (an affiliate of Alibaba) threatened the Party's grip on the financial system by providing consumers with access to loans (although there may have been reasons to curb Ant's lending outside political concerns alone). "Is China Right to Tame Ant?," *The Economist*, January 2, 2021, https://www.economist.com/finance-and-economics/2021/01/02/is-china-right-to-tame-ant.

22. Li Yuan, "Why China Turned Against Jack Ma," *New York Times*, December 24, 2020, https://www.nytimes.com/2020/12/24/technology/china-jack-ma-alibaba.html.

23. Carl Benedikt Frey, "How Culture Gives the US an Innovation Edge over China," *MIT Sloan Management Review*, February 8, 2021, https://sloanreview.mit.edu/article/how-culture-gives-the-us-an-innovation-edge-over-china/.

24. Gerard DiPippo et al., "Red Ink: Estimating Chinese Industrial Policy Spending in Comparative Perspective," Center for Strategic and International Studies, May 23, 2022, 17–18, https://csis-website-prod.s3.amazonaws.com/s3fs-public/publication/220523_DiPippo_Red_Ink.pdf?VersionId=LH8ILLKWz4o.bjrwNS7csuX_C04FyEre.

25. "What Is a Government Guidance Fund? What Is the Difference Between Government Guidance Funds and Industry Funds? [什么是政府引导基金？政府引导基金和产业基金的区别在哪？]," Sha'an Xi Net [中陕网], May 26, 2023, http://zx.dsww.cn/zixun/2023/0526/122797.html.

26. Barry Naughton, *The Rise of China's Industrial Policy: 1978 to 2020* (Mexico City: Catedra Mexico-China, 2021), 19.

27. Naughton, *The Rise of China's Industrial Policy*, 44.

28. "Medium- and Long-Term Program of Science and Technology (2006–2020) [国家中长期科学和技术发展规划纲要(2006–2020年)]," State Council of the People's Republic of China [中华人民共和国中央人民政府], http://www.gov.cn/gongbao/content/2006/content_240244.htm.

29. "Medium- and Long-Term Program of Science and Technology."

30. Sebastian Heilmann and Lea Shih, "The Rise of Industrial Policy in China, 1978–2012," *China Analysis*, no. 100 (2013): 1–25.

31. Naughton, *The Rise of China's Industrial Policy*, 59–64.

32. "China in Focus: Lessons and Challenges," Organization for Economic Cooperation and Development, 2012, 76–77, https://www.oecd.org/china/50011051.pdf.

33. Like the Innovation-Driven Development Strategy (IDDS); Naughton, *Rise of Chinese Industrial Policy*.

34. "'Made in China 2025' Plan Issued," State Council, May 19, 2015, http://english. www.gov.cn/policies/latest_releases/2015/05/19/content_281475110703534.htm; Xi Jinping [习近平], "The 20th National Congress of the Communist Party of China Opens in Beijing Xi Jinping Reports to the Congress on Behalf of the 19th Central Committee [（二十大受权发布）中国共产党第二十次全国代表大会在京开幕 习近平代表第十九届中央委员会向大会作报告]," *Xinhua.com* [新华网], October 16, 2022, http://www.news.cn/politics/leaders/2022-10/16/c_1129067252.htm.

35. Li Keqiang [李克强], "Government Work Report [政府工作报告]," March 5, 2023, http://www.gov.cn/zhuanti/2023lhzfgzbg/index.htm.

36. "35 Key 'Stranglehold' Technologies ['卡脖子'的35项关键技术]," Ministry of Education of the People's Republic of China [中华人民共和国教育部], September 24, 2020, https://www.edu.cn/rd/zui_jin_geng_xin/202009/t20200924_2016 138.shtml; Xi Jinping [习近平], "Accelerate the Construction of a Scientific and Technological Power to Achieve High-Level Self-Reliance and Self-Reliance in Science and Technology [加快建设科技强国 实现高水平科技自立自强]," Qiushi [求是], April 30, 2022, speech delivered May 28, 2021, http://www.qstheory.cn/ dukan/qs/2022-04/30/c_1128607366.htm.

37. Xi Jinping [习近平], "Major Issues Concerning China's Strategies for Mid- to Long-Term Economic and Social Development [国家中长期经济社会发展战略若干重 大问题]," Qiushi [求是], October 31, 2020, http://www.qstheory.cn/dukan/qs/2020-10/31/c_1126680390.htm.

38. "Watch Xi Jinping's Important Speeches to Understand the 'Big Circulation' and 'Dual Circulation.'"

39. Gerard DiPippo et al., "Red Ink: Estimating Chinese Industrial Policy Spending in Comparative Perspective," Center for Strategic and International Studies, May 23, 2022, 10–11, 33.

40. "China's Increasingly Cheap Wind Turbines Could Open New Markets," S&P Global, September 26, 2022, https://www.spglobal.com/marketintelligence/en/news-insig hts/latest-news-headlines/china-s-increasingly-cheap-wind-turbines-could-open-new-markets-72152297.

41. For example, Liu Shejian [刘社建], "Inspiration from the Four Asian Tigers [亚洲四 小龙的启示]," *South Reviews* [南风窗], no. 3 (2006): 43–44; Peng Xingzhi [彭兴智], "Examining the Purpose of East Asian Authoritarian Regimes from the Economic Take-off of 'Four Asian Tigers' [从"亚洲四小龙"经济的腾飞看东亚威权政体的存 在意义]," *Business* [商], no. 11 (2016): 123.

42. DiPippo et al., "Red Ink," 9, 31.

43. Sean O'Connor, "How Chinese Companies Facilitate Technology Transfer from the United States," US-China Economic and Security Review Commission, May 6, 2019, 7–8, https://www.uscc.gov/sites/default/files/Research/How%20Chinese%20Co mpanies%20Facilitate%20Tech%20Transfer%20from%20the%20US.pdf.

44. Keith Bradsher, "How China Obtains American Trade Secrets," *New York Times*, January 15, 2020, https://www.nytimes.com/2020/01/15/business/china-technology-transfer.html.

45. Kathrin Hille and Richard Waters, "Washington Unnerved by China's 'Military-Civil' Fusion," *Financial Times*, November 8, 2018, https://www.ft.com/content/8dcb534c-dbaf-11e8-9f04-38d397e6661c.

46. US Department of State, "The Chinese Communist Party on Campus: Opportunities and Risks," September 2020.

47. "APT1: Exposing One of China's Cyber Espionage Units," Mandiant, February 2013, https://www.mandiant.com/sites/default/files/2021-09/mandiant-apt1-report.pdf.

48. Office of the US Trade Representative, "Findings of the Investigation into China's Acts, Policies, and Practices Related to Technology Transfer, Intellectual Property, and Innovation Under Section 301 of the Trade Act of 1974," March 22, 2018, 153, https://ustr.gov/sites/default/files/Section%20301%20FINAL.PDF.

49. Office of the US Trade Representative, "Findings of the Investigation into China's Acts, Policies, and Practices," 6–7.

50. IP Commission, "The Report of the Commission on the Theft of American Intellectual Property," National Bureau of Asian Research, 2013, 2–3, https://www.nbr.org/wpcontent/uploads/pdfs/publications/IP_Commission_Report.pdf.

51. "2022 American Business in China White Paper," *American Chamber of Commerce in the People's Republic of China*, 2022, https://www.amchamchina.org/wp-content/uploads/2022/05/WP2022-Final.pdf.

52. Robert Atkinson and Ian Clay, "Wake Up, America: China Is Overtaking the United States in Innovation Output," Hamilton Center on Industrial Strategy, November 2022, 1, https://www2.itif.org/2023-us-v-china-innovation.pdf.

53. Soumitra Dutta, INSEAD, and Simon Caulkin, "The World's Top Innovators," *World Business*, January–February 2007, 26–37; "China Ranks 11th Among the 132 Economies Featured in the GII 2022," Global Innovation Index, 2022, https://www.wipo.int/edocs/pubdocs/en/wipo_pub_2000_2022/cn.pdf.

54. "Foreign Direct Investment Statistics: Data, Analysis and Forecasts," OECD, https://www.oecd.org/investment/statistics.htm, accessed July 26, 2023; "Global Foreign Direct Investment Flows over the Last 30 years," United Nations Conference on Trade and Development, May 5, 2023, https://unctad.org/data-visualization/global-foreign-direct-investment-flows-over-last-30-years.

55. "Digest of Japanese Science and Technology Indicators 2022—Executive Summary," National Institute of Science and Technology Policy, August 2022, https://www.nistep.go.jp/en/wp-content/uploads/NISTEP-RM318-SummaryE_R.pdf.

56. "Japanese Science and Technology Indicators 2010," National Institute of Science and Technology Policy, January 2011, https://www.nistep.go.jp/en/wp-content/uploads/Indicator2010_tex.pdf.

57. "China Pathfinder: Annual Scorecard," Rhodium Group and Atlantic Council Geoeconomics Centers, October 2022, 4, https://www.atlanticcouncil.org/in-depth-research-reports/report/china-pathfinder-2022-annual-scorecard/.

58. Soumitra Dutta et al., eds., *Global Innovation Index 2022: What Is the Future of Innovation-Driven Growth?*, 15th ed. (Geneva: World Intellectual Property Organization, 2022), https://www.wipo.int/edocs/pubdocs/en/wipo-pub-2000-2022-en-main-report-global-innovation-index-2022-15th-edition.pdf.

59. "China Daily: China's Photovoltaic Industry Has Entered a Period of High-Quality Development [中国光伏产业不如高质量发展期]," *China Daily* [中国日报], December 24, 2019, https://cn.chinadaily.com.cn/a/201912/24/WS5e01bd77a3109 9ab995f3640.html.

60. "Fact Sheet: Commerce Finds Dumping and Subsidization of Crystalline Silicon Photovoltaic Cells, Whether or Not Assembled into Modules from the People's Republic of China," International Trade Administration, Department of Commerce, October 10, 2012, https://enforcement.trade.gov/download/factsheets/factsh eet_prc-solar-cells-ad-cvd-finals-20121010.pdf.

61. "Executive Summary—Solar PV Global Supply Chains—Analysis," IEA, 2022, https://www.iea.org/reports/solar-pv-global-supply-chains/executive-summary.

62. Rachel Tang, "China's Auto Sector Development and Policies: Issues and Implications," Congressional Research Service, June 25, 2012.

63. "Global Electric Car Stock, 2010–2021," International Energy Agency, October 26, 2022, https://www.iea.org/data-and-statistics/charts/global-elect ric-car-stock-2010-2021.

64. Christoph Nedopil Wong, "China Belt and Road Initiative (BRI) Investment Report 2023 H1," Fudan University Green Finance and Development Center, August 1, 2023, https://greenfdc.org/china-belt-and-road-initiative-bri-investment-report-2023-h1/.

65. "A Battery Supply Chain That Excludes China Looks Impossible," *The Economist*, July 17, 2023, https://www.economist.com/asia/2023/07/17/a-battery-supply-chain-that-excludes-china-looks-impossible.

66. Naughton, *The Rise of China's Industrial Policy*, 60–61.

67. Graham Allison and Eric Schmidt, "China's 5G Soars over America's," *Wall Street Journal*, February 16, 2022, https://www.wsj.com/articles/chinas-5g-america-stream ing-speed-midband-investment-innovation-competition-act-semiconductor-biot ech-ai-11645046867.

68. "The 5G Ecosystem: Risks and Opportunities for DoD," Defense Innovation Board, April 2019, 13, https://media.defense.gov/2019/Apr/03/2002109302/-1/-1/0/ DIB_5G_STUDY_04.03.19.PDF.

69. Financial Research Center of the Fudan Development Institute, "Frontiers of Financial Academics: Talking About the Difficulties of the Development of China's Semiconductor Industry and the Way Out [金融学术前沿：浅谈中国半导体产业发展的困境和出路]," Fudan Development Institute [复旦发展研究院], April 23, 2022, https://fddi.fudan.edu.cn/bc/f0/c18985a441584/page.htm.

70. Yu Huimin [余惠敏], "Seize the Must-Have for the Development of High Technology [抢占高科技产业发展必争之地]," *People's Daily* [人民网], January 8, 2023, http://theory.people.com.cn/n1/2023/0108/c40531-32601964.html.

71. "Made in China 2025 Technical Area Roadmap ['中国制造2025'重点领域技术路线图]," National Manufacturing Power Construction Strategy Advisory Committee [国家制造强国建设战略咨询委员会], September 29, 2015, https://www.cae.cn/cae/ html/files/2015-10/29/20151029105822561730637.pdf.

72. "State Council Notice on the Publication of the National 13th Five-Year Plan for S&T Innovation [国务院关于印发'十三五'国家科技创新规划的通知]," State Council of the People's Republic of China [中华人民共和国中央人民政府], August 8, 2016, http://www.gov.cn/zhengce/content/2016-08/08/content_5098072.htm.

73. Financial Research Center of the Fudan Development Institute, "Frontiers of Financial Academics"; Yu, "Seize the Must-Have for the Development of High Technology."

74. Wei Zhongyuan [魏中原], "The Science and Technology Innovation Board Promotes the 'Evolution' of Domestic Semiconductors, and the Trend of the Third Transfer of the Semiconductor Industry to China Will Not Change [科创板推动国产半导体'进化', 第三次半导体产业转移向中国趋势不改]," Yicai [第一财经], August 22, 2022, https://m.yicai.com/news/101513312.html.

75. "Measuring Distortions in International Markets: The Semiconductor Value Chain," OECD, December 2019, OECD Trade Policy Papers no. 234, doi:10.1787/8fe4491d-en. China's State Council explicitly instructs Chinese state-owned banks to provide capital to Chinese semiconductor firms. China's State Council, "Guideline for the Promotion of the Development of the National Integrated Circuit Industry," June 2014, https://members.wto.org/CRNAttachments/2014/SCMQ2/law47.pdf.

76. John VerWey, "Chinese Semiconductor Industrial Policy: Past and Present," *Journal of International Commerce and Economics*, July 2019, 13, https://www.usitc.gov/publications/332/journals/chinese_semiconductor_industrial_policy_past_and_present_jice_july_2019.pdf.

77. Julie Zhu, "Exclusive: China Readying $143 Billion Package for Its Chip Firms in Face of U.S. Curbs," Reuters, December 13, 2022, https://www.reuters.com/technology/china-plans-over-143-bln-push-boost-domestic-chips-compete-with-us-sources-2022-12-13/.

78. Debby Wu, "Engineers Found Guilty of Stealing Micron Secrets for China," *American Journal of Transportation*, June 12, 2020, https://ajot.com/news/engineers-found-guilty-of-stealing-micron-secrets-for-china; Chris Miller, *Chip War: The Fight for the World's Most Critical Technology* (London: Simon & Schuster Ltd, 2023), 305–310.

79. "SIA Whitepaper: Taking Stock of China's Semiconductor Industry," Semiconductor Industry Association, July 2021, https://www.semiconductors.org/wp-content/uploads/2021/07/Taking-Stock-of-China%E2%80%99s-Semiconductor-Industry_final.pdf.

80. Gregory C. Allen, "Choking off China's Access to the Future of AI," Center for Strategic and International Studies, October 11, 2022, https://www.csis.org/analysis/choking-chinas-access-future-ai.

81. "How Military-Civil Fusion Steps Up China's Semiconductor Industry—DigiChina," DigiChina, April 1, 2022, https://digichina.stanford.edu/work/how-military-civil-fusion-helps-chinas-semiconductor-industry-step-up/.

82. Helen Toner, Jenny Xiao, and Jeffrey Ding, "The Illusion of China's AI Prowess," *Foreign Affairs*, June 2, 2023, https://www.foreignaffairs.com/china/illusion-chinas-ai-prowess-regulation?gad=1&gclid=Cj0KCQjw8NilBhDOARIsAHzpbLBqdnZAlvl4ZQA0GC8L6CSTEuXKBf7dtpS5UlwpykqSrXS9uAm13MMaAguQEALw_wcB.

83. Tan Tieniu [谭铁牛], "Lecture 7 of the Special Lectures of the Standing Committee of the Thirteenth National People's Congress: Innovative Development and Social Impact of Artificial Intelligence [十三届全国人大常委会专题讲座第七讲:人工智能的创新发展与社会影响]," The National People's Congress of the People's Republic of China [全国人民代表大会], October 29, 2018, http://www.npc.gov.cn/c12434/c541/201905/t20190521_268525.html.

84. "Xi Jinping on Artificial Intelligence [习近平谈人工智能]," CASIA [中国科学院自动化研究所], December 23, 2020, http://www.ia.cas.cn/dqyd/xxyd/202012/t20201223_5837241.html.

85. Jia Zhenzhen [贾珍珍], Ding Ning [丁宁], and Chen Fangzhou [陈方舟], "The Advent of Intelligent Warfare Is Accelerating [智能化战争加速到来]," PLA Daily [解放军报], March 17, 2022.

86. Gregory C. Allen, "Understanding China's AI Strategy: Clues to Chinese Strategic Thinking on Artificial Intelligence and National Security," Center for a New American Security, February 2019.

87. Elsa B. Kania and Lorand Laskai, "Myths and Realities of China's Military-Civil Fusion Strategy," Center for a New American Security, January 28, 2021, https://www.cnas.org/publications/reports/myths-and-realities-of-chinas-military-civil-fusion-strategy.

88. "Communiqué on National Expenditures on Science and Technology in 2021," National Bureau of Statistics in China, September 1, 2022, http://www.stats.gov.cn/english/PressRelease/202209/t20220901_1887829.html.

89. "The Central Committee of the Communist Party of China and the State Council Issued the 'Party and State Institutional Reform Plan' [中共中央国务院印发'党和国家机构改革方案']," Xinhua.com [新华网], March 16, 2023, http://www.news.cn/politics/zywj/2023-03/16/c_1129437368.htm.

90. "35 Key 'Stranglehold' Technologies."

91. Regina M. Abrami, William C. Kirby, and F. Warren McFarlan, "Why China Can't Innovate," Harvard Business Review, March 2014, https://hbr.org/2014/03/why-china-cant-innovate.

92. Chang Sheng [常盛], "Don't Just Worry About a Few Bundles of Cabbage, the 'Sea of Stars' and Technological Innovation Is Even More Exciting [别只惦记着几捆白菜,科技创新的星辰大海更令人心潮澎湃]," People's Daily [人民日报], December 12, 2020, https://www.sohu.com/a/438055555_650579.

93. Cat Tarnoff, "The Marshall Plan: Design, Accomplishments, and Significance," Congressional Research Service, January 18, 2018, 2, https://sgp.fas.org/crs/row/R45079.pdf; George S. Marshall, "The 'Marshall Plan' Speech Delivered at Harvard University, 5 June 1947," OECD, accessed April 6, 2023, https://www.oecd.org/general/themarshallplanspeechatharvarduniversity5june1947.htm.

94. Ilyana Kuziemko and Eric Werker, "How Much Is a Seat on the Security Council Worth? Foreign Aid and Bribery at the United Nations," Journal of Political Economy 114, no. 5 (2006): 905–930.

95. "U.S. Agency for International Development: An Overview," Congressional Research Service, January 3, 2023, https://crsreports.congress.gov/product/pdf/IF/IF10261.

96. "U.S. Agency for International Development: An Overview."

97. Many countries labeled both as "not free" and/or a "consolidated authoritarian regime" by Freedom House received over $500 million in USAID funds in FY2022, including Ethiopia, Somalia, Syria, Uganda, and Yemen. "Democracy, Human Rights, and Governance," US Agency for International Development, https://www.usaid.gov/democracy, accessed November 29, 2023; "Countries and Territories," Freedom House, https://freedomhouse.org/countries/nations-transit/scores, accessed November 29, 2023; "U.S. Foreign Assistance by Country," Foreign Assistance, https://www.foreignassistance.gov/cd/ethiopia/, accessed November 29, 2023.

98. "Poverty Headcount Ratio at $2.15 a Day (2017 PPP) (% of Population)—China," World Bank, https://data.worldbank.org/indicator/SI.POV.DDAY?locations=CN, accessed July 18, 2023.

99. Sun Yun [孙云], "Why Is China's Foreign Aid So Secretive [中国对外援助为何神神秘秘]," China-US Focus [中美聚焦], December 27, 2017, http://cn.chinausfocus.com/foreign-policy/20171027/22213.html.

100. For China's most recent white paper on foreign aid and development, see "China's International Development Cooperation in the New Era," PRC State Council Information Office, January 2021, http://english.scio.gov.cn/whitepapers/2021-01/10/content_77099782_3.htm.

101. Gu Guan-Fu, "Soviet Aid to the Third World: An Analysis of Its Strategy," *Soviet Studies* 35, no. 1 (January 1983): 71–89.

102. Norman A. Graebner, "Foreign Aid: A Strategy in the Cold War," paper presented at the Farm Foundation's conference "Increasing Understanding of Public Problems and Policies," 1959, 21.

103. Dennis T. Yasutomo, "Why Aid? Japan as an 'Aid Great Power,'" *Pacific Affairs* 62, no. 4 (Winter 1989): 490–503; Robert M. Orr Jr., "The Aid Factor in U.S–Japan Relations," *Asian Survey* 28, no. 7 (1988): 740–756.

104. Robert D. Blackwill and Ashley J. Tellis, "A New U.S. Grand Strategy Towards China," National Interest, April 13, 2015, https://nationalinterest.org/feature/wake-america-china-must-be-contained-12616.

105. Michael J. Green, *By More than Providence: Grand Strategy and American Power in the Asia Pacific since 1783* (New York: Columbia University Press, 2017), 538.

106. Li-Han Chan, "Soft Balancing Against the US 'Pivot to Asia,'" *Australian Journal of International Affairs* 71, no. 6 (2017): 569.

107. "Lou Jiwei Answers Reporters' Questions on the Establishment of AIIB [楼继伟就筹建亚洲基础设施投资银行答记者问]," Ministry of Finance of the People's Republic of China [中华人民共和国财政部], March 7, 2014, http://www.mof.gov.cn/zhengwuxinxi/caizhengxinwen/201403/t20140307_1053025.htm .

108. "AIIB Welcomes Mauritania as New Prospective Member," Asian Infrastructure Investment Bank, January 9, 2023, https://www.aiib.org/en/news-events/news/2023/AIIB-Welcomes-Mauritania-as-New-Prospective-Member.html.

109. Tang Lixia [唐丽霞], "Practices and Experiences of China's 70 Years of Foreign Assistance [新中国70年对外援助的实践与经验]," *Frontiers* [学术前沿], no. 2 (2020): 75–77.

110. Receiving Chinese aid in 2000–2014 brought recipient countries more in line with Beijing's voting patterns at the United Nations, leading to an increase in local residents' favorable views of China. Che Yi [车翼], He Xiaoyu [贺晓宇], and Zhang Yan [张燕], "Foreign Aid and International Influence: Evidence from the Economic Rise of China [对外援助与国际影响力：来自中国经济复兴的证据]," *Journal of Finance and Economics* [财经研究], no. 7 (2023): 122–137.

111. Nadege Rolland, *China's Eurasian Century: Political and Strategic Implications of the Belt and Road Initiative* (Seattle, WA: National Bureau of Asian Research, 2017), 93–109.

112. ChinaPower Team, "How Will the Belt and Road Initiative Advance China's Interests?," ChinaPower, May 8, 2017, updated August 26, 2020, https://chinapower. csis.org/china-belt-and-road-initiative/.

113. Liu Xiangfeng [刘翔峰], "AIIB and 'One Belt, One Road' [亚投行与一带一路战略]," *China Finance* [中国金融], no. 9 (2015): 41–42, http://www.cqvip.com/QK/96434X/20159/664541240.html.

114. Liu Xiangfeng [刘翔峰], "AIIB and the Belt and Road Strategy" [亚投行与一带一路战略], *China Finance* [中国金融], no. 9 (2015): 41–42

115. Yougang Chen, Stefan Matzinger, and Jonathan Woetzel, "Chinese Infrastructure: The Big Picture," McKinsey and Co., June 1, 2013, https://www.mckinsey.com/featured-insights/winning-in-emerging-markets/chinese-infrastructure-the-big-picture.

116. ChinaPower Team, "How Are Foreign Rail Construction Projects Advancing China's Interests?," ChinaPower, November 12, 2020, https://chinapower.csis.org/rail-construction/.

117. Huang Meibo [黄梅波] and Wang Jiejia [王婕佳], "International Aid Evaluation System and China's Foreign Aid [国际援助评价体系及中国的对外援助]," *Overseas Investment and Export Credits* [海外投资与出口信贷], no. 6 (2022): 9.

118. Li Xiaoyun [李小云], *The Future of Development Assistance: The Dilemma of Western Model and China's New Role* [发展援助的未来：西方模式的困境和中国的新角色] (Beijing: CITIC Press [中信出版集团], 2019), chap. 3.

119. Li Xiaoyun [李小云], "Global Poverty Reduction Needs More of China's Voices [世界减贫需要更多中国声音]," in Li Xiaoyun [李小云], *The Future of Development Assistance: The Dilemma of Western Model and China's New Role* [发展援助的未来：西方模式的困境和中国的新角色] (Beijing: CITIC Press [中信出版集团], 2019).

120. Li, "Global Poverty Reduction Needs More of China's Voices"; Wang Zhao [王钊], "The Symbiosis Between China's Infrastructure Aid and International Development System [中国的基础设施建设援助与国际发展援助的"共生"]," *Foreign Affairs Review* [外交评论], no. 2 (2020): 51–81.

121. Rolland, *China's Eurasian Century*, 93–109.

122. "Official Development Assistance (ODA)," OECD, https://www.oecd.org/dac/financing-sustainable-development/development-finance-standards/official-development-assistance.htm, accessed July 18, 2023.

123. Ammar A. Malik et al., "Banking on the Belt and Road: Insights from a New Global Dataset of 13,427 Chinese Development Projects," AidData, September 29, 2021, 37, https://docs.aiddata.org/ad4/pdfs/Banking_on_the_Belt_and_Road__Insights_from_a_new_global_dataset_of_13427_Chinese_development_projects.pdf.

124. Zhou Shangsi [周尚思] and Xu Zhiming [徐之明], "Comparative Analysis of China's and US Official Development Assistance to Africa [中国与美国对非洲官方发展援助模式的比较分析]," *Shandong Social Sciences* [山东社会科学], no. 12 (2021): 160.

125. Malik et al., "Banking on the Belt and Road."

126. Malik et al., "Banking on the Belt and Road," 18–19.

127. Malik et al., "Banking on the Belt and Road," 3.

128. "China Rethinks Developing World Largesse as Deals Sour," *Financial Times*, October 13, 2016, https://www.ft.com/content/5bf4d6d8-9073-11e6-a72e-b428cb934b78, quoted in Malik et al., "Banking on the Belt and Road," 37.

129. *China's Foreign Assistance* (2014) [中国的对外援助 (2014)], State Council Information Office of the People's Republic of China [中华人民共和国国务院新闻办公室], July 2014. From 2007 to 2015, Chinese companies won contracts for 30 percent of the World Bank's infrastructure projects. In the ranking of global construction contractors in 2017, seven of the top ten were Chinese companies. Li Xiaoyun [李小云], "How to Understand China's Foreign Aid [如何理解中国的对外援助]," in Li Xiaoyun [李小云], *The Future of Development Assistance: The Dilemma of Western Model and China's New Role* [发展援助的未来：西方模式的困境和中国的新角色] (Beijing: CITIC Press [中信出版集团], 2019).

130. "Does China Dominate Global Investment?," ChinaPower, https://chinapower.csis.org/china-foreign-direct-investment/#breakdown-of-chinese-outbound-fdi-by-sector.

131. "Budget Dataset," US Department of State and USAID, https://www.foreignassistance.gov/data, accessed March 17, 2023.

132. "Fiscal Year (FY) 2023 President's Budget Request for the United States Agency for International Development (USAID)," USAID, 2022, https://www.usaid.gov/sites/default/files/2022-05/USAID_FY_2023_BudgetRequest_FactSheet.pdf.

133. Zhou and Xu, "Comparative Analysis of China's and US Official Development Assistance to Africa," 160.

134. "China and the World in the New Era [新时代的中国与世界]," State Council Information Office of the People's Republic of China [中华人民共和国国务院新闻办公室], September 27, 2019, http://www.gov.cn/zhengce/2019-09/27/content_5433889.htm; "Xi Jinping: Promoting 'One Belt, One Road' Cooperation to Deeply Benefit the People [习近平:推动共建'一带一路'走深走实造福人民]," Xinhua News Agency [新华社], August 27, 2018, http://www.xinhuanet.com/politics/2018-08/27/c_1123336562.htm.

135. Ana Horigoshi et al., "Delivering the Belt and Road: Decoding the Supply of and Demand for Chinese Overseas Development Projects," AidData, October 2020, 20, https://www.aiddata.org/publications/delivering-the-belt-and-road.

136. Malik et al., "Banking on the Belt and Road," 1.

137. Yufan Huang and Deborah Brautigam, "Putting a Dollar Amount on China's Loans to the Developing World," *The Diplomat*, June 24, 2020, https://thediplomat.com/2020/06/putting-a-dollar-amount-on-chinas-loans-to-the-developing-world/.

138. "Belt and Road Initiative," European Bank for Reconstruction and Development, n.d., https://www.ebrd.com/what-we-do/belt-and-road/overview.html.

139. Lingling Wei, "China Reins In Its Belt and Road Program, $1 Trillion Later," *Wall Street Journal*, September 26, 2022, https://www.wsj.com/articles/china-belt-road-debt-11663961638?mod=article_inline; Malik et al., "Banking on the Belt and Road," 2.

140. Malik et al., "Banking on the Belt and Road," 2.

141. Christopher Balding, "Why Democracies Are Turning Against Belt and Road: Corruption, Debt, and Backlash," *Foreign Affairs*, October 24, 2018, https://www.foreignaffairs.com/articles/china/2018-10-24/why-democracies-are-turning-against-belt-and-road.

142. "Xi Jinping: Promoting Belt and Road Cooperation to Deeply Benefit the People."

143. François de Soyres et al., "How Much Will the Belt and Road Initiative Reduce Trade Costs?," Federal Reserve Board of Governors, International Finance Discussion Papers 1274, 2020, https://doi.org/10.17016/IFDP.2020.1274; *Belt and Road Economics: Opportunities and Risks of Transport Corridors* (Washington, DC: World Bank, 2019), 5.

144. Maryla Maliszewska and Dominique van der Mensbrugghe, "The Belt and Road Initiative: Economic, Poverty and Environmental Impacts," World Bank Policy Research Working Paper 8814, April 2019, 3.

145. Sebastian Horn, Carmen M. Reinhart, and Christoph Trebesch, "China' Overseas Lending," NBER, July 2019, https://www.nber.org/system/files/working_papers/w26050/revisions/w26050.rev0.pdf.

146. Ren Xiao [任晓] and Guo Xiaoqin [郭小琴], "Interpreting China's Foreign Assistance: A Preliminary Theoretical Analysis [解析中国对外援助:一个初步的理论分析]," *Fudan Journal* [复旦学报], no. 4 (2016).

147. Axel Dreher et al., "Apples and Dragon Fruits: The Determinants of Aid and Other Forms of State Financing from China to Africa," *International Studies Quarterly* 62, no. 1 (2018): 182–194.

148. Wang Da [王达], "AIIB: China's Considerations and Global Significance [亚投行的中国考量与世界意义]," *Northeast Asia Forum* [东北亚论坛], no. 3 (2015): 63; see appendix on Development Finance Institutions at www.orianaskylarmastro.com/upstart; Zhang Monan [张茉楠], "The Multiple Implications of AIIB on the Transition of Global Financial Governance [亚投行之于全球金融治理变革的多重意义]," *China.com.cn* [中国网], January 25, 2016, http://finance.china.com.cn/news/special/zgjjqjzw/20160125/3561348.shtml.

149. "China's Global Development Initiative Is Not as Innocent as It Sounds," *The Economist*, June 9, 2022, https://www.economist.com/china/2022/06/09/chinas-glo bal-development-initiative-is-not-as-innocent-as-it-sounds.

150. Marek Jochec and Jenny Jenish Kyzy, "China's BRI Investments, Risks, and Opportunities in Kazakhstan and Kyrgyzstan," in *China's Belt and Road Initiative and Its Impact in Central Asia*, ed. Marlene Laruelle (Washington, DC: George Washington University, Central Asia Program, 2018), 69.

151. "The Central Committee of the Communist Party of China and the State Council Issued the 'National Standardization Development Outline' [中共中央国务院印发'国家标准化发展纲要']," Xinhua News Agency [新华社], October 10, 2021, https://www.gov.cn/zhengce/2021-10/10/content_5641727.htm; "Notice on Issuing the Action Plan for Implementing the 'Outline of National Standardization Development' [关于印发贯彻实施'国家标准化发展纲要'行动计划的通知]," State Council of the People's Republic of China [中华人民共和国国务院], July 8, 2022, https://www.gov.cn/zhengce/zhengceku/2022-07/09/content_5700171.htm.

152. Yi Wu, "China Standards 2035 Strategy: Recent Developments and Implications for Foreign Companies," China Briefing, July 26, 2022, https://www.china-briefing.com/news/china-standards-2035-strategy-recent-developments-and-their-impli cations-foreign-companies/.

153. Malik et al., "Banking on the Belt and Road," 19; "UN Comtrade Database," United Nations Comtrade, https://comtrade.un.org/data/, accessed April 3, 2023.

154. Malik et al., "Banking on the Belt and Road," 3.

155. Liang Fang [梁芳], "What Are the Risks to the 'Maritime Silk Road' Sea-Lanes? [今日'海上丝绸之路'通道风险有多大？]," Defense Reference [国防参考], March 13, 2015, http://www.81.cn/jwgd/2015-02/11/content_6351319.htm.

156. China has supplemented these strategies with foreign direct investment. According to the American Enterprise Institute and the Heritage Foundation's China Global Investment Tracker, between 2005 and 2019 China invested just over $130 billion in European and North American energy projects—about one-fifth of its total FDI during that period. ChinaPower Team, "Does China Dominate Global Investment?," ChinaPower, September 26, 2016, updated January 28, 2021, https://chinapower. csis.org/china-foreign-direct-investment/.

157. "Blue Dot Network," US Department of State, https://www.state.gov/blue-dot-netw ork/, accessed July 31, 2023.

158. "FACT SHEET: Roadmap for a 21st-Century U.S.-Pacific Island Partnership," The White House, September 29, 2022, https://www.whitehouse.gov/briefing-room/sta tements-releases/2022/09/29/fact-sheet-roadmap-for-a-21st-century-u-s-pacific-island-partnership/.

159. "Real and Heavy Achievements—A Side Note of General Secretary Xi Jinping's Attendance at the Third 'One Belt, One Road' Construction Symposium [实打实、沉甸甸的成就—习近平总书记出席第三次'一带一路'建设座谈会侧记]," Xinhua.com [新华网], November 21, 2021, http://www.news.cn/2021-11/21/c_112 8084028.htm.

160. Luo Zhaohui [罗照辉], "China's Foreign Aid and International Development Cooperation in a COVID-19 Pandemic World [大疫情背景下中国对外援助和国际发展合作]," *China International Studies* [国际问题研究], no. 1, January 15, 2022, 18.

161. Jane Nakano, "Greening or Greenwashing the Belt and Road Initiative?," Center for Strategic and International Studies, May 1, 2019, https://www.csis.org/analysis/greening-or-greenwashing-belt-and-road-initiative.

162. Chinese media articulates that GDI is still primarily a conceptual framework, while the BRI is a concrete means of realizing it. Another interpretation is that GDI has a global focus and corresponds directly to the United Nations Sustainable Development Goals and is considered to express the Chinese government's overarching understanding and policy agenda for global development, whereas the BRI focuses on specific regions and issue areas. Wang Junsheng [王俊生], "Implementing 'One Belt, One Road' and Global Development Initiative [落实'一带一路'倡议与全球发展倡议]," *Guangming Daily* [光明日报], April 26, 2023, http://cn.chinadiplomacy.org.cn/2023-04/26/content_85255281.shtml.

163. Joseph Lemoine and Yomna Gaafar, "There's More to China's New Global Development Initiative than Meets the Eye," Atlantic Council, August 18, 2022, https://www.atlanticcouncil.org/blogs/new-atlanticist/theres-more-to-chinas-new-global-development-initiative-than-meets-the-eye/. GDI seems to be a smaller effort than BRI—China's National Development and Reform Commission is the main coordinating body behind the BRI, whereas the GDI is run by the Ministry of Foreign Affairs and the China International Development Cooperation Agency. "Xi's New Global Development Initiative," Center for Strategic and International Studies event, September 12, 2022, https://www.csis.org/events/xis-new-global-development-initiative.

164. Michael Schuman, Jonathan Fulton, and Tuvia Gering, "How Beijing's Newest Global Initiatives Seek to Remake the World Order," Atlantic Council, June 21, 2023, https://www.atlanticcouncil.org/in-depth-research-reports/issue-brief/how-beijings-newest-global-initiatives-seek-to-remake-the-world-order/.

165. Andrew Scobell et al., "At the Dawn of Belt and Road," RAND Corporation, 2018, 215.

Conclusion

1. For examples, see Fang Cai, *The China Miracle: Development Strategy and Reform* (Hong Kong: Chinese University of Hong Kong Press, 2003); Nicholas L. Lardy, *China's Unfinished Economic Revolution* (Washington, DC: Brookings Institution Press, 1998); and Barry Naughton and Kellee S. Tsai, *State Capitalism, Institutional Adaptation, and the Chinese Miracle* (Cambridge, UK: Cambridge University Press, 2015).

2. Xi Jinping, "20th Party Congress Work Report," Ministry of Foreign Affairs of the People's Republic of China, October 16, 2022, https://www.fmprc.gov.cn/eng/zxxx_662805/202210/t20221025_10791908.html.

3. Pei Changhong [裴长洪], and Liu Hongkui [刘洪愧], "How China Can Become a Powerful Country in International Trade: A New Analysis Framework [中国怎样迈向贸易强国:一个新的分析思路]," *Economic Studies* [经济研究], no. 5 (2017): 26–43.

4. Li Gang [李钢], "China's Strategic Path Toward Becoming a Trade Great Power [中国迈向贸易强国的战略路径]," *Journal of International Trade* [国际贸易问题], no. 2 (2018): 11–15; Alicia García-Herrero, "Could the RMB Dislodge the Dollar as a Reserve Currency?," MarshMcLennan, BrinkNews, July 8, 2021.

5. Mu Rongping [穆荣平], Fan Yonggang [樊永刚], and Wen Hao [文皓], "Innovation Development: Way to Build China a Major S&T Power [中国创新发展：迈向世界科技强国之路]," *Journal of Chinese Academy of Sciences* [中国科学院院刊] 32, no. 5 (May 15, 2017): 512–520, https://doi.org/10.16418/j.issn.1000-3045.2017.05.010.

6. "Jin Yinan: They Are Afraid Because the Cost Is High [美国永不与中国开战？金一南:代价太大,自然会怕]," Huanqiu.com [环球网], September 17, 2021, https://mil.huanqiu.com/article/44oDAJnRaiX; Luo Fuqiang [罗富强], "What Are the Costs and Conditions for Foreign Countries if They Dare to Intervene in China's Unification by Force [统一之战,外国若敢干预会付出怎样的代价和条件]," Sina News [新浪新闻], August 16, 2018, https://jmqmil.sina.cn/dgby/doc-ihhtfwqs0284397.d.html?vt=4.

7. "Not the Partner You Were Looking For," *The Economist*, March 1, 2018, https://www.economist.com/leaders/2018/03/01/how-the-west-got-china-wrong.

8. Da Wei [达巍] and Cai Hongyu [蔡泓宇], "50 Years of China-US Relations Under US National Security Strategies [美国国家安全战略视阈下的中美关系 50 年]," *Journal of International Security Studies* [国际安全研究], no. 2 (2022): 38.

9. Chun Han Wong, Keith Zhai, and James T. Areddy, "China's Xi Jinping Takes Rare Direct Aim at U.S. in Speech," *Wall Street Journal*, March 6, 2023, https://www.wsj.com/articles/chinas-xi-jinping-takes-rare-direct-aim-at-u-s-in-speech-5d8fde1a.

10. Yuan Peng [袁鹏], "The Coronavirus Pandemic and the Great Changes Unseen in a Century [新冠疫情与百年变局]," *Contemporary International Relations* [现代国际关系], no. 5 (2020): 1–2.

11. Hal Brands and Michael Beckley, *Danger Zone: The Coming Conflict with China* (New York: W. W. Norton, 2022).

12. Jonathan Fenby, *Will China Dominate the 21st Century* (Medford, MA: Polity Press, 2014); Melvin Gurtov, *Will This Be China's Century? A Skeptic's View* (Boulder, CO: Lynne Rienner, 2013); David Shambaugh, *China Goes Global: The Partial Power* (New York: Oxford University Press, 2013); David Shambaugh, ed., *China and the World* (New York: Oxford University Press, 2020); Robert Sutter, *Chinese Foreign Relations: Power and Policy Since the Cold War* (Lanham, MD: Rowman and Littlefield, 2007).

13. Kenneth Waltz, *Theory of International Politics* (Long Grove, IL: Waveland Press, 1979), 195.

14. Andy W. Marshall, *Long-Term Competition with the Soviets: A Framework for Strategic Analysis* (Santa Monica, CA: RAND Corporation, 1972), viii.

15. Jan-Michael Ross and Dmitry Sharapov, "When the Leader Follows: Avoiding Dethronement Through Imitation," *Academy of Management Journal* 58, no. 3 (2015): 658–679.

16. Michael E. Porter, "Stop Imitating, and Get to the Real Strategy," *Bank Advertising News*, January 12, 1998, 6.

17. I would like to thank Thomas Fingar for encouraging me to emphasize this point.

18. Walter Russell Mead, "The Return of Geopolitics," *Foreign Affairs,* April 17, 2014, https://www.foreignaffairs.com/articles/china/2014-04-17/return-geopolitics.

19. Paul Scharre, "America Can Win the AI Race," *Foreign Affairs,* April 4, 2023, https://www.foreignaffairs.com/united-states/ai-america-can-win-race.

20. Oriana Skylar Mastro, "Conflict and Chaos on the Korean Peninsula: Can China's Military Help Secure North Korea's Nuclear Weapons?," *International Security* 40, no. 3 (Winter 2015–2016): 7–53.

21. G. John Ikenberry, *After Victory: Institutions, Strategic Restraint, and the Rebuilding of Order after Major Wars* (Princeton: Princeton University Press, 2001); Stephen G. Brooks and William C. Wohlforth, "The Rise and Fall of the Great Powers in the Twenty-First Century: China's Rise and the Fate of America's Global Position," *International Security* 40, no. 3 (Winter 2015–2016): 7–53; Michael C. Beckley, "China's Century? Why America's Edge Will Endure," *International Security* 36, no. 3 (Winter 2012): 41–78.

22. Yuan, "The Coronavirus Pandemic and the Great Changes Unseen in a Century."

23. Mary E. Lovely, "The Trouble with Trans-Pacific Trade," *Foreign Affairs*, January 23, 2023, https://www.foreignaffairs.com/united-states/trouble-trans-pacific-trade.

24. "Economic Power Play: Assessing China's Trade Policies," The Economist Intelligence Unit, 2021, https://impact.economist.com/perspectives/sites/default/files/economic_power_play_assessing_chinas_trade_policies_0608.pdf.

25. André Sapir and Petros C. Mavroidis, "China and the WTO: An Uneasy Relationship," Center for Economic Policy Research, April 29, 2021, https://cepr.org/voxeu/columns/china-and-wto-uneasy-relationship.

26. Matthew Reynolds and Matthew P. Goodman, "Deny, Deflect, Deter: Countering China's Economic Coercion," Center for Strategic and International Studies, March 2023, https://csis-website-prod.s3.amazonaws.com/s3fs-public/2023-03/230321_Goodman_CounteringChina%27s_EconomicCoercion.pdf?VersionId=UnF29IRogQV4vH6dy6ixTpfTnWvftd6v.

27. Arzan Tarapore et al., "Minilateral Deterrence in the Indo-Pacific," *Asia Policy* 17, no. 4 (2022).

28. Oriana Skylar Mastro, "Testimony of Dr. Oriana Skylar Mastro," testimony before the Senate Foreign Relations Committee Hearing on a New Approach for an Era of US-China Competition, March 13, 2019, https://www.foreign.senate.gov/imo/media/doc/031319_Mastro_Testimony.pdf.

29. Duncan Hollis, "China and the US Strategic Construction of Cybernorms: The Process Is the Product," Hoover Working Group on National Security, Technology,

and Law, Aegis Paper Series No. 1704, July 7, 2017; Ines Kagubare, "Cyberspace Plays Key Role in Growing US-China Tension," *The Hill*, June 6, 2023, https://thehill.com/policy/cybersecurity/4032479-cyberspace-plays-key-role-in-growing-us-china-tension/.

30. James A. Lewis, "Creating Accountability for Global Cyber Norms," Center for Strategic and International Studies, February 23, 2022, https://www.csis.org/analysis/creating-accountability-global-cyber-norms.

31. Ankit Panda and Benjamin Silverstein, "The U.S. Moratorium on Anti-Satellite Missile Tests Is a Welcome Shift in Space Policy," Carnegie Endowment for International Peace, April 20, 2022, https://carnegieendowment.org/2022/04/20/u.s.-moratorium-on-anti-satellite-missile-tests-is-welcome-shift-in-space-policy-pub-86943.

32. "New Generation Artificial Intelligence Development Plan [国务院关于印发新一代人工智能发展规划的通知]," State Council of the People's Republic of China [中华人民共和国中央人民政府], September 20, 2017, https://www.gov.cn/zhengce/content/2017-07/20/content_5211996.htm.

33. Adrian Pecotic, "Whoever Predicts the Future Will Win the AI Arms Race," *Foreign Policy*, March 5, 2019, https://foreignpolicy.com/2019/03/05/whoever-predicts-the-future-correctly-will-win-the-ai-arms-race-russia-china-united-states-artificial-intelligence-defense/.

34. Walter J. Ferrier, Ken. G. Smith, and Curtis M. Grimm, "The Role of Competitive Action in Market Share Erosion and Industry Dethronement: A Study of Industry Leaders and Challengers," *Academy of Management Journal* 42, no. 4 (August 1999): 376.

35. Kenneth Arrow, "Economic Welfare and the Allocation of Resources for Invention," in *The Rate and Direction of Innovative Activity*, ed. R. R. Nelson (Princeton, NJ: Princeton University Press, 1962).

36. Richard N. Foster, *Innovation: The Attacker's Advantage* (New York: Summit Books, 1986), 21.

37. Yun Jiang and Jordan Schneider, "The United States Needs More Wine to Stand Up to Chinese Bullying," *Foreign Policy*, December 10, 2020, https://foreignpolicy.com/2020/12/10/united-states-australian-wine-chinese-bullying-strategic-shiraz-reserve/.

38. For example, see Oriana Skylar Mastro and Sungmin Cho, "How South Korea Can Contribute to the Defense of Taiwan," *Washington Quarterly* 45, no. 3 (2022): 109–129; Oriana Skylar Mastro, "The Taiwan Temptation," *Foreign Affairs*, June 3, 2021, https://www.foreignaffairs.com/articles/china/2021-06-03/china-taiwan-war-temptation; Oriana Skylar Mastro, "Reassurance and Deterrence in Asia," *Security Studies* 31, no. 4 (2022): 743–750.

39. "Philippines Announces Four More Military Bases US Troops Can Use," *Straits Times*, April 4, 2023, https://www.straitstimes.com/asia/se-asia/philippines-announces-four-more-military-bases-us-troops-can-use.

40. Seth G. Jones, "America's Looming Munitions Crisis," *Foreign Affairs*, March 31, 2023, https://www.foreignaffairs.com/united-states/americas-looming-munitions-crisis;

Michael Brown, "Taiwan's Urgent Task," *Foreign Affairs*, January 25, 2023, https://www.foreignaffairs.com/china/taiwan-urgent-task-new-strategy-to-keep-china-away.

41. Jake Sullivan, "Remarks by National Security Advisor Jake Sullivan at the Special Competitive Studies Project Global Emerging Technologies Summit," White House, September 16, 2022, https://www.whitehouse.gov/briefing-room/speeches-rema rks/2022/09/16/remarks-by-national-security-advisor-jake-sullivan-at-the-special-competitive-studies-project-global-emerging-technologies-summit/.

42. For more recommendations, see Oriana Skylar Mastro, *The Costs of Conversation: Obstacles to Peace in Wartime* (Ithaca, NY: Cornell University Press, 2019), 126–142.

43. Men Honghua [门洪华] and Li Ciyuan [李次园], "Great Power Competition in International Relations: A Strategic Research Agenda [国际关系中的大国竞争: 一项战略研究议程]," *Journal of Contemporary Asia-Pacific Studies* [当代亚太], no. 6 (2021): 41–42.

44. Rohan Mukherjee, "Rising Powers and the Quest for Status in International Security Regimes" (PhD dissertation, Princeton University, May 2016), 140.

45. See Oriana Skylar Mastro, "In the Shadow of the Thucydides Trap: International Relations Theory and the Prospects for Peace in U.S.-China," *Journal of Chinese Political Science*, no. 24 (2019): 25–45.

46. Ikenberry, *After Victory*.

47. For example, see Evan Montgomery, *In the Hegemon's Shadow: Leading States and the Rise of Regional Powers* (Ithaca, NY: Cornell University Press, 2016); Dale Copeland, *The Origins of Major Wars* (Ithaca, NY: Cornell University Press, 2000).

48. Another point of intense debate is the source of these intentions. Those with a pre-disposition toward Sinology and cultural essentialism argue that China's ancient history and political culture have set it toward a modern iteration of its ancient Middle Kingdom tributary system. Henry Kissinger, *On China* (New York: Penguin Books, 2011); Martin Jacques, *When China Rules the World: The Rise of the Middle Kingdom and the End of the Western World* (New York: Penguin Books, 2009). Others point to grand strategy as the result of rational conclusions drawn through rational decision-making by Communist Party leaders who want to maintain and expand domestic power and legitimacy—and foreign policy is thus a tool of domestic politics. Bates Gill, *Daring to Struggle: China's Global Ambitions Under Xi Jinping* (New York: Oxford University Press, 2022); Suisheng Zhao, *The Dragon Roars Back: Transformational Leaders and Dynamics of Chinese Foreign Policy* (Stanford, CA: Stanford University Press, 2022).

49. Avery Goldstein demonstrates that Chinese grand strategy is largely an attempt to shape and respond to US strategy when he argues that Xi Jinping is reassuring, reforming, and resisting. Avery Goldstein, "China's Grand Strategy Under Xi Jinping: Reassurance, Reform, and Resistance," *International Security* 45, no. 1 (2020). Rush Doshi argues that China engaged in *blunting* (that is, impeding US power) beginning at the end of the Cold War, and later commenced *building* (that is, actively strengthening a regional presence) in the early twenty-first century. Rush Doshi, *The Long Game: China's Grand Strategy to Displace American Order* (Oxford: Oxford

University Press, 2021). See chaps. 3 through 6 on blunting and chaps. 7 through 10 on building. M. Taylor Fravel argues that the degree of internal consensus as well as assessments of the changing nature of warfare determine when and how China changes its military strategy. Taylor Fravel, *Active Defense: China's Military Strategy Since 1949* (Princeton: Princeton University Press, 2019).

50. "In Their Own Words: Foreign Military Thought—Science of Military Strategy (2013)," China Aerospace Studies Institute, February 8, 2021, https://www.airunivers ity.af.edu/CASI/Display/Article/2485204/plas-science-of-military-strategy-2013/, 303–306; translated from Shou Xiaosong [寿晓松], *The Science of Military Strategy* [战略学] (Beijing: Military Science Press [军事科学出版社], 2013), 241–244.

Index